Rhetoric of extermination, 344-345.
Rhetorical functionalism, 27-29.
Rhetorical system, 5, 29.
Richards, D.F., 108.
Richardson, Albert, 109.
Riddlebarger, Mathew, 103-104.
Rocky Mountain News: as a source of "key symbols," 14; history of, 23; recruitment role, 115; founding, 133-134; passim, 131-195; reporting of Camp Weld Council, 258-259.
Roman Nose, 226-227, 228, 256, 322, 328.

Schell, Jonathan, 341.
Schofield, General, 226, 227, 228, 247.
Scudder, John, 108.
Sheehan, Bernard W., 20.
Shoup, Colonel George, 118, 291, 295.
Shulman, Robert, 11, 55.
Sievers, Michael, 18.
Simpson, Matthew, 219.
Situation, rhetorical, 6, 17.
Smiley, Jerome, 110, 112.
Smith, Jack, 294-295, 297.
Smith, John, 226, 250, 254, 294, 298, 323, 324.
Sohm, Rudolf, 28.
Soule, Silas, 292, 294, 295, 323, 324, 346.
Spotted Horse, 248.
Stanley, Harry, 339.
Stanton, E.M., Secretary of War, 190, 227, 228, 229, 231-233, 241-243, 290.
Stanton, William, 59, 70.
Stock (or Steck), Amos, 254, 255-256, 259.

Terry, Michael, 340.
Trade and Intercourse Acts, 1790-1799, 80.
Treaty of 1861, 154-155, 223-224.
Treaty of Fort Laramie, 154, 223.
Tritch, George, 172.
Turner, Frederick Jackson, 105.

Ubbelohde, Carl, 23.
Unitary creation, 59-63, 70.
Unrau, William, 155.

Virginia Company, 2, 3.

Wallace, Anthony, 46.
Washburn, Wilcomb, 20, 22.
Washington, George, 81.

Waterhouse, Edward, 2-3.
Weiss, Richard, 21.
West, Charles, 338, 339.
Wharton, J.E., 115.
White Antelope, 254, 255, 256, 259.
Whitley, Simeon, 162, 190, 254, 256, 258-259.
Wirt, William, 85.
Wooten, "Uncle Dick," 108, 110, 116, 134.
Wynkoop, Edward, 180-181, 184, 194, 195, 252, 257, 258, 259, 260, 284, 287-288, 290, 291, 293, 301, 324, 332, 346.

DEDICATION

For my family; especially Linda and Andrea

ACKNOWLEDGEMENTS

Professor and Dean David Zarefsky of Northwestern University provided invaluable suggestions and comments which helped to guide this study. The recommendations provided by Professor Thomas Farrell, G. Thomas Goodnight and Lee Griffin, also of Northwestern, were helpful in refining the study.

Portions of Chapter IV originally appeared as "The 'Rocky Mountain News' and the Indians," an article published in the July 1988 edition of JOURNAL OF THE WEST. Copyright 1988 by Journal of the West Inc. Used by permission.

Material quoted from Seymour M. Hersh, MY LAI 4, A REPORT ON THE MASSACRE AND ITS AFTERMATH. Copyright Random House Inc., 1970. Used by permission.

Material quoted from Murray Edelman, POLITICS AS SYMBOLIC ACTION: MASS AROUSAL AND QUIESCENCE. Copyright Academic Press Inc., 1971. Used by permission.

Special thanks to the Administration of Adams State College, Alamosa, Colorado, for providing financial support without which this study could not have been published.

TABLE OF CONTENTS

I. INTRODUCTION — 1

    Purpose of the Study — 6
    Justification for the Study — 15
    Literature Review — 18
    Methodology — 24
    Limits of the Study — 30
    Notes — 32

II. PARKMAN, MORTON AND GOVERNMENT CONSTITUTIONS: KEY SYMBOLS OF NATIVE AMERICANS — 45

    The Conspiracy of Pontiac — 45
        Indian Nature — 46
        Pontiac — 51
        Plot — 53
        Key Symbols — 57

    Crania Americana — 58
        Background — 58
        Unitary Creation — 61
        Indian Nature — 63
        Josiah Nott — 70
        Key Symbols — 75

    Native Americans, "Constitutions" and Extra-Constitutional Assumptions — 76
        Constitutions Before 1787 — 76
        Constitutions After 1787 — 78
        Cherokee Indian Removal — 83
        Key Symbols — 90
        Notes — 91

III. THE AUDIENCE — 101

    Denver and Colorado Territory — 101
    The Colorado Militia — 113
    Notes — 122

IV. THE 'ROCKY MOUNTAIN NEWS' AND THE SYMBOLS OF EXTERMINATION — 131

    Background — 131
    Symbols of 1859-1861 — 134
    Symbols of 1862 — 146
    Symbols of 1863 — 149
    Symbols of 1864 — 157
        War Declared — 157
        The Hungate 'Massacre' — 160
        The Election of 1864 — 166
        Sand Creek Reported — 180

	Conclusions	188
	Notes	198
V.	GOVERNOR JOHN EVANS: ELITE SYMBOLS OF NATIVE AMERICANS AND THE LEGITIMATION OF EXTERMINATION	219
	Background	219
	White Audience	222
	Evans to Government Agencies	222
	Evans to the People of Colorado	235
	Evans to American Indians	244
	War Declared	246
	The Camp Weld Council	252
	Notes	263
VI.	COLONEL JOHN CHIVINGTON: ELITE SYMBOLS OF NATIVE AMERICANS AND THE LEGITIMATION OF EXTERMINATION	281
	Background	281
	Official Correspondence	283
	Unofficial Messages	289
	Sand Creek Reported	296
	Summary	303
	Notes	308
VII.	CONCLUSIONS AND IMPLICATIONS: FROM SAND CREEK TO MY LAI 4	319
	Conclusions Specific to Sand Creek	319
	Extermination and the "Deficient Indian"	320
	Myth and Reality in Colorado White/ Native American Relationships	322
	The Myth and Choice	323
	White Rhetoric and Native Americans	328
	Implications for White/Non-white Rhetoric	335
	The "Deficient Vietnamese Savage"	336
	The Vietnamese as Enemy	337
	Charlie Company and Captain Medina's Rhetoric	338
	A Rhetoric of Extermination	343
	Areas for Further Study	345
	Notes	348
APPENDIX:	Chronology: Important Events Before and After Sand Creek	357
SELECTED BIBLIOGRAPHY		359
INDEX		376

ILLUSTRATIONS

Handbill, ATTENTION INDIAN FIGHTERS   100

Map: INDIAN RESERVES, Established
      by 1851 Ft. Laramie Treaty and
      by 1861 Ft. Wise Treaty   218

SAND CREEK AND THE RHETORIC OF EXTERMINATION:

A CASE STUDY IN INDIAN-WHITE RELATIONS

Introduction

The "dialectic of civilization" on the North American continent was a battle between diverse Native cultures and White European/Americans who sought to impose control upon an environment devoid of their vision of order.[1] Initially (although grudgingly), White Europeans treated Native Americans as possible equals. When John Rolfe became party to an interracial marriage with Pocahontas in 1614, the couple was presented at the Royal Court of England.[2] English clergy self-consciously examined the "right" for Whites to acquire Native land. As the Reverend Robert Gray queried in 1609, "By what right or warrant can we enter into the land of these savages, take away their rightful inheritance from them and plant ourselves in their places being unwronged or unprovoked by them?"[3]

Early accounts of first contact with the Native Americans, while judgmental regarding "Indian" heathenism, were optimistic in their perception of Native American potential. Richard Hakluyt (the younger), in dedicating Jacques Cartier's travel accounts, concluded that although Native Americans were "destitute of the knowledge of God or any good laws" they were "yet of a nature gentle and tractable and most apt to receive, willingly, the Christian religion."[4] Both Hakluyts (the elder, a lawyer and the younger, a geographer) were supported in their positive judgments of Native Americans by officials of the Virginia Company.[5] Another supporter, the Reverend Samuel Purchas, provided one answer to Robert Gray's question when he boasted of how carefully the members of the Virginia Company had conciliated the "salvages" and of how the settlers paid in fair exchange for all the land they occupied, "a thing of no small consequence to the conscience, where the milde Law of Nature, not that Violent Law of Armes, layes the foundation of their possession."[6] Although the term "savage" was used extensively by men like Purchas, Hakluyt and Cartier, the "name" did not carry the pejorative overtones it acquired after 1622. Savages were persons of the forest, rude, bestial and sometimes cruel; yet they were still persons of some potential.[7]

Obviously, early representatives of the Virginia Company and the Clergy had motives to present Native Americans as "ignoble" but not threatening. Colonization was expensive and some settlers were necessary to trade for Indian goods. Scaring investors and colonists away with frightening judgments of the Natives made little sense. For the early Jesuits and some Puritan preachers, the Indian possessed some potential for God's kingdom. In 1585 the elder John Hakluyt stated in his "inducements to the Liking of the Voyage intended towards Virginia" the goals of such a voyage: "1, to plant Christian religion; 2, To Trafficke; 3, To Conquer; or to do all three."[8] Certainly "milde and tractable Indians" would be ideal to accomplish such goals.

However, when the Virginia Company changed its concern from the fur trade to acquiring land on which to grow the new profitable discovery, tobacco, the quality of the cant regarding Native Americans changed. Between 1618 and 1622 the number of English settlers doubled, giving the English greater firepower and the possibility of winning a confrontation with the Natives. The increase in English settlers alarmed Opechancanough and in 1622 the Powhatan confederacy rebelled and killed one-third of the Virginia colonists. Several historians have noted the "grim satisfaction" which could be detected in English accounts of the conflict.[9] The necessity for land changed the White man's burden from conversion and trade to the "violent law of Armes." As colonist Edward Waterhouse reacted:

> Our hands which before were tied with gentleness and faire usage, are now set at liberty by the treacherous violence of the savages . . . So that we, who hitherto have had possession of no more ground than their waste and our purchase at a valuable consideraton to their own contentment gained; may now by right of Warre, and law of Nations, invade the Country, and destroy them who sought to destroy us; whereby we shall enjoy their cultivated places, turning the laborious

Mattocke into the victorious sword (wherein there is more ease, benefit and glory) and possessing the fruits of others (which are sitiate in fruitfullest places of the land) shall be inhabited by us, whereas heretofore the grubbing of woods was the greatest labour.

Waterhouse and others believed that the "massacre" "will be good for the Plantation, because now we have just cause to destroy them by all meanes possible." The Virginia Company used the massacre to order a war against the Indians. However, the company's orders were not necessary. The Governor and Council wrote, "Wee have anticipated your desire by settinge uppon the Indyans in all places." Furthermore, all means possible came to include: poison in the wine offered to the Indians at a treaty session; "burning their corne . . . burning their Boats, Canoes and Houses . . . by pursuing and chasing them with our horses, and blood-hounds to draw after them, and Mastives to teare them." Moreover, ". . . neither fayre warr nor good quarter is ever to be held" against such enemies.[10] Thus was the European notion of unlimited warfare introduced to North America and its inhabitants.

In this earliest conflict between White settlers and Native Americans a pattern of rhetoric and action was established which characterized the relationship between Native Americans and Whites. In this pattern, White settlers moved (usually illegally) onto Native-occupied land. In repeated <u>faits accompli</u>, White settlers would negotiate with Natives for coveted land already settler-occupied. Eventually, first the Crown and later the American Federal Government recognized White demands; the government would promise that White settlers would respect subsequent legally established boundaries and threaten punishment against unruly Whites. The government rhetoric in such covenants is written in a tradition of equal respect for concerned persons and property, both White and Native American. However, the central government usually lacked the resources and willingness to enforce such promises. White frontiersmen and Natives would eventually clash with terrible depredations performed by both sides.

This "dialectic of civilizaton" (or "civilization versus savagism" as Roy Harvey Pearce has described it), was embedded with the need to rationalize or to speak about past and future actions. First the English and then White Americans sought to rationalize their attempts at control of Native Americans. Initially there was little opportunity for English colonists to engage in such rationalization. Groups of Native Americans were in a position of dominance with sheer numbers providing them with possessory rights to the continent. During this period, Native Americans were treated as sovereign nations whose generous forebearance allowed Whites to gain a foothold. As the balance of power shifted, however, Whites were faced with justifying the displacement of their Native breathren. The broad rhetorical problem which the now dominant Whites faced has been noted by Italian political scientist Gaetano Mosca when describing one function of myth in power maintenance:

> . . . In fairly populous societies that have attained a certain level of civilization, ruling classes do not justify their power exclusively by de facto possession of it, but try to find a moral and legal basis for it representing it as the logical and necessary consequence of doctrines and beliefs that are generally recognized and accepted.[11]

Since no clear "warrant" was provided by the existing state of affairs -- Native Americans were the obvious holders of the "new" land -- reasons had to be invented which justified White control of the situation. The reasons provided had to have utility in situations where land was willingly ceded to the Whites and in situations when land was gained by force. Further, Anglos were faced with the problem of how to respond to the continued presence of Native Americans after negotiation and conquest had gained for the Whites the desired land. According to some theorists, this continued presence was especially upsetting since, in the "Savage," some Whites perceived a darker image of themselves, a "wild man within," which the brutalizing effects of their new environment threatened to release. Thus, as Gary Nash explains, "Not to control the Indians, . . . was to lose control of one's new environment and ultimately of oneself."[12]

Therefore, discourse which Whites used to control and to rationalize their treatment of Native Americans also had to function to control the needs of its originators. However no student of rhetoric has examined this rhetorical system. Although materials for study abound, most are fragmented and general. Few conflicts between Natives and Whites have been documented enough in depth to allow for systematic study. One exception is the so-called Sand Creek "Massacre."

In the early dawn of November 29, 1864, a regiment of Colorado Volunteers led by Colonel John M. Chivington attacked an encampment of Cheyenne and Arapahoe Indians near a bend of "Big Sandy" or Sand Creek about nine miles northeast of the site of present-day Chivington, Colorado. The controversy regarding Sand Creek began almost as soon as the last bullet was fired. Some critics accepted the events at Sand Creek as a "massacre." Based upon evidence drawn from both military and Congressional hearings, the encounter is described as a "merciless slaughter" of men, women and children of proven friendly demeanor, who believed they were under the protection of the Colorado authorities.[13]

Those writers who supported an opposing viewpoint generally accept Chivington's interpretations of the "battle."[14] He claimed to have killed between 400 and 500 Indians, mostly warriors, hostile to Colorado settlers and responsible for many frontier "depredations."[15] Various stories of stolen White property and a "white man's scalp not more than three days old," were interpreted as evidence of these depredations.[16] Finally, a "conspiracy" among all of the Plains tribes was referred to as proof that the band of Indians at Sand Creek was hostile.[17] The initial controversy over the nature of Sand Creek has resulted in a large number of records available for examination.[18]

As Colorado was organized as a Territory, White elites within the Territory politicized attempts to deal with Native Americans. Some elites saw glory to be had in seeking conquest of the Indians. Others sought public confidence by exposing the inhumane treatment of the poor Indians by their political opponents. Both factions actually sought the same ends -- power. In the process, the truth of what happened at Sand Creek was subordinated to this end.

But for the Indians the pattern of events and rhetoric was still the same. Indian land was illegally occupied before legal concessions provided Whites with the best land. Indian depredations were detailed and reported when only minor infractions had occurred and the Indians "true to their nature" were pronounced hostile before they committed hostile acts. Eventually a few good men went off to Sand Creek to do battle with the "red devils." Whether the battle was justified or not, the rhetoric surrounding it provides an opportunity to examine a process by which Colorado Whites concluded that "more Sand Creeks were needed." While historians have quibbled over the question of whether Sand Creek was a "battle" or a "massacre," they have ignored the perception of the White audience that exterminaton of Native Americans was a necessity and a positive good.[19] Furthermore, there has been no attempt to examine the Sand Creek incident as it relates to the larger process by which a dominant culture sought to define and justify a relationship with Native Americans "unlike that of any two people in existence."[20]

Purpose of the Study

This study examines discourse concerned with the "unique" relationship between Native and White Americans. The rhetoric which influenced events at Sand Creek and which was generated by the resulting controversy will be examined as a case study to provide generalizations regarding this interaction. The major questions will be: How did the ideas and images present in the rhetoric of Sand Creek function within the "situation" of Sand Creek; and, what do these ideas and images reveal about the relationship of Native and White Americans?[21] Accordingly, the following hypotheses will be examined:

1. Mythic racist assumptions characterized nineteenth century rhetoric regarding Native Americans.

2. The White Coloradan audience in the 1860's was favorably disposed towards violent methods of problem solving.

3. Atrocity stories printed in the Rocky Mountain News between 1860 and 1864 reinforced negative images of Indians.

4. Elite messages sent before, during and after the battle of Sand Creek functioned so as to allow for the extermination of American Indians at that site.

Each of these hypotheses is discussed below.

Hypothesis I

Several writers have commented on the preoccupation with "race" as an explanatory force in nineteenth century rhetoric.[22] Moreover, it has been argued that such explanations were fictions or "myths" and therefore difficult to falsify.[23]

Myth

In The Republic, Plato provides the first discussion of the importance of myth in binding the "guardians" with the entire body politic. While Plato admits to the necessity for the rulers sometimes to deliberately mislead the community, he prefers that the rulers and the community share the necessary "fictions." By alluding in a metaphorical fashon to common "dreams," "fictions" or "myths," nourish the ties of cohesion between young and old.[24] Political theorists have expanded somewhat upon Plato's conception of myth.

Murray Edelman defines "myth" as "an unquestioned belief held in common by a large group of people that gives events and actions a particular meaning."[25] Similarly, Jacques Ellul defines myth as "an all-encompassing, activating image . . . which displaces from the consciousness all that is not related to it. Such an image pushes man to action precisely because it includes all that he feels is good, just and true."[26] Accordingly every society has its myths which serve important cultural functions. Joseph Campbell has indicated three such functions of myth:

1. To waken and maintain in the individual a sense of 'mystical' participation in the universe.

2. To provide an image of the universe that will be in accord with the knowledge of the time.

3. To validate, support and imprint the norms of a given specific moral order.[27]

Thus, myth "explains the past, present and future." Although there may be different variants of myth, these functions tend to remain the same.[28]

It has been argued that, in western civilization, history and its form is our myth.[29] This is not to say that history is comprised totally of false narratives or that its mythic functions always imply distortion. It is to say that historical consciousness dominates the thought of western man.[30]

Given that western man is especially conscious of, and susceptible to, historical information as mythic form, it might be expected that "elites" would manipulate history to take advantage of this potential rhetorical power. Such manipulation takes the form of "historical myth" -- information which purports to describe historical events and people which has been fabricated or distorted, consciously or unconsciously. Further, historical myth is comprised of sacral, ideological and historical elements.[31] The sacral emphasizes the mystical functions of myth, the ideological provides the orientation and normative mythic functions, and the historical element provides believabililty.

Through the sacral element the <u>dramatic personae</u> of an historical myth achieve the stature of divine beings. The Washingtons, the Patrick Henrys and the Pontiacs become superior to either ourselves or the norm, performing great deeds during momentous times. The sacral also allows the historical myth to become didactic in the sense that we are expected to either emulate the mythic hero or the "lesson" of the myth. There is an additional realization of participation. Mircea Eliade explains this sense of historical myth when he writes:

> In other words, a myth is a true history of what came to pass at the beginning of time, and one which provides the pattern for human behavior. In imitating the exemplary acts of a God, of a

mythic hero, or simply by recounting their adventures, the man of archaic society detaches himself from profane time and magically re-enters the Great Time, the sacred time.[32] Thus, the sacral allows historical myths to be "immutable;" it is difficult to deny a "true" history. Moreover, if basic assumptions are unchallengeable, a myth cannot be disproven.

Historical myth may also contain elements of ideology. Although there appears to be little consensus upon what exactly comprises an "ideology,"[33] the perspective of Jurgen Habermas can be usefully applied. Habermas synthesizes Marxian and Freudian theory into an interpretation of ideology as a structure of systematically distorted communication or a communication system in which key semantic contents are sheltered from the light of critical examination. While the sacral meaning of an historical myth may be consciously applied, ideological meaning, in Habermas' view, is derived from unconscious "delinguisticized" motives. Unconscious motives and repressions remove key semantic concepts from the possibility of critical examination while simultaneously providing an explanation for these semantic concepts which is correct and real.[34] Thus particular norms and validity claims are proven by a world view which assumes their very existence. Therefore any ideological claim demands "the compulsory suspension of doubt about its claims to validity."[35] Such statements usually take the form of appeals to "self evident truths," appeals to tradition or to the natural order of things.

The ideology present in many historical myths is based upon collective beliefs but, unlike the sacral, is time-bound and practical. While the sacral element stresses the concepts of participation and mystification that transcend time, the ideological element refers to historical and political events in a materialistic way to evaluate past actions based upon present ideology. Meaning is given to the present by making the past consistent with it. Muller implies this conclusion when he defines ideologies as "integrated belief systems which provide explanation for political reality and establish the collective goals of a class or group, and in the case of a dominant ideology, of society at large. They have an evaluative component in that they attach either negative or positive judgments to conditions in society and to political goals."^{36} Thus, the ideological component of historical myth is the result of unconscious repression, defies discursive test of validity, is both materialistic and time-bound, and is comprised of evaluative statements. Such a conceptualization of the ideological component in historical myth helps to explain the need for elites to recast history in their own mold and therefore the constant "revision" of history which occurs with the passage of time.

The last element of historical myth is that of the actual historical event around which the myth is created. Although historical myth may be "immutable" because of the sacral and untestable because of ideological influences, it will be believable only if elements of truth are present. The dramatis personae cannot be totally fictional and the deeds they perform, while great, must be possible. As Bruner has observed about myth, "Its power is that it lives on the feather line between fantasy and reality. It must be neither too good nor too bad to be true, nor must it be too true."^{37}

These three elements of historical myth work together to comprise an essentially powerful rhetorical tool since "by knowing the myth, one knows the origin of things and hence can control them and manipulate them at will."^{38} Lasswell, Lerner and Pool further emphasize the importance of myth when they write:

> The myth is part of the predisposition that determines response . . . it provides a structure of goal values, identifications, and expectations -- held with varying degrees of elaboration and intensity -- for society as a whole. Since we interpret all responses according to the postulate of maximization, it is clear the myth may influence the chain of communication at every link.$_{39}$

Myths become the grounds for belief and part of perceived history to be drawn upon to influence human actions. However, as implied throughout the discussion of sacral and ideological elements, historical myth selectively interprets and constructs an historical reality which presents a danger of illusion. Robert Shulman warns: "Myths pattern our perception: they endow some acts with significance and make others appear irrelevant and because they speak to and express our basic feelings and ideals, they influence what we do, what we see and the way we see it."[40] Murray Edelman has also explained the "disposition of the anxious mind to take perceptions of present constraints as immutable: to avoid explorations of alternative possibilities." Thus, conflict and anxiety energize the attachment of myth and "anxious people prove eager to organize their perceptions of the world so as to reinforce the myth."[41] A "myth," according to Edelman, provides a "collective course of action to allay the anxiety." For individuals who are anxious, myths provide "a vivid account of who are friends, who are enemies, and what course of action must be pursued to protect the self and significant others." Thus, an examinaton of the world of myths is a relatively simple one. In contrast to the "complicated network of competing influences in the empirical world," a study of the myths "revolves around hostile plotters and benevolent leaders. . . ." Archetypal "themes" in myth include the identification of the benevolent leader capable of saving the "commonwealth," and the "corollary" that victory is only possible through obedience and self-sacrifice. Such myths occur in the rhetoric of elites or authorities and are expressed by "key symbols."[42]

Therefore, the purpose of the chapter related to this hypothesis will be to analyze several authoritative sources for the myths and key symbols related to the American Indian. The authoritative sources for preliminary analysis will include Francis Parkman's <u>History of the Conspiracy of Pontiac</u>, Samuel George Morton's <u>Crania Americana</u> and governmental "constitutions" made for Native Americans.[43]

<u>History of Conspiracy of Pontiac</u>

Francis Parkman has been labeled as an historian of "timeless example" and the "Greatest of all" American historians.[44] His works were as popular during their day as the fiction of Cooper and Melville. A review of Pontiac in the contemporary North American Review is instructive:

> It gives a more complete and accurate picture of Indian character and life, and of Indian warfare such as it was a century ago, than has yet appeared in print. And it is written with so much spirit and picturesque effect that it is as entertaining as a nursery tale.[45]

Indeed the "children's edition" of Pontiac survived seven printings.[46]

While Parkman's "History" more recently has been the subject of controversy, even his critics grudgingly admit that he was a "master craftsman" who made an exhaustive search of the sources. Critics generally agree that the History is a "classic."[47]

Crania Americana

Morton's Crania Americana has been described as the most influential work regarding racial make-up and origins until Darwin "shattered the work of the American school."[48] Moreover, Crania Americana provided apparent "scientific evidence" for those who denied the literal interpretation of creation and argued for innate physical differences between the races. Such physical differences, Morton implied, illustrated inherent inequalities beyond the control of environmental changes.[49] Prior to the publication of Morton's research, few argued for the unimprovability of Native Americans, but by the end of the 1840's the deficient, immutable Indian was a common symbol in debates regarding American Indian policy.[50]

Constitutions

Kenneth Burke has discussed the idea of a "constitution" as an "idealistic anecdote" in the "enactment of human wills." He defines a constitution as an "authoritative ordinance, regulation or enactment." Furthermore, "A written constitution . . . is a calculus of motives. It is a terminology, or set of coordinates, for the analysis of motives." The texts of various ordinances, treaties and laws intended to define the "wishes" of the central government toward the Indians fall within these definitions. There can be no doubt that these ordinances and treaties were acts "(or enactments), done by <u>agents</u> (such as rulers, magistrates, or other representative persons) and designed (<u>purpose</u>) to serve as motivational ground (<u>scene</u>) of subsequent actions, it being thus an instrument (<u>agency</u>) for the shaping of human relations."[51] Lasswell, Lerner and Pool explain that Laws are easily discovered:

> In the United States we turn to the codes of the Federal, State or local government, depending upon the detail appropriate to a given investigaton. There are also collections of court decisions and opinions which must be taken into consideration when we summarize the sense of the sentences found in the statutes.[52]

The "key symbols" located in government constitutions will provide a legal symbolization of Native Americans by White Americans. The "authoritativeness" of such documents is established by their interpretation as "law."[53]

Hypothesis II

This hypothesis also is a descriptive one. The intent of the chapter related to this hypothesis is to describe the White Coloradan audience of the early 1860's. This description will include: audience characteristics, attitudes expressed towards themselves, their surroundings and, especially, Native Americans. The relationship of a specific group to this larger audience -- the Colorado Third Regiment -- will also be examined. It will be argued that early White Colorado society was pervaded by violence and that violence was an acceptable form of problem solving. Establishing the nature of the audience will be helpful in discerning how given messages and symbols may have functioned within the situation that was Sand Creek.

Hypothesis III

Kenneth Burke has written that atrocity stories arise naturally in war time and that the human mind

13

will gravitate towards the imagination of the perfect atrocity story.[54] Yet, perhaps because White Americans have never really perceived the various military campaigns against the Indians as wars against foreign nations, accounts of so-called Indian "depredations" which might be categorized as atrocity stories have not been isolated or studied in any systematic way.[55] Certainly the role of atrocity stories in the Sand Creek affair deserves examination. Moreover, the examination of the role of other agencies (besides agents, Chivington and Evans) and their potential function within the situation of Sand Creek would make a useful contribution to the literature regarding Sand Creek.[56]

The Rocky Mountain News has been selected for this analysis for several reasons. The News was the first elite institution in Colorado. Its publication predated the establishment of Colorado Territory and the incorporation of Denver.[57] It was selected as the "official" newspaper of the territorial legislature and has remained in continuous publication since April, 1859. The longevity of the News has allowed for the most complete collection of relevant historical issues available. Moreover, its continuous publication during the early tumultuous years of the Territory while other newspapers languished indicates a level of representativeness lacking in the other publications.[58] Its founder, editor and policymaker was William Newton Byers, who became a close friend of Governor John Evans and a supporter of John Chivington. Beginning with Evans' appointment, Byers supported, without question, "official" territorial policy towards the Indians. As a result, Byers found himself required to justify Sand Creek as a positive good, which he continued to do as late as 1880.[59]

Therefore, issues of the Rocky Mountain News from approximately 1860 until 1864 will be examined for the occurrence of the "key symbols." The nature of these key symbols and their distribution relative to external events will be noted. Additionally, it will be theorized that these symbols functioned so as to reinforce negative White Coloradan perceptions of Native American nature.

Hypothesis IV

Many studies of Sand Creek are devoted to placing blame for the purported slaughter upon either Colonel

Chivington or Territorial Governor John Evans. Certainly both of these individuals attempted to control events prior to, during and after Sand Creek. However, the nature of the official and unofficial rhetorical acts these two men engaged in, which may have functioned to influence events at Sand Creek, has not been analyzed. Additionally, the role of other communications from higher authorities has been ignored. From statements of White participants in the fight, however, it seems apparent that some members of the Colorado Volunteers believed that "extermination" was the order of the day.[60] Official correspondence between the appropriate authorities is readily available.[61] Therefore an analysis of the "key symbols" in these messages ought to be made. Similar to the previous hypothesis, the nature, and distribution of these symbols will be noted. Moreover, it will be argued that the symbols used by various authorities allowed for White depredations committed at Sand Creek.

Justification for the Study

This study is a contribution to the scholarly literature concerned with White racism in the U.S. Racism may be defined as "the belief that one or more races have innate superiority over other races."[62] Racism provides a rationale for derogating other races and "prejudice" is the expression of this rationale.[63] Racism and prejudice are phenomena requiring special study within the context of American experiences. Certainly the expression of racism in its varying degrees, from antilocution to attempts at extermination, contradicts the expression of the equality of all men found in the Constitution, the Bill of Rights and interpretations of these documents. The process by which statements of equality are devalued or negated for some individuals or groups deserves analysis otherwise the risk exists that such guarantees will lose all meaning for all peoples. Moreover, White racism expressed toward Native Americans is unique in that it progressed to calls for and actual attempts at extermination. However, there is little analysis of White racism and Native Americans. Most studies of racism in the United States devolve to White treatment of Blacks and other minorities "closer" to the mainstream of American life.[64] This lack of study is surprising since White experiences with Indians predated other direct experiences with other minorities. As Professor McWilliams states:

> Any consideration of colored minorities in the United States must perforce, start with the American Indian. Apart from historical or chronological considerations, the Indian problem is central to the whole question. It represents not only the point of departure, but the point to which any discussion of the larger problem must ultimately return. For it was with the Indian that our patterns of 'color reaction' and 'color behavior' were first conditioned. So deep-seated and ingrained have these patterns become that it seldom occurs to the average American that a large part of his race psychology might be traced to the experience of his ancestors with Indians . . . .[65]

Thus, the "color reaction" first displayed by White Americans toward Native Americans may hold implications for all other colored minorities encountered by White Americans. The White experience with the American Indian may suggest that any perceived increased militance on the part of a colored or cultural minority group results in reciprocal White violence at a level far beyond the capabilities and provocation of the minority group.[66] As a prototype for our "color reactions" and culture reactions, the pattern of Native and White American relations deserves study. As McWilliams implies above, a solution to White racism may escape us until this pattern and its implications are understood.

This study will also make a unique contribution to an emerging scholarly literature concerned with Native American and White American relations. Although historians have attempted "to present the ideas and imagery used by whites to understand the peoples they call Indians," such studies have been descriptive in nature.[67] Moreover, these studies seem to stress a particular era in Indian-White relations, or else to generally review particular ideas or images as they occur throughout history.[68] The analysis resulting from these studies may be called rhetorical only by accident rather than by design.[69] This is not to say such studies have no value, only that the studies tend to classify "ideas" and "images" but without examining how such ideas and images functioned to influence the choices made by White actors and the implications of those choices. Therefore, this study will contribute to a rhetorical history of the relationship between Native and White Americans rather than to a "history of ideas" about Native Americans.

An examination of the rhetoric of Sand Creek is warranted by another consideration. The interaction of a relatively non-technological culture and a more intensively technological culture generates a recurring rhetorical situation. This interaction brings about rhetoric by which the dominant culture seeks to justify actions taken "for" and "against" the dominated culture. However, once it is assumed that the dominant culture is superior (perhaps because of the existence of technology),[70] actions taken both for and against the less developed culture may have the same outcomes: at the very least, disruption and internal conflict; in the extreme, destruction and extermination.[71]

Although the Colorado society of the 1860's was obviously not as technological as that of today, it is clear that White Americans at this time were greater users of technology than Native Americans. An assumption upon which the rhetoric of Sand Creek was based was that White culture was superior to that of the "savage Indians." Moreover, because of this superiority, it was assumed that Native Americans should accept White attempts to civilize them. Those Indians who were unwilling to do so should, as stated in the Rocky Mountain News, be[72] subject to "A few months of active extermination."

In the future as well as in the past, Americans will make contact with less developed cultures. Therefore, the rhetoric which was used to justify Sand Creek specifically and treatment of Native Americans generally deserves exposure and explanation. The "red Devils" who terrorized Colorado may be removed only in time from the "gooks" of Vietnam. The Sand Creek "massacre" or "battle" may differ only in time and place from the My Lai "massacre," not in ideology of inception. What is important to consider is not the reality of the situation, that is whether there were battles or massacres, necessary or unnecessary, but the process by which an ideology was created and used which brought about the intended or unintended destruction of another culture.[73] Francis Jennings aptly summarizes the task of the critic and the justification for this study:

> Reason must struggle to break the bonds of ideology so long established and so firmly fixed. National and racial religions of the present day are no less powerful than the crusader religions of days past in their grip on men's minds. The very words used to express thought give it shape and direction as well as symbolic substance, and the words evolved from centuries of conquest have been created for the purposes of conquest rather than the purposes of knowledge. To call a man savage is to warrant his death and to leave him unknown and unmourned.[74]

To critique this "ideology" and its related myths will free us from the limitations imposed by past mistakes.

Literature Review

Sand Creek Massacre

No dissertation concerning Sand Creek specifically has been discovered. In fact, until the appearance of Stan Hoig's <u>The Sand Creek Massacre</u> in 1961, no full-length narrative account of the incident was available. Michael Sievers, in his review of historiographic literature concerning Sand Creek, explains the reasons for the paucity of comprehensive literature:

> Perhaps the primary reason for the lack of comprehensive study has resulted from historians' overt specialization in one aspect or view of the incident . . . Perhaps part of the reason for overspecialization can be attributed to the controversial nature of the event. Some writers well may have felt duty-bound either to defend or to condemn the incident, while others finding the debate too hot have avoided forming any significant conclusions. Also the very complexity of the event and, at the same time its minuteness have contributed to detailed accounts.[75]

18

The extant literature concerning Sand Creek can be organized around the major questions about the event: Were the Indians at Sand Creek hostile?; Was there a conspiracy among the Plains tribes to rise up against White settlers?; Were atrocities committed by Whites at Sand Creek?; Who was responsible for Sand Creek?[76] However, a careful review of this historiographical literature reveals a major concern among historians as to <u>what</u> happened and <u>who</u> was responsible. An analysis as to <u>how</u> such an event came about and was supported by a large number of people is lacking.[77]

Beyond these specific studies of Sand Creek, secondary sources in four other categories deserve mention: general background books concerning Native and White American relations, studies of racism and Native Americans, ethnohistorical books concerning the Cheyenne and general books regarding Colorado history.

Indian-White Relations

An excellent introduction to a historical perspective on Native and White American relations is provided by Professor William T. Hagan. In a brief but concise narrative Hagan tells the story of the clash between the two cultures. He traces the different stages in the conflict and his description of the changing attitude of White settlers toward Native Americans is especially valuable.[78]

In his book, <u>The White Man's Indian</u>, Robert F. Berkhofer Jr. discusses "Persistent Fundamental Images and Themes" which have characterized White interpretation of Native Americans: "the idea of the Indian;" the "deficient savage" and moral evaluation of Native American culture.[79] His study is useful in explaining the predominance of racial explanations of the state and potential of Native Americans to be discussed in the second chapter.

In his text, <u>The Invasion of America: Indians, Colonialism and the Cant of Conquest</u>, Francis Jennings seeks to expose the ideology of "Amerindian-Euramerican acculturation" during the colonial period. He indicates that the "official records" of Native and

19

White American relations during this period were rife with ideology and that this "ideology of conquest" is still present in historical records and popular interpretations.[80]

Bernard W. Sheehan also offers a conception of Native American and White American relations. His interpretation concentrates upon "how the White American's conception of himself" influenced both his perception of the Native American and the subsequent policy directed at the Native American.[81]

In his book Red Man's Land/White Man's Law, Wilcomb Washburn discusses the relationship between White and Native Americans "primarily in legal terms." He traces the legislative history of the conflicting cultures. He argues that the assumptions "that Christians and Christianity had both a moral and legal authority to overspread the world" have influenced much of subsequent White policy. Professor Washburn's study will contribute to this investigation in the legal symbols it reveals regarding Native and White American relations.[82]

The last general study to be discussed is Roy Harvey Pearce's Savagism and Civilization: A Study of the Indian and the American Mind. It is the history of a belief or idea which seeks to account for "The Metaphysics of Indian Hating." His major thesis is that the myth of savagism contrasted with the myth of the bearers of a "true civilization" so distorted White Americans' perceptions of reality that they met consistent frustration in dealing with any issue pertaining to the presence of Native Americans.[83]

Pearce's idea of "savagism" is both assumed and built upon by many of the studies previously mentioned.[84] The idea of the ignoble savage permeates the rhetoric to be studied. A knowledge of Pearce's study will help to isolate this image and help to explain its effect upon rhetorical choices.

Racism

Description of the "pattern" of Native and White American relations has been left largely to historians similar to those previously mentioned. However, several sociological studies helpful to the concerns of this study do exist.

Gary Nash and Richard Weiss seek to illumine the "role of racial attitudes in shaping the American experience." These editors strive to determine what White racial attitudes are, their origins, their changing nature and the functions they have served.[85] In nine essays, White racial attitudes from the Colonial period to the twentieth century are analyzed. Nash's essay, "Red, White and Black; The Origins of Racism In Colonial America," is especially helpful in analyzing early patterns of White European and Native American interaction.

In addition to Nash's essay, Philip Borden's essay, "Found Cumbering the Soil: Manifest Destiny and the Indian in the Nineteenth Century" is also enlightening. His description of changing attitudes toward Native Americans through the nineteenth century is helpful in providing a context for Sand Creek.[86]

The final essay, Peter Lowenburg's "The Psychology of Racism," determines "the unconscious as well as the conscious elements in individual race prejudice and suggests how racism functions in American society as a whole."[87] He argues that "prejudice is a learned behavior." He explains the "self-fulfilling prophecy" and "projection" as generators of continued prejudice. Especially important to this study is his explanaton of "anxiety" and its relation to prejudice.[88] Certainly White Americans were in situations, personal and social, which could arouse great anxiety. Citizens of Colorado in 1864 perceived the very elements rising against them, feared attack from Rebel forces, saw their own military ordered East to do battle on a "more important" front and feared an ill-defined conspiracy among all of the Plains tribes.[89]

While Lowenburg provides explanation for racism and prejudice at the individual level, a study by Daniels and Kitano provides an explanation at the social level. In examining "extraordinary" outcomes of racism, they argue that there is a "sequence -- a process beginning with a two-category system and its inherent prejudice, leading to discrimination, then progressing to more drastic behaviors."[90]

21

Ethnohistory

In assessing the rhetoric of White American and Native American relations, it is important to adopt what has been described as an ethnohistorical point-of-view. Wilcomb Washburn provides an excellent summary of ethnohistory when he writes:

> Any human event is composed of an act and the interpretation put upon it . . . Traditionally, the historian has applied unconsciously his own attitudes to the act . . . The ethnohistorian (whether anthropoligist or historian) would first of all try to determine whether the act did in fact occur. Then he would attempt to decide what the significance of the act was in the culture setting in which it was performed.[91]

Such methodology also stresses the importance of change and diversity. Historical methods and materials can be used to determine the nature and causes of change in a culture brought on by contact with another culture.[92]

Preston Holder, in his study, examines cultural change on the Great Plains as a result of White intrusion. He explains that there was little cultural uniformity among the various inhabitants of the Plains and remarks on the effects of increasing European contacts in bringing about the collapse of village economies and increased Native American dependence on White technology. He also provides a brief history of the Cheyennes, revealing their original agricultural background. For more detailed information he refers to George Bird Grinnell as the "greatest authority" on the Cheyennes.[93]

Grinnell's work is certainly the definitive study regarding the culture of the Cheyenness. While his narrative of the customs and history of this tribe is as accurate as a study of this nature can be, Grinnell's sympathies clearly are with the Cheyennes in any mention of conflict between White and Native Americans. But there is also much value in the noncontroversial ethnographic data contained in the study which is important in validating claims in White rhetoric about Sand Creek. For example, Chivington and others claimed that one proof of the hostility of

22

the band camped at Sand Creek was the existence of[94] "fortifications" such as rifle pits and trenches. Grinnell and other experts indicate that these pits had been dug by people trying to save their lives. The Plains tribes, especially[95] the Cheyennes, did not fortify an encampment.

Colorado History

It is not enough to apply the assumptions of ethnohistory only to Native cultures. It must also be realized that the White Colorado culture of 1864 was not the culture of 1980. To "understand" a culture on its own terms is to view the situation as an actor rather than only as an observer. To help establish this viewpoint, a basic knowledge of the scene is important. Two texts useful in providing both a broad history of Colorado and a more specific narrative which concentrates on mid-nineteenth century in Colorado are Carl Ubbelohde's A Colorado History and Robert L. Perkin's The First Hundred Years: An Informal History of Denver and the Rocky Mountain News.

Professor Ubbelohde's text ranges from a discussion of the first dwellers of Colorado at Mesa Verde to a discussion of more recent events. It is obviously a very general study[96] but is useful in establishing background material.

Robert Perkin's book is especially useful in relating the Denver "audience" to both the Rocky Mountain News and events leading to the incident at Sand Creek. Perkin tells both the story of the founding of the Rocky Mountain News and early Denver and the relationship of the two institutions to each other. Drawing from a wide variety of primary sources, he vividly describes early Denver and its inhabitants. He also takes a position critical of the role of the Rocky Mountain News in exacerbating events leading to the Sand Creek battle. Although titled as an "informal history," the work is a painstaking reconstruction of life in Denver in the 1860's and the[97] only available history of the Rocky Mountain News.

Several other works also contain useful information regarding early Colorado and are recognized as "standard" texts. However, many of these studies seek to defend Sand Creek -- particularly by referring to the hostility of the Cheyennes. That is, these texts all tend to support a "conspiracy theory" of events leading to Sand Creek. According to this interpretation, the group of Cheyennes and Arapahoes at Sand Creek was part of a large conspiracy which sought to eradicate White settlers on the Plains while the bulk of Federal troops were busy fighting the Civil War. All of these texts should be used with caution, for they may be more a part of the rhetoric of Sand Creek, pro or con, than the incident's objective recorders.[98]

Primary Sources

The primary sources for Chapter Two will include: Francis Parkman's history of Pontiac's "Conspiracy" and the Indian war of 1763-1765; Samuel George Morton's Crania Americana, a study on "craniology" which purports scientific proof that Native Americans were savage and intractable; and the texts of various "constitutions" (including acts, ordinances and proclamations) made by the Federal government regarding Native Americans.[99]

The primary sources for Chapter Three will include the 1860 census and contemporary accounts and letters from the scene.[100]

Issues of the Rocky Mountain News between 1860 and 1865 will be the primary source for the analysis in Chapter Four.

As already indicated, records of the United States War Department will be the primary source material for Chapter Five. Additionally, statements of Governor Evans and other authorities printed in the Rocky Mountain News and other official statements recorded in the subsequent Army and Congressional hearings not recorded in the "Rebellion Records" will be utilized. For example, verbal statements attributed to officers immediately before and during the Sand Creek fight will also be examined.[101]

Methodology

Harold Lasswell's seminal model for message analysis will be adapted to guide this study. "Who says what to whom in what channel with what function," will help to organize and gather the data. A rhetorical functionalism derived from writings by Robert Berkhofer, Kenneth Burke and others will aid in the interpretation of the symbolic choices made by the actors to be studied.

Lasswell, Lerner and Pool believe that "What men say . . . is a major part of what they do." They also believe that the study of symbols and myth is the proper focus for the study of communication which is an attempt of one elite group to ensure continued control of the "commonwealth." They recommended that such myths and symbols be sought in "specific acts of speaking or of writing" which occur during a given period of time.[102] To locate such myths, they suggest a process of content analysis. Content analysis may be defined as "the systematic, objective, and quantitative characterization of content variables manifest or latent in a message."[103] Lasswell, Lerner and Pool recommend three major steps in their explanation of content analysis:

1. Selection of "authoritative sources" and the isolation of "key symbols."

2. Selection of a "representative and accessible" channel of communication.

3. Notation and analysis of the distribution of the "key symbols" in this channel.[104]

Step 1

The first step of this content analysis is the selection of influential authorities or sources of communication. The key question in this determination is "Is this individual (agency or document) authoritative?"[105] While Lasswell, Lerner and Pool are rather unclear as to the exact criteria to be employed in this selection, the influence and pervasiveness of a given authority during a given period of time would seem to help answer the question as to who is authoritative. Once the authorities are selected they can be analyzed for the "key symbols" relevant to the research hypothesis.

Key symbols are "focal points for the crystallization of sentiment, uniting child with adult, layman with expert, philosopher with lawyer, the speculative man with the man of action." Moreover, the key symbol is the "common denominator" of the sacral, ideological and historical elements of Historical myth. Such symbols "can be classified into those referring to persons and groups (symbols of identification), to preferences and volitions (symbols of demand) and to the assumptions of fact (symbols of expectations)."[106] Thus in examining authoritative sources of Chapter Two, a qualitative search will be made for symbols referring to Native Americans, for evidence of the different authorities' attitudes toward them and for symbols of fact regarding Native Americans. Additionally the "larger themes" or myths which contain such symbols will also be noted.

Step 2

The second step in this system of content analysis is to locate the "most representative and accessible channels of communication." The Rocky Mountain News and the Rebellion Records both seem to meet implicit criteria provided by Lasswell et al. These theorists state that a newspaper is a desirable channel "because we can be relatively sure of who controls and reads the news." Moreover, "In nearly all states some papers are understood to be leading organs of the party in office and of the government." Additionally, since a newspaper, like the Rocky Mountain News, appears regularly and frequently, the flow of symbols, their distribution and covariation with external events are measurable.[107] The Rebellion Records also seem to meet the criteria for representativeness and accessability. The sources of the various messages are identifiable as is the flow of symbols.

Step 3

Once the channels for study have been selected, they can be analyzed for the occurrence of the "key symbols." For the purposes of this study, although trends in usages will be clearly noted, qualitative changes will most commonly be the topic of discussion.

26

As Alexander George has pointed out, "Inferences from content to noncontent variables . . . need not always be based on the frequency values of content features." A "content characteristic" or "content syndrome," may be important to the study because of its mere presence or absence.[108] Application of a strict quantitative measurement would assign no importance to a singular occurrence.

Interpreting the Data

While Lasswell's model provides a convenient method for describing the make-up of symbolic messages, it provides no guidance for extrapolating from the observed variable (symbol, myth or message) to nonobserved motivational variables (why a given symbol or myth was invoked). Moreover, Lasswell provides no theoretical linkages that explain the potential ramifications of specific message choices. A "half hearted" rhetorical functionalism is one model of symbolic behavior which allows the critic to account for both manifest (conscious) and latent (unconscious/unintended) functions of rhetorical choices.

Robert Berkhofer supports the use of a "loose" or "half hearted" systems analysis to determine the relationship of wholes and parts. Rather than adopting a specific model, his interpretation is a guide which stresses the specific context of the situation under study and the manner in which specific events "function" within that situation.[109] The ethnohistorical approach mentioned above complements Berkhofer's suggestions since both are situational in nature. Additionally, Berkhofer's interpretation allows for a rhetorical viewpoint of the situation and for the use of specific analytical tools to determine the relationship of "parts" within the whole of the rhetorical context.

A "loose" functionalism allows for functions which promote structural persistence which actors may not recognize. Although interpretation of the situation by an actor seeking possible choices (rhetorical or otherwise) may be conscious, other unconscious motives may also account for the choices made. Berkhofer does not explain nonempirically measured methods for relating wholes to parts. He only cautions that explanation based solely upon a conscious situational interpretation is "incomplete."[110] However, he urges that behavior, "be understood, then, both in terms of the actors' situational interpretation and the observer's theory about those actions." That is, "good reasons" provided by the observer for particular actions and choices on the part of the actor are a part of a complete explanation of how those actions and choices function within the whole. Berkhofer admits value in the study of "unconscious personal, social and physical environmental processes."[111]

The "Unconscious" and Latent Functions

The importance of unconscious motivations and latent effects to the study of rhetorical history is implied by Rudolf Sohm's comment that "The greatest and most far-reaching revolutions are not consciously observed at the time of their occurrence."[112] More problematic is establishing a method to "complete" the explanation of the situational interpretation. Lasswell, Lerner and Pool write of the study of the "subtle unconscious patterning of speech" or "style" as a way to gain insight into the "currents of history." However, other than a vague reference to historical psychoanalysis, they provide no clear guidance.[113] Richard L. Merritt suggests "qualitative content analysis" as an explanation of what is meant by the phrase "unconscious patterning of speech." He explains that it is similar to the "psychoanalyst's search for the lapsus linguae, 'the slip of the tongue,' or the unexpected appearance of key words and phrases."[114] He believes the study of "the mass of unconscious elements . . . word usage, syntax and contextual configurations" to be extremely important since "the unconscious or latent structure of a message may outweigh its manifest content." But, other than alluding to "intelligence and insight" in the application of qualitative analysis, he provides no systematic explanation.[115] A critic whose work is consistent with rhetorical functionalism and aids in the explanation of qualitative analysis is Kenneth Burke.

A Burkeian methodology which seeks human motives, "via a methodical inquiry into cycles or clusters of terms and their functions," is one method of accounting for more than the conscious.[116] Furthermore, Burke believes that rhetorical works are "strategic stylized answers to questions posed by the situation in which they arise."[117] For Burke, the characteristic "invitation to rhetoric" arises out of the physiological differences between people. However, each <u>specific</u> situation generates the need to resolve these differences anew and Burke clearly believes the efforts to bring about "congregation" can be both conscious and unconscious. Burke believes the manifest content ("facts") of a message can be masked by the latent content ("analogic.")[118] Burke has attempted to make "the analysis of literary symbolism as systematic as possible . . . to allow for the determination of a speaker's attitude." He directs the critic to:

> Note all striking terms for acts, ideas, attitudes, images, relationships . . . Note oppositions . . . Pay particular attention to beginnings and endings of sections or subsections . . . Watch names, as indicative of essence . . . Watch also for incidental properties of one character that are present in another . . . Note internal forms . . . Watch for a point of 'farthest internality' . . . Note details of <u>scene</u> that may stand 'astrologically' for motivations affecting charcter, or for some eventual act in which character will complete himself . . . Note expressions marking secrecy, privacy, mystery, marvel, power, silence, guilt . . . Look for 'moments' at which, in your opinion, the work comes to fruition.[119]

Such "systemization," Burke cautions, is necessary so that the critic will keep "inferences under control."[120] However, the extent to which Burke can be systemized is limited.

This methodology assumes the existence of two rhetorical systems. One, the smaller system, was generated by the rhetorical situation of Sand Creek and has long since decayed in its urgency. The other, larger system encompasses discourse concerned with the relationship of Native and White Americans which draws urgency from the apparent imperfections of this relationship. The situation of Sand Creek will be examined as a case study which illustrates the "pattern" of the larger rhetorical system.

Limits of the Study

The system of rhetoric to be studied is limited in two ways. First of all, it concerns only rhetoric by White Americans directed at a mostly White audience. In all probability Native Americans also sent important messages which affected the relationship of Whites and Natives Americans. However, a focus upon White-originated rhetoric is adopted for several reasons. Practically, Native American rhetoric defies traditional methods of rhetorical analysis. Few valid Indian messages have survived for analysis. The few that have survived are White versions of Indian rhetoric and are of questionable value for analysis. Such rhetoric is not really directly pertinent to a study which seeks to understand the pattern of White racism. As Jerry Muskrat points out, "Most of the problems of Native Americans emanate from the external world, that is, the Anglo-American culture." Therefore, the rationale behind these problems can be described by studying White rhetoric.[121]

The second limitation is dictated by the materials for study regarding Sand Creek. The primary sources are almost exclusively of institutional origin. Therefore most of the discourse available for examination is "official" -- although some of the rhetoric interpreted as "official" by White audiences may have been informal statements made by persons occupying an authority role. Some notion of "popular rhetoric" may be gleaned from the newspaper analysis, but data regarding the extent of such a popular rhetoric are unavailable. Materials for study in the third chapter are less official and will help to establish popular assumptions regarding Native Americans.

Finally, it is necessary to caution the reader that it is not the argument of this study that White Anglos were/are the sole actors/speakers in the racist history of humankind. For narrative purposes, the study will dichotomize between White Anglos and Native Americans (sometimes referring to Native Americans as "Indians" or "American Indians" for stylistic variety). The elements of race hatred that helped lead to incidents like Sand Creek and My Lai 4 are not just restricted to Whites. The war of extermination by the Iroquois against the Hurons has been well-documented. Additionally, thousands of Blacks and Native Americans served in Vietnam and many probably shared the same attitude toward the "deficient Vietnamese Savage" as their White comrades. Ethocentric race hatred and its justification is a human characteristic, not simply a "White" character trait.[122]

CHAPTER I

NOTES AND REFERENCES

[1] Roy Harvey Pearce, *Savagism and Civilization: A Study of the Indian and American Mind* (Baltimore: The Johns Hopkins Press, 1965), p. 3.

[2] Roger Daniels and Harry H.L. Kitano, *American Racism: Exploration of the Nature of Prejudice* (Englewood Cliffs, N.J.: Prentice-Hall, Inc., 1970), p. 4.

[3] Robert Gray, *A Good Speed to Virginia* (London, 1609) quoted in James Axtell, "Through a Glass Darkly: Colonial Attitudes Toward Native Americans," *Essays From Sarah Lawrence College*, 2 (October, 1973), p. 3; For a review of argument used to justify dispossession of Native Americans of their lands see Wilcomb Washburn, "The Moral and Legal Justification for Dispossessing the Indians," in James Morton Smith, ed., *Seventeenth Century America Essays in Colonial History* (Chapel Hill: University of North Carolina Press, 1959), pp. 15-32.

[4] Richard Hakluyt, quoted in Francis Jennings, *The Invasion of America: Indians, Colonialism and the Cant of Conquest* (Chapel Hill: University of North Carolina Press, 1975), p. 75.

[5] Jennings, p. 77.

[6] Samuel Purchas, *Purchas, his Pilgrimage*, 4th ed. (London, 1626), p. 836.

[7] See: Jennings, pp. 74-76; Pearce, pp. 1-49; Gary B. Nash, "Red, White and Black: The Origins of Racism in Colonial America," in *The Great Fear: Race in the Mind of America* (Chicago: Holt, Rinehart and Winston, 1970), p. 1-26.

[8] Jennings, p. 76.

[9] Axtell, p. 14; Jennings, p. 80; Pearce, p. 7; Nash, p. 5; Gary B. Nash, *Red, White and Black, The Peoples of Early America* (Englewood Cliffs, New Jersey: Prentice-Hall, 1974), p. 62.

[10] See Susan M. Kingsbury, ed., The Records of the Virginia Company of London (Washington D.C., 1906-1935), III: 556-557; 221-222.

[11] Gaetano Mosca, The Ruling Class, trans. H.D. Kahn (New York: McGraw-Hill, 1939), p. 70.

[12] Nash, 1970, p. 8; 1974, p. 319.

[13] See: George Bird Grinnell, The Fighting Cheyenne (1915; rpt. Norman: University of Oklahoma Press, 1958), pp. 165-180; Stan Hoig, The Sand Creek Massacre (Norman: University of Oklahoma Press, 1961); Donald J. Berthong, The Southern Cheyenne (Norman: University of Oklahoma Press, 1963); Dee Brown, Bury My Heart at Wounded Knee: An Indian History of the American West (New York: Bantam Books, 1971), pp. 85-91.

[14] Reginald S. Craig, The Fighting Parson: The Biography of Colonel John M. Chivington (Los Angeles: Westernlore Press, 1959); Irving Howbert, Indians of the Pikes Peak Region (1914; rpt. Glorietta, New Mexico: Rio Grande Press Inc., 1970), pp. 93-186.

[15] United States War Department, The War of the Rebellion: A Compilaton of the Official Records of the Union and Confederate Armies, Series 1, Vol 34, part 1 (Washington D.C.: G.P.O., 1880-1901), p. 948; hereafter cited as Rebellion Records.

[16] Rebellion Records, p. 948.

[17] "Evans to Dole, November 10, 1863," Rebellion Records, Series I, Vol 34, part 4, p. 100; "Evans to Major General Curtis, June 16, 1864," Rebellion Records, Series I, Vol 34, part 4, pp. 421-22.

[18] United States Senate, "Sand Creek Massacre," Report of the Secretary of War, Senate Executive Document 26, 39th Cong. 2d sess. (Washington D.C.: G.P.O., 1867); United States Congress, House of Representatives, "Massacre of Cheyenne Indians," Report on the Conduct of the War, 38th Cong. 2d sess. (Washington D.C.: G.P.O., 1865); United States Senate, "The Chivington Massacre," Reports of the Committees, 39th Cong. 2d sess. (Washington D.C.: G.P.O., 1867).

[19] See issues of the contemporary Rocky Mountain News, November 30, December 20, 1865. A "soldiers vindication ticket" was proposed in 1865 pledged to the "vindication" of the battle. The majority of the candidates pledged to the ticket were elected.

[20] Chief Justice John Marshall quoted in Robert F. Berkhofer, Jr., The White Man's Indian (New York: Alfred A. Knopf, 1978), p. 163.

[21] In this study "situation" is used in a sense explained by Robert F. Berkhofer, Jr., in A Behavioral Approach to Historical Analysis (New York: The Free Press, 1969), pp. 33-45.

[22] See: Thomas F. Gossett, Race, the History of an Idea in America (Dallas: Southern Methodist University Press, 1963), pp. 244-250; Lewis H. Carlson and George A. Colburn, eds., In Their Place: White America Defines Her Minorities 1850-1950 (New York: John Wiley and Sons, 1972), p. 32; Berkhofer, White Man's Indian, pp. 25-32; Reginald Horsman, "Scientific Racism and the American Indian in the Mid-Nineteenth Century," American Quarterly, 27 (May, 1965), 153-54; Nash, 1974, p. 5.

[23] Roy Harvey Pearce, Savages and Civilization, pp. v-vii.

[24] Eric H. Warmington and Philip G. Rouse, eds., Great Dialogues of Plato, trans. W.H.D. Rouse (New York: New American Library of World Literature, 1956), pp. 214-215.

[25] Politics as Symbolic Action (Chicago: Markham, 1971), p. 14.

[26] Jacques Ellul, Propaganda: The Formation of Men's Attitudes (New York: Alfred A. Knopf, 1969), p. 31.

[27] Joseph Campbell, "Mythological Themes in Creative Literature and Art," in Myths, Dreams and Religion, ed. Joseph Campbell (New York: E.P. Dutton, 1970), pp. 138-140.

[28] Bill Kinser and Neil Kleinmen, The Dream that was no More a Dream: A Search for Aesthetic Reality in Germany 1890-1945 (Evanston: Harper and Row,

1969), p. 13; Bass and Cherwitz differentiate between what they describe as "sacred myth" and "political myth" arguing that political myth is composed of elements of sacred myth and ideology. Jeff D. Bass and Richard Cherwitz, "Imperial Mission and Manifest Destiny: A Case Study of Political Myth in Rhetorical Discourse," Southern Speech Communication Journal, 43 (Spring, 1978), 218. See also G.S. Kirk, Myth: Its Meaning and Functions in Ancient and Other Cultures (Cambridge, Berkeley and Los Angeles: University of California Press, 1970), pp. 1-42.

[29] W. Taylor Stevenson, History as Myth (New York: The Seabury Press, 1969), p. 16; see also Ellul, p. 40.

[30] Stevenson, p. 17.

[31] This analysis was inspired by Bass and Cherwitz, See especially pp. 214-218.

[32] Mircea Eliade, Myths, Dreams and Mysteries (New York: Harper and Row, 1960), p. 23.

[33] Burke lists seven meanings all of which "are quite different in insight and emphasis," A Rhetoric of Motives (1950; rpt. Berkeley: University of California Press, 1969), p. 104.

[34] Jurgen Habermas, The Legitmation Crises, trans. Thomas McCarthy (Boston: Beacon Press, 1973).

[35] Trent Schoyer, The Critique of Domination: The Origins and Development of Critical Theory (Boston: Beacon Press, 1973), p. 163.

[36] Claus Mueller quoted in Bass and Cherwitz, p. 216.

[37] Jerome Bruner, "Myth and Identity," in Henry A. Murray, ed., Myth and Mythmaking (New York: Braziller, 1960), p. 279.

[38] Mircea Eliade quoted in Stevenson, p. 17.

[39] Harold D. Lasswell, Daniel Lerner, and Ithiel de Sola Pool, The Comparative Study of Symbols, An Introduction (Stanford: Stanford University Press, 1952), p. 19.

[40] Robert Shulman, "Parkman's Indians and American Violence," The Massachusetts Review, 12 (1971), 222.

[41] Edelman, pp. 31, 77.

[42] Edelman, pp. 54, 77-78. See the discussion of method for explanation and justification of this procedure.

[43] Francis Parkman, The Conspiracy of Pontiac and the Indian War after the Conquest of Canada (New York: Charles Scribner's Sons, 1915), 2 vols; Samuel George Morton, M.D., Crania Americana; or A Comparative View of the Skulls of Various Aboriginal Nations of North and South America; to which is Prefixed an Essay on the Varieties of the Human Species (Philadelphia: J. Dobson, Chestnut Street, 1839); Wilcomb Washburn, The American Indian and the United States: A Documentary History, 4 vols (New York: Random House, 1973).

[44] Robert L. Gale, Francis Parkman (New York: Twayne Publishers, Inc., 1973), p. 165; James Truslow Adams, The March of Democracy: A History of The United States (New York: Random House, 1965), II, 225.

[45] Francis Bowen, "Review of the History of the Conspiracy of Pontiac," North American Review (October, 1851), p. 495. For a summary of Parkman's contributions and critical acclaim see S. Austin Allibone, Critical Dictionary of English Literature and British and American Authors (Philadelphia: J.P. Lippincott and Co., 1872), p. 1508.

[46] Samuel Elliot Morison, The Parkman Reader (Boston: Little, Brown and Company, 1955), ix.

[47] Wilbur R. Jacobs, Dispossessing the American Indian: Indians and Whites on the Colonial Frontier (New York: Charles Scribner's Sons, 1972), p. 92.

[48] Horsman, p. 156. For a summary of the contemporary critical reaction see Allibone, pp. 1376-1377.

[49] Morton, p. 260.

[50] Horsman, pp. 154-155.

[51] Kenneth Burke, A Grammar of Motives (1945; rpt. Berkeley: University of California Press, 1969), pp. 323, 379, 341.

[52] Lasswell, Lerner and Pool, p. 13.

[53] Lasswell, Lerner and Pool, p. 13.

[54] Kenneth Burke, Language as Symbolic Action: Essays on Life, Literature and Method (Los Angeles: University of California Press, 1966), p. 384.

[55] By an atrocity story I mean an account of apparent deliberate "depredations" purported to have been committed by Indians. This account should include (all or in part): Massacre, mutilation or torture of White Americans. For a brief analysis of the "motive and means" of atrocity stories see James Morgan Read, Atrocity Propaganda, 1914-1919 (New York: Arno Press, 1972), pp. 1-21.

[56] Michael A. Sievers, "Sands of Sand Creek Historiography," Colorado Magazine, 49 (Fall, 1972), 140.

[57] Robert L. Perkin, The First Hundred Years: An Informal History of Denver and the Rocky Mountain News (Garden City, N.Y.: Doubleday, 1959), pp. 10, 17; Douglas C. McMurtrie and Albert H. Allen, Early Printing in Colorado (Denver: A.B. Hirshfield Press, 1935), pp. 19, 23.

[58] Robert G. Athern, The Coloradans (Albuquerque: University of New Mexico Press, 1976), pp. 45-46.

[59] W.N. Byers, "The Sand Creek Affair," handwritten manuscript and columns from the New York Tribune in "Byers papers" a special collection in the Western History Department of the Denver Public Library.

[60] Lonnie J. White, "From Bloodless to Bloody," Journal of the West, 6 (October, 1967); Statement of Morse H. Coffin regarding an attack on a Cheyenne village on Sept. 23, 1864; "The idea was very general that a war of extermination should be waged against the Indians without regard to age or sex," p. 556.

[61] Rebellion Records, Series 1, Vol 34, part 3 includes most of this correspondence. For a complete listing see Chapter Five.

[62] Daniels and Kitano, p. 2.

[63] Harry L. Kitano, Race Relations (Englewood Cliffs, New Jersey: Prentice Hall, 1974), pp. 17-18.

[64] For example, in Nash and Weiss's bibliography for further reading only 8 volumes out of 83 specifically relate to Native Americans. Nash, The Great Fear, pp. 202-207. Reginald Horsman writes, "In writing on the development of concepts of racial inferiority in pre-civil war America, American Historians have substantially neglected the American Indian," pp. 125-6.

[65] Carey McWilliams, Brothers Under the Skin (Boston: Little, Brown, 1944), p. 50.

[66] This conclusion would be consistent with Daniels and Kitano, see especially, pp. 11-12.

[67] Berkhofer, White Man's Indian, p. xiv.

[68] Roy Harvey Pearce's study is an example tracing a general image through history.

[69] For example, Berkhofer's White Man's Indian.

[70] Daniels and Kitano explains, "Europeans came to associate their undeniable technological success with some kind of innate superiority, a belief that was substantiated by their established control over the non-European people." Daniels and Kitano; p. 3. H. Craig Miner makes a similar argument in The Corporation and the Indian: Tribal Sovereignty and Industrial Civilization in Indian Territory, 1865-1907 (Columbia: University of Missouri Press, 1976), p. ix. See also Nash, 1974, p. 26.

[71] For two studies in this vein see: Robert F. Berkhofer Jr., Salvation and the Savage: An Analysis of Protestant Missions and American Indian Response, 1787-1862 (New York: Atheneum, 1972); Bernard W. Sheehan, Seeds of Extinction: Jeffersonian Philanthrophy and the American Indian (Chapel Hill: University of North Carolina Press, 1973).

[72]"Evans to Patriotic Citizens of Colorado," Rocky Mountain News, August 10, 1864.

[73]Daniel Boorstin has referred to Native and White American relations as a "pre-enactment" of contact between western civilizations and underdeveloped countries. See William T. Hagan, American Indians (Chicago: University of Chicago Press, 1961), pp. v-vi. Likewise, Robert Shulman argues that White violence against Native Americans was the prototype for violence against the Vietnamese and other nonwhite people. "Parkman's Indians and American Violence," The Massachusetts Review, 12 (1971), 221-39.

[74]Jennings, p. 12.

[75]Sievers, p. 140. For a more recent discussion of the Sand Creek incident see Michael H. Harnish, "The Sand Creek Massacre: Toward a Settlement," Thesis, Wichita State University, 1980.

[76]Michael Sievers organizes his review of the extant literature around these questions. It is a thorough review and there is little need to repeat it here.

[77]In the Spring of 1865, the Union Administration Party, the dominant political party in Colorado at this time, approved resolutions calling for "more Sand Creek battles." In the subsequent election, Union Administration Candidates were generally successful. White, p. 575.

[78]Hagan, pp. 107-108.

[79]Berkhofer, The White Man's Indian, pp. 25-32.

[80]See above, note number 4.

[81]Sheehan, pp. 12, 276-79.

[82]Red Man's Land/White Man's Law: A Study of the Past and Present Status of the American Indian (New York: Charles Scribner's Sons, 1971), pp. vii, 4, 23.

[83]Pearce, pp. vi-vii.

[84]Washburn and Hagan do not. Berkhofer, White Man's Indian, p. 109; Jennings, p. 10; Sheehan, p. 201.

[85]Nash, The Great Fear, p. vii.

[86]Borden in The Great Fear, pp. 70, 79.

[87]The Great Fear, pp. 187-201.

[88]Lowenburg in The Great Fear, p. 197.

[89]McWilliams notes: "Fear and anxiety were unquestionably factors . . . in racism; fear of the unknown peril of the wilderness and its equally unknown inhabitants," p. 53. For description of events creating anxiety in Colorado see White, pp. 542-45 and Chapter Four.

[90]Daniels and Kitano, pp. 11, 12.

[91]Wilcomb E. Washburn, "Ethnohistory: History 'In the Round'," Ethnohistory, 8 (Spring, 1961), 34.

[92]James T. Axtell, "The Ethnohistory of Early America: A Review Essay," William and Mary Quarterly, 35 (January, 1978), pp. 113-115.

[93]Preston Holder, The Hoe and the Horse on the Plains: A Study of Cultural Development Among North American Indians (Lincoln: University of Nebraska Press, 1970).

[94]Craig, p. 193; "Chivington Testimony," Senate Document 142, p. 102.

[95]Grinnell, p. 561. Additionally both Hoig, p. 151 and White, p. 561, indicate that it "was unheard of" for Plains Indians to fortify a camp.

[96]Carl Ubbelohde, A Colorado History (Boulder: Pruett Press, 1965).

[97](Garden City, N.Y.: Doubleday, 1959).

[98]Wilburn Fisk Stone, ed., History of Colorado, 4 vols (Chicago: S.J. Clarke Publishing Co., 1918), I; p. 90; James H. Baker and LeRoy R. Hafen, eds., History of Colorado, 5 vols (Denver: Linderman Co.,

Inc., 1927), 276-377; Katherine L. Craig, Craig's Brief History of Colorado for Teacher and Student, 2nd ed. (Denver: Welch-Haffner Printing Co., 1923), p. 68; William N. Byers, Encyclopedia of Biography of Colorado (Chicago: Century Publishing and Engraving Co., 1901), pp. 70-71; Frank Hall, History of the State of Colorado, 4 vols (Chicago: Blakely Printing Co., 1899), I; pp. 327-28; Jerome C. Smiley, ed., Semi-Centennial History of the State of Colorado, 2 vols (Chicago: Lewis Publishing Co., 1913), I; pp. 411-19.

[99] See above, note number 81.

[100] U.S. Department of the Interior, Census Office, Population of the United States in 1860 (Washington D.C.: U.S. Government Printing Office, 1864), p. 549; LeRoy R. Hafen, ed., Colorado Gold Rush, Contemporary Letters and Reports, 1858-59 (Glendale, California: Arthur H. Clark, 1941); LeRoy R. Hafen and Ann W. Hafen, eds., Reports From Colorado, The Wildman Letters 1859-1865 with Other Related Letters and Newspaper Reports, 1859 (Glendale, California: Arthur H. Clark: 1961).

[101] Reply of Governor Evans of the Territory of Colorado to that Part Referring to Him of the Report of "The Committee on the Conduct of the War" Headed 'Massacre of Cheyenne Indians,' Executive Department and Superintendency of Indian Affairs, Colorado Territory, Denver, August 6, 1865. This reply is also found in Reports of the Committees, pp. 77-87; John Chivington, "Speech at the Pioneer Meeting, September 14, 1883," in Alice Polk Hill, Tales of the Colorado Pioneers (Denver: Pierson and Gardiner, 1884), pp. 89-92; John Chivington, "Testimony to the Joint Committee on the Conduct of the War," pp. 101-108.

[102] Lasswell, Lerner and Pool, pp. 1-2.

[103] Richard L. Merritt, Systematic Approaches to Comparative Politics (Chicago: Rand McNally, 1970), p. 64.

[104] Lasswell, Lerner and Poole, pp. 1-25.

[105] Lasswell, Lerner and Poole, p. 16.

[106] Lasswell, Lerner and Poole, pp. 14-15.

[107] Lasswell, Lerner and Pool, pp. 16-17.

[108] Alexander L. George, "Quantitative and Qualitative Approaches to Content Analysis," in Ithiel de Sola Pool, ed., Trends in Content Analysis (Urbana: University of Illinois Press, 1959), pp. 9-10.

[109] Berkhofer, A Behavioral Approach, pp. 193-95.

[110] A Behavioral Approach, p. 43.

[111] A Behavioral Approach, p. 44.

[112] Quoted in Lasswell, Lerner and Poole, p. 21.

[113] Lasswell, Lerner and Poole, pp. 21-22.

[114] Merritt, pp. 70-71. For a discussion of psychoanalysis and history see Philip Rief, "Psychoanalysis," In American History and the Social Sciences, ed. Edward N. Saveth (New York: The Free Press, 1964), pp. 110-126.

[115] Richard L. Merritt, Symbols of American Community 1735-1775 (New Haven: Yale University Press, 1966), p. xiii.

[116] Kenneth Burke, "Interaction-Dramatism," in David L. Sills, ed., International Encyclopedia of the Social Sciences (New York: Macmillan, 1968), p. 445.

[117] Richard L. Johannsen, ed., Contemporary Theories of Rhetoric: Selected Readings (Evanston: Harper and Row, 1971), p. 361. Also see Kenneth Burke, "The Rhetorical Situation," in Communication: Ethical and Moral Issues, ed. Lee Thayer (New York: Gordon and Beach, 1973), p. 264.

[118] Kenneth Burke, "Fact, Inference and Proof in the Analysis of Literary Symbolism," in Lyman Bryson, ed., Symbols and Values: An Initial Study (New York: Cooper Square Publishers, 1964), p. 285.

[119] Burke, "Fact, Inference," pp. 296ff.

[120] Burke, "Fact, Inference," p. 283.

[121] Jerry Muskrat, "The Constitution and American Indian: Past and Prologue," Hastings Constitutional Law Quarterly, 3 (Summer, 1976), 676.

[122] See George T. Hunt, *The Wars of the Iroquois: A Study in Intertribal Trade Relations* (Madison: University of Wisconsin Press, 1940), pp. 66-87 for the fairest account of this conflict. Thomas Dunlay in *Wolves for the Blue Soldiers: Indian Scouts and Auxiliaries with the U.S. Army* (University of Nebraska Press, 1982) recounts the recruiting of Indian Scouts, warriors and policemen by the U.S. Army for help in subjugating fellow Indian peoples who resisted White encroachment.

CHAPTER II

PARKMAN, MORTON AND GOVERNMENT CONSTITUTIONS:

KEY SYMBOLS OF NATIVE AMERICANS

The "Conspiracy" of Pontiac

Wilbur Jacobs has stated, "Probably no more pseudo-historical view of the past has been invented than the conspiracy theory of Indian war and politics, an unfortunate oversimplification of historical causation that looms behind misunderstanding and bitterness in early frontier Indian-White relations."[1] In physical conflicts with Native Americans, Whites attempted to justify their actions, casting the natives in the roles of "treacherous savages" seeking to satiate their "native thirst for blood." The myth of the Indian conspiratorial tactics began with the 1622 uprising mentioned in the introduction but exists as a prototype in Francis Parkman's The Conspiracy of Pontiac.

Parkman organizes his history around events that were factual. Since the late 1600's the British and the French had been attempting to diminish one another's trade empires in North America. The actual balance of power, however, was held by the "Six Nations:" the Senaca, Cayuga, Onondaga, Oneida, Mohawk and the Tuscarora Indian Nations. For practical reasons, both the French and the British recognized the Six Nations and for almost forty years the Six Nations "played off" the British and the French against each other.[2]

However, in the 1740's a "critical imbalance" in the system came about when the Iroquois miscalculated and granted the English too-extensive trading rights in the Ohio country. The French reacted negatively to this imbalance and attacked English settlements and the French and Indian war "was on." During the war the Six Nations unsuccessfully attempted to play their old role; fighting both for and against both sides. The results were that:

The end of the war found the French expelled, British troops stationed . . . in the Iroquois domain as well as in posts outside the Iroquois sphere of influence and a new spirit of economy pervading Indian affairs. No longer were Iroquois promises bought with tons of hardware and 'dry goods;' 'presents' were now limited. The old free trade was like-wise curtailed, there were fewer traders, and powder and lead were sold only at government factories by surly public servants . . . The play off system was out; a bargaining system was in.

The British now sought a <u>firm</u> alliance with the Iroquois, but with the crown as the <u>dominant</u> partner.[3]

According to two historians and Parkman, the loss of their "French Brothers" greatly upset the Natives in the Ohio Country.[4] While all three writers agree that the subsequent uprising was general among the Indians in the Ohio Country, only Parkman attributes the Indian War of 1763 to a master conspiracy directed by Pontiac. Professor Jacobs indicts Parkman's evidence for such a "conspiracy," Professor Wallace calls the label "conspiracy," inaccurate and another historian, Howard Peckham, argues that "there was no grand conspiracy."[5] Parkman isolates probable causes for the unrest and conflict such as English mistakes, increased White settlement of land claimed by Indian tribes, French agitation and the urgings of a Native "Prophet;" but it is clear that he considers inherent Indian nature to be the sufficient condition for upheaval.

Indian Nature

Because of their "restless and warlike" nature, Parkman indicates that the Natives responded "at once" when they learned "that the King of France had ceded all their country to the King of England." Furthermore:

Within a few weeks a plot was matured such as was never . . . conceived or executed by a North American Indian. It was determined to attack all the English forts upon the same day; then, having destroyed their garrisons, to turn upon the defenceless frontier, and ravage and lay waste the settlements, until, as many of the Indians fondly believed, the English should be driven into the sea, and, the country restored to its primative owners.[6]

The actual events of the uprising included destruction of forts at Venango, LeBoeuf and Presqu' Isle as well as the annihilation of two British detachments on the Niagara Falls road by the Senaca. Other historians assign Pontiac only an incidental role while Parkman credits him with being the "prime mover."[7]

From the first page of his "History", Parkman's negative judgment of the character of all Native Americans is apparent. There is no doubt as to where the "nature" of the Natives will lead them. Parkman writes:

> The conquest of Canada was an event of momentous consequence in America history . . . they [Native Americans] were destined to melt and vanish before the advancing waves of Anglo-American power, which now rolled westward unchecked and unopposed. They saw the danger and led by a great and daring champion [Pontiac] struggled fiercely to avert it. The history of that epoch, crowded as it is with scenes of tragic interest, with marvels of suffering and vicissitude, of heroism and endurance, has been as yet unwritten, buried in the archives of governments . . . To rescue it from oblivion is the object of the following work. It aims to portray the American forest and the American Indian at the period when both received their final <u>doom</u> [emphasis added].[8]

In this opening description of Parkman's history, a cluster of symbols occurs which is repeated at the end of the two volumes -- images of the destruction of Native Americans. Through superior Anglo conquest the unlucky natives will receive their final doom. However, the terms "melt" and "vanish" are passive reactions to the dilution of inherently weak Native cultures by a superior Anglo American power. That the Indians will "melt" and "vanish" is inevitable. Throughout, Parkman avoids direct mention of overt extermination of Indians by Whites. Although "Anglo-Power" rolls unchecked, it is no more to blame for the doom of the Natives than an ocean for the power of its tides. Ultimately, the superior nature of White culture will overcome the inferior nature of Native culture and the "gulf" between the two races will disappear along with the Red Man.

Parkman develops his argument by referring to the "immutability" of the Indians. Like aspects of nature itself they never change. They are "hewn out of a rock" and true to their intrinsic nature are responsible for their own fate:

> Races of inferior energy have possessed a power of expansion and assimilation to which he [the Indian] is a stranger; and it is this fixed and rigid quality which has proven his ruin. He will not learn the arts of civilization, and he and his forest must perish together.[10]

Thus, the immutability of Indian nature removes any blame from White Americans and Parkman for the treatment and conditions of Native Americans. For Parkman, replacing "doomed savagism" with civilization is constructive and the failure of Natives to adopt civilized ways is evidence of their immutability.

With the defeat of the "Conspiracy" images of doom reappear. Parkman muses over Pontiac's thoughts as he travels to negotiate with his White conquerors:

> Little could he have dreamed and little could the wisest of the day have imagined that, within the space of a single human life, that lovely lake (Lake Erie) would be studded with the sails of commerce; that cities and villages would rise upon the ruins of the forest; and that the poor mementoes of his lost race -- the wampum beads, the rusty tomahawk, and the arrowhead of stone, turned up by the ploughshare -- would become the wonder of school boys, and the prized relics of the antiquary's cabinet. Yet it needed no prophetic eye to foresee that, sooner or later, the doom must come. The star of his people's destiny was fading from the sky; and, to a mind like his, the black and withering future must have stood revealed in all its desolation.

Later, after the visit, Pontiac's "hopes of resistance" are "scattered to the winds," and

> . . . the tide of British power rolled westward in resistless might; while the fragments of the rival empire, which he would fain have set up as a barrier against the flood lay scattered a miserable wreck; and while the remnant of his people melted away or fled for refuge to remoter deserts. For them the prospects of the future were as clear as they were calamitous. <u>Destruction or civilization -- between these two lay their choice; and few who knew them could doubt which alternative they would embrace</u> [emphasis added].11

Thus, Parkman attributes the choice for their own destruction to Indian "nature." Like their "poor mementoes" they would soon lie beneath the soil which would support the cleansing tide of British Civilization.

In his conclusion, Parkman makes his final argument for Indian doom, asserting in an example that Pontiac himself was responsible for the disappearance of the Illinois tribes. Additionally, with Pontiac established as the "best" champion the Indians could offer, Parkman points to the eternal inferiority of savages by literally setting White civilization to trampling on Pontiac's grave:

> Thus basely perished [killed by a renegade Indian bribed by liquor] this champion of a ruined race. But could his shade have revisited the scene of murder, his savage spirit would have exulted in the vengeance which overwhelmed the abettors of the crime. Whole tribes were rooted out to expiate it. Chiefs and sachems, whose veins had thrilled with his eloquence; young warriors, whose aspiring hearts had caught the inspiraton of his greatness, mustered to revenge his fate, and from the north and east, their united bands descended on the villages of the Illinois . . . over the grave of Pontiac more blood was poured out in atonement than flowed from the veins of the slaughtered heroes on the corpse of Patroclus; and the remnant of the Illinois who survived the carnage remained forever after sunk in utter insignificance.
> Neither mound nor tablet marked the burial-place of Pontiac. For a mausoleum, a city has

risen above the forest hero; and the race whom he hated with burning rancor trample with unceasing footsteps over his forgotten grave.$_{12}$

Through "conquest" and his own nature the Native American achieved his doom as civilizaton triumphed over savagism. Parkman might have yielded some shred of sympathy for a race doomed only because of their own immutability. However, he provides justification for their condemnation in his symbols of the dark, bloodthirsty, treacherous savage. The components of the violent, hostile and treacherous savage are present in Parkman's discussion of their appearance, living conditions and motives.

Parkman's Indian is "full of contradictions" and "presents a darker mantle of his own inscrutable reserve." He is a "dark" image, blotting but not seriously threatening the light of civilization. "Stamped . . . with a hand and stern physiognomy" the Indian warrior may present an air of "haughty indolence" as he "lounges naked" in his "dark" hovel. However, his "black eyes" hide darker intentions. Whereas in his first discussion of Indians, <u>The Oregon Trail</u>, Parkman had painted a clear picture of the "wolfish savage," in <u>The Conspiracy</u> the savage becomes blurred, presenting a "dark" impression of "brooding mischief."

Parkman's naturalistic metaphors, adjectives and verbs also present an uncomplimentary picture of a savage, uncontrollable because of his nature. The individual Indian creeps about like a "Lynx," "panther," or "wolf" but his unchangeable nature is "hewn" in stone. War "fires" his being while he hides his emotions under a "mask of icy coldness." Moreover, when gathered together in large groups, Indians are "brutes" converging in a "wild multitude," that might erupt in a "wild frenzy" at any moment. Unlike the "feeble, nursling settlers" who are "ill-fitted" to frontier life yet make "steady progress," the "wild tribes" of "motley barbarians swarm" over the plains in "hordes." Additionally, the Indian's living conditions reinforce his unredeemable nature. His "dark lodges" are pits of "degeneracy and decay" where numberless "starveling urchins" crouch in "black recesses."

In his attribution of motive to the Indians, Parkman completes an "inner-Indian" consistent with his external impression. "Instinct, ferocious passions and fierce caprice" energize the dark image provided by Parkman. "Blood and war" are the ends sought by uncontrollable urges. His "native thirst for blood" makes the "subtle savage" completely untrustworthy. Moreover, "ambition, revenge, envy and jealousy" are the Indian's ruling passions and "treachery" the means for fulfilling their instincts. "Dark, cold and sinister," an Indian would prefer to make a secret stab rather than an open blow." The stereotype is made total when Parkman writes ". . . all savages, whatever may be their country, their color or their lineage, are prone to treachery and deceit."[13] Thus, while Native Americans outwardly might appear to be either friendly or hostile, one function of Parkman's conspiracy myth is to "prove" that Indians were inwardly identical: violent, hostile and treacherous. Finally, in the character of Pontiac, Parkman provides the perfected treacherous savage.

Pontiac

Parkman carefully constructs Pontiac "in strongest light and shadow" to epitomize the best the Indians could offer, flawed not by the worst but by faults "common to his race." Like heroes of old, Pontiac exercises "despotic" power over those around him partly based upon his position as "principal chief" but mostly based upon the personal merits of "Courage, resolution, address and eloquence . . ."[14] In this, the lighter side of Pontiac, even motivated by "patriotism," Parkman creates an image necessary to the dramatic impact of the conspiracy myth. Given the limitations he imposes upon the character of the savage, doomed by its own nature, he must provide an exception (or nearly so) if the concerted action of savages was to be threatening. As Parkman himself recognizes, "With them, the war was a mere outbreak of fury, and they turned against their enemies with as little reason or forecast as a panther . . . But the mind of Pontiac could embrace a wider and deeper view." Although Pontiac is a "thorough savage," Parkman awards him the ability to think and conjecture whereas the "average Indian" can only see and react.

Pontiac is the "prime mover of the plot" without whom "the whole might have ended in a few troublesome inroads upon the frontier and a little whooping and yelling under the walls of Fort Pitt." Cast as a noble warrior of the forest, Pontiac came forward to command the conspiracy against the English: ". . . his muscular figure was cast in a mould of remarkable symmetry and vigor."[15] Illustrating eloquence and sagacity, Pontiac united the tribes, arousing "their native thirst for blood," appealing to their superstitious natures and:

> At the close of the year 1762, he sent ambassadors to the different nations. They visited the country of the Ohio and its tributaries, passed northward to the region of the upper lakes, and the borders of the river Ottawa; and far southward towards the mouth of the Mississippi. Bearing with them the war-belt of wampum broad and long, as the importance of the message demanded, and the tomahawk stained red, in token of war, they went from camp to camp, and village to village. Wherever they appeared, the sachems and old men assembled, to hear the words of the great Pontiac. Then the chief of the embassy flung down the tomahawk on the ground before them, and holding the war-belt in his hand, delivered, with vehement gesture, word for word the speech with which he was charged. It was heard everywhere with approval; the belt was accepted, the hatchet snatched up, and the assembled chiefs stood pledged to take part in the war. The blow was to be struck at a certain time in the month of May following, to be indicated by the changes in the moon. The tribes were to rise together, each destroying the English garrison in its neighborhood, and then, with a general rush, the whole were to turn against the settlements of the frontier.[16]

In these events, although Pontiac was no "stranger to the high emotion of the patriot hero," Parkman chooses to present him not as a George Washington but as "the Satan of this forest paradise" in whom "uncurbed passions" churned as he instigated "the treacheries which, to his savage mind, seemed fair and honorable."[17] Parkman's symbols heighten Pontiac's ominous nature by providing contrast between his muscular figure and his color: "His complexion was darker than is usual with his race." Thus Parkman hints at the "blackest treachery" which marked Pontiac's conduct. Parkman despairs of Pontiac's limitations:

> . . . one cannot but lament that a commanding and magnanimous nature should be stained with the odious vice of cowards and traitors. He could govern with almost despotic sway, a race unruly as the winds. In generous thought and deed, he rivalled the heroes of ancient story; and craft and cunning might well seem alien to a mind like his. Yet Pontiac was a thorough savage and in him stand forth . . . the native faults and virtues of the Indian race.[18]

Like all savages, Pontiac is motivated by "bloodlust" and utilizes "treachery and deceit" to fulfill his ends. Moreover, his notion of "military virtue" dictates the use of circumvention and "sneak attack."

When Pontiac's plot to take and sack Detroit is discovered and overturned, Parkman metaphorically provides for the destruction of even the light side of Pontiac: "An entrapped wolf meets no quarter from the huntsman; and a savage, caught in his treachery, has no claim to forbearance." Ultimately, like all savages, Pontiac had no chance against the advancing tide of civilization. He was deluding himself in imagining that the British would "give way before the rush of his savage warriors; when in truth, all the combined tribes of the forest might have chafed in vain rage against the rock-like strength of the Anglo-Saxon."

Thus, in the conspiracy myth, Parkman creates Indians immutable, and therefore immune from civilization: [19]"He will not learn the arts of civilization . . ." Additionally, Indian immutability dictates that he will naturally succumb to superior Anglo-Saxon civilization. Moreover, this victory of civilization is justified as all Indians are characteristically savage, hostile and treacherous.

Plot

The various episodes within <u>The Conspiracy of Pontiac</u> have provided a mythic prototype for the plot-line of Indian-White conflicts. While such conceptions say more about their adherents than about Native and White American relations, their implications are important to this study. Parkman qualitatively creates expectations, provides a point-of-view and specific roles within the drama of The Conspiracy.

He prepares his readers for the machinations of Pontiac, explaining, "To the credulity of Mankind each great calamity has its "prognostics." Just as the gods provided warnings and signs in the great Greek tragedies so Parkman relates "prognostics" to the "New England Puritans" of impending disaster including: "Signs and portents in the heavens, the vision of an Indian Bow and the figure of a scalp imprinted on the disk of the moon . . ." The Puritans, however, ignored these signs, and Pontiac and his warriors "burst" upon them like Philip and his Macedonian army. The "blackness" of the atmosphere prepares Parkman's reader for the "dark" evil to come:

> In October, 1762, thick clouds of inky blackness gathered above the fort and settlement of Detroit. The river darkened beneath the awful shadows and drops of rain began to fall of strong sulphurous odor, and so deeply colored that the people it is said collected them and used them for writing . . . Throughout the winter, the shower of black rain was the foremost topic of their fireside talk; and foreboding of impending evil disturbed the breast of many a timourous matron.[20]

Nature, in providing hints of the future, is established as Parkman's secular "God." "Nature" has predetermined the outcome of the clash between Savagism and Civilization. That civilization will triumph in "rolling across" the continent is a function of "nature," not any action taken by Anglo-Americans. "Nature" has provided the "rock-like strength" of the Anglo-Saxon. The Indian's flawed nature will determine his doom.

Thus, "Nature" directs the plot in The Conspiracy. Parkman first set his stage, "History," and once the inferior "nature" of the Indian character is established the sequence of events moves inexorably forward. Episode follows episode of Indian-Pontiac treachery, subsequent threat and temporary success or failure of the "plots." But the plot always moves toward final Anglo victory. Although Parkman uses "nature" to absolve himself and Anglos from any guilt incurred as a result of the treatment of American Indians, the point-of-view in The Conspiracy is a totally White point-of-view.

This White point-of-view follows a two-value system. The world is perceived as a conflict between Whites and Nonwhites. In this conflict, the primary problem is[21] how to maintain order -- White superiority. White values such as individualism, hard work, rationality and assimilation are contrasted with Indian culture which contains nothing of value. Therefore, in Parkman's plot, the protagonist is the civilized White; the antagonist, the "savage" Indian.

Parkman's development of the plot-line of the myth sets a logical mold which gives the myth great potential power. Simply put, in his "history," "defenceless White settlers" are "prey" to treacherous savages. The treachery and violence of all savages is proven by their "very nature." If no depredations have been committed, they will be, since that is the savage's nature. If acts of violence have been committed by the "red skins," this is proof of their treacherous nature. Furthermore, one such action indicates the potential for conspiracy among many tribes. As Professor Shulman explains the logic, "In the manner of self-validating systems of belief, almost any enemy action thus reinforces our original expectations and makes us even more destructive."[22] The proof burden for such a conspiracy is minimal, especially if the assumption regarding Indian treachery is accepted. For example, with this assumption, Parkman relies upon only <u>one</u> letter written by a M. D'Abbadie dated, simply 1764 to prove the "conspiracy." Wilbur Jacobs explains that:

> . . . nobody has succeeded in locating (the letter) since Parkman's time. D'Abbadie arrived in Louisiana from France on June 29, 1763 and was hardly in a position to give accurate information on Pontiac's sending of war belts in the year 1762. It is odd that Parkman should rely chiefly upon a letter written in 1764, two years after

Pontiac had sent his wampum ambassadors 'from camp to camp and village to village,' since this is a major source used to confirm his thesis of the 'conspiracy,' Parkman might well have given a complete description of the letter.$_{23}$ Failure to correctly document his major assumption, however, does not diminish the functions of this myth.

Each episode (with one exception) of conflict between Whites and Indians is arranged so that Anglo-American forces are defending themselves against the unprovoked attack and atrocities of numerically superior Indian forces. With the scene so designed, violence, especially lurid, bloodthirsty violence, is only characteristic of the "savage." Moreoever, the Indian appears to use violence of a larger scale than does the Anglo. Parkman adds to this impression by giving account after detailed account of unprovoked Indian violence. He dwells on Indian violence in an obsessive way. Yet, he barely mentions White violence against Native Americans. Absent his atrocity stories, his "history" would be only three-fourths as long.

In his one presentation of White violence against Indians Parkman does give specific details. He illustrates fifty armed frontiersmen, the "Paxton Boys," murdering six Indians at Conestoga Manor. Stressing the provocation of the Whites, "It is not for those living in the tranquility of polished life fully to conceive the depth and force of that unquenchable, indiscriminate hate which Indian outrages can awaken," he narrates that the "furious ruffians shot, stabbed and hacked to death all whom they found there." Later the same frontiersmen killed the fourteen surviving Indians from the first attack, firing so close to the unarmed men, women and children "that the brains were scattered by the explosion." However, Parkman hints darkly that the suspicions of the Paxton men against these Indians (that they had abetted the uprising by acting as "spies") "were not wholly unfounded." $_{24}$Their "general complaints were founded in justice."

Therefore Parkman portrays White violence as a rational reponse to Indian outrages -- as the only means of control an Indian can understand. For soldiers and settlers who fight the Indians with "deadly, cool determination," violence is a routine non-extraordinary matter. However, Indian violence against Whites is unprovoked out of a "rage . . . too deep to be quenched" and "outrages" illustrate "unabated ferocity." Indian violence is irrational and uncontrollable. Such a mythic conceptualization reinforces the characterization of the Native American "as the antithesis of civilization . . . a demonic force (rather) than a living person, a rampaging demiurge, not just a member of a primitive culture with deficient manners."[25] Therefore, the most extreme response was justified by the White frontiersman.

In addition to the immutable, treacherous savage, the conspiracy myth provides a plot-line in which demonic savages threaten "defenceless Whites." White soldiers are forced to "do their duty" and "kill" Indians while Indians vividly "murder" innocent Whites. With their wagons drawn in a circle, Whites labor to defend themselves from savages consistently and constantly conspiring against them. Therefore these key symbols are illustrated by Parkman's <u>Conspiracy of Pontiac</u>:

1. Indian cultures are doomed.

2. Indians cannot/will not accept White values (civilization).

3. <u>All</u> Indians are, by nature, hostile, savage and treacherous.

4. Indians are irrationally violent.

5. White violence is a rational reaction to Indian "depredations."

6. Indian tribes conspire and plot against Whites.

Crania Americana

Background

Parkman's prototype provided mythic justification for the treatment of the Native American. While such a myth might fill important functions for those on the "cutting edge" of the frontier anxious for themselves and their safety, overtly it could not fulfill similar manifest functions for those for whom an intellectual rationale was needed to justify the realities of control.[26] Therefore the intellectual elite turned to "Science" and "empiricism" to validate their ideological beliefs in Anglo-Saxon superiority; the subsequent controversy spread through the rest of society. The importance of scientific symbols is emphasized by Professors Carlson and Colburn:

> No single group did more to legitimatize race stereotyping than did scientists. Through their supposedly objective studies of craniology, physiogonomy, eugenics, and ethnology, intelligence and social behavior, these scholars, operating from a basically Anglo-Saxon norm, attempted to prove that popular images of minorities were scientifically correct. Their work on behalf of Anglo-Saxon superiority, however, only proved that their racial prejudice was stronger than their scientific dedication.[27]

That their symbolizaton went beyond mere academic debate and entered society at large is explained by Reginald Horsman:

> . . . but America in the age of Manifest Destiny also bred its scientific prophets who provided an intellectual rationale for the realities of power. Whatever the views of the philanthropists, the scientists' ideas of permanent racial inferiority, widely disseminated in books and magazines, permeated political and diplomatic arguments of the late 1840's and become of key importance in the controversy over American expansion.[28]

Opposition to scientific arguments for racial inferiority was centered squarely in Jeffersonian thought and a literal interpretation of the Old Testament. In the words of the Declaration, it was a "self evident truth that all men are created equal." And, as William Stanton explains, "These words did not mean to Jefferson simply that men ought to enjoy equality of opportunity or equality before the law. They meant precisely that men had been Created [emphasis original] equal. That equality of rights derived from the Biblical Creation."[29]

However, there was not a consensus regarding the equality of the races. In the 1830's a direct onslaught on the inferiority of Native Americans was originated by Dr. Charles Caldwell. Caldwell was a prominent physician in Kentucky and became the first important phrenologist. He challenged the Biblically based Unitary Creation theory. He asserted that there were four distinct species of man -- Caucasian, Mongolian, Indian and African. Each species inherited specific abilities and potential. Moreover, Caldwell insisted that the abilities and potential of Indians were "inferiorly organized and endowed," and that "the years of this race [the Indians] are not only numbered; they are comparatively few."[30] While such an outspoken challenge to the unitary creation theory was rare in the 1830's various other scientists, critics and interested parties began to engage in theorizing, "If all men were related, how could their various differences be accounted for?" Because of the immanent presence of Blacks and Native Americans, every citizen, elite or not, became an ethnologist or "at least a speculator on matters of race."[31] However, in 1839, there appeared a text which was hailed as a solution, "to establish permanent organic principles" to the confused and sometimes vitrolic speculation about the origin of the races.[32] Moreoever, if the thoughts of Francis Parkman provided qualitative justificaton for the destruction of the Native American, the painstaking measurements in Samuel George Morton's [33] Crania Americana provided a quantitative rationale.

Morton's earliest publication revealed an interest in geology stimulated by Robert Jameson's lectures at Edinburgh. In 1834 he published his Synopsis of the Organic Remains of the Creataceous Group of the United States. In this text he analyzed the fossils gathered by the Lewis and Clark expedition. However, Morton did not concentrate his energies all in one area of investigation. Although plagued by ill-health his entire life, he engaged in a large practice in Philadelphia, lectured as a Professor of Anatomy at Pennsylvania Medical College and published books and articles in scientific journals on anatomy, medicine and vertebrate palenontology, as well as geology and craniology.[34] In the 1820's he developed an interest in craniology. Aroused, he said, when preparing a lecture on the "Five Races of Man," he found he had no example crania. At his request friends and acquaintances all over the world sent him example crania; some even robbing Indian graves at the risk of their own skulls. He soon had established in Philadelphia an American Golgotha; the world's largest scientific collection of human skulls. But Morton was solely dependent upon others for compilation of his collection and never went into the field himself.[35] After Morton's collection of Crania reached more than one hundred, he began planning a craniological work on the American Indians. Accordingly, in 1837, he sent out a Prospectus, as was customary at that time, describing his planned text and requesting more skulls and "subscriptions." Two years later the work was ready for the printer. Described as nonargumentative and of retiring nature, Morton was an unlikely candidate "to foment revolution in American science, to provide the boots and saddles and spurs with which to ride the mass of mankind."[36]

Crania Americana consists of an introductory chapter, "On the Varieties of the Human Species," and a lengthy descriptive chapter on the crania and customs of the Indian nations. Additionally, the text contains a summary of anatomical measurements, seventy-one lithographic plates and an essay by George Combe, a well-known phrenologist.

Throughout the text Morton is nonargumentative. He prefers to let the reader "draw his own conclusions." However, it is clear that Morton was impressed with the accomplishments of the Anglo-Saxon race. Caucasians have "peopled the finest portions of the earth and given birth to its fairest inhabitants." Using his symbols, Caucasians are "Fair, great, robust, large, remarkable, prominent and beautiful." Moreover, "this race is distinguished for the facility with which it attains the highest intellectual endowments." However, the American Race (Native Americans) are "averse to cultivation and slow in acquiring knowledge; restless, revengeful, and fond of war . . ." They are "brown, dark," with "low brows and small skulls."[37]

Morton does not overtly judge, as did Parkman, Rather, his symbols reveal that he shared in the social myth of White supremacy. However, if one accepts the principles of craniology which Morton legitimizes and Morton's findings (his "measurements"), the only conclusion that can follow is that Native Americans (and Blacks and Orientals) are inherently intellectually inferior to Anglos.

In his "Preface," he symbolizes his overt intentions: "The principal design has been to give accurate delineations of the crania of more than forty Indian nations." He is also interested in determining "by the evidence of osteological facts, whether the American aborigines, of all epochs, have belonged to one race, or to a plurality of Races." How this determination is to be made is unclear -- especially since Morton refers to Phrenology, apologetic for his own "inability to do justice to the subject." Morton included an essay on phrenology from George Combe. Combe had written this "memoir" without recourse to Morton's measurements or even knowing what Morton had written. The reader, by means of Combe's essay, could apply the Phrenological rules to "every skull" within Morton's study.[38]

Unitary Creation

Morton's next section is a long "Introductory Essay," concerning the varieties of the Human species. He relates the nearly complete peopling of the earth, regardless of the geographical climate. There are a few uninhabited countries because of "choice" not coercion. Thus,

> The Eskinmau, surrounded by an atmosphere that freezes Mercury, rejoices in his snowy desert, and has pined in unhappiness when removed to more genial climes. On the other hand, the native of the torrid regions of Africa, oppressed by a vertical sun, and often delirious with thirst, thinks no part of the Earth as desireable . . .[39]

Additionally migration is rare, except in temperate zones, although the "spirit of migratory enterprise" is without limit in modern times. Moreover, the inhabitants of every extended locality exhibit physical and moral traits common only to themselves:

> The Arabians are at this time precisely what they were in the day of the patriachs; the Hindoos have altered in nothing since they were described by the earliest writers: nor have three thousand years made any difference in the kind and hair of the Negro. In like matter the characteristic features of the Jews may be recognized in the sculpture of the temples of Luxor and Karnack, in Egypt where they have been depicted for nearly thirty centuries.[40]

Subsequently, Morton notes the popular belief in the Unitary Creation and environmental adaption of each recognizable human species. However, rather than confronting these issues directly, he finesses his way around them:

> Without attempting to pursue this intricate question in detail, we may inquire, whether it is more consistent with the known government of the universe to suppose, that the same Omnipotence that created man, would adapt him at once to the physical, as well as to the moral circumstances in which he was to dwell on earth? It is indeed difficult to imagine that an all-wise Providence, after having by the deluge, destroyed all mankind excepting the family of Noah, should leave these to combat and with seemingly uncertain and inadequate means, the various external causes that tended to oppose the great object of their dispersion: and we are left to the reasonable conclusion, that each Race was adopted from the beginning to its peculiar local destination. In other words, it is assumed, that the physical characteristics which distinguish the different Races are independent of external causes.[41]

He also recognized "mixed races" as a result of migrations, mentions controversies over the names and numbers of the various Races of Man but is "unprepared to offer anything new" on this subject. As subnations within the five Races he proposes, for the sake of study, twenty-two families or "groups of nations possessing to a greater or lesser extent, similarity of physical and moral character and language."[42]

Thus, Morton sidesteps the most controversial racial issues of the 1830's and does not directly argue regarding Unitary Creation. He concludes that a wise Creator would engage in economic and sound craftsmanship. He maintains that such economy would be served best by physically adapting each race to its environment. He concludes, reasonably, that the characteristics of each race were "independent of external causes." He provides one additional argument for this independence. Assuming literal Biblical chronology which assigned the Creation of Man to about 4,000 B.C., Morton notes that Egyptian art, dating perhaps to 3,000 B.C., already clearly illustrated separate races. It would seem a physical impossibility that races might have developed in the thousand-odd intervening years. However Morton does not state this conclusion in the text but argues for this "physical impossibility" in a "note." By denying the environmental hypothesis, he allows for the permanence of racial characteristics.[43]

Indian Nature

Initially Morton establishes that Native Americans are identifiable, "possessed of certain physical traits that identify them in localities remote from each other." Additionally he provides a preliminary judgment of their "character" which illustrates his belief in the superiority of "Caucasian" civilization. "In character these nations (The Appalachian Branch which includes all the nations of North America excepting the Mexicans) are warlike, cruel and unforgiving. They turn with aversion from the restraints of civilized life and have made but trifling progress in mental culture or the useful arts."[44] As will be noted, Morton does defend Indians against several charges. But the assumptions of White superiority, inferiority of Native cultures, Native violence and cruelty, and their intellectual inferiority are apparent in his discussion. However, he does not refer to his "measurements" as proof of these assumptions. He cites other researchers and their "concurrent testimony." Although he attempts to provide a diversity of opinions, particularly on the improvability of the Indians, he concludes with Parkman as to the inherent "gulf" between the two races.

In purely "scientific" symbols he discusses the physical traits of the American Family.[45] He is most at home with such descriptions, obviously preferring the "minutia" of pedantic classification to expressing theoretical judgments. He also discusses the "deficient beard" of the native tribes and explains their color. As a literal observer he rejects the adjective "red" as applied to Native Americans. He believes this misnomer may be a result of the "war paint" popular in many tribes and instead points out that "no epithet derivable from the color of the skin, so correctly describes the Americans collectively as that of Brown Race." Additionally, he discusses the stature and "keen senses" of the Natives, indicating correctly the diversity between individuals and different tribes. It is clear that Morton recognizes physical differences among Indians. He finds fault with those "closet naturalists" who had argued for the physical inferiority of the Indian:

> How idle is the theory which attributes to these people less hardiness of constitution than belongs to the European! What, in truth, can exceed their endurance of fatigue, of hunger, of thirst, and of cold? By day and by night, in summer and winter, over mountains, and through rivers and forests they pursue their determined course, whether the object be revenge on an enemy, or food for their families at home. It has been assumed in evidence of their weakness that they sunk under the labor of the mines much sooner than either Europeans or Negroes: but it must be borne in mind that the Indian is incapable of servitude, and that his spirit sunk at once in captivity, and with it his physical energy: while on the other hand, the more pliant Negro, yielding to his fate, and accomodating himself to his condition, bore his heavy burthen with comparative ease. Thus it was that a moral influence destroyed thousands of Indians in Hispaniola, until the race of islanders became extinct, while their fellow laborers lived and multiplied in defiance of oppression.[46]

Not only does Morton "celebrate" the hardy constitution of the Indians, but he defends them against charges of cowardice and treachery. He explains that, by education, the Indian is taught "to consider a successful strategem more honorable than open victory." Retreat and subterfuge are "tactics" which the Indian has used successfully. But there is no doubt about the courage of the Native American:

> The courage of the Indian is evident in his desperate resistance to a superior force; by his choice of death to capitulation, even when he has every guaranty of personal safety; and by that unshrinking firmness with which he sees and feels the approach of death under the most cruel torments. To be whole days and nights fastened to a stake and subject to incessant but gradual mutilation -- to sustain this load of misery with fortitude and even with cheerfulness, and finally to sink into death without losing for a moment his indomitable self-possession, are surely sufficient proofs of the courage of Indians.

Indians are thus not cowards but "perpetually vigilant."[47]

Surprisingly, Morton does not share Parkman's view of the "treacherous" nature of Native Americans. In a long passage he defends the Indians against such charges and makes a strong negative judgment against Anglo policy:

> It is usual to charge the Indians with treachery: but in most instances it will be found that they have only retorted the perfidiousness that has been heaped upon them by others. The annals of Indian history are ample evidence of this fact. A system of encroachment and oppression has been practised upon them since the first landing of Europeans on the shores of America: their lands have been seized upon the most frivolous pretences and they have had no redress at the hand of the White man: wars have been fomented among them to procure their mutual destruction: and when they have been weakened by the conflict, the common enemy has stepped in and seized upon their possessions. They have been taken in their villages, or inveighed on ship-board, to be sold

> into slavery; and in fact every art that cupidity could devise has been put into practice to deprieve them of liberty and of life. Is it surprising that a people thus oppressed should retaliate on their oppressors? Or shall we stigmatise them as treacherous when they have received so much treachery at our hands?[48]

Morton clearly has sympathy for the "Indian," but such sympathy does not grant equality.

As if embarrassed by his defenses, Morton's tone changes. Although he may not share Parkman's view of the "treacherous" Indian, he does share belief in the violent, demonic savage:

> It is not, however, to be denied that they are unfeeling by nature and cruel by education. To spill the blood of an enemy, to torture him to death by slow degrees is the supreme pleasure of the American savage. He wreaks his vengeance with equal fury on all kindred of his adversary. Old age, the helplessness of infancy or the charms of youth, have no power to check his destroying spirit. His is, in truth, a demonic love of slaughter which delights in the shriek of the wounded and groan of the dying. Revenge is his ruling passion, and it is the first lesson a father inculcates in his child.

Moreover, like Parkman, Morton sees the prime energizing force of the Native American to be war:

> It must in truth be confessed that the Indian is least to be admired at home; for in him the domestic virtues are but partially expanded. War and the chase, on the other hand, call forth his energies. Hunger, fatigue and toil are encountered without a murmur, and the mind, goaded on by the powerful impluse of ambition or revenge, becomes untiring and indomitable. The firmness of purpose, its attendant privations, and the final contest with a courageous adversary, gives seductive exaltation to the character of the American savage.

Absent motivating force, Morton pictures the savage "at home:"

> Behold him lounging under the shade of a tree, the victim of apathy and sloth, too vain to cultivate his fields, or to raise a hand for his own support, while he looks with complacency on the toils of a mother, a wife, or a daughter, whom the barbarous usages of Indian thralldom have condemned to perpetual slavery.

So hateful and miserable is this "thralldom" that, Morton asserts, squaws kill their female babies to prevent them from suffering this fate and commit suicide themselves.[49] He comments positively on Indian religion. However, he continues a negative value judgment when he provides his view of the intellectual potential of the Native American. This comment is not presented as an argument but as an anthropological description, not related to his study:

> The intellectual faculties of this great family appear to be of decidedly inferior cast when compared with those of the Caucasian or Mongolian races. They are not only averse to the restraints of education, but for the most part incapable of a continued process of reasoning on abstract subjects. Their minds seize with an avidity on simple truths while they at once reject whatever requires investigation and analysis. Their proximity, for more than two centuries to European institutions has made scarcely appreciable changes in their mode of thinking or their manner of life; and as to their own social condition, they are probably in most respects what they were at the primitive epoch of their existence.

Moreover, Indians have an inherent inability to understand anything regarding numbers which explains their misunderstanding of many treaty settlements.[50]

Morton concludes his description by examining the problem of Indian improvability. Like Parkman, he believes there is a "separation" between the White and Indian mind. He doubts that the Indian can be "civilized," although he does not reject the possibility if "education had been bestowed on a single family through several generations." However, for his evidence here (besides several anecdotes) he cites Professors Laurance and Caldwell. Caldwell's position has already been described. Laurence observed, not optimistically:

> To expect that the Americans can be raised by any culture to an equal height in moral sentiments and intellectual energy with Europeans, appears to me quite as unreasonable as it would be to hope that the bull-dog may equal the greyhound in speed; that the latter may be taught to hunt by scent like the hound; or that the mastiff may rival in talents and acquirements the sagacious and docile poddle.[51]

Morton's description does not reduce the Indian to the animalistic state, for the purpose of execution, that Parkman's did. However, it does clearly state the deficient nature of the savage. Morton's judgments are a probable result of the undeveloped methodology of anthropological observation contaminated by unconscious racism. Morton, as stated, never went into the field himself; he probably did not travel west of Philadelphia. Therefore, he not only relied upon others to complete his collection, but also for the scientific description of the "American Race." Such methodology would be inexcusable today but was common in the last century.[52] Morton presented social judgments of Indian character not as conscious racism but as apparent anthropological fact based upon "concurrent testimony." Although there was no guarantee that the "anecdotes" that he relied upon for proof were representative of Indian character, they were the best proof available. It is surprising that he defended Native Americans from charges of physical inferiority, treachery and cowardice. He does not cite a source in these defenses; therefore it is difficult to determine his reasons or bases for such judgments. However, his rejection of the charges of the physical inferiority of the Indian is not surprising. His knowledge of physiology and "osteological fact" makes this theory the most falsifiable and one instance in which he does have the theory to apply confidently. He leaves these "observations" and turns to his real purpose -- measurement.[53]

Based upon a summary of his detailed measurements he makes three relatively non-controversial conclusions:

1st. That the American Race differs essentially from all others, not excepting the Mongolian; nor do the feeble analogies of language, and the more obvious ones in civil and religious institutions and the arts, denote anything beyond casual or colonial communication with the Asiatic nations; and even these analogies may be perhaps accounted for, as Humboldt has suggested, in the mere coincidence arising from similar wants and impulses in nations inhabiting similar latitudes.
2nd. That the American nations, excepting the Polar tribes, are of one Race and one species, but of two great Families, which resemble each other in physical, but differ in intellectual character.
3rd. That the cranial remains discovered in the Mounds, from Peru to Wisconsin, belong to the same race, and probably the Toltecan Family.

With these conclusions he establishes Native Americans as a separate race and defeats the popular thesis that they belonged to the "Mongol Race." Furthermore, all Native Americans illustrate shared racial characteristics and the "Mound Builders" possessed these characteristics. Again Morton does not explicitly state the obvious conclusion; that the Indians were a distinct species of man. He allows his measurements to speak for themselves especially regarding "internal capacity:"

RACES	No. of Skulls	Mean Internal Capacity	
Caucasian	52	87	
Mongolian	10	83	
Malay	18	81	
American	147	82	
Ethiopian	29	78	54

He relates that he "rejected" the skulls of idiots and persons under age in researching these measurements. That he was partly aware of one ramification of his study -- the apparent superior intellectual capacity of the Caucasian (if this tenet of phrenology is applied), is obvious. He implies that the differential may be underestimated, writing, "with a single exception," the skulls of the Caucasians measured were "derived from the lowest and least

69

educated class of society." Furthermore, he indicates that "the Hindoo skulls measured may have decreased the Caucasian mean because the skulls of these people are probably smaller than those of any other existing nation." He does not directly state this underestimation. It is up to the reader to draw conclusions regarding Caucasian superiority.[55] But, the reader is overwhelmed with tables of Anatomical and Phrenological measurement. The non-phrenologist is naturally forced to the small "mean" table, previously cited, to give meaning to the study. This logical emphasis is predetermined by the extent to which the chart reinforces Anglo superiority, upholds racial stereotypes and avoids controversy regarding creation theory.

Focusing narrowly upon "osteological facts" functions to draw the reader onto Morton's ground, as well as to emphasize an unstated but undeniable conclusion. Professor Stanton explains:

> The question of specific unity or diversity was left to the reader. But on the evidence presented, who could decide for unity? One might still insist that climate could change color, but who could say that climate could change the osteological character of the individual, determine the capacity of the skull or the angle the face makes with the horizontal? Here was a portion of the human frame which, protected from the rays of the sun and fetid air of marshes, could not be influenced by environment. Here was the line of demarcation between the old anthropology and the new: mathematical measurement was suplanting aesthetic judgement.[56]

Controversy existed regarding Unitary Creation and an individual seeking to deny it had to deny the collective nineteenth century belief in the Bible and the book of Genesis. This is not to say that most individuals and scientists believed in the equality of White, Red and Black and those shades in between. It is to say that most Americans were eager to accept and extend Morton's findings to their "logical" conclusion.[57] One such American was Josiah Nott.

Josiah Nott

Nott of Mobile, Alabama was one of the South's leading surgeons and defender of polygenesis and Anglo superiority. Between 1844 and 1857, Nott reached an international reputation by writing on race.[58] In addition to his concern for the perpetuation of Southern slavery, Nott used Morton's findings regarding the Indian, along with those of other theorists, to argue for inherent Indian inferiority. In his first publication Nott's racism is apparent. He asserts, "History and observation both teach that in accordance with this defective organization, the Mongol, the Malay, the Indian, and the Negro, are now and have been in all ages and all places inferior to the Caucasian."[59] For his "proof" for these conclusions, Nott turns to Morton:

> Dr. S. G. Morton, by a long series of well-conceived experiments, has established the fact, that the capacity of the crania of the Mongol, Indian, and Negro, and all dark-skinned races, is smaller than that of the pure White man. And this deficiency seems to be especially well-marked in those parts of the brain which have been assigned to the moral and intellectual faculties.[60]

Nott, however, was selective in the proofs he drew from Morton. While Morton had distinguished between the barbarous and semi-civilized tribes of North and South America, respectively, Nott made no such distinction. The polemics of his language are clear. Nott recalled that Cortez had illustrated how five hundred ". . . Caucasian arms and heads were worth more than millions of these miserable creatures." The bee and the beaver, he declared, displayed as much genius at construction as the Mexican, ". . . everything in the history of the Bee shows a reasoning power little short that of a Mexican." He had no reservations regarding the fate of the North American Indians. This inherent savage remained so after all attempts at civilization; perhaps even more "worthless and corrupt." Moreover, ". . . whatever improvement exists in their condition is attributable to a mixture of races. Their chiefs and Rulers are Whites and mixed bloods, and the full-blood Indian is now what he always has and always will be."[61]

In 1854, Nott and the Egyptologist George Gliddon edited a work dedicated "to the Memory of Morton." <u>Types of Mankind</u> went through ten editions and "attempted to present all the evidence which had been advanced to prove that distinct races had existed from the beginning of time and that they had been created separately, with different intellectual, moral and physical capacities."[62] Nott and Gliddon broke completely with Biblical traditions. They did not argue indirectly, as had Morton, but stated that it was the responsibility of every Christian to inquire "honestly" into the unitary/polygenetic question using the tools of science rather than disputed scriptures. However, the cant of racism permeates their "study," most significantly for the Negro, but the Indian is not neglected.

Whereas Morton wished for his reader to draw his own conclusions, Nott and Gliddon leave no conclusion unstated. In their scientific conception of Race and relationship between races, cranial capacity justifies the elevation of the Caucasian race. This is not just "science" but destiny:

> Nations and races, like individuals, have each an especial destiny: some are born to rule, and others to be ruled. And such has ever been the history of mankind. No two distinctly marked races can dwell together on equal terms. Some races, moreover, appear destined to live and prosper for a time, until the destroying race comes, which is to exterminate and supplant them. Observe how the aborigines of America are fading away before the exotic races of Europe.

While they reject biblical explanation of Creation, they are all too-willing to invoke the Creator's hand in explaining the dominance of the Anglos:

> These groups of races heretofore comprehended under the generic term Caucasian, have, in all ages been the rulers; and it requires no prophets eye to see they are destined eventually to conquer and hold every foot of the globe where climate does not interpose an impenetrable barrier. No philanthropy, no legislation, no missionary labors can change this law; it is written in man's nature by the hand of the Creator.

Just as the Caucasian is destined to control the world by Divine appointment, so the Indian is destined to disappear and melt. And, as Parkman indicated, this is a result of the immutability of the Indian or his unimprovability:

> In America, the aboriginal barbarous tribes cannot be forced to change their habits, or even persuaded to successful emigration: they are melting away from year to year; and of the millions which once inhabited that portion of the United States east of the Mississippi river, all have vanished, but a few scattered families; and their representatives, removed by government to the Western frontier, are reduced to less than one hundred thousand. It is clear as the sun at noon day, that in a few generations more, the last of these Red Men will be numbered with the dead. We constantly read glowing accounts, from interested missionaries, of the civilization of these tribes; but a civilized <u>full-blooded</u> [emphasis original] Indian does not exist among them . . . No human ingenuity can induce them to become educated, or to do an honest day's work: they are supported entirely by begging, besides a little traffic of the squaws in the woods. To one who has lived among American Indians, it is vain to talk of civilizing them. You might as well attempt to change the nature of the buffalo.[63]

For Nott, Buffalo and Indians alike are limited by their inherent makeup and both submit more readily to extermination than to change. Moreover, apparent change is false, as it originates not in the character of the Indian but through alteration of genetic makeup:

> It has been falsely asserted, that the <u>Choctaw</u> and <u>Cherokee</u> Indians have made great progress in civilization. I assert positively, after the most ample investigation of the facts, that the pure-blooded Indians are everywhere unchanged in their habits. Many white persons, settling among the above tribes, have intermarried with them; and all such trumpeted progress exists among these whites and their mixed breeds alone. The pure-blooded savage still skulks untamed through the forest, or gallops athwart the prairie. Can anyone call the name of a single pure Indian of the <u>Barbarous</u> tribes who -- except in death, like a <u>wild cat</u> -- has done anything worthy of remembrance?[64]

Thus, pure blood dooms the Indian to "death," but Nott is not proposing miscegenation as a solution to the Indian's unimprovability. As the author of the "the Mulatto a Hybrid -- Probable Extermination of the Two Races," he would recoil in horror from the marriage between John Rolfe and Pocahontas, Royal presentation or not. Rather, he would prefer a race war, but even this conflict would not civilize these "types":

> Looking back over the world's history, it will be seen that human progress has arisen mainly from the war of races. All the great impulses which have been given to it from time to time have been the result of conquests and colonizations. Certain races would be stationary and barbarous forever, were it not for the introductions of new blood and novel influences; and some of the lowest types are beyond the reach even of these salutary stimulants to melioration.$_{65}$

Ethnographic and physiological "proofs" are included among these statements but "cranial capacity" overshadows all, as it is the osteological fact which proves Anglo superiority. Nott goes one step further -- although the skull reflects cranial capacity, examination of the brain itself should reflect obvious physical proof of the "graded" differences between the races. In comparing plaster casts of European and Native American brains, he notes:

> If the anterior lobe manifests the intellectual faculties -- the middle lobe, the propensities common to man with the lower animals -- and the posterior lobe, the domestic and social affections -- and if size influences the power of manifestation, the result will be that in the Native American intellect will be feeble -- and in the European strong; in the American animal propensity will be very great -- in the European more moderate; while in the American, the domestic and social affections will be feeble and, in the European, powerful . . .

Moreover, such differences are consistent with their external features:

> The above comparison of two human brains illustrates anatomical divergences between European and American races. Could a complete

series of engravings embracing specimens from each type of mankind, be submitted to the reader, his eye seizing instantaneously the cerebral distinctions . . . [which] would compel him to admit that the physical differences of human races is as obvious in their internal brains as in their external features.[66]

That is, Native American and other non-caucasian races bear external stigma of their inferiority. One function of Nott's extension and statement of Morton's measurements is to provide proof of the internal inferiority of Native Americans. Just as Parkman created an Indian whose internal ugliness was consistent with Parkman's view of the Indian's external appearance, Nott provides an Indian internally inferior as signified in external features. Thus, Morton and Nott's "science" provided key symbols which rationalized White superiority and innate intellectual Indian inferiority. In periodicals and publications of the 1840's and 1850's, Americans were constantly reminded that the external differences between races were meaningful. These "key symbols," while apparently "scientifically" based, were essentially similar to those symbols included in Parkman's conspiracy myth:

1. Indian physical differences are proof that they belong to a race apart from Anglos.

2. Indians are inferior, intellectually and physically, to Anglos.

3. Indians are genetically unchangeable.

4. Indians are doomed.

5. Indians are savage and violent.

As Reginald Horsman concludes, "Many to whom Indian inferiority, inability to be civilized, and ultimate extinction seemed evident now were supplied with scientific proofs."[67] Such beliefs ultimately found their way into Government policies directed at the Native American.

Native Americans, "Constitutions" and Extra-Constitutional Assumptions

We shall now examine key governmental symbols of Native Americans as expressed in "Constitutions." Additionally, the Cherokee removal will be analyzed to determine the effects of extra-constitutional assumptions on "constitutional" policy making. Comparing "Constitutional clauses" with extra-constitutional assumptions should be enlightening, since, as Burke explains:

> . . . the survival of the Constitutional titles or clauses through radical reconstructions of the national situations will give us testimony about the nature of unity and division that serves pretty much as the overall category for everything and certainly for human relations.[68]

The "promises" made in the constitutions regarding American Indians are examined chronologically as they functioned within the conflict between Anglos and Native Americans.

Constitutions Before 1787

During the Revolution, the various Indian tribes, although urged by the colonies to remain neutral, generally fought on the side of the "tories." Even when the Indians did not do so, the colonists were all too willing to believe that the British were instigating, through the Indians, the murder of "defenceless" women and children. This suspicion of English/Indian conspiracy remained through the War of 1812 with some factual basis.[69] The result of these suspicions as well as actual Indian aid to the British was that the central government's Indian Affairs policy originated while the Indians were regarded as "enemy nations." The subsequently utilized treaty making process enhanced this perception.[70]

The end of the Revolution found Native Americans in a legal limbo. They had not been "conquered" but the Peace of Paris made no mention of the Indians. Early American policy reflected the resulting confusion over the exact status of the Indians and their relationship to first the "Confederation" and then to the United States.

Article IV of the Articles of Confederation stated that Congress had "the sole and exclusive right and power of . . . regulating trade and managing all affairs with the Indians, not members of any of the states, provided that the legislative right of any state within its own limits be not infringed or violated . . ."[71] Professor Hagan explains the implications of this clause:

> The weakness of the Articles of Confederation was nowhere more apparent than in its feeble efforts to cope with the Indian problem. Apparently barred by the language of the Articles from infringing upon a state's rights to abuse Indians resident within its own boundaries, Congress was equally futile in dealing with the Indians beyond state boundaries.
> . . . Both Indians and whites simply bypassed the inadequate forces Congress stationed along the disputed frontier.[72]

Of course, under the Articles, the states were virtually the only level of enforcement. If a state did not wish to cooperate with the Congress, it simply did not. Thus the ambiguity and weakness of the Articles made it impossible for the Continental Congress to develop a coherent Indian policy. However, the precedent for maintaining the responsibility for "Indian affairs" in Congress was established. Moreover, the Congress utilized the British custom of negotiating for Indian land by diplomatic treaty and issuing "ordinances" to enforce these treaties. The implication of this custom was that the Indians were sovereign nations and at least as powerful as the Whites. The framers of the clause indicated that Congress would manage all affairs <u>with</u> the Indians, not "of" or "for" the Indians.

Concern in the central government for establishing clear jurisdiction and ameliorating fraudulent land practices by Whites with Indians was illustrated in the Northwest Ordinance of 1787. The Ordinance also provided the basic policy for the government of territories and the process by which these territories might become states, "on an equal footing with the original states, in all respect whatever." Moreover, the Ordinance set forth a bill of rights that was similar to the future Bill of

Rights in the Constitution. The rights were guaranteed as "articles of compact" between the original states and the people of the territories. These rights included: religious liberty, a writ of habeas corpus and trial by jury and protection against "cruel and unusual punishments." The framers of the Ordinance also emphasized that "no man shall be deprived of his liberty or property but by . . . the law of the land . . . [and with] full compensation." The Ordinance neither included nor excluded Native Americans from these guarantees in Article II. However, in Article III the framers, at least, recognized the Indian's right of property and to be let alone. The framers also asserted in this article an "ideal wish" towards which future relations with Native Americans should strive:

> The utmost good faith shall always be observed toward the Indians; their lands and property shall never be taken from them without their consent; and, in their property, rights, and liberty, they never shall be invaded or disturbed, unless in just and lawful wars authorized by Congress; but laws founded in justice and humanity shall, from time to time, be made for preventing wrongs being done to them and for preserving peace and friendship with them.[73]

Implicit in this article is the recognition of Indian tribes as separate nations since to Congress was preserved the right to make "just and lawful wars." However, paternalism is also apparent in the "wish" to prevent "wrongs being done to them." As a "constitution," the Ordinance was unique in the conscious manner in which at least minimal human rights were promised to Native Americans. Subsequent documents made promises regarding obligations and requirements but not at the level of human rights.

Constitutions After 1787

Perhaps Native Americans might have had some legal chance, had the minimal "wishes" incorporated in the Northwest Ordinance been included in the Constitution and Bill of Rights. However, the framers of the Constitution had even less to say regarding the Native Americans. Indians are mentioned in only two clauses of the original Constitution. In section three of Article I, "Indians not taxed," are excluded from apportionment for Congressional representation. In section eight, the framers reserve to Congress the power to regulate commerce "with the Indian tribes." Additionally, in the records of the discussion and debates leading to the adoption of the Constitution, there is no evidence of Native American rights specifically being discussed. For example, in <u>The Federalist</u>, Madison, Hamilton and Jay only mention "the Indian problem" as a reason for a standing militia and example of the weakness of the Articles.[74] In the actual debates at the 1787 convention, attention was given to Indians and their "exclusion from the basis of apportionment" and their importance to the commerce clause. There is a slim indication that the framers envisioned some potential for Native American participation in Constitutional guarantees. The framers exclude "Indians not taxed," implying that Indians might at some future time own their land in "fee simple."[75] Fee simple was a legal concept derived from English land law of the late Middle Ages and signified "absolute ownership, or the right of the owner to sell the land to anyone, or to allow it to be inherited by his heirs." Private property was envisioned as an instrument of civilization. As both Henry Knox, Secretary of War during both the Articles and in Washington's administration, and Thomas Jefferson were to argue, ownership in fee simple among the Indians would stimulate them to acquire "civilized" techniques to enhance the value of the property. However, in the event civilization was not acquired, Whites encroaching upon Indian land would kill the game upon which the Natives depended and the Indians would sell their land and move further west.[76]

Knox and Jefferson's ideal provided a "constitution-beneath-the-constitution" which admitted the equality of the Native Americans but sought to make over Indian societies into copies of White society and eventually to absorb Indians into the mainstream. This process was to be a peaceful one and a useful by-product would be the acquisition of land needed for expansion. Their ideal policy, however, was a failure in its attempts to civilize the Indians. But the assumption that Native Americans should be improved and "civilized" remained a bulwark of Federal Indian policy into the twentieth century. Moreover, the Lockean assumptions regarding the power of private ownership of land, while unsuccessful in bringing about the civilization and assimilation of Native Americans, were successful in justifying the dispossession of most Indian lands.[77]

Knox's influence is clear in the four temporary Trade and Intercourse Acts passed between 1790 and 1799.[78] The functions of these Acts were to regulate trade by means of licensing procedures, to distinguish "White" land from Indian land and to control White encroachments onto Indian lands and thereby provide "peace and progress" for all. These laws were designed to assure implementation of the various treaties and to provide enforcement against obstreperous Whites. For example, the Intercourse Act of July 22, 1790 cautioned:

> That if any citizen or inhabitant of the United States, or of either the territorial districts of the United States, shall go into any town, settlement or territory belonging to any nation or tribes of Indians, and shall there commit any crime upon, or trespass against the person or property of any peaceable and friendly Indian or Indians, which if committed within the jurisdiction of any state or within the jurisdiction of either of the said districts, against a citizen or white inhabitant thereof, would be punishable by laws of such state or district, such offenders shall be subject to the same punishment, and shall be proceeded against in the same manner as if the offence had been committed within the jurisdiction of the state or district to which he or they may belong, against a citizen or white inhabitant thereof.

Additionally, the purchase of lands from the Indians by private parties was outlawed unless accomplished at a public treaty with the United States.[79]

Similar to the Northwest Ordinance, there was some attention granted to Indian rights, although only "friendly" and "peaceable" Indians were protected. As long as they were "friendly," they would be protected as any citizen from crimes against person and property. However, such protection was extended only while they remained in "Indian country." If the

Natives went beyond legally established borders, they lost not only this protection but became "unfriendly" and "unpeaceable."

Hamilton's attempts to place the new government on sound financial footing made little allowance for the massive resources needed for enforcement and Whites committed outrages upon Indians who responded in kind. For many tribes, revenge for loss of blood relatives was an important cultural requirement. Such revenge could include either the murder and torture of the responsible party or parties or representatives thereof or the kidnapping and "adoption" of the responsible individual to literally replace the lost relative.[80] Whites, of course, had no understanding of such "savage" customs and natives who entered "White land" to engage in such actions only guaranteed their stereotype as hostile and unfriendly. Additionally, natives who left their assigned land to engage in traditional blood feuds with other Indian tribes also illustrated their savage nature. The lurid accounts of such practices provided by rescued White captives of the various Indian tribes contributed greatly to White misunderstandings of such customs.[81] Thus, although this law guaranteed the protection of Indian rights, it provided no allowance for Indian customs which would result from the inability of the Federal government to control encroaching frontiersmen.

In his message to Congress on October 25, 1791, Washington did not abandon the hope that he and Knox had for peaceful dealings with the Indians. Although the military had been used to "restrain" Indians and to defend Whites on both Northern and Southern frontiers, Washington hoped to avoid all need of coercion in the future. He intended, he said, "to advance the happiness of the Indians and to attach them firmly to the United States." The benevolent influences of both Knox and Jefferson were apparent in Washington's plan.[82] However, referred to a special committee the bill died without debate. The Act of 1790 continued in force but was a temporary measure only, "for the term of three years . . ."

In 1793, Congress did enact stronger legislation, incorporating tenets of the 1790 law with many of Washington's recommendations. The President was authorized to give goods and money to the various tribes, "to promote civilization . . . and to secure the continence of their friendship." To accomplish this civilizing influence, he was authorized to spend twenty thousand dollars a year. Moreover, the Act provided for specific punishments for Whites who committed crimes in Indian country and attempted irregular purchases of Indian land. In 1796 and 1799 the Intercourse Act was renewed, each time strengthening the President's powers. The 1796 Act drew specific boundaries of Indian country and gave the President broad powers to use force against Whites encroaching on Indian lands. Although these Acts were temporary, they did help to establish the precedent for the Federal government and especially the President as a protector of Indian land rights.

In 1802, President Jefferson urged that the temporary measures in the previous Intercourse Acts be made permanent. The result was "An Act to Regulate Trade and Intercourse With the Indian Tribes, and to Preserve Peace on the Frontiers." The Act with twenty-two sections remained in force until 1834.[83]

The Act contains the usual clauses designating "boundaries" outlawing private sale or acquiring of Indian land, outlining trade restrictions and promoting civilization. Additionally guarantees are provided Indian life and property with specific punishments provided for White incursions. Any White who commits a crime of property against an Indian must pay "a sum equal to twice the value of the property" taken or damaged. The "Treasury of the United States" will provide payment for claims which an offender cannot pay. However, in the same section, any Indian who "sought private revenge or [attempted] to obtain satisfaction by any force or violence" forfeits such payment. The Act also provides the "death penalty" for any citizen who kills an Indian or Indians "in amity with the United States." Ironically, the Act does not contain a like penalty for Indians guilty of murdering Whites. Rather, section XIV provides a lengthy process whereby a "representative attorney" under direction of the President will "make application to the nation or tribe" for restitution. It is no wonder that frontier Whites simply enforced their own laws by identifying all Indians as unfriendly, whatever their demeanor. Moreover, while the literal enforcements threatened against Whites were greater both in quality and quantity than threats made against Indians, covert justification was given in the Act for handling Whites leniently. In section VI, the military is designated as the enforcement mechanism against obstreperous White squatters. However, in providing such enforcement, officers and soldiers are cautioned to treat offenders "with all the humanity which circumstances will possibly permit." The penalty for maltreatment was court martial. The result was, in Professor Hagan's words, that "For army officers in a civilian-dominated military establishment this was sufficient warning. If Indian and White interests conflicted, the Indian was sacrificed."[84] The extent to which such interests would be sacrificed is exemplified in the case of Cherokee Indian removal.

Cherokee Indian Removal

During the Revolution, the Cherokees were in alliance with the British. Attacked by an American Southern militia, the tribe sued for peace. In May of 1777, a treaty was signed at Dewitt's Corner in which the Cherokees admitted defeat by the Americans and gave up a section of their lands included within the boundaries of South Carolina.[85] This was the first of fourteen formal treaties between the new country and the Cherokee Nation by which thousands of square miles of Cherokee land were ceded to the United States in return for tribal annuities and various gifts and goods.[86] Furthermore, although these natives came to embody a symbol of Jefferson's and Knox's policies of civilizing the Indians, the Cherokees were finally forcibly "removed" west of the Mississippi.

Immediately after the Revolution and in direct conflict with the Articles, the Cherokees ceded to Georgia land around the sources of the Oconee River. To the continued frustration of Georgia's White citizens, this was the last bit of land the Cherokees willingly ceded <u>directly</u> to Georgia. Although frequently approached and feted by the Georgia government, the Cherokees maintained their Georgia lands. By the Hopewell Treaty in 1785 the Cherokees recognized that they were "under the protection of the United States of America, and of no other sovereign whatsoever." Additionally, in Article IV, they agreed to specified boundaries but no grant of land was made concerning Georgia. The treaty also granted the

Cherokees the right to punish White squatters who remained six months after the ratification of the treaty, "as they please"; protected the Cherokees from capital crimes initiated by White citizens and warned against revenge inflicted on the "innocent." Article Twelve allowed the Cherokees "the right to send a deputy of their choice, whenever they think fit to Congress." This treaty was "signed and sealed" between representatives of the United States and the Cherokee Nation."[87] The symbol "Cherokee Nation" closes this treaty and in the subsequent treaties made between the United States and these Native Americans the designation "Cherokee Nation" appears throughout all articles. While this symbol indicates the recognition by the Federal government that the Cherokees were a "sovereign nation," the appearance of the terms "cede" and "relinquish" following Cherokee Nation in the treaties made after 1802 is a reflection of the decreasing power of the Cherokees. Moreover, while the maintenance of peace appeared to be the overt purpose of most of these treaties, all of the treaties were concerned with the ceding or relinquishment of land by the Cherokees to the U.S. Government. In the last three treaties (1817, 1819 and 1824) the symbols "peace" and "friendship" do not occur. Rather, the purpose of these treaties is to remove "doubts" regarding specific boundaries and clarify the method whereby lands in the west could be exchanged for Indian lands in Georgia.[88]

Although the Federal government had, on a number of occasions, encouraged and sought the voluntary removal of the Cherokees through the previously mentioned treaties, a simultaneous policy, "a most laudable effort," in Professor Kennedy's words," was made to promote the civilization, and, with it, the permanent establishment of these Indians upon the soil which they now inhabited."[89] This contrary "wish" was proven more effective in its influence upon the Cherokees. In 1820, President Monroe, pressured by Georgia, requested monies from Congress to extinguish by treaty Indian title to all land occupied by the Cherokees in the limits of Georgia. But, when approached by White commissioners in 1823, the Council of Chiefs of the Cherokees replied, "It is the fixed and unalterable determination of this nation never again to cede one foot more of our land."[90] The leaders of the Cherokees had learned all too well the lessons their White "friends and fathers" had taught them regarding the value of the land. As related in the memoirs of William Wirt:

> We have an account of the condition of these people from the pen of one of their own children, an educated Indian, written in 1825; one who, seven years before, was a savage, and who, at the date of this letter, was engaged in translating the New Testament into the Cherokee language. 'Apple and peach orchards are quite common,' he writes, 'and gardens are cultivated. Butter and cheese are seen on the Cherokee tables. There are many public roads in the nation, and houses of entertainment kept by natives. Numerous and flourishing villages are seen in every section of the country. Cotton and woollen cloths are manufactured here. Almost every family in the nation grows cotton for its own consumption. Industry and commercial enterprises are extending themselves in every part. Nearly all the merchants are native Cherokees. The Christian religion is the religion of the nation . . . Our system of government founded on republican principles, secures the respect of the people. New Town, pleasantly situated in the centre of the nation, is the seat of government. A printing-press is soon to be established; also a national library and museum.'[91]

The missionaires to the Cherokees detailed similar accounts of Cherokee progress.[92] The Cherokees took other self-conscious steps to prove their civility. In 1826, the Cherokees held a constitutional convention at which a constitution similar to the U.S. Constitution was adopted. It was declared that the Cherokees were one of the sovereign and independent nations of the earth and that they maintained sole jurisdiction over land within their own territory. The constitution also provided for a representative government modeled after that of the United States.[93]

Before any further action could be taken, an extra-constitutional discovery doomed any chance the Cherokees might have had to maintain their Georgia holdings. Gold was discovered in northeastern Georgia and by the summer of 1830, in excess of 3,000 White men from various states were illegally digging gold on Cherokee land. Although the presence of these Whites was illegal under the laws of all three governments claiming jurisdiction -- the Federal government, the Cherokee Nation and the State of Georgia -- none of these governments had the ability to check the illegal White encroachments.

In the meantime, President Adams' term and expired. Although not a real friend of the Cherokees, he had refused to use force in removing them. Andrew Jackson, or "Sharp Knife" as he was called, took office in 1829. Jackson spoke forthrightly to the problem of Cherokee removal. In his first message to Congress on December 8, 1829, he examined the "Condition and Ulterior Destiny of the Indian Tribes."[94] It is clear that he favored removal as a policy. For example, Jackson stated that the only hope of the avoidance of extermination of the Cherokees was their removal: "Surrounded by the Whites with their arts of civilization, which by destroying the resources of the savage doom him to weakness and decay, the fate of the Mohegan, the Narragansett and the Delaware is fast overtaking the Choctaw, the Cherokee and the Creek."[95] That is, the only benevolent and humanitarian policy was one which would remove the Indians from the debilitating vices and influences of the Whites because the Indians were inherently a weak people and susceptible to such vices. Reconciling this argument with past policy which emphasized the civilizing influence of private ownership of land and proximity of White culture was one of the problems faced by removal advocates.

Following Jackson's message, Georgia pressed even more strongly for removal and Jackson acquiesced to Governor Gilmer's request to withdraw the few Federal troops attempting to control White gold seekers in Cherokee Georgia. Eventually, both the House and Senate introduced an Indian Removal Bill with the House version being dropped in favor of the Senate Bill. In the ensuing debate, "constitutional" promises granted by treaty to the Cherokees were reaffirmed by John Marshall and the Supreme Court.

Georgia took political steps to pressure fulfillment of the Federal promise made in 1802. These included passage of restrictive state laws to make the Cherokees as uncomfortable as possible and pressure on Congress for a bill providing monies and administrative assistance for exchanging Cherokee holdings for western lands. Georgia also[96] sought the authority to use force to secure removal. The first step was within Georgia's realm and the Cherokees could be made extremely uncomfortable before the legality of such actions was ruled upon. After Jackson's message, the debate was already on-going regarding the second step. However, the third step, or the use of force, was seldom discussed and never given constitutional respectability in any legislation. Yet force was used in the final removal of the Cherokees. Debates regarding removal were characterized by promises of benevolence by both pro and antiremoval forces. Every White person, from President Jackson down, seemed concerned with "commiseration" for the Indians. But violence was an inevitable outcome when it became clear that the Cherokees would cede no more land. As Helen Hunt Jackson observed:

> So long as they would cede and cede, and grant and grant tract after tract, and had millions of acres still left to cede and grant, the selfishness of white men took no alarm; but once consolidated into an empire, with fixed and inalienable boundaries, powerful, recognized and determined, the Cherokee Nation would be a thorn in the flesh to her white neighbors. The doom of the Cherokees was sealed when they declared once and for all, officially as a nation, that they would not sell another foot of land.[97]

For the majority White group of Georgia, the Cherokees became a threat, and the situation "extraordinary" with the establishment of the Cherokee Constitution. Georgia branded the constitution a "presumptuous document"; a sign that the Indians they had tolerated for so long were getting "uppity." White incursions upon Cherokee land became even more common with house burnings, floggings and other direct retaliatory actions serving to "warn" the Cherokees that they had gone too far. One Indian, an accused horse thief, was hung by Georgia authorities in direct defiance[98] of Federal due process guarantees in solemn treaties.

Years before, Thomas Jefferson had predicted the natural injustice of White attempts to justify the procurement of Indian-occupied land:

> Whoever shall attempt to trace the claims of the European Nations to the Countrys in America from the principles of Justice, or reconcile the invasions made on the native Indians to the natural rights, of mankind . . . will find that he is pursuing a Chimera, which exists only in his imagination, against the evidence of indisputable facts.[99]

But the removal forces were successful in constructing symbols which justified Cherokee removal and the removal bill passed both the House and the Senate. However, the "Chimera" they constructed did not serve as logic or argument for John Marshall and the Supreme Court. Although the Court did rule against the Cherokee Nation in the Cherokee Nation v. Georgia, it did so only because it did not find the status of the Cherokees to be similar to that of a foreign, sovereign nation. Rather, in Marshall's words, it found that the Cherokees were a "domestic, dependent nation" and to that extent the Court had no jurisdiction. However, in Worcester v. The State of Georgia, the Court ruled that Georgia did not have the right to extend her laws over the Cherokees. Marshall wrote, in the majority opinion:

> The Cherokee nation then, is a distinct community, occupying its own territory, with boundaries accurately described, in which the laws of Georgia can have no force, and which the citizens of Georgia have no right to enter, but with the assent of the Cherokees themselves or in conformity with treaties and with the acts of Congress.[100]

He had carefully reviewed every argument for and against removal as legally established in the previous treaties and Trade and Intercourse Acts. However, Jackson refused to enforce Marshall's decision and forced removal was carried out during which 4,600 Cherokees died.[101] It is ironic that the Jacksonian Era coincided so closely with what has been described as the "Age of Reform in America." For the Cherokees, expediency proved to be stronger than reform attempts to help the Indians.

Subsequent legislation did assume the reality of Indian removal from the east. As the framers of the Intercourse Act of 1834 indicated: "That all the part of the United States west of the Mississippi and not within the states of Missouri and Louisiana, or the territory of Arkansas, and also, that part of the United States east of the Mississippi river, and not within a state to which Indian title has not been extinguished, for the purposes of this act [shall] be taken and deemed to be Indian country." The same bill contained support for continuing to treat the various tribes as if they were sovereign nations. This practice continued until 1871 and its ending coincided with the end of the threat from the Plains tribes.

A bill accompanying the new Intercourse Act was also debated and would have provided for the organization of an Indian Territory "of the same kind and regulated by the same rules, that the Territories of the United States are now governed."[102] This bill was the last "constitutional" attempt to guarantee Indian rights to self-government, life and liberty in the nineteenth century. When it failed, supported by the same forces that had opposed removal and opposed by many who had favored removal, in Father Prucha's words:

> . . . there was little hope that the pledge given to the Indians upon removal that they would be protected in the permanent enjoyment of the Western lands could be fulfilled or that the new intercourse act would enjoy much better enforcement than its predecessors.[103]

Indeed the words of William Ellsworth spoken against the removal bill proved prophetic, "Not twenty-five years will pass, before the Indians on those rich lands will be in some white man's way." Absent real constitutional guarantees, Native Americans would always be at the mercy of easily shifted opinion.[104]

The image of the Indian as enemy underlies most early constitutions. Although his demeanor might appear friendly, his nature, savage and violent, did not change. As Burke mentions, constitutions involve an enemy implicitly or explicitly and the establishment of constitutions purely on White grounds suggests that Indians were the enemy. Restrictions upon the Indians suggested that they might act otherwise. Although restrictions were also placed on Whites, clauses urging "humane treatment" made Whites less an enemy than Native Americans.[105]

89

"Key Symbols" manifestly stated in government constitutions offer some apparent contrast to the symbols located in the two previous authoritative messages. Constitutionally, American Indians were:

1. "Nations" and "Sovereign entities."

2. "Savages" but capable of adopting "civilization."

3. Possessors of and capable of relinquishing the land.

4. Deserving of, and granted the protection of the U.S. government.

The actual treatment of Native Americans, however, was determined by the extra-constitutional assumptions implied by the "key symbols" utilized by Parkman, Morton, Nott and, to an extent, Jackson.

CHAPTER II

NOTES

[1] Wilbur R. Jacobs, Dispossessing the American Indian: Indians and Whites on the Colonial Frontier (New York: Charles Scribners' Sons, 1972), p. 13.

[2] Anthony F.C. Wallace, The Death and Rebirth of the Senaca (New York: Vintage Books, 1972), p. 112. For a detailed explanation of trade between these parties see George T. Hunt, The Wars of the Iroquois: A Study in Intertribal Trade Relations (Madison: University of Wisconsin Press, 1940).

[3] Wallace, p. 114.

[4] Francis Parkman, The Conspiracy of Pontiac and The Indian War After the Conquest of Canada (New York: Charles Scribners' Sons, 1915), I, pp. 179-189; Jacobs, p. 85; Wallace, pp. 114-115.

[5] Jacobs, p. 84; Wallace, p. 115; Howard H. Peckham, Pontiac and the Indian Uprising (Princeton: Princeton University Press, 1947), pp. 107-111.

[6] Parkman, I, p. 189.

[7] Parkman, I, pp. 194-196; Wallace writes that "Pontiac himself had not actually organized a pan-Indian uprising" but had acted more as a catalyst, p. 115. Jacobs indicts the evidence for Pontiac's role, p. 84, and Peckham concludes, "As for a general uprising of all the western tribes against all the British western posts, Pontiac may have thought of it but his abilities were taxed in uniting his immediate neighbors and devising a surprise assault on one fort." p. 108.

[8] Parkman, I, pp. ix, x.

[9] Parkman, I, pp. x, xi, xiii.

[10] Parkman, I, p. 48.

[11] Parkman, II, pp. 317, 323-324.

[12] Parkman, II, pp. 329-331.

[13] See Francis Parkman, The Oregon Trail: Sketches of Prairie and Rocky Mountain Life (New York: Charles Scribners' Sons, 1915), pp. 125, 177, 396, 330-331, 419, 425. For Parkman's specific discussion of Indian character see The Conspiracy, I, pp. 43-49.

[14] The Conspiracy, I, pp. 238, 190-191.

[15] The Conspiracy, I, pp. 193-194, 198, 190, 213-214.

[16] The Conspiracy, I, pp. 194-196.

[17] The Conspiracy, I, pp. 226-225.

[18] The Conspiracy, I, pp. 210, 237-238.

[19] The Conspiracy, I, pp. 238, 237, 226, 48.

[20] The Conspiracy, I, pp. 220-221.

[21] For example see Robert Shulman, "Parkman's Indians and American Violence," The Massachusetts Review, 12 (April, 1971), 228. Much of my analysis is based upon Shulman's conclusions.

[22] Shulman, p. 222.

[23] Jacobs, p. 84.

[24] The Conspiracy, II, pp. 127, 131, 135, 128.

[25] Shulman, p. 225.

[26] Bernard W. Sheehan, Seeds of Extinction, Jeffersonian Philanthropy and the American Indian (Chapel Hill: The University of North Carolina Press, 1973), pp. 185-212. Also see Reginald Horsman, Race and Manifest Destiny, the Origins of Anglo Saxonism (Cambridge: Harvard University Press, 1981), p. 109.

[27] Lewis H. Carlson and George A. Colburn, eds., In Their Place: White America Defines Her Minorities 1850-1950 (New York: John Wiley and Sons, 1972), p. 32.

[28] Reginald Horsman, "Scientific Racism and the American Indian in the Mid-nineteenth Century," American Quarterly, 27 (May, 1965), 153-154.

[29] William Stanton, The Leopard's Spots: Scientific Attitudes Toward Race in America 1815-59 (Chicago: The University of Chicago Press, 1960), p. 2.

[30] Charles Caldwell, M.D., Thoughts on the Original Unity of the Human Race (New York: E. Bliss, 1830), pp. 134, 135, 146, 151, 173.

[31] Stanton, p. 10.

[32] London Medico-Chirurgical Review, October, 1840, quoted in J.C. Nott and George R. Gliddon, Types of Mankind; or, Ethnological Researches Based upon the Ancient Monuments, Paintings, Sculptures and Crania of Races, and upon Their Natural, Geographical, Philological and Biblical History (Long: Trubner & Co., 1854), p. xxxiv.

[33] Samuel George Morton, M.D., Crania Americana; or A Comparative View of the Skulls of Various Aboriginal Nations of North and South America: to Which is Prefixed An Essay on the Varieties of the Human Species (Philadelphia: J. Dobson, Chestnut Street, 1839).

[34] Stanton, p. 25.

[35] Stanton, p. 28.

[36] Stanton, p. 27.

[37] Morton, pp. 6, 7-23, 63-82.

[38] Morton, pp. iii-v.

[39] Morton, pp. 1-2.

[40] Morton, pp. 2-3.

[41] Morton, p. 4.

[42] Morton, pp. 3-5.

[43] Morton, p. 88.

[44] Morton, p. 64.

[45] Morton, p. 65.

[46] Morton, pp. 68, 75.

[47] Morton, p. 77.

[48] Morton, p. 78.

[49] Morton, pp. 78-79, 80.

[50] Morton, pp. 81-82.

[51] Morton, pp. 81-83.

[52] Annemarie De Waalmalefijt, Images of Man: A History of Anthropological Thought (New York: Alfred A. Knopf, 1974), p. 220.

[53] Morton, p. 253.

[54] Morton, p. 260.

[55] Morton, p. 261.

[56] Stanton, p. 33.

[57] Horsman, "Scientific Racism," writes, "Americans in general were delighted to accept new interpretations which provided a rationale for the failure of American Indian policy and a justification for the seemingly ruthless appropriation of both Indian and Mexican land." p. 153.

[58] Stanton, pp. 65-72.

[59] Nott, Two Lectures on the Natural History of the Caucasian and Negro Race (Mobile: Thompson, 1844), p. 35.

[60] Nott, Two Lectures on the Connection Between the Biblical and Physical History of Man (1843; rpt. New York: Negro Universities Press, 1969), p. 36.

[61] Two Lectures on the Natural History, pp. 36-36. Also see Nott, "Diversity of the Human Races," De Bow's Review, 10 (Feb. 1851), 129-130.

[62] Horsman, "Scientific Racism," pp. 159-160.

[63] Nott and Gliddon, pp. 79, 69.

[63] Nott and Gliddon, p. 461.

[65] Nott and Gliddon, p. 53.

[66] Nott and Gliddon, p. 465.

[67] Horsman, "Scientific Racism," p. 160.

[68] Kenneth Burke, A Grammar of Motives (1945); rpt. Berkeley: University of California Press, 1969), p. 338. Burke implies the legal conflict between whites and Native Americans when he writes, "Yet when, in the realm of the practical a given case comes before the courts, you promptly find this merger or balance or equilibrium among the Constitutional clauses becomes transformed into a conflict among the clauses -- and to satisfy the promise contained in one clause, you must forego the promise contained in another." Burke, Grammar, p. 349.

[69] William T. Hagan, American Indians (Chicago: University of Chicago Press, 1961), pp. 31-65. In the Declaration an image of Native Americans is offered which demonstrates the belief of the founding fathers that the Indians were conspiring against them. Jefferson wrote "He [George III] has endeavored to bring on the inhabitants of our frontiers the merciless Indian savages, whose known rule of warfare is an undistinguished destruction of all ages, sexes, & conditions." For a discussion of the development of this statement see Garry Wills, Inventing America: Jefferson's Declaration of Independence (Garden City, New York: Doubleday and Company, 1978), pp. 71-75.

[70] Donald L. Burnett Jr., "An Historical Analysis of the 1968 'Indian Civil Rights' Act, " Harvard Journal on Legislation, 9 (May, 1972), 558.

[71] "Articles of Confederation," in Wilcomb E. Washburn, ed., The American Indian and the United States: A Documentary History (New York: Random House, 1973), III, p. 2140.

[72] Hagan, p. 40.

[73]"Northwest Ordinance of July 13, 1787," in A Documentary History, III, pp. 2145, 2147, 2148.

[74]See The Federalist, ed. Jacob E. Cook (Middletown, Conn: Wesleyan University Press, 1961), pp. 37, 156-158, 161, 262, 282.

[75]See Max Farrand, ed., The Records of the Federal Convention of 1787 (New Haven: Yale University Press, 1937), I, pp. 193, 201, 227, 229, 236; II, pp. 183, 352, 571, 590, 651.

[76]Wilcomb Washburn, Red Man's Land/White Man's Law: A Study of the Past and Present Status of the American Indian (New York: Charles Scribners' Sons, 1971), p. 62. Hagan, pp. 43-44.

[77]For a discussion of events which influenced Jeffersonian policy see George Dewey Harmon, Sixty Years of Indian Affairs: Political, Economic and Diplomatic (Chapel Hill: University of North Carolina Press, 1941), pp. 80-93; Reginald Horsman, Expansion and American Indian Policy, 1783-1812 (East Lansing: Michigan State University Press, 1967), pp. 104-114. For Locke's arguments regarding the value of land as a civilizing influence see John Locke, An Essay Concerning the True Original Extent and End of Civil Government (1690), Chapter V, "Of Property."

[78]For discussion of the background and development of these four Acts see: Hagan, pp. 44-45; Harmon, pp. 101-103; Horsman, Expansion and American Indian Policy, pp. 62-64; Prucha, American Indian Policy, pp. 45-49; Washburn, Red Man's Land, pp. 59-61. The Acts themselves are available in Washburn, A Documentary History, III, pp. 2151-2163 and Francis Paul Prucha, ed., Documents of United States Indian Policy (Lincoln: University of Nebraska Press, 1975), pp. 14-20.

[79]Washburn, A Documentary History, III, pp. 2152-2153.

[80]See Wallace, The Death and Rebirth of the Senaca, pp. 44-48.

[81]Sheehan, pp. 185-212.

[82] See "President Washington's Third Annual Message October 25, 1791," in Prucha, Documents, pp. 15-16.

[83] Washburn, A Documentary History, III, pp. 2154-2163.

[84] Hagan, pp. 44-45; Also see Donald R. Englund, "Indians, Intruders and the Federal Government," Journal of the West, 13 (April, 1974), 97-104.

[85] Ulrich Bonnell Phillips, "The Expulsion of the Cherokees," in Filler and Guttman, p. 1.

[86] These treaties are available in Richard Peters, The Case of the Cherokee Nation Against the State of Georgia; Argued and Determined at the Supreme Court of the United States, January Term 1831 (Philadelphia: John Grigg, 9 North Fourth Street, 1831), pp. 249-281.

[87] "Treaty of 28 November 1785," in Peters, pp. 249-251.

[88] "Treaty of 8 July 1817," "Treaty of 27 February 1819," "Treaty of 24 October 1824," in Peters pp. 265-273. Samuel Carter III in Cherokee Sunset, A Nation Betrayed: A Narrative of Travail and Triumph Persecution and Exile (New York: Doubleday & Company, 1976) indicates that both the 1817 and the 1819 treaties included attempts by Whites to bribe and manipulate Cherokee representatives into larger land cessations, pp. 27-40.

[89] John Pendleton Kennedy in The Collected Works, Memoirs of the Life of William Wirt (New York: G.P. Putnam and Sons, 1872), II, p. 244.

[90] Quoted in Phillips, p. 3.

[91] Kennedy, pp. 244-246.

[92] "Resolution and Statements of the Missionaries," in Louis Filler and Allen Guttman, eds. The Removal of the Cherokee Nation: Manifest Destiny or National Dishonor? (New York: Robert E. Krieger, 1977), pp. 53-60.

[93] Phillips, p. 5. Carter, pp. 69-70, writes, "It [the constitution] would climax all the progress they had made in government. It would fit the pattern of

democracy in other countries. But most of all, perhaps, it would be something thay could hold up to the world -- a shield, a battle standard, a declaration to Georgia, among others, of the permanence of their establishment."

[94] Andrew Jackson, "The Condition and Ulterior Destiny of the Indian Tribes, December 8, 1829," in Filler and Guttman, pp. 14-17.

[95] "Ulterior Destiny," p. 17.

[96] Albert K. Weinberg, Manifest Destiny, A Study of Nationalist Expansionism in American History (Glouchester, Massachusetts: Peter Smith, 1958), p. 82.

[97] Helen Hunt Jackson, A Century of Dishonor (New York: Harper and Row, 1966), p. 272.

[98] Carter, pp. 92, 104-106.

[99] Quoted in Washburn, "The Moral and Legal Justifications for Dispossessing the Indians," in Seventeenth-Century America: Essays in Colonial History, ed. James Morton Smith (Chapel Hill: University of North Carolina Press, 1959), p. 26.

[100] "John Marshall: The Cherokee Nation Vs. The State of Georgia," and "John Marshall: Worcester Vs. the State of Georgia," both in Filler and Guttman, pp. 62-61; pp. 69-78.

[101] Reportedly, Jackson responded to Marshall's decision, "John Marshall made his decision, now let him enforce it." Quoted in Hagan, p. 75.

[102] Prucha, American Indian Policy, pp. 262, 271. Two basic reports underlay the proposed Law of 1834: The first, the proposals for reorganizing the administration of Indian Affairs submitted by William Clark and Lewis Cass is available in Senate Document 72, 20th Congress, 2d session, Feb. 10, 1829, ser. 181; the second is in the Report of the House Committee on Indian Affairs which introduced the bills, see House Report 474, 23rd Congress, 1st session, May 20th 1834, ser. 263. See also: Annie H. Abel, "Proposals for an Indian State, 1778-1878," Annual Reports of the American Historical Association for 1907 (Washington: U.S. G.P.O., 1908), I, pp. 87-103.

[103] Francis Paul Prucha, American Indian Policy in the Formative Years: The Indian Trade and Intercourse Acts, 1790-1834 (Cambridge: Harvard University Press, 1962), p. 273.

[104] "Speech of William Ellsworth," in Washburn, A Documentary History, II, p. 1099.

[105] Burke, 357-360.

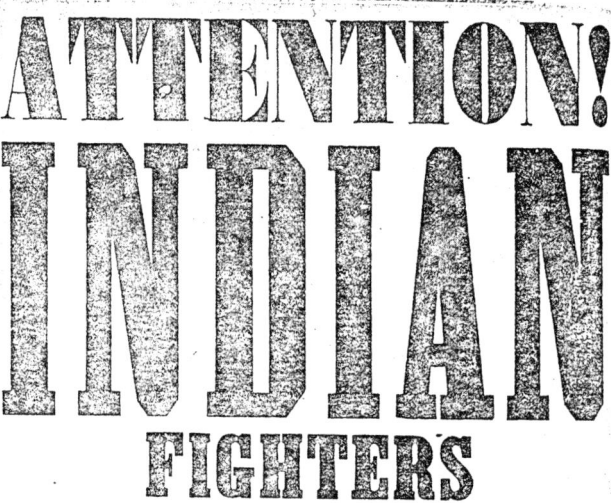

CHAPTER III

THE AUDIENCE

Denver and Colorado Territory

It would be impossible to draw an absolutely accurate composite picture of the population of Colorado Territory in the late 1850's and early 1860's. However, the 1860 census, the early occupants themselves and outside observers are all sources of evidence as to the characteristics and attitudes of the Colorado population. For the most part, the inhabitants themselves spoke more favorably of their environment and their own characteristics than did outside observers.

Try as he might, William N. Byers, editor of the Rocky Mountain News, could not change the characteristic restless nature of many of Denver's early occupants. Although the 1860 census numbered the population of Colorado at 34,277, it has been estimated that three times that number came and left. A sample of just under three thousand adults living in the Rockies illustrated that little more than half (55.6%) were born in the United States and the majority of these were male, young and declared a Protestant religion. This American-born population came from Ohio, New York, Illinois, Missouri and Indiana in that order. However, the points of origin are deceptive since these locations were not always places of birth, only the last "permanent" address of the young, male wanderers.[1] Most of those questioned in Colorado for the 1860 census stated their occupation to be "miners," although many were "greenhorns," having never mined before. Actually only about one-third (33.7%) were experienced miners from either Georgia or California. Augusta Tabor, the wife of H.A.W. Tabor who would find the largest gold mine in Colorado, declared, "I never saw a country settled with such greenhorns as Colorado . . . they were mostly from farms and some clerks. They were all young men from 18 to 30. I was here a good many years before we saw a man with gray hair."[2] Nevertheless, the fact that 22,000 of those sampled indicated their occupation to be miners implies that the majority believed their fortune was, ideally, to be found in the mineral wealth of Colorado. However, most of the population managed only to make a living -- rather than discovering a fortune -- by "mining the miners." Land speculators, merchants, blacksmiths, lawyers, doctors, preachers, teachers and even journalists were included among those who provided goods and services to the miners. On one occasion Byers cynically evaluted the population to be "thirty active miners, ten merchants and saloon keepers, five mechanics, fifty loafers, gamblers and fancymen. [The city was] Lousy with lawyers, pettifoggers and scrub doctors."[3] Mrs. Tabor was correct in observing the predominance of young men in the area. The median age was slightly over thirty-three years and in 1860 the census taker found approximately 33,000 men and 1,600 women in the area. Although the proportion would change radically by 1870 when there would be roughly 25,000 men and 15,000 women, most of this shift would occur after the Civil War and well after Sand Creek.[4] Therefore, the law of supply and demand enhanced the social value of female companionship for the early male pioneers. "I tell you, sir," remarked one inhabitant of a remote mining town, "when I first came down from the gulches into Denver, I would have given a ten-dollar piece to have seen the skirt of a servant-girl a mile off."[5] During the summer of 1859, bored men looking for inexpensive amusement conducted mock legislatures in the evenings. As Professor Athearn relates:

> For example, House Bill No. 323 provided for chartering the Leavenworth City, St. Joseph and Pikes Peak double-track railroad, both branches to Taos to accommodate the whiskey trade, and to Salt Lake City to import a supply of women. As an indication of which was the most pressing need, a separate resolution was passed authorizing the presiding officer . . . to negotiate with the governor of Massachusetts for the delivery of approximately a thousand schoolma'ams for the purpose of teaching the population of the territory. The measure was immediately amended to strike the word 'teaching' and to insert 'marrying,' after which it passed unanimously.[6]

Although this was a motion made in jest, Byers seriously proposed the formation of a female emigration society to bring women to Colorado by the

102

carload.[7] Byers and others associated the presence of women with a more civilized, permanent society.[8] "Left by themselves, men degenerate rapidly and become rough, harsh, slovenly -- almost brutish," Reverend William Goode declared after a visit to Colorado. Frank Hall, a Colorado editor and historian, concluded that a society of many men and few females could not maintain any system of civil order.[9] Although early Denver did have problems establishing "order," the lack of women was more probably a result of disorder than a cause. Moreover, the scarcity of women with the resultant increased valuation of their persons required that Colorado men react violently to real harm or threats to their female companions.

This young, male society also expressed optimism regarding the potential for success in their new surroundings. The values which they sought to fulfill were materialistic with competition viewed as the suitable means for achieving this success. Their slogan "Pikes Peak or Bust" is well-known and as an optimistic expression of a goal has been remembered more readily than the "Busted, by God" slogan of the "Gobacks." Their optimism is apparent in recorded correspondence from the young miners. A portion of a letter written by John Buell in November of 1858 is typical. He writes:

> Our cabin is completed today. Kennedy and myself have done all the work. We have been amazingly industrious. The city from which I write, is a new but prosperous burg. The lands around this city are splendid for farming purposes. The soil produces everything and the climate is luxurious. Opposite my cabin, miners are making from five to eight dollars a man a day . . .
> It is the general opinion hereabouts by those well qualified to judge, that this South Park region at the headwaters of the Rio Grande, Colorado, Arkansas and South Platte rivers will produce a new El Dorado . . . .[10]

Although intervening events would dampen the optimism of some who would "goback," subsequent strikes the next summer would preserve the optimism and confidence of those men who stayed. Mathew Riddlebarger, a journalist, wrote to his sister in June of 1860:

. . . for the past week the reports from the mines have been of the most exciting and cheering kind -- for instance, about six days ago Jim Winchester arrived from the mountains and reported that he saw five men take out near two thousand dollars in one day. This started nearly everybody in town for the mountain diggings. Today I was informed by reliable (so I consider them) men that, on last Saturday, three men in one day made $260, and that five men made $590. And this is vouched for by several men who came down from the mountains. Still again claims have been sold for from two thousand to eleven thousand dollars. One company from Chicago sold two claims for $21,000, and yet the returning crowd will swear there is no gold in the country. I am satisfied, and I care not how many come or go. Mark my words, the gold is here and will be found.[11]

Optimistic, although sometimes hyperbolic expressions concerning Colorado's climate, the caliber of its people and its great potential characterized these early messages from Colorado. Moreover, many of the "fifty-niners" came west with the intention to remain permanently in the new region -- or at least until a bigger "strike" was rumored somewhere else. Some quickly declared their loyalty to their new abode, sharing Byers' hopes for a new community in the wilderness. "There is no use talking, but verily, Denver City is now a great place and a great institution in business and social respects," recorded one of the fifty-niners. In the new, fresh environment old things, such as despair and hopelessness, were done away with and "behold all things are novel and new."[12] Although some miners expressed reservations regarding the less desirable occupants of Denver, they hoped time would lead these elements away. It was explained that crudity was common in new communities, but that time would sort the good from the bad.[13] While there were bound to be number of shiftless people ("floaters") on any frontier, Colorado was recorded to be more than fortunate in the quality of her emigrants. Readers of midwestern periodicals were appraised, in late 1859, that "we have a hundred per cent, and I might have said five hundred per cent, more educated, enterprising businessmen of all departments, more intelligent and refined city men and women, and more of the essential elements of success for a sound and social state of things . . . than any other municipal corporation within the scope of our knowledge and observation anywhere." Indeed, "more" became a favorite adjective of Western boosters.[14]

Frontier "spaciousness" has been credited with instilling a special sense of democracy, self-reliance and especially independence upon the frontier population. Frederick Jackson Turner has described his version of the democratizing influence of the frontier. He explains:

> It was not only a society in which the love of equality was prominent: it was also a competitive society. To its socialist critics it seemed not so much a democracy as a society whose members were 'expectant capitalists' . . . It was based upon the idea of a fair chance for all men, not on the conception of leveling by arbitrary methods and especially [leveling] by law.[15]

Moreover, according to Turner, the frontier tended to alter the character, quality and attitudes of the individuals and of the societies which they created. Western society was conditioned and patterned by the forces which gave it birth.[16] Turner writes that some of the more prominent traits developed in individuals were:

> The coarseness and strength combined with acuteness and inquisitiveness; that practical, inventive turn of mind, quick to find expedients; that masterful grasp of material things, lacking in the artistic but powerful to effect great ends; that restless, nervous energy, that dominant individualism, working for good and for evil, and withal that buoyancy and exuberance which comes with freedom -- these are traits of the frontier, or traits called out elsewhere because of the existence of the frontier.[17]

As will be demonstrated, the Denver population in particular sought expedient solutions which may have worked evil. While Turner's thesis has been criticized, it is predictive in describing the self-perceptions held by specific members of the Denver population.[18]

One fifty-niner, Matthew Dale, indicated that he believed that his surroundings imparted a special character to its inhabitants. He wrote to his brother in 1861, "you cannot gain that self-reliance and independence under all circumstances a few years here would impart, by remaining anywhere in the east."[19] Moreover, the mountain named for Lieutentant Pike came to symbolize the "Eldorado" sought by those who called themselves "young America." As one young prospector wrote, "it stood for the whole country, from Mexico to our northern line .... It represented gold, and plenty of it; it spoke of influence, power and position in our middle age, and ease and comfort in our decline. I think that with the first view of the celebrated mountain we felt the first quickening of a definite purpose."[20] Thus, for the early population of Denver, individualism indicated the right to seek personal capitalistic success. Some members perceived that their surroundings simultaneously symbolized their goals and literally contained the ingredients for achieving success. As Byers would write, it was the "destiny" of civilization to inherit the mountains from the wild animals and savages. At a Christmas celebration in 1858, the "toasts" were dedicated to the "wish" that "all the emigration to this El Dorado find comfortable quarters as we have in this beautiful camp and may they succeed in realizing their brightest golden anticipations." Moreover, the "destiny" of the emigrants was poetically noted, "Our destiny -- westward the star of empire takes her way, and she has now lodged in the Rocky Mountains."[21]

Therefore, this optimistic population sensed their destiny among the mountains of Colorado. As "expectant capitalists," they were prepared to risk a "fair chance" for some members of the diverse races and nationalities that also sought their fortune in early Colorado. Although transplanted White Americans made up the majority of the population a quarter (25.6%) came from England, Ireland or Germany, and the remainder from Italy, France, Poland and other parts of the world.[22] As a rule, the smaller a given minority and the less threatening it was, the less prejudice which was expressed toward it. For example, a small band of Jewish merchants had traveled west with the fifty-niners and were accepted as an unobtrusive part of the community. They were eventually awarded what Byers in the Rocky Mountain News described as a "high place" in the region and acceptance in "the best metropolitan society."[23]

The 1860 census also listed 46 blacks in the Denver area. The census of the following year, ordered by Governor Gilpin, found 89.[24] Like their Jewish brethern, these blacks found acceptance because of their small numbers. They performed the usual menial tasks as well as operating and sometimes owning small private businesses. In 1859 a reporter indicated that Denver's Eldorado saloon was managed and operated by J.G. Sims,[25] "a colored gentleman and wealthy, from Cincinnati." When blacks gathered to mourn Lincoln's assassination the News noted that "the colored citizens of this place are about as patriotic as any class of people in the country." William J. Hardin, a mulatto from Kentucky, became well-known as a local Denver orator and garnered personal praise from the White population.[26]

Although both Jewish and black populations achieved qualified acceptance in early Denver, other larger minority groups were not so lucky. While the blacks were not persecuted, Spanish-speaking Americans were openly distained. Anglos in pioneer Colorado took the position that Mexican-Americans were a naturally inferior people. As Robert Athearn explains:

> The relaxed easy going way of life of these people, their apparent lack of aggressiveness in business matters, and certainly their Catholicism grated upon the nerves of transplanted New England Puritans, whose rigid moral, religious and economic beliefs differed so widely from those of a Latin background.[27]

Mexicans, or "greasers" as they were commonly called, were described as "prone to indolence, drunkenness, filthiness and gaming" (although there was no mention of the Anglos' penchant for gaming and drinking).[28]

Other minorities such as the Chinese, the Mormons and later the Italians and the Irish also were treated with varying levels of prejudice by the White population.[29] All minorities eventually would experience negative treatment but the intensity of the prejudice expressed was dependent upon the threat posed by the specific group. Any anxiety engendered by the above-mentioned minorities was probably a result of economic threat. However, the anxiety experienced because of Native Americans grew out of fears for personal safety.[30]

Initially the fifty-niners expressed nervousness regarding the Indians but tolerated their demands for sugar, coffee and tobacco. D. F. Richards wrote to the Omaha Times, "We saw a great many Indians both Cheyennes and Sioux, but experienced no difficulty with them more than having to drive late sometimes to get away from them to camp."[31] Similarly, John Graves and Josiah Hinman stated that they were wary of the Indians but did not "fear them much."[32] Thousands of miners immigrated to the Denver region without experiencing trouble with the natives. Some of the early arrivals were impressed with the Indians' hospitality and readiness "to point out the road."[33] Others sought immediately to ensure protection from the perceived danger posed by the Indians. One man, John Scudder, traveled to Fort Laramie "to solicit the aid and protection of the commanding officer at that post from the Indians." He wrote that "they have not troubled us much this winter, but we are entirely at their mercy . . . ."[34] This early "nervous" attitude was best summarized by "Uncle Dick" Wooten, an inhabitant of the original cabin settlement that became Denver, when he stated, "They [the Indians] are about as wild by nature as any other animal found roaming through the forest and jungle. They have never recognized any law but the law of force and the difference between a 'wild Indian' and a 'civilized Indian' is about the difference between the tiger at large, and the tiger in a cage."[35]

Mixed with these fears of Indian nature were attitudes of contempt and amusement for Indians and Indian ways. One newsman described the Arapahoes as "squalid and conceited, proud and worthless, lazy and lousy," and he predicted that "they will strut out or drink out their miserable existence and, at length afford the world a sensible relief by dying out of it."[36] Some miners and newly arrived inhabitants regarded the Indians as an amusement and quaint in their behavior. Members of one party were entertained when a visting Indian declared his love for the wife of one of the Whites and solemnly offered to buy her.[37] On January 28, 1859, a "feast" was provided by the White inhabitants of Auria for the Arapahoe Indians. The motivations for this event have not been recorded. However, Rufus Cable was amazed at the huge amounts of food which could be consumed by the visiting Indians. Cable declared, "I have never seen men eat til now. I have heard that one [Indian] man could eat an antelope at one meal, and I verily believe one Indian called, 'Heap of Whips,' could eat a whole ox! It is worth one year's travel to witness such a scene."[38]

Besides the inhabitants' descriptions of themselves and their surroundings, visitors to Colorado also recorded descriptions of Colorado's life and times. Many of these descriptions stressed the lawless and violent nature of the settlers of the early 1860's.

A.K. McClure, Pennsylvanian journalist, recorded a less than favorable opinion of Denver citizens, declaring that ". . . nine tenths of those who came at first were either fugitives or adventurers. In one mingled mass came the honest bankrupt, the fugitive from justice, the gambler and the loafer."[39]

Albert Richardson, in a description of his travels in <u>Beyond the Mississippi</u>, preserved a partial picture of <u>Denver and its citizens</u> in 1859. The best "hotel" in town was the Denver House, a large tent which also doubled as a saloon with a swept earthen floor. The bar of this establishment, Richardson observed, was "always crowded with swarthy men armed and in rough costumes." Enormous amounts of "cigars and liquors" were sold and a half a dozen gaming tables were populated by gamblers day and night. "I saw the probate judge of the county lose thirty Denver lots in less than ten minutes, at cards, in this public saloon on Sunday morning," he wrote, "and afterward observed the county sheriff pawning his revolver for twenty dollars to spend in betting at faro." Additionally, Richardson recalls the "mix" of the population and some common eccentric amusements:

> Denver society was a strange medley. There were Americans from every quarter of the Union, Mexicans, Indians, half-breeds, trappers, speculators, gamblers, desperados, broken-down politicians and honest men. Almost every day was enlivened by its little shooting match. While the great gaming saloon [the Denver House] was crowded with people, drunken ruffians sometimes fired five or six shots from their revolvers, frightening everybody pell-mell out of the room, but seldom wounding any one. One day I heard the bar-keeper politely ask a man lying upon a bench

to remove. The recumbent replied to the request with his revolver. Indeed firing at this bartender was a common amusement among the guests. At first he bore it laughingly, but one day a shot grazed his ear. Whereupon remarking that there was such a thing as carrying a joke too far and that his was 'about all played out,' he buckled on two revolvers and swore he would kill the next man who took aim at him. He was not troubled afterwards.[40]

Uncle Dick Wooten agreed with Richardson's judgment that gaming was nearly universal among the first wave of emigrants. Moreover, Uncle Dick, an old-time trapper and Indian scout, was used to hard types and an eye-witness to the development of early Denver. However, he still pronounced a large portion of the Denver population to be "utterly lawless." He declared that murders were "almost everyday occurences" and "stealing was the only occupation of many members of the population."[41]

Horace Greeley's observations of Denver were consistent with Richardson's, McClure's, and Wooten's. Greeley's analysis was frank: ". . . I apprehend that there have been, during my two weeks sojourn, more brawls, more fights, more pistol shots with criminal intent in this log-city of one hundred and fifty dwellings, not three-fourths completed nor two-thirds inhabited, nor one-third fit to be, than in any community of no greater numbers on earth."[42] While these descriptions are all of early Denver, statements as late as 1867 despaired of the lawlessness and violence of the Denver community.[43]

Not all observers agreed with the picture painted of Denver by such negatively tinged descriptions. Jerome Smiley conceded to such judgments only in part. He agreed that in a way every fifty-niner was an adventurer, "but to assert or imply that, as a whole, the mass was composed of bankrupts, criminals, gamblers and loafers is stupid, ignorant nonsense, formulated for the stories it was once common to relate of many places in the west."[44] Smiley, a consistent booster of Denver, was probably correct regarding the tendency of outside and short-term observers to misperceive Denver society. But a careful reading of the records of the day indicates that violence was a common event in early Colorado.[45]

The early Rocky Mountain west was a harsh place and, while hospitality was easily given and gratefully accepted, individuals were expected to "mind their own business" and to "solve their own problems." The requirement that individuals solve their own problems at times resulted in unfettered social violence. Colorado was not organized as a legal Territory until 1861 and until that time and considerably after the "rule of force" was the arbiter on civil and criminal questions. By the time Denver was only two years old and with a population of only around 4,000 persons, records existed of "fifteen murders (one by axe, another by butcher knife and the remainder prosaic shootings), two duels . . . innumerable acts of mayhem of ingenious variety (one man had his ear bitten off in a catch-as-catch-can competition, another lost the tip of his nose), and assorted thievery which carried off everything that could be lifted."[46] Although such behavior was to be expected of such a "reckless, unprincipled set of men," it was not long before the inhabitants of "illegal Denver" sought to control the situation as expediently as possible. To settle disputes and to establish the truth on questions of "justice," first the "Miner's Courts" and later the Committee for Safety with its "People's Court" were improvised.[47]

The Miner's Court was established on the basis of a few terse principles:

> Sec. I. Any person guilty of wilful murder upon conviction thereof shall be hung by the neck until he is dead.
>
> Sec. II. Any person guilty of manslaughter or homicide shall be punished as a jury of twelve men may direct.
>
> Sec. III. Any person shooting or threatening to shoot another, using or threatening to use any deadly weapon except in self-defense, shall be fined a sum not less than Fifty nor more than Five Hundred Dollars and receive in addition as many stripes on his bare back as a jury of six men may direct, and be banished from the district.
>
> Sec. IV. Any person found guilty of grand larceny shall be fined in a sum double the amount

stolen and receive not less than fifteen nor more than three hundred lashes on his bare back, and be banished from the district and such other punishment as a jury of six men may direct.[48]

Edward Dunklee describes the general manner in which these "principles" were applied and correctly identifies the type of law which these legal trappings barely concealed. He writes:

> Frequently such courts were held in a depression or valley, and those favoring the lynching of the alleged murderer would be asked to stand on one side to the creek and those opposing the other. If the vote was in the affirmative, the lynching was speedy, often carried out within the hour. Not infrequently the entire incident -- murder, capture, trial, sentence and execution -- occurred within twenty-four hours.[49]

Approximately the same procedures were followed by Denver's People's Courts, although in at least one instance, the "trial" was dispensed with.[50] There were few acquittals in cases involving capital offenses. As Professor Perkin points out, it would have taken a "brave and rash" man to vote for acquittal when "all about him were yelling 'Aye.'"[51]

These systems of justice have been defended and praised for their swiftness and certainly of punishment. Jerome Smiley has written of "the majesty of aroused, outraged public sentiment" which resulted in the "swift, terrible and unrelenting execution" of the "more wanton ruffians" which convinced similar men "that they could not successfully defy the whole community."[52] However, among the few acquittals rendered during this time was the freeing of Charley Harrison who "boasted that he planned to kill twelve men so that he would have a jury of peers in hell."[53] Moreover, the "swiftness and certainty" of publicly endorsed violence did not deter the daily violence which continued unabated throughout the reign of the People's Court.[54] As late as 1865, well after Colorado had become an official Territory with an established legal system, Coloradans were still willing to hastily construct People's Courts to expedite "justice."[55]

In 1859 the Pikes Peakers held several elections to form their own government to help establish some order. They voted against statehood because it was too expensive, declared the creation of "Jefferson Territory," wrote their own constitution and elected their own office holders. When Kansas Governor Denver sent "outsiders" to administer justice in the new city, its independent inhabitants expressed displeasure at this arrangement and maintained their own institutions, ignoring the new arrivals. Not until the region was officially recognized as Colorado Territory on February 28, 1861, did the provisional officers relinquish their "power" (although they also were mostly ignored by their fellow citizens). Moreover, so prevalent was violence as a way of life in Colorado that outgoing "Governor" Steele noted its existence in his proclamation to his subordinates which directed them to

> yield unto Caesar the things that are Caesar's . . . and further I advise and recommend to all law and order loving citizens to submit to the laws of the United States and restrain themselves from deeds of violence which so long have made our peculiar position almost a bye word in the eyes of the civilized world.[56]

Thus, characteristic of early Coloradans was a willingness to seek expedient solutions to complex problems. Moreoever, violence was a dominant fact of life both as a problem and a solution. The "justice" inflicted upon those individuals who appeared to have broken the basic code of Denver and were unlucky enough to have been apprehended is an example of this type of frontier problem solving. Rather than waiting for help from the east or constructing more long-term solutions, independent citizens of Colorado attempted to swiftly solve their own problems and even resented interference from the outside.[57] Their approach to problems demanding military solutions was characterized by the same sense of expediency.

The Colorado Militia

The Colorado Volunteers were a specific portion of the Denver audience which had access both to the messages presented in the Rocky Mountain News and the elite messages to be analyzed in Chapters Five and Six. Although a majority of the soldiers who were present at the Sand Creek campaign were so-called

"100-dayzers" or citizens of Colorado who had enlisted for one hundred days, they were officially associated with the Colorado First Regiment.

The Colorado First (also comprised of volunteers) had achieved fame early in the Civil War. In 1862, at Apache Pass near Glorietta, New Mexico, the First had helped to turn back a Confederate attempt to conquer the Southwest. In what has been described as the "Gettysburg of the West," a band of "wild Pikes Peakers" from the Denver area apparently saved the southwest from the clutches of the gold-poor Confederacy.[58] This first embodiment of Colorado volunteer military labeled themselves as "uncommon soldiers." As one private colorfully replied to a Captain who had made a remark concerning the quality of the "common soldier:" "G-d d--d old white livered whiskey tub! If you don't eat them words in three winks of a louse's tail, we'll tear you limb from gut! By G-d! youl'll find we're uncommon soldiers . . . ."[59] Orvando Hollister's history of the group does illustrate that the Third deserved the label "uncommon soldiers."[60]

After their victory, the Pikes Peakers returned to Denver where they were received with wild acclaim. Their newly promoted Colonel Chivington, credited with inspiring the victory, proceeded to Washington to demand a generalship and that his regiment be attached to Pope's army for regular duty. Chivington and his regiment were rebuffed by the War Department and spent the next two years sitting out the war near Denver. During these two years there was continued tension between the townspeople and the "uncommon soldiers," scurvy on the post, poor living conditions, and boredom for the remaining heroes of Glorietta.[61] For the First Regiment the victory at Glorietta became a high point against which future exploits of the First would be measured. In late 1863, portions of the Colorado infantry were moved to Missouri and portions of the First Colorado Cavalry ordered to Kansas. To Chivington and his demoralized, poorly equipped force was left the task of keeping the Colorado portion of the Overland Stage route open and protecting the Territory from rebel guerrillas and hostile Indians.

In the Spring of 1864, amid apparent increased Indian depredations, Chivington and Governor John Evans made frantic appeals to the War Department for authority to raise an additional mounted regiment.[62] Evans and Chivington were ignored for nearly two months, but the War Department finally granted its permission. The result was the Colorado Third Regiment, 1200 men to be recruited and attached to the remaining portions of the Colorado First and stationed at Camp Evans.

Recruiting officers were quickly commissioned by Governor Evans and Territorial newspapers called upon loyal citizens to enlist.[63] A handbill of the day posted to attract respective recruits was blunt about the purpose of the enlistment. Its largest invitation read "ATTENTION INDIAN FIGHTERS," and promised that those who chose to serve against "hostile Indians" would receive a salary of $.40 a day and "be entitled to all horses and plunder taken from the Indians." In spite of vigorous support by the Rocky Mountain News, speeches by Chivington and efforts by other "heroes" of Glorietta, recruiting was slow in Denver. On August 17, 1864, with a bid for election to Congress only three weeks away, Chivington declared the Denver area under martial law. This declaration severely restricted the operation of businesses but also allowed the Provost Marshall to enroll all able-bodied males in some type of military service.[64] The News had advocated this action early in August to "yank those fellows out of their holes and off their front steps."[65] Chivington's action allowed the needed enrollment to be completed within a week, although some recruits were discharged later because they apparently had enlisted only because of threats by the Provost Guard.

The type of citizen "attracted" into the Colorado Third has been characterized by contemporary J.E. Wharton as consisting of "floaters" or the less stable population of the Denver area.[66] Professor Hugh Carey, who has made a detailed study of the make-up of the Third from "Muster-out Rolls of Civil War Volunteers," classed many of the non-commissioned officers and privates as "men whom the hard school of frontier existence had taught pronounced independence, self-reliance, brutality and rowdiness."[67] Nor was the "brutality" of this population reserved only for the treatment of Indians. A company of the Third was ordered to take five captured rebel guerrillas from Denver to Fort Wise, south of Denver. But the unfortunate captives reportedly were shot while

115

"attempting to escape." Uncle Dick Wooten traveled by the area of "escape" a few weeks later and reported seeing skeletons tied to trees with bullet holes in their skulls.[68]

The recruits' attitudes towards American Indians probably were not any less hostile than those of the more stable citizens who had managed to perform their "military service" in ways which kept them from volunteering. The Colorado population in general had been terrified and outraged by apparent Indian attacks of the Spring and early Summer of 1864. Publicity in the News concerning Indian massacres of Whites near and far let no Coloradan forget the nature of the "red devils." Therefore it is difficult to isolate the attitudes of the recruits apart from this publicity -- especially since similar publicity was a part of the recruitment process.[69] However, helpful records of relevant attitudes are available for analysis.

Orvando Hollister served with the First Colorado Regiment from its initial organization through its campaign in New Mexico and its return to the Denver area. While he was "mustered out" in 1863, his attitudes provide some insight into the mentality of the citizen-soldier prior to 1864. In his "history" of the Colorado Volunteers in New Mexico, he "intended to mirror the feelings of the soldiers as faithfully as possible."[70] He mirrored an equally dim view of "officers . . . Jews, Catholics, Mexicans and Confederates."[71] Not to be excluded was his attitude toward "Indian Character." He wrote:

> Whatever of savage grandeur in the Indian character . . . conjured from the records of history or romance, was speedily dissipated on entering a lodge. The squaws, miserable and emaciated, were baking human excrement on shingles for food. While the bucks were usually engaged lousing themselves. The squalid misery of these wasted creatures is past belief, and must be seen to be appreciated. Utter and speedy extinction is their only cure.[72]

Hollister remained in Denver after he left the volunteers. At different times he edited two rival newspapers to the Rocky Mountain News and was editor of the News for a time during 1868 while Byers was busy with other matters. As editor of the Black Hawk

Daily Mining Journal, Hollister declared, "If there be one idea that should become an axiom in American politics it is That the Red Man Should be Destroyed" [emphasis original].[73] Hollister also was one of the "heroes" of Glorietta who actively supported the recruitment process in 1864.[74]

Irving Howbert was a volunteer of the Colorado Third in 1864 and participated in the Sand Creek engagement when he was eighteen years old. He later wrote a "history" of the Indians of the Pikes Peak Region in which he related his version of the events at Sand Creek. His motive, he wrote to a friend, was "to place before the world, as far as possible, the true story of the battle of Sand Creek." The book contains two chapters which relate his version of the battle and defend its White participants.[75]

Like Parkman, he labeled the Indian as "merely a child" in most matters. He recorded that the "sole occupation" of the nomadic Indian was killing other human beings. So "fiendish" were the tortures which were inflicted upon innocent White captives that White men fighting the Indians "seldom failed to reserve one last shot in their revolvers with which to end their lives if capture was imminent, and in many instances men have shot their wives and children rather than allow them to fall into the hands of the Indians." Moreover, he declared the squaws "were even more diabolical than the warriors."[76] His solution was implicit but he clearly believed acts of "forebearance" to be self-defeating and argued that "it would have required only a few cases of summary punishment such as we gave them at Sand Creek, to have settled Indian troubles for all time."[77] Thus, while he denied the indiscriminate murder of Indian women and children at Sand Creek, he implicitly admitted the savage nature of the White attack.[78]

Another participant in the battle at Sand Creek, Morse Coffin, has directly denied Howbert's contention that there was no indiscriminate killing of women and children at Sand Creek. Written when he was an old man in the late 1890's but not published until 1965, the book also provides a record of the "general" public sentiment of the day toward the Indians. Moreover, the record largely has been ignored by historians in their evaluations of that battle. Regarding Howbert's denial of indiscriminate slaughter of Indians by Whites, Coffin wrote:

> . . . neither Col. Chivington or Col. Shoup (not to mention others) have been honest in this matter; but have pretended that the killing of women and children in this battle was entirely unavoidable; could not be helped, as all were in the rifle pits together, etc. etc. . . . Now I know a part of this is true, and that many were unavoidably killed; that it was not easy to distinguish the sexes during the fight, and that it would have been impossible to help killing many women and children; and I also know perfectly well (and nearly every other man who was in the Sand Creek fight must be satisfied of it) that it was the purpose during the battle to kill old and young of both sexes. This is the fact of the case, and it is useless to shirk it, or pretend it was all accident.[79]

He accounted for this "purpose" by referring it to the "general opinion" of the time:

> I now desire to mention a few things in order to make plain the general opinion among the people at that time regarding Indian killing, and thus account in some degree for the scalping indulged in at Sand Creek . . . . At the time the 3rd Colorado regiment was raised, the idea was very general that a war of extermination should be waged; that neither sex nor age should be spared; and women held these views in common with men . . . and one often heard the expression that 'nits make lice, make a clean thing of it.' Of course there were some exceptions . . . . I propose to show that both officers and soldiers but carried out the general sentiment. . . .[80]

Coffin's statements are especially important since he had denied initially that Sand Creek had been a massacre.[81] These admissions indicted his behavior along with that of his cohorts. Thus, his statements may be the "best evidence" of the nature of events at Sand Creek while providing a measure of the opinion of the day towards Native Americans. Yet, even in granting the White excesses which he says occurred at Sand Creek, Coffin lays most of the blame on Chivington (where it may lay) and insists that the Cheyennes and Arapahoes at the site were hostile. In his mind their apparent hostility justified their disfigurement but there is an aura of confession around his statements such as: "[I] did not see a solitary warrior not scalped . . . I know this is not to the credit of myself and others who did it; but it is the truth, and I am disposed to shoulder my share of it. At this time it was deemed all right and proper . . . ."[82]

Hollister, Howbert and Coffin are not necessarily reflective of the majority opinion of the Third. Rather, their expressions have survived those times and are available for examination. As I illustrate later, several officers and men of the Third clearly had positive attitudes towards the Indians at Sand Creek and sought to prevent violence there. However, other statements and evidence reinforce the probability that attitudes in the Third were generally negative toward all Indians, that most members had joined up with the desire to fight Indians, that personal experience and knowledge intensified their hatred of Native Americans and that "extermination" was considered a popular solution to the Indian problem.

As citizen-soldiers the recruits brought to their service attitudes reflective of the general attitudes of the Denver population. Therefore they were at least as "nervous" regarding Indians as Howbert, as contemptuous regarding Indian ways as Hollister, and as ready to be guided by the general sentiment as Coffin. Some members, who were "floaters," were more prone to violence than Denver's more stable citizens and apparently joined up with the sole purpose of fighting Indians. On September 29, 1864, with rumors of a potential treaty with the Indians making the rounds because of the Camp Weld Conference, the News reported, "we understand that a serious misapprehension exists at Camp Evans today which came very near ending in mutiny. The boys were informed that a treaty of peace had been arranged yesterday with the Indians and there would be no fighting. As that was what they enlisted for they desire to active service in the field."[83] However, no treaty was made (at least as the Whites perceived it) and one and one-half months later, portions of the Colorado First and Third left on the expedition to Sand Creek.

The salience of the need to fight Indians may have also been increased by personal experience and knowledge. Howbert explains that

Among the members of our regiment, there were many who had had friends and relatives killed, scalped and mutilated by these Indians, and almost every man sustained financial loss by reason of their raids; Consequently it is not surprising they should be determined to inflict such punishment upon the savages as would deter them from further raids upon our settlement.[84]

Byers provides a similar justificaton in his defense of extermination as a solution.[85] Moreover, reports from Denver during approximately the same period reinforce Coffin's statements regarding the general feeling towards Indians.

In September, 1864 the Reverend William Crawford gave a measure of the intensity of the attitude. He reported, "There is but one sentiment in regard to the final disposition which shall be made of the Indians: 'Let them be exterminated men, women and children together.' They are regarded as a race accursed, like the ancient Canaanites, and like them, devoted of the almighty to utter destruction. Of course I do not myself share in such views."[86] Although he was less objective than Reverend Crawford, Nathaniel Hill revealed a similar judgment when he wrote to his wife in Rhode Island in August of the same year:

There is no sentimentality here on the frontier respecting Indians. Cooper and Longfellow are regarded with disgust. Indians are all the same, a treacherous and villainous set. I would rejoice, as would every man in Colorado to see them exterminated.[87]

The recruits to the Third would have been especially sensitive to community pressure calling for such a "solution." Their relations with the citizens of Denver were strained throughout September and October of 1864. The War Department was occupied with a war on a more important front and did not provide the newly raised regiment with proper arms or mounts. Therefore the Third was limited in the military maneuvers in which it could engage and the recruits who had "hurried up" to enlist were not covering themselves with glory as had their forerunners at Glorietta but waiting for action. Moreover, as their inactivity stretched beyond fifty days of their enlistment period, they were insultingly dubbed the "Bloodless Third" by fellow citizens, tired of the antics of the bored soldiers.[88] It can be easily imagined that a group of "uncommon soldiers," independent, brutal and impatient of purpose would seek to dispel the label "bloodless" as expediently as possible.

CHAPTER III

NOTES

[1] Robert G. Athearn, The Coloradans (Albuquerque: University of New Mexico Press, 1976), p. 17; Elliott West, The Saloon on the Rocky Mountain Mining Frontier (Lincoln: University of Nebraska Press, 1979), pp. 5, 6. For a detailed discussion of population development see Colin B. Goodykoontz, "The People of Colorado," in LeRoy Hafen, ed., Colorado and Its People (New York: Doubleday and Co., 1948), II, pp. 77-120. See also U.S. Department of the Interior, Census Office, Population of the United States in 1860 (Washington D.C.: U.S. Government Printing Office, 1864), p. 549.

[2] West, p. 5; Augusta Tabor, "Cabin Life in Colorado," Colorado Magazine, 4 (March, 1927), 22-28.

[3] Daily Rocky Mountain News, August 29, 1861. Hereafter this source will be cited as RMN.

[4] Athearn, p. 34.

[5] Quoted in Athearn, p. 37.

[6] Athearn, pp. 37-38.

[7] RMN, March 7, 1866.

[8] RMN, March 7, 1866; Athearn, p. 37.

[9] Reverend William H. Goode, Outposts of Zion with Limnings of Mission Life (Cincinnati: Poe and Hitchcock, 1864), p. 438; Frank Hall, History of the State of Colorado, 4 vols (Chicago: Blakely Printing Co., 1889), I, pp. 206-207.

[10] LeRoy R. Hafen, ed., Colorado Gold Rush, Contemporary Letters and Reports 1858-1859 (Glendale, California: Arthur H. Clark, 1941), p. 160.

[11] Hafen, Letters and Reports, p. 366.

[12] "Correspondent to the Missouri Democrat, from Denver, December 15, 1859," in LeRoy R. Hafen and Ann W. Hafen, eds., Reports From Colorado, the Wildman

Letters 1859-1865 with Other Related Letters and Newspaper Reports, 1859 (Glendale, California: Arthur H. Clark Company, 1961), p. 224; and "Thomas Wildman to his sister, January 4, 1860," in Reports From Colorado, p. 240.

[13]"Augustus Wildman to Lucy Starr Haskins, December 16, 1860," in Reports from Colorado, p. 272.

[14]"Correspondent to the Missouri Democrat, writing from Denver, December 15, 1859," in Reports From Colorado, p. 229.

[15]Turner, The United States, 1830-1850; The Nation and Its Sections (Gloucester Mass: Peter Smith, 1958), p. 20.

[16]Turner, The Frontier in American History (New York: Holt, Rinehart and Winstone, 1921), p. 205.

[17]Frontier in American History, p. 37.

[18]For an excellent compilation and guide to the Turnerian point of view see: O. Lawrence Burnette, Jr., ed., Wisconsin Witness to Fredrick Jackson Turner, A Collection of Essays on the Historian and the Thesis (Madison: The State Historical Society of Wisconsin, 1961); In this volume see especially J.A. Burkhart, "The Turner Thesis: A Historian's Controversy," pp. 160-173. Among the most important evaluations of Turner's thesis are: Avery O. Craven, "Fredrick Jackson Turner," in The Marcus W. Jernegan Essays in American Historiography (Chicago: University of Chicago Press, 1937), pp. 252-270; Joseph Schafer, "Turner's Frontier Philosophy," Wisconsin Magazine of History, 16 (June 1933), 451-469 and Frederic L. Paxson, "A Generation of the Frontier Hypothesis," Pacific Valley Historical Review, 2 (March 1933), 34-51.

[19]Quoted in Duane A. Smith, Rocky Mountain Mining Camps, the Urban Frontier (Bloomington: Indiana University Press, 1967), p. 22.

[20]Quoted in Athearn, p. 18.

[21]Recorded by A.O. McGrew in a letter to the Omaha Times, February 17, 1858, in Hafen, Letters and Reports, 1858-1859, p. 196.

[22] West, p. 5.

[23] Quoted in Athearn, pp. 27-28.

[24] Athearn, p. 28.

[25] Reports From Colorado, pp. 200, 240.

[26] RMN, August 2, 1864 and April 17, 1865. See also Eugene H. Berwanger, "William J. Hardin: Colorado Spokesman for Racial Justice, 1863-1873," Colorado Magazine, 52 (Winter, 1975), 52-65.

[27] Athearn, p. 173.

[28] Henry Villard quoted in Athearn, p. 173.

[29] See Athearn, pp. 171-188 and Smith, pp. 29-42.

[30] Such a conclusion is consistent with observations made by A.K. McClure, Three Thousand Miles Through the Rocky Mountains (Philadelphia: J.P. Lippincott, 1869), pp. 66, 67, 73, 74-76, 83-84, 86-87.

[31] Hafen, Letters, p. 144.

[32] Hafen, Letters, pp. 145, 158; also see pp. 201, 204.

[33] Hafen, Letters, p. 230.

[34] Hafen, Letters, pp. 245-46.

[35] Quoted in Howard Lewis Conrad, "Uncle Dick" Wooten (Chicago, 1890), p. 119.

[36] Quoted in Athearn, p. 72.

[37] John H. Edwards, in LeRoy R. Hafen, ed., Overland Routes to the Gold Fields, 1859 From Contemporary Diaries (Glendale, California: Arthur H. Clark, 1942), pp. 311-12.

[38] Hafen, Letters, p. 219.

[39] McClure, p. 124.

[40] Albert D. Richardson, Beyond the Mississippi (Hartford, Conn: American Publishing Co., 1867), pp. 177-178, 186.

[41] Quoted in Robert L. Perkin, The First Hundred Years, An Informal History of Denver and the Rocky Mountain News (Garden City, NY: Doubleday and Co., 1959), p. 50.

[42] Quoted in Perkin, p. 123.

[43] J. William Hepworth Dixon, New America (Philadelphia: J.B. Lippincott, 1867), pp. 92, 96, 97.

[44] Quoted in Perkin, p. 52.

[45] See Hafen, Letters, pp. 147, 216-17, 339, 356-57; Hafen, Reports, pp. 59, 67, 250-52, 260, 271, 287, 291, 295.

[46] Perkin, pp. 174-75; For detailed descriptions of some of these "crimes" see Edward V. Dunklee, "Justice Comes to Denver," The Westerners Brand Book 1949 (Denver: The Artcraft Press, 1949), pp. 195-204; See also Francis S. Williams, "Trials and Judgements of the People's Courts of Denver," Colorado Magazine, 27 (October, 1950), 294-302 and Calvin W. Gower, "Vigilantes," Colorado Magazine, 41 (Spring, 1964), 93-104.

[47] Hafen, Reports, pp. 271-272.

[48] Quoted in Dunklee, p. 200.

[49] Dunklee, p. 198.

[50] Dunklee, p. 199.

[51] Perkin, p. 175.

[52] Jerome C. Smiley, ed., Semi-Centennial History of the State of Colorado, 2 vols (Chicago: Lewis Publishing Company, 1913), I, pp. 349. Also see statements in Dunklee, pp. 200-201.

[53] Perkin, p. 178. Harrison was also recorded to have said that he wouldn't count the eleven "mexicans

and niggers" he had slain. He apparently achieved acquittal by threatening and buying off the eyewitnesses against him. See RMN, July 25, 1860.

[54]This is Perkin's conclusion, p. 176. It is consistent with another study. See Lee Casey, ed., Denver Murders (New York: Alfred A. Knopf, 1946).

[55]See RMN, October 24, 1865.

[56]Quoted in Thomas L. Karnes, William Gilpin, Western Nationalist (Austin: University of Texas Press, 1970), p. 259.

[57]"G.N. Hill to the Kansas City Journal of Commerce, January 15, 1859," in Letters and Reports, 1858-59, pp. 173-74.

[58]Perkin, pp. 236, 237-249; For a first hand account see Orvando J. Hollister, Colorado Volunteers in New Mexico, 1862 (1863; rpt. Chicago: The Lakeside Press, 1962), pp. 97-124.

[59]Quoted in Hollister, p. 38.

[60]See especially pp. 37-39.

[61]Janet Lecompte, "Sand Creek," Colorado Magazine, 41 (Fall, 1964), 316; RMN, August 6, 1862.

[62]See Chapters Five and six of this study for an analysis of these communications.

[63]RMN, August 13, 1864.

[64]Raymond G. Carey, "The 'Bloodless Third' Regiment, Colorado Volunteer Cavalry," Colorado Magazine, 38 (October, 1961), 279.

[65]RMN, August 1, 1864.

[66]J.E. Wharton, History of the City of Denver (Denver: Byers and Dailey, 1866), p. 155.

[67]Carey, p. 282.

[68]Chivington had written to Major S.S. Curtis regarding the guerrillas: "Have five notorious guerrillas. Will try by military commission. If

convicted can I approve and shoot them?" Curtis replied that only the department commander had the power and that it could not be delegated. So the captives had to be taken to Fort Wise. Rebellion Records, Series 1, Vol 41, part 2, pp. 828, 843; Wooten's discovery related in Perkin, p. 251. John Dailey gives an account of this event in his diary but found that the prisoners were shot by the guard while attempting to escape. "Entry for Monday, September 5, 1864," Dailey Diaries, Unpublished MS in Denver Public Library, Western History Collection, no page number.

[69] Carey, p. 287.

[70] Hollister, p. xvii.

[71] Hollister, p. xviii.

[72] Hollister, p. 31.

[73] Black Hawk Daily Mining Journal, August 30, 1864.

[74] Carey, p. 287.

[75] Irving Howbert, The Indians of the Pikes Peak Region (1914; rpt. Glorietta, New Mexico: The Rio Grande Press, Inc.: 1970); "Howbert to William B. Thom, June 12, 1915," in Thom Collection, Unpublished Letters in Western History Collection, Denver Public Library.

[76] Howbert, pp. 180-82.

[77] Howbert, p. 184.

[78] Howbert, pp. 184, 113.

[79] Morse H. Coffin, The Battle of Sand Creek (Waco, Tex: Wm. Morrison, 1965), p. 89.

[80] Coffin, pp. 9-10.

[81] RMN, October 9, 1904, p. 9, col 1.

[82] Coffin, p. 36.

[83] RMN, September 29, 1864.

[84] Howbert, pp. 110-111.

[85] RMN, July 24, 1865.

[86] Quoted in Colin B. Goodykoontz, "Colorado As Seen by a Home Missionary, 1863-1868," Colorado Magazine, 12 (March, 1935), 66.

[87] "Nathaniel P. Hill Inspects Colorado Letters Written in 1864," The Colorado Magazine, 34 (January, 1957), 35-36.

[88] Carey, p. 289.

CHAPTER IV

THE 'ROCKY MOUNTAIN NEWS' AND

THE SYMBOLS OF EXTERMINATION

> " . . . don't credit and above all, don't circulate stories calculated to excite and inflame the public."
> Rocky Mountain News,
> Sept. 6, 1861

> "This war of civilization . . . is the irrepressible conflict and those whose opportunity has ever been best for observation have invariably arrived at one conclusion, that it admits of but one solution: that [of] the extermination of the red man . . ."
> Rocky Mountain News,
> July 24, 1865

Background

As Robert Perkin has illustrated, the early history of the Rocky Mountain News was directed by William Newton Byers. He was its founder and "policy maker." In the pages of the News, he sought to direct Denverites to proper courses of action. A self-made man, he firmly believed others should follow his example of "temperance, truth and high moral living."[1] Born in Madison County, Ohio on February 22, 1831, Byers was the oldest of six children. He educated himself from books "begged and borrowed" as did Lincoln whom he supported for President in the 1860's. By intense application, Byers developed a knowledge of practical surveying which he made his initial avocation. In 1860 he was appointed deputy United States surveyor for Iowa and surveyed some of the original western lines of that state. Byers was a consistent keeper of journals and a note in an 1852 journal reveals something of the inner, young Byers. From Pope he notes,

131

>   Health exists of with Temperance alone consists
>   And Peace, O virtue is all thine one.[2]

He would later, editorially, lecture his obstreperous White Denver audience regarding the virtues of agrarian hard work and "temperance."

During 1850 he followed Francis Parkman's trail west through Nebraska, Wyoming, Idaho and into what was to become the states of Washington and Oregon. In Oregon Territory, again he was instrumental in "laying out" the first section lines in a western state. After November, 1853, he traveled through California, visiting San Francisco with which he was "agreeably dissapointed," and "Sackramento," "a brisk and pleasant place." Eventually he arrived back "home," now Muscatine, Iowa, where he helped his father on the family farm and was soon married. By early October of 1854, he and his new bride were located in Omaha. The Omaha *Arrow* related the arrival of

> . . . W. N. Byers, formerly of Muscatine, Iowa, an old stager on the Oregon frontier who brings with him one of the best solar compasses for field surveying in the west. He proposes making our soil his home . . . .[3]

The twenty-five year "old" stager, again appointed a deputy U.S. surveyor for a new state, helped survey and map Omaha. Byers also was elected to the first Nebraska Territorial Legislature and in 1857 served as a town alderman in Omaha.

In winter, 1858, Byers, now a member of a land agents firm, Poppleton and Byers, edited a western "Guidebook."[4] The panic of 1857 and rumors of gold in the Rockies made "argonauts" out of many broke farmers and merchants. Thousands of young men streamed west both persuaded by and informed by guidebooks like that edited by Byers.

In his guide Byers informed his "greenhorn" audience that he was also going west to seek his fortune and engaged in a bit of editorializing in this advice to his gold-stricken audience:

> In conclusion, we would say to all who go to the mines, especially to the young, <u>Yield not to temptation</u>. Carry your principles with you;

132

leave not your character at home, nor your Bible; but you will need them both, and even grace from above, to protect you in a community whose god is Mammon, who are wild with excitement and free from family restraints [emphasis original].[5]

In March of 1858, Byers travled to the head of the Platte River, leading an outfit consisting of two oxen-pulled wagons, one loaded with a printing press. Although his guidebook had been his sole experience with journalism, by the end of April Byers was in the Denver area "babying, boosting, and scolding it and jealously protecting it from all slanders," through the pages of his Rocky Mountain News.[6]

Byers' partner and "anchorman" in founding the News was John Dailey. Also born in Ohio, Dailey brought practical experience to the paper as publisher and printer. He had worked at several newspapers in Indiana, Ohio and Iowa and helped found the Iowa Citizen which became the Des Moines Register. He met Byers in Omaha while both were working on a survey party and eventually joined Byers in Denver first as head-printer of the News and later as full partner. He worked faithfully with Byers until 1870 except for a brief hiatus in 1864 when he enlisted in the Third Colorado Calvary. He was present at the Battle of Sand Creek.[7] As stated, Byers was the "editorialist" of the two men while Dailey was the printer/workman. Most of the policies supported by the News, political and otherwise, were originated by Byers.

The founding of the News actually predated both the formation of Colorado Territory and the official naming of "Denver city." Although the first issue of the News was published on April 23, 1859 (some twenty minutes before its short-lived rival, the Cherry Creek Pioneer), Colorado did not legally become a Territory until 1861 and Denver was not incorporated until December, 1859. The News was designated as the "official" paper of the Territory before a territory was legally created, making the News the oldest continuing institution in Colorado.[8] Moreover, Byers was among Colorado's first elite. He supported statehood and was instrumental in helping to establish the permanent institutions he felt should accompany any great city. He became a close friend of Governor John Evans who was reportedly his silent partner and was rescued by John Chivington during the "Great Flood in Cherry Creek" in 1864.[9]

Throughout his editorial career with the News, Byers championed statehood for Colorado, sometimes linking the issue with other political concerns of the day. The remarkable success of the Rocky Mountain News was illustrated by its endurance. While numerous other newspapers were published in and around Denver only to languish, the News survived, at times the only newspaper in the area. While Byers did attempt to change opinion, the causes he campaigned for usually reflected assumptions held by the majority of his local audience. Although Byers would write occasionally for Eastern consumption -- most often in defense of Denver and its inhabitants -- his emphasis was focused upon his local audience held hostage by its isolation. Without exaggeration it could be said that through famine, fire and flood the News survived because it fulfilled important functions for its audience.[10] Byers' hopes for statehood remained unfulfilled until 1876. However, as his goal statehood remained paramount until that time. He retired from journalism in 1878 only after the goal had been achieved.[11]

To gain statehood for Colorado, Byers sought to attract, maintain and mold the necessary population to achieve his goal. He examined emerging problems of the day as they affected his statehood goal and the continued existence and prestige of the News as an influential institution in the Denver community. As an emerging problem of policy, the relationship between Indians and White Coloradans was defined and redefined by the News in symbols which aided the cause of statehood and the continued influence of the News. These symbols may best be studied, chronologically, as they changed with the concerns of the day.

Symbols of 1859-1861

Byers' concern for boosting Colorado statehood was apparent in the first issue of the News, printed in the leaky-roofed attic of "Uncle Dick" Wooten's cabin. In this first issue, Byers promised that in just a few "months," Colorado "would be a great community knocking at the door of the Union for admission as a sovereign state. However, it was also clear that Byers, at least implicitly, limited membership in this "state" to Whites. Like Parkman, Byers symbolized the "wild Indian" receding "before the advancing wave of Anglo Saxon enterprise and civilization, where soon we fondly hope will be erected a great and powerful$_{12}$ state, another empire in the sisterhood of empires." Although Byers and the other "fifty-niners" were squatting illegally on land promised to the Cheyennes and Arapahoes, these promises were of little consequence; such displacement was "destiny." As Byers explained it:

> . . . the hum of busy men is heard in the mountains so lately rising lonely in the majestic silence; the cheerful tones of a multitude fill the air that but lately echoed only the occasional voice of a weary wanderer; the Buffalo and Deer that but yesterday scarely feared the form of man are already driven by the presence of men, from the boundless plains where they had roamed almost undisturbed for a thousand years; the wandering savages, often an object of fear to the pilgrim travelers, are themselves, in the twinkling of an eye, trembling before the coming wave of countless emigration. The poor Indian, heretofore quietly displaced by treaty, is now pushed rudely on by the resistless rush of Yankee enterprise; and ere the year shall close, the Indians of Kansas and Nebraska will have closed by a leap, almost the last space between them and their mournful destiny.$_{13}$

In this first issue, Byers also provided overt reasons for founding the News which reflected both pecuniary interests and rhetorical impulses:

> We know enough, however, to believe that a large population will settle here at once, and prosper, and we believe that this will be a reading and intelligent population. Believing this we have at great trouble brought a printing press and all necessary fixtures over 500 miles, at an inclement season, and over roads freezing at night and thawing by day. We have done this because we wished to collect and send forth reliable information, because we wished to mould and organize the new population, and because we thought it would pay . . . .$_{14}$

Byers and Dailey's first problem involved proving the authenticity of reported gold strikes in the area. They could hardly "mould and organize" a population which did not remain. The first emigrants had gone west to the Rockies with unrealistic expectations regarding the accessibility and amount of available gold. The writers of popular guidebooks were not above exaggerating the ready availability of gold. Of course, when the emigrants arrived on Cherry Creek and found that not all its grains were gold and that mining was as hard as or harder than pushing a plow, they became discouraged and bitter and some "went back."[15]

Although Byers had declared "accurate and truthful information" to be the all embracing policy of the News, because he had published one of the guidebooks, he found himself regarded as "one of the most capable and dangerous liars in the country."[16] Assuring an adequate population base was a necessary condition for his hopes for statehood, therefore Byers had to solve the problem of returning emigrants. In an editorial titled "The Returning Emigration," Byers addressed the still remaining population:

> . . . all this has been brought about by the action of a few restless spirits who are of no advantage to any country. They arrive in the vicinity of the mining region, stop a few hours or a day or two, perhaps prospect a little in places most unlikely in the world for finding gold, and because they cannot shovel gold nuggets like they have been accustomed to dig potatoes, they raise the cry that all is humbug . . .[17]

Byers also addressed those eastern newspapers that had labeled him a "liar." When the Davenport, Iowa Gazette charged Byers with lying himself "black in the face" regarding the "Pikes Peak humbug," Byers replied:

> We defy the world to point to one single editorial statement in the news which we are unable to substantiate literally as set forth. So pitch in, gentlemen, your abuse is powerless to harm us . . .
> The papers denounce the 'Pikes Peak humbug,' as they are pleased to call it, basing their opinion in the main upon the lying reports of men who have never seen this region of country -- men who have turned back and made their way home

> howling like whipped curs -- creatures who should never have been unloosed from their mothers' apron strings . . . .[18]

As reports of "humbug" in the Rockies became increasingly common, Byers responded even more strongly:

> GOBACKS
>
> We hope this class are all again safely at home with their Pa's and Ma's, their sweethearts, or 'Nancy and the babies'; there they may dwell in sweet seclusion, retirement, and repose, and whilst they sit around the chimney corner they can fight their battles again . . . Farewell to those 'gobacks' they have had their day and soon will be forgotten.[19]

Byers' directness often would get him into trouble. He would be attacked by opposition newspapers or even, on one occasion, kidnapped and shot at.[20] The migration away from Denver was halted, not just by Byers' persuasion, but with the help from Horace Greeley, who traveled to the scene in June of 1859 and pronounced some of the gold strikes near Denver to be genuine.[21]

Quantitatively, "Indians" as a topic occupied only a small percentage of the potential space in the early editions of the News. When symbols related to Native Americans were used they reflected an anglo ethnocentric bias and some of the constituents of the conspiracy myth. As noted, Byers believed that the Indians would "melt away" before the "advancing tide" of Anglos. But no one was to blame for this "melting away;" it was "destiny" that a "white empire" would replace and chase our "inferiors, physically, morally, [and] mentally." Although Byers expressed some reservations and nervousness regarding Native Americans, he favored "peaceful relations" with them.[22] However, their inferiority, in his early view, did not justify their deliberate destruction by the Whites. Rather, a "civilized and enlightened people" had the special burden of avoiding "an agressive and tyrranous course." Thus, Native Americans were symbolized as "our Indian neighbors," the "Poor Indian," observed on "Indian Expeditions," imbued with "Childlike curiousity" and of "nobel countenance." The term "savage" was often applied, not necessarily in a pejorative sense, but as a statement of the Indians' condition. As "red skins" or "dusky sons of the forest," they occasionally committed "depredations," but during this period seldom were guilty of "outrages." When they did stray, they were described as "vagabonds," and "rascels" or "drunken savages." Moreover, such incidents were often attributed to the provocation of the White "squatters," "bummers," "gamblers" or "miscreants" illegally selling liquor to the Indians.[23]

Byers' initial position regarding the treatment of Native Americans was overtly based upon "prudence and discretion." Certainly Byers' position may have been influenced by altruistic concerns since he admitted "white injustices" against the Indians. But he was also concerned with maintaining emigration into his new community in the wilderness. Prospective emigrants were less likely to be frightened off by favorable and nonthreatening reports of friendly Indians than by reports of Indian treacheries.

While Byers shared the "nervous" attitude regarding the danger of Native Americans, he initially debunked any chance of a larger scale uprising. On August 27, 1860, the News reported:

> A story was circulating in the city this morning that 2,000 Cheyenne and Arapahoes were coming up the Platte with the design of attacking and burning the city tonight. We have no doubt a large party of Indians are in the neighborhood, but have no idea that they meditate any harm, other than their natural dispositions to beg and steal.[24]

In fact, Byers was to argue, the Indians were not to blame for reported depredations; rather "recent depredations on stock ranches on which some animals have been stolen and others shot with arrows have invariably been the work of white men . . . ."[25] Additionally, when Indians actually had committed depredations, the blame fell upon the Whites and their liquor trade with the Indians:

> It is time this liquor traffic with the Indians should be stopped. Every man, woman and child in this country is in danger if it is allowed to

continue. Shall a few soulless miscreants, who wish to make favorable bargains with half-drunken savages be permitted to sow firebrands . . . over this now peaceful country? . . . the people have rights and they will most assuredly maintain them in this matter.[26]

Byers concluded with a threat that those who failed to "take warning" would be dealt with by the "citizens" rather than the "City courts." A few weeks later the News reported an unsuccessful conviction but successful punishment of such offenders, "The three Mexicans who were on trial last Monday for selling liquor to Indians were acquitted for lack of evidence . . . some time during the night [they] were all badly beaten either by one another or by other parties . . . ."[27]

So, the News agreed with old Indian scout Jim Beckwourth that most Indian troubles were caused by or were the fault of White men. On April 18, 1860, the News published an indignant letter from Beckwourth demanding "Justice to the Indians." Beckwourth related that a group of White "drunken devils" and "bummers" had attacked a band of "Appache" and Cheyenne Indians who had come peaceably to Denver to visit Beckwourth. In the attack the Whites had committed "acts of violence which in any other country would condemn the perpetrators to ignominy and shame . . . ." Beckwourth concluded with some advice, based upon his forty years of living with Indians:

The Indians are keenly sensible to acts of injustice, as they are tenacious of revenge, and it is more humiliating to them to be the recipients of such treatment upon their own lands, which they have been deprived of, their game driven off and they made to suffer by hunger, and when they pay us a visit, abused more than dogs. My advice is, that municipal regulations be made, prevent the sale of intoxicating drinks to them, with such penalties as would make the law respected. And all emigrants who are on their way here ought to, most religiously, refrain from giving Indians whisky, or trading it to them for their horses; for if he sells his pony, he will steal one from the next white man that comes along. All our Indian troubles are produced by the impudent acts of unprincipled white men . . . . [emphasis original].[28]

In the same edition, the News supported Beckwourth's complaints and advice in an editorial titled "Lo the Poor Indian:"

> We earnestly invite the attention of our citizens to the communication to be found in our columns, from Capt. Beckwourth, in reference to the outrage committed upon the Indians lately encamped in our city for the purpose of peaceful trade . . .
> We hope the suggestions contained in the Capt.'s letter will be heeded . . . Cannot some public expression of our municipal authorities or of the people be had, condemning the outrage, so that Capt. Beckwourth may bear to them such redress as it is in our power to make? . . .[29]

In later circumstances, the News would use the phrase "The poor Indian" with consistent irony rather than sympathy.

Another account in September of 1861 related the trailing and subsequent hanging of a horse thief. The account is surprising not because of the violence of the justice applied but because the horse that was taken was stolen from a Cheyenne "noted for his friendship to the whites."[30]

During this period, some Indians were symbolized by the News as capable of friendship with Whites. One Indian, Left Hand, was reported by Byers to be a "friend." Left Hand, an Arapahoe, had reported to a Mr. Rice that the Kiowas were "coming to wipe out the settlers throughout the country." Because Left Hand was ignored, Byers implied, a "massacre" took place.[31] In its reporting of this incident the News admitted the presence of "hostile" Indians and illustrated the vivid manner in which such Indian depredations were reported. Under the title "Indian Outrages, Two Citizens Murdered," the News reported that:

> On the 29th a party of about 20 Indians supposed to be Kiowas, attacked H.J. Rice and H. Pierson at their cabin on Running Creek . . . and killed them both, threw their bodies into the cabin and then burned it, together with the remains of their murdered victims . . . . outside of where the house stood they [Mr. Young and "some assistants"] found the scene of violent struggle.

Lying on the ground were some bullets recognized as belonging to Mr. Pierson's guns, three bloody arrows, a piece of broken and bloody war club and part of a man's brains where no doubt Pierson had fallen. Rice had apparently fallen near the door . . . The bodies were dragged into the cabin and burned. The bones were found . . . .[32]

In his editorial in the following issue, Byers tried to gather support for an expedition against the "murderers of Rice and Pierson." Although he called for a "prompt and summary lesson," Byers clearly distinguished between hostile and friendly Indians. He also concluded that Denver would never be "seriously threatened" and that more attention should have been paid to Left Hand's report.[33] A bit later in Denver history Byers would make no such distinctions between hostile and friendly Indians.

In summary, throughout this early period Byers debunked accounts of Indian hostility as "grossly exaggerated," and insisted that Indian "outrages" always "grow as they go."[34] By engaging in this debunking he was not simply serving the value of "prudence" but also was attacking the policies of a rival newspaper, the Denver Herald. Byers, in his usual blunt manner, protested the efforts "in certain quarters" to arouse the public against the Indian.[35] Thundering that the sources of such efforts sought only to "gain a little notoriety," Byers warned that:

> Let the report go back to the Missouri River, that there is serious trouble here with the Indians, and Emigration will cease at once. Shall the folly and rashness of a few inconsiderate persons, who wish to gain a little personal notoriety, be allowed to embroil us in a war with the Indian? We trust not [emphasis added].[36]

This charge of an irresponsible Indian policy was only one of many that Byers would hurl at the rival newspaper -- his primary competition for the public printing contract let by the newly established Territory of Colorado.[37] The Herald had been successful, initially, in gaining the contract, but Byers fought to gain back the right which had been given him by the "illegal" legislature of Jefferson Territory (as the independent inhabitants of the region had originally dubbed themselves) in 1859. Characteristically, Byers name-called the "toady organ," as having "neither public respect nor public confidence, a groveling, hireling sheet which hesitates at nothing to attain its ends." The editor of the Herald was a "natural liar, -- the most unmitigated and reprehensible one it has ever been our fortune to meet."[38] Regaining the printing contract for the News would help to improve the tenuous financial condition of the paper and provide the News with the increased credibility due an institution with a direct link to the new government. Since both the News and the Herald were essentially Republican and pro-Union in their sentiments, it was difficult for Byers to find issues on which the two newspapers were not in essential agreement. Therefore the "Indian question" was ideal for Byers' purposes. If the Herald supported a policy which resulted in the end of immigration, it certainly did not deserve to be the "official" organ of the Territorial Legislature. Moreover, if stories regarding Indian depredations were debunked by the News and actions which might exacerbate relations with the Indian condemned, hesitant emigrants might "come along," assuming Colorado Territory to be a safe place. Additionally, by supporting an enlightened Indian policy, Byers could increase the credibility of the News (dubbed the "Rocky Mountain Liar" by the Eastern press) by appealing to an audience with generally more humanitarian attitudes toward Indians. Nor would a "lenient" approach alienate his Colorado audience, who, as yet, did not favor harsh treatment of "their" Indians.[39] Until the spring of 1864, more Whites were injured or murdered within the Denver city limits than Whites harmed by the Arapahoes and Cheyennes during the same period.[40]

In September of 1861, the News was still warning of the "effect" of negative publicity upon the future of the Territory. However, there was some measure of sincerity in these attempts of the News to soothe a population nervous over the breakup of the Union and Colorado's role in the conflict. The News indicated that:

> Almost every hour in the day we hear some idle rumor, originating, no one knows how, of intended immediate attack upon this city by Texas Rangers, or Indians or traitors in our midst . . . . We

do not believe there is a Texas Ranger within Five Hundred miles of this city, today, nor can there be extensive organization of Indian warriors in close proximity . . . . Be prepared for any emergency and always be on the alert, but don't credit and above all don't circulate stories calculated to excite and inflame the public.[41]

The threat posed to Byers' goal of statehood by the war is obvious. Just as portions of the rest of the country were confronting questions of loyalty to the Union, so too was the newly designated Territory of Colorado. Byers was a Union man and shortly after the rebellion began, he placed a woodcut of Old Glory at the head of the editorial column in the News. But it was not clear, early on, that Colorado Territory would remain loyal to the Union. The first Territorial governor, William Gilpin, (who would incur Byers' wrath for giving the printing contract to the Herald), was reportedly ordered by President Lincoln to "leave immediately for Denver and protect the mountain region from secession."[42] When Gilpin took office in 1861, one observer declared that Denver was equally divided on secession and another reported that "Denver has a great many rebel sympathizers."[43] Byers' earliest competition had come from the Denver Mountaineer, "A rampant Secession organ," and for a time there was some doubt as to how Colorado would "go." Prior to the Territorial election in 1861, Colorado was thought to be "Democratic" but, in the end, most moderate Democrats voted Republican and the "secesh" Mountaineer sold out to Byers and its editor headed east to join the Southern cause.[44] However, Byers and the News appeared to downplay any probability of secession, perhaps fearing that it would stop the already slowing migration from the east. Thus, Byers eventually would write that the Territory was "indifferent" to the "Jeff Davis school of thought" and that "Copperheadism, under the specious guise or name of Democracy, is played out in Colorado."[45] However, there was one fear regarding the war which Byers consistently would circulate -- the fear of conspiracy among Confederates and the Indians of Colorado. Byers' initial statement of this concern was restrained and focused blame on the "unholy cause" of the Confederates rather than the "peaceful tribes." He wrote (under the title of "Barbarous Warfare"):

To the honor of most of the peaceful tribes be it
said, they cannot be seduced from their fealty to
the United States. But we should not forget that
there are a few tribes whose restlessness and
mischievous disposition may prompt them to accept
the propositions of unprincipled men who claim to
act on the authority of a powerful Confederacy.
Here in this remote territory we are not as
secure in this particular as many be generally
believed. A subtle and malignant agent of the
Secessionists might succeed in convincing the
tribes arund us that we are infringing upon their
rights, and that unless we were driven off, the
home and place of the red man would soon be known
no more.

The "subtle and malignant agent" isolated by the News
as responsible for the plot was "Albert Pike . . . a
man [once] regarded by Northerners, ever, as the sole
of honor."[46] The information the News circulated was
correct in this instance. General Pike had signed
treaties with the Seminoles and ordered them to attack
Ford Larned. However, the "conspiracy" failed when
the Seminoles grew tired of the White man's military
and simply "melted away."[47] Moreover, an Indian, Lean
Bear, warned the commanding officer at Fort Larned of
the plot, once again proving that Indians could be
friendly. Lean Bear's warning was apparently the
source of Byers' information.

    For Byers and the population of Colorado, the
fear of an alliance between the Plains tribes and
Confederate forces was very real. Byers was convinced
enough of the possibility to support Governor Gilpin's
attempt to raise a militia.[49] Although he had
initially welcomed the appointment of Gilpin as a
fellow member of the elite who envisioned greatness
for the west, Byers did a turnabout when Gilpin's
Territorial secretary awarded the printing contract
solely to the Herald.[50] Thereafter, Gilpin found
himself associated with "bummers," "liars," and the
disloyal in the pages of the Rocky Mountain News.
When rumors began circulating regarding Gilpin's use
of Federal Indian Funds, the News was quick to
capitalize:

    Is Gilpin the hightoned honorable man his friends
represent him? Will a true Union man rob the
Government of money entrusted him as disbursing

agent? But that is not the whole of his perfidy -- the Indian money was deposited in this city in Gilpin's own name, and checked out upon his private checks to defray his private expenses .... This is the fund upon which he is running for Congress, buying buggies and votes.[51]

But the charge which was real ammunition for the News' attack was the initial refusal of the Federal government to redeem the "drafts" which Gilpin used to pay and outfit what became the Colorado First. The News cried that the "Bogus Gilpin Drafts" had created a debt which oppressed the loyal people of Colorado with a war debt greater than that of "any other" community in the United States. "More than half a million dollars," the News reported was "advanced by a few hundred people who have waited for their pay over six months."[52] Byers' real grievance against Gilpin, however, probably is more accurately reflected in these words: "In ignoring the advice and confidence of the oldest, most substantial and best known citizens, and in failing to lower himself to a familiarity with the people, he showed a remarkable want of judgement, if not of taste" [emphasis original].[53] Of course, Byers was one of the "oldest most substantial and best known citizens." Thus Gilpin's crime was not one of policy, but of ignoring Byers and the News.

At the height of the acrimony between the News and the Herald, Byers took time out to reassure "Those Seeking a New Home." Probably fearing that reports of Confederate movements in New Mexico (where the Colorado First was), rumors of Indian conspiracies, and reports of governmental problems would affect prospective emigrants, Byers declared:

> We desire to emphatically contradict the prevalent impression throughout the northwestern states, that Colorado Territory (Pikes Peak) is in a state of revolution -- such reports have no truth whatever. On the contrary, the utmost peace prevails, with no probable prospect of its being interrupted . . . .[54]

Thus, the early years of the Rocky Mountain News manifestly were concerned with assuring an adequate population and creating for itself a position of influence. During this time, American Indians, although considered inferior, were symbolized in the News in a neutral or positive manner. The reasons for this relatively positive symbolization may have included altruistic motives and a real concerns "for our Indian friends" (and the fact that there were few "real" Indian threats at this time). Byers' experiences during his travel west as a young man certainly provided him with the first-hand experience, similar to Jim Beckwourth's which implied that "prudence and discretion" was the wisest policy. However, presenting Indians in a friendly rather than a hostile light may also have functioned so as to facilitate continued immigration and as an issue of difference between the News and the Herald.[55]

A few months before Gilpin was removed from office, Byers managed to recapture the coveted printing contract. The addition of two new relatively wealthy partners and the printing contract placed the News on an improved financial footing. The fortunes of the Herald declined significantly along with the fortunes of its editor's "silent partner" William Gilpin.[56] Byers, however, was soon to acquire a "silent partner" of his own. When he described the new Governor, John Evans, as "Just the man for Governor of Colorado," he was describing a man who would seek Byers' advice and support and was thus, "just the man for William Byers."[57] The two men could do much for each other. Byers desired above all else to be a decisive influence in Colorado's bid for Statehood. Evans wished to be a Senator from the State of Colorado. With complementary goals, the two men soon became close friends.[58]

Symbols of 1862

After Gilpin was replaced by Evans, the News began a slow drift away from "prudence and discretion" and a conciliatory policy towards Indians to more negative symbolizations of the same. Governor Evans had been in Colorado just a little more than a month, when the News reported him in the field with Colonel Leavenworth, dealing with reported "serious [Indian] depredations a few miles down the Platte." However, the News cautioned that "Rumors are abundant, but we shall enter into no detail until we learn reliably the particulars of the case." Later, the News reported that the Governor had been "entirely successful."[59] A week later the News expressed its first real concerns regarding "Prospects of Indian Troubles," noting, "A growing animosity to the white settlers is manifest in the dispotision of our immediate neighbors, the Arapahoes and Cheyennes . . . ." Moreover, the News reported that the Indians were "moody and reserved, evidently brooding mischief." However, ominous as the news appeared to be, Byers mostly was concerned with the lack of military protection available in Colorado. The Colorado First was in New Mexico and, as the News declared:

> Colorado has raised nearly two thousand volunteers for the war . . . but no sooner are they in a condition to do service than they are called to Mexico, so that today there is not a squad of ten soldiers who can be called out to defend the lives, homes and property of the citizens of Colorado, in case of an Indian war.[60]

Such a statement seems out of place coming from an institution that a short time before had worried about the effects of negative publicity on potential emigrants. Who would want to emigrate to an area where there was a "Prospect of Indian Troubles," and hardly "ten soldiers" to protect the population? But Byers had apparently put that concern behind him -- along with ex-Governor Gilpin and the Herald. Indeed, in the spring and summer of 1862, reports of Indian depredations increased in the News; including reports from afar and local reports.[61] Reports of Indian depredations continued through 1862. These reports were relatively restrained with the News urging caution -- "we are inclined to think the reports are much exaggerated . . ." -- but the News concluded that "there is a danger, and a sufficient military force to afford efficient protection to the scattering settlements should at once be recalled to the Territory."[62] Although early in the spring the News was likely to refer to our "Indian neighbors," as the summer progressed the term "Indian" increasingly became followed by the term "depredation" and specific Indians were as often referred to as "thieves" as "friends." By the middle of July the News was labeling Arapahoes and Cheyennes as "treacherous vagabonds" engaged in "predatory operations" and "Indian outrages." The News also predicted extensive depredations to come.[63] However, a careful reading of these "reports" reveals no deaths (White or Indian), no serious injuries and only vague references to robbery and theft. The only detailed "outrage" concerned a certain Peter Shook who was "set upon" by "sixty" Indians so "savage" that when the White ladies present "with great bravery, rushed to the rescue of the young man, encircling his person with their arms . . . ," they (the Indians) retreated.[64] The Shook incident, however, illustrated that at the heart of the White man's interpretation of these early "outrages" was a resentment of the Indians' lack of deference to the Whites. Even the News admitted that "stories of their depredations had been grossly exaggerated . . . [they had] burned a few old house logs -- of no value to anyone . . . ." But the News peevishly complained that "They [the Arapahoes and Cheyennes] are very surly and impudent . . . ." The Indians were arrogant and bold in the thievery they practiced upon smaller groups of White settlers but were no more "arrogant" in their petty thefts than were the Whites squatting illegally upon Indian land. However, the News cited "the repetition of these outrages . . ." as a reason for alarm and appealed to the nervous attitudes of its audience:

> If they see fit, the Indians can sweep the settlers of Colorado from the face of the earth, and the military authorities of the western Department do not seem disposed to raise their hands to prevent it. It is high time the people were taking some steps to check their [the Indians] murderous and marauding forages.[65]

The willingness and ability of the "people" to protect themselves had already been illustrated by the "Peoples' Courts." Both Byers and the Governor would later call for a similar "justice" for the "hostile" Indians.

Byers was correct regarding the small number of troops available for defense in the Territory. Certainly if the Indians had "seen fit," they could have wiped Colorado clean of White encroachers during this time. However, the Cheyennes and the Arapahoes were more concerned with their traditional enemy, the Utes.[66] Some of the News' worries were relieved the following month when the Territorial Legislature passed a militia law. In the meantime, a bloody and widely reported Sioux uprising in Minnesota, in which a sizeable portion of the White population was killed, gave increased credence to such worries regarding Indian propensities. After this well-publicized event, few frontier editors were willing to support conciliatory policies with their "Indian neighbors."[67] Byers and the News, although clearly more negative than the previous year, were not ready yet to declare their Indians hostile.

Upon his assumption of the Governorship, John Evans declared it his intention to extinguish Indian land title by "authorized" treaties with the "Ute, Apache, Kiowa and Camanche Indians."[68] He was supported in this quest by Byers in the News. Throughout 1862 and 1863, the News missed no opportunity to report Evans at work on this task; all the while expressing confidence in the Governor's ability to acomplish this stated goal:

> It has been our fortune to live under various Territorial governments and their administrations . . . and [we] can freely say that in all our experience we have seen none other as successfully conducted as that of Governor Evans . . . . A treaty with the Indians will soon be held and the present misunderstanding satisfactorily settled.[69]

In a later issue, it was stated that "The Governor's well-known diplomatic tact" would result in a "satisfactory and advantageous treaty."[70] Similar, although more martial praise, was provided for Byers' other good friend, John Chivington, "Our distinguished fellow-citizen, the gallant Major who lead the Colorado boys . . . ."[71] However, as if hedging against the failure of the treaty negotiations to resolve the land question, during 1863, Byers and the News increased reports of "Indian massacres" which symbolized the hostile, treacherous savage and proposed "extermination" as a solution. Most of the Indians thus described were not local Indians but other Indians to the south and west of the Territory.

Symbols of 1863

Stories concerning Indians in the Rocky Mountain News available for examination from 1863 may be judged as decidedly negative. Of twenty-seven stories

149

concerned directly or indirectly with Indians, ten overtly favored "extermination" of Indians and only two may be judged as positive in tone.[72] A story published on March 24, 1863 is typical of the type of story which the News was now circulating. It was bluntly titled "Exterminate Them," and the News reported:

> The New Mexican published at Santa Fe advocates the extermination of the Indians in that Territory, as the most effective method of security for life and property. It may not be a very popular suggestion but we have long been of the opinion that treaties with the Indians, distribution of presents, etc., was a criminal waste of time and money. We have yet to see the first redskin who could be trusted. So long as they can gratify their gluttinous propensities at the expense of the general government and receive yearly installments from the hands of Indian agents, they may affect friendship and pretend to be loyal. But even while receiving their annuities from the agent they allow no good opportunity for robbery and plunder to go unimproved. They are a dissolute, vagabonish, brutal and ungrateful race, and ought to be wiped from the face of the earth. A few such men as Col. Conner could do more to quiet the Indians than a thousand Indian agents with immense trains of annuities to back them [emphasis original].[73]

If Byers had "long been of the opinion," he must have forgotten his position of March 26, the year before, when he favored "sufficient means to buy corn and wheat to feed the Indians" as a way of avoiding an "outbreak." Moreover, his last two statements in the 1863 story appear to be more general in their application than to simply the Indians of Sante Fe. Certainly Byers illustrated the nineteenth-century preoccupation with "race" as an explanation for physical and mental characteristics. In this instance, the traits "dissolute, vagabondish and brutal" were attributed to the "Indian race." As if providing proof for the negative judgment of Native American character, a few days later, the News described an "Indian Massacre on the Overland Route." The story followed the plot-line set forth by Parkman. A small group of White frontiersmen was set upon by a larger group of Indians and "a most horrible Indian massacre" was a result. However, against almost overwhelming odds, after a "life and death" race, several Whites made good their escape. As it would whenever the "details" were available, the <u>News</u> described, in vivid close-up, the wounds, suffering, and bravery of the assaulted Whites:

> The passenger was shot through the head and had fallen down into the boot [of the coach], while blood and brains bespattered over the entire front part of the coach. The driver was shot through the body in the region of the heart, but still manfully retained his post and performed his duty. Judge M. took the reins and assisted the driver down into the boot under the seat, where he continued to assist and advise the management of the team until he died, which was in less than half an hour.

Later, after the coach reached "Deep Creek Station," the <u>News</u> reported that:

> The driver was found to be dead but the other man was still alive up to the time Judge M. left, which was near twenty-four hours after, although his brains were oozing from the wounds in the top of his head. It was subsequently learned that the Indians had killed and scalped two men at the station before the coach came up.

Judging that there was a "fair probability" of the Indians being punished, the <u>News</u> declared emphatically, "we hope they may be exterminated."[74] Although the cleverness and bravery of White participants was carefully detailed, Indian motives were not examined. Rather, the raid was symbolized as a result of the demonic nature of the Native Americans. The provocation of White occupation and travel across Indian land was not mentioned. However, it would have been surprising if this story, and others like it during that spring and summer, were told from anything other than a White point of view.[75]

On April 4th, the <u>News</u> specified the "feeling" that had become "general" as a result of the overland raid. The "only way," the <u>News</u> declared, of dealing with such hostile action was to "wage upon them [the Snake Indians] <u>a war of extermination</u> [emphasis original]." But, as if to make up for the general condemnation of March 24th, the News differentiated Colorado's Indians: "Fortunately for Colorado, the Indian tribes within the Territory are at present on friendly terms with the whites . . . .", but the News warned that those "best acquainted with Indian character" did not guarantee the indefinite "amity and goodwill" of Colorado's Indians. However, should the Indians in Colorado "ever forget themselves" and commit outrages, the News promised a "speedy and summary vengance."[76]

The News was not including Colorado's natives in its favored war of extermination to which it later wished "God speed the great humane work!"[77] But, on April 6, 1863, it suggested that the Arapahoes needed "a drubbing." Throughout the spring and summer of 1863, the News catalogued and detailed further examples of the "savage ferocity" of Indians in Utah, New Mexico and the "southern" part of the Territory. Especially emphasized was the overland route between Denver and Bannock city, the locaton of the "new mines." Byers had some motive to warn of the potential "calamity and fatal danger" along this route, since some of those traveling along it were leaving Denver, to which emigration had all but ceased. As Byers calculated it on April 24th, of the twenty-eight persons who had started to the new mines "25 have been murdered on the road by the Indians."[78] Based upon previous reports in the News, this figure was inflated by approximately twenty deaths.

In the meantime, the News reported regarding some "Indians talks at Washington." A party of Utes, Colorado's far western natives, had been invited to Washington by Commissioner Dole to negotiate a new treaty. But the Utes stubbornly refused such negotiations and demanded that the Federal government drive the Whites out of "their country."[79] A few days later, the News utilized its interpretation of this event to justify a subtle but significant shift in its attitude toward the Territorial tribes. Under the title "Indian Outrages," the News editorialized:

> It is useless to disguise the fact that the Indian tribes of the great Rocky Mountain Range are more hostile this season than ever before . . . . Especially are emigrants to new mining sections, considered by the savages their best prey on account of the rich plunder obtained

in arms, provisions, whiskey and stock. There seems to be a combination among the Indians to interfere with and annoy gold seekers and up in the vicinity of Bannock city, the tribes have sworn to extermination all whites who dare to attempt to settle in their country. As a significant indication of the feeling of the Indians, it is only necessary to allude to the spirit manifested by the chiefs of our own territorial tribes, during their later conference with our government officials at Washington. The leading orator of the party emphatically demanded that the government should drive all the whites from this country, and stop spending time and money in the distribution of annuities and present. This is the first instance ever known where the Indians have expressed a wish to give up presents and annuities, and it is by no means a pleasant augury for the future. <u>There is reason to apprehend serious difficulty with the red-skin vagabonds, and we cannot be too vigilant and guarded in all our intercourse with them</u> [emphasis added].$_{80}$

Thus, again the News emphasized the dangers of travel to Bannock City. Byers once had repudiated the circulation of negative publicity regarding Indian depredations to preserve emigration to Denver. He now was willing to circulate such stories to decrease movement westward from Denver. Nor was the illegal status of Bannock City by treaty mentioned. Byers also alluded to a mysterious "combination" among the tribes. Of course, <u>which</u> tribes were in combination was unclear. It could hardly have been among the Shoshones, Utes, Navajos, Arapahoes and Cheyennes, since varying amounts of continuing enmity existed among all of these tribes (except for the Arapahoes and Cheyennes who were traditional allies). Yet, in the last paragraph, <u>one Ute orator</u> was interpreted as having spoken for <u>all</u> the territorial tribes -- a ridiculous assertion since the Utes were the worst enemy of the Arapahoes and Cheyennes. Therefore, Byers used the actions and words of <u>other</u> Indians to justify an increased vigilance against <u>all</u> of Colorado's tribes. While, externally, <u>Colorado's</u> Indians had been peaceful and friendly, reports of the behavior of other Indians functioned to remind Byers' audience that, inwardly, all Indians were identical: hostile, treacherous and savage.$_{81}$

During most of this time, the News supported gaining land concessions from the Territorial tribes through negotiation. Byers and other White occupants of the area were especially sensitive to the land question since the Treaty of Fort Laramie in 1851 granted all land east of the Rockies between the North Platte and the Arkansas to the Arapahoe and Cheyenne Indians. Moreover, the Kansas-Nebraska Act of 1854 repromised that such Indian hunting grounds were not available for White entry until the Indians had given their permission.[82] Thus, Byers and the other settlers were illegal squatters upon Indian lands. On September 6, 1860, the News had nervously commented that "we trust no action will be taken tending to confirm the hasty opinion that the whites of Pikes Peak country were tresspassers and that Government aid would be furnished to drive them from the settlements if the Indians so requested."[83] Such worries on the part of the News, while probably not realistic, were constitutionally based. The 1834 Trade and Intercourse Act promised that the Federal Government would remove illegal interlopers from Indian lands.[84] Painfully aware of the early "illegal" nature of settlement in Colorado, Byers worried that, "If the different tribes around us should once become satisfied that our government sympathized with them . . . they would feel emboldened to the commission of outrages of an aggravated character . . . It is hoped . . . steps will be taken to extinguish the redman's title to these lands on fair and satisfactory terms."[85] Nor did the eventual legal Territorial organization include a solution for Byers' worries. The organic Territorial Act stated that "nothing in this act shall be construed to impair the right of person and property now pertaining to the Indians in said territory. So long as such right shall remain unextinguished by treaty between the United States and such Indians."[86]

As late as 1864 Byers continued to worry regarding the eventual disposition of Indian land claims. Although a treaty session was held in 1861 at Fort Wise, only a few unimportant Cheyenne and Arapahoe Chiefs actually signed the treaty. Moreover, there were differences of opinion, even among the Whites, as to exactly what the treaty had established. Governor Evans and the News insisted that the treaty "extinguished the title to all the country between the North Fork of the Platte and the Arkansas rivers, from

154

the junction of the former with the South Platte and the Cimerone crossing of the latter to the summit of the Snowy Range; or if it did not no land whatever was ceded by that treaty." In essence, this was all the land east of the Rockies to the Kansas border.[87] Moreover, Evans and Byers favored extending this interpretation of the treaty to all non-signatory Arapahoe and Cheyennes by further treaty negotiation and concentrating all of these Indians on a small reservation near Sand Creek. The News expressed optimism regarding the final success of the Governor in achieving a treaty. But at the conclusion of the Governor's attempts in the Fall of 1863, the News reported regretfully that the Governor was "not entirely successful . . . ."[88] Just a few weeks later Evans began besieging Washington with reports of "hostility" among the Cheyennes and Arapahoes.[89]

Throughout the summer and fall of 1863, while predicting success for the treaty making, the News had continued its reports of various "outrages," "massacres" and depredations by other Indian tribes. It is difficult, if not impossible, to confirm or deny the validity of these stories. However, William Unrau reports that miners and farmers were circulating inaccurate stories, apparently to "incite" a solution to the boundary question.[90] That some of these "rumors" found their way into the pages of the News is likely. More problematic is accounting for the very obvious change in Byers' position regarding Indians from 1860 to 1863 and his vivid reporting of the apparent actions of other Indians.[91]

Stories of Indian/White relations were "news" on the frontier. Certainly in 1862-63 some "depredations" did happen. It␣was inevitable that as the number of contacts between Whites and Indians increased, increased misunderstandings would occur. To maintain its credibility, the News would have been expected to report on Indians, since Indian/White relations was a topic which concerned all of its reading audience. With an absence of local White/Indian incidents in 1862-63, or success in negotiations, Byers filled the gap by picking up "old stories" concerning Indians published in other frontier papers. Besides serving as information, such stories had entertainment value for the isolated Denver and Colorado audience. Newspapers were often passed from reader to reader in isolated settlements and read again and again. A vivid style helped to maintain the attention of an audience which was accustomed to hyperbole. Thus a single White death, justified or not, at the hand of any group of Indians became symbolized as a "most horrible massacre" and minor thefts of cattle and food became "more Indian outrages."

Many of the war-making customs of the Plains Indians were cruel and bloody (although such customs fulfilled important cultural functions for their practitioners), but made ideal topics which maintained White audience interest. Thus, even while Byers was urging "prudence" as the guiding value for an Indian policy in 1860, he published the report of the murder of Rice and Pierson which was vividly dripping with the blood and gore of the dead Whites. Moreover, the same attention to bloody details can be seen[92] in the reporting of Whites murdered by other Whites. Thus, such vividness was not unique to reports of Indian depredations but was the style of the day. However, such a style coupled with a totally White point-of-view of every incident of Indian/White relations guaranteed that the conspiracy myth was reinforced for the White audience. After 1863, information contrary to the conspiracy myth seldom appeared in the pages of the News.

It is clear that shortly after John Evans became Governor of Colorado Byers abandoned caution he had exercised in the first years when he reported and editorialized regarding American Indians. Certainly the "extermination position" which he developed in 1863 was unjustified by local experience and was a change from his original position. Few in Byers' local audience (except, perhaps, Jim Beckwourth)[93] would disagree with the change in Byers' position. His audience disagreed on a myriad of other issues, but could be united in fear by "Indian scalping stories." Robert Perkin believes that Byers' stories regarding Indian depredations served to scare Coloradans "like a troop of Boy Scouts scaring themselves with scalping stories around a campfire . . . ."[94] However, in 1863, with Colorado Indians at relative peace, such overstated stories also served to remind Byers' audience of the racial immutability of Indian savagery. In 1864, Governor Evans' communications would tend to illustrate, to a distracted Federal government, that the Indians of Colorado were

156

hostile.[95] But his ally in the Rocky Mountain News had already established the threat posed by Indian nature to the home audience. The Indians described by Byers in 1863, mostly, were not Colorado's Indians. However, it would involve only a small step to include these Native Americans in the hostile category if Evans was not successful in achieving the desired land concessions by an ordinary treaty-making process.[96]

Symbols of 1864

If Byers in the Rocky Mountain News was at a loss for topics of local events in 1863, 1864 was a year which provided no shortage of "interesting" items. Early in the year, the News predicted an Indian "war" with its own Cheyennes and Arapahoes. Local Indian depredations were reported with regularity and mangled and mutilated bodies of "innocent" White emigrants were brought to Denver as proof of Indian savagery. As if to provide "prognostics" of events to come, natural disasters such as the "Great Flood in Cherry Creek" in May and the grasshopper plague of the later summer placed White settlers on the defensive. Further, 1864 was a political year for the Territory during which statehood was to be voted upon by Territorial voters. The future political lives of Byers' favored friends, John Evans and John Chivington, were also linked to the statehood question and since the News had "never been beaten," so was the prestige of the News.[97] So, in 1864, Indians were symbolized in ways which could have functioned to further Byers' statehood goal and to provide continued prestige for Evans, Chivington and Byers.

"War" Declared

Stories published in the Rocky Mountain News during 1864 may be judged as overtly negative regarding most Indians, particularly the region's Cheyennes and Arapahoes. Although many records and stories from this period were lost in the Great Flood, of approximately sixty-three stories concerned directly or indirectly with American Indians published in the News, only five symbolized Indians in a positive fashion. The majority of the stories (37) related atrocities against Whites performed by Indians. Twenty-five of these accounts regarded

Territorial depredations, with the twelve remaining ones concerned with Indian depredations in other areas. Other stories called for the "extermination" of Colorado's Indians, hinted at "conspiracies" struck among various Plains tribes and between White rebel guerrillas and Indians and generally reported on "The Indian War." Moreover, by August, 1864, other stories indirectly linked those Whites opposing statehood with the blame for the Indian "war."[98]

The News started out the year where it had left off the previous fall. A story in the January 8th edition rejoiced in the outcome of a battle between Whites and Navajos in New Mexico. A "decisive victory" for the Whites was "about as severe a chastisement as the murdering, thieving Navajoes have received in a long while." The January 9th and January 11th editions carried stories regarding the 1862 uprising in Minnesota in which "over eight hundred men, women and children were butchered by the Indians."[99] But, between the middle of January and the second week in April of 1864, there was little mention of Native Americans in the pages of the News.

With the spring thaw, however, opportunities for Indian/White conflict increased, allowing Byers to air his views regarding Indian nature. On April 12th, the News reported "Horrible Murders" in Pueblo, Colorado. A "wily savage, true to his nature and education, . . . literally chopped to pieces" two sleeping Whites "universally respected" in the Territory.[100] Subsequently the News noted an uncertain "Rumor of Indian Fighting," but in the next issue pronounced a more certain point of view in its leading editorial: "The Indian War."[101]

In this pronouncement, Byers was more correct than he knew at the time. The engagement between Indians and Whites that was the stimulus for the "rumors" was identified later by both Indian and White authorities as the genesis of the "Indian War of 1864." Two cases of reported cattle theft were blamed upon a group of local Cheyennes and White troops were ordered not merely to investigate the thefts but to "punish" the accused Indians.[102] On April 12, 1864, an engagement occurred between a company of White troops under the command of Lieutenant Clark Dunn and a group of Cheyennes. This expedition culminated in what came to be called the "Battle of Fremont's

Orchard." The expedition had been undertaken at the request of a White rancher named Ripley who had reported various Indian "depredations" along Bijou Creek and the theft of some stock. But his reports of "depredations" were never substantiated. Black Kettle, a neutral party in this struggle, later admitted that the Indians in question had "found some loose stock" and were in the process of returning it when discovered by the White soldiers.[103] Although the "encounter" began on friendly terms, a fight broke out when Dunn attempted to disarm one of the young "Dog Soldiers." A Plains Indian might willingly surrender arms as a sign of friendship but an attempt to take his arms was an automatic violation of friendship and a signal for a fight.[104] White insensitivity to Indian customs was a common stimulus for conflict.

Chivington's reaction to the report of Dunn's encounter in which two White soldiers died is instructive in the orientation provided for subsequent "expeditions" that spring. "Look out for them," Chivington ordered, "and kill them."[105] On April 16th, Major Jacob Downing (Dunn's commander) entered into the pursuit. After an encounter with Indians, in which Downing claimed to have killed twenty-five warriors, he reported, "Though I think we have punished them pretty severely in this affair, yet I believe now is but the commencement of war with this tribe, which must result in exterminating them."[106]

During approximately this same time period, Lieutenant George Eayre was in the field west of Denver, in pursuit of Indians who reportedly had stolen 175 head of cattle from two government contractors. While seeking the "guilty" Indians, Eayre had several encounters with Cheyenne bands. In one instance a "friendly Indian," Lean Bear, was killed. Lean Bear had recently returned from Washington with a medal from the "great father." Probably recalling the praise he had received two years before when he warned the Territory regarding rebel recruitment of the Seminoles, Lean Bear had ridden alone toward a group of nervous soldiers holding up his medal as proof of his friendliness. He was shot for his trouble.[107] Indian versions of these encounters generally place blame upon Whites for the stimulus to violence and the level of violence. In later interviews, surviving Cheyenne and Arapahoe

159

chiefs stated that any depredations occurring in April and May were in revenge for the killing of Lean Bear. Regardless of where the real blame should be placed, between April 12, 1864 and May 16, 1864, troops under Chivington's command had three major fights with the Cheyennes, destroyed four Cheyenne villages and killed a head chief who was proud of his friendship with the Anglos.[108] The White, "official" reports of these events found their way into the pages of the News.

Ironically, a commentator in the News on April 14th had remarked on the provacative nature of such "encounters." The News cautioned that:

> It requires men of much sagacity and common sense, with arms or without them, to fool around Indians. They have to judge of us as we have to do them, when we see them advancing, by the 'looks of things'; and other things being unsettled, the first opportunity is generally seized by both the red and white skins.[109]

But, as mentioned, the News failed to heed its own advice. Based upon only "two brushes" with Indians who were "supposed to be Cheyennes," Byers seized the "Opportunity" to declare "The Indian War." As a title this symbol exaggerated the extent of hostilities in April, 1864. But a "war" between Whites and Territorial Indians functioned to prove that Colorado's Indians had succumbed to their nature. Byers and the News were only predicting what most believed was the inevitable solution to problems between Whites and Native Americans.[110] If any of the White population had doubts regarding the hostile nature of all Indians, events in May and June proved the reality of Byers' "Very Promising Indian War." Byers' symbols in this regard reflect Jerome Bruner's theory that "Life then produces myth and finally imitates it."[111]

The Hungate "Massacre"

The offices of the News had successfully survived the first of Denver's natural disasters. On April 19, 1863, a "great fire" destroyed much of Denver. The News escaped the fire primarily because of its location -- perched on stilts over Cherry Creek. Although warned by a "Friendly Indian" of occasional "big water" in the usually dry creek-bed, Byers and the offices of the News remained confidently aloft over the stream. Moreover, as the town rebuilt, the office of the News was joined by other businesses clustered about the banks of the dry creek or built upon pilings over the white sand. In mid-May 1864, rainfall was constant over the headwaters of Cherry Creek.[112] Denver received only small amounts of rain which settled the dust and the town's population went to sleep on May 19th, "snoring," it was recorded by a sometimes contributor to the News, "in calm security." Around midnight a gigantic "water engine of death" rushed down and over the bank of Cherry Creek destroying all in its path, including the

> dear old office of the Rocky Mountain News, the pioneer of hardship and of honor, which here nobly braved the battle and the breeze for five full years and a month, regularly without intermission or intimidation, and down it sank, with its union flag staff, into the maelstrom of the surging waters . . .

This "Sketch of the Great Deluge in Denver" was published in the Daily Commonwealth and Republican of May 24, 1864.[113] Also published the next day was this item:

> Deeply sympathizing with our neighbors of the Rocky Mountain News in the calamity which has fallen upon them (more heavily, perhaps, than any other of our citizens) we have placed the Commonwealth office at their disposal until the arrival of their new printing office, which will be ordered forthwith. The plan determined upon is at present to issue but one paper, the Daily Commonwealth, with which the subscribers of the News will be furnished. During this arrangement the paper will be published in the evening instead of the morning.[114]

However, Byers sought a more rapid solution and with the financial backing of John Evans (who had also provided shelter for Byers and his temporarily homeless family, rescued from the flood by John Chivington) purchased the "plant" of the Commonwealth sometime between May 19 and June 26, 1864. Meanwhile, the "Indian War" continued and the combined "persona" of the Rocky Mountain News and the Commonwealth reported the murder of the Hungate family.[115]

On June 11, 1864, a party of Arapahoes traveling to their village on the North Platte, savagely butchered a White family of four about twenty miles from Denver. All the evidence at the time was interpreted so as to blame the Cheyennes -- the marauders in the White/Indian encounters of April and May.¹¹⁶ News of the attack reached Denver in the June 15th edition of the Commonwealth. The initial report of the event was restrained and noted the "wild rumors" circulating in the city and provided an undetailed account of the murders:

> On Saturday afternoon, the buildings on the ranche of Mr. Van Wormer, of this city, on Living Creek, thirty miles south east of Denver, were burned down by Indians, as were the buildings of the next ranche. Mr. Hungate and family, who occupied Mr. Van Wormer's ranche, were barbarously murdered by the Indians. The bodies of Mrs. H. and two children were found near the house -- they had been scalped, and their throats cut. A later report brings news of the discovery of Mr. Hungate's body, about a mile from the same place. Mocassins, arrows, and other Indian signs were found in the vicinity. The bodies of these will be brought to the city this afternoon, and will, at the ringing of the Seminary bell, be placed where our citizens can all see them.₁₁₇

The story concluded with an appeal to expedite organization of the militia so as to be ready at a moment's warning "to put after the murdering thieves." This story lacked the vividness and bloody details of the stories of earlier depredations related in the News. One might speculate that this story was the handiwork of Simeon Whitley type-set early on the morning of Wednesday the fifteenth, since he had been used to publishing a morning paper. Later that day apparently the seminary bell did ring and, as one observer wrote, "everybody saw the four [murdered pioneers] and anger and revenge mounted all day long as the people filed past or remained to talk over Indian outrages and means of protection and reprisal."¹¹⁸

The change in sentiment after the mangled bodies were viewed was clearly evident in another story in the same edition of the Commonwealth, written later in the day. The vivid style is similar to the stories provided by Byers in earlier editions of the News. The account is reproduced in its entirety for later reference:

A HORRIBLE SIGHT! The bodies of those four people that were massacred by the Cheyennes on Van Wormer's ranch, thirty miles down the Cut-off, were brought to town this morning, and a corner's inquest held over them. It was a most solemn sight indeed, to see the mutilated corses [sic], stretched in the stiffness of death, upon that wagon bed, first the father, Nathan Hungate, about 30 years of age, with his head scalped and his either cheeks and eyes chopped in as with an axe or tomahawk. Next lay his wife, Ellen, with her head also scalped through from ear to ear. Along side of her lay two small children, one at her right arm and one at her left, with their throats severed completely, so that their handsome little heads and pale innocent countenances had to be stuck on, as it were, to preserve the humanity of form. Those that perpetrate such unnatural, brutal butchery as this ought to be hunted to the farthest bounds of these broad plains and burned to the stake alive, was the general remark of the hundreds of spectators this forenoon. Mr. Hungate's body was found about a mile and a half from Van Wormer's ranch, where he was residing as herder, and his family were found close to the house, which was burned. They were from the state of Illinois. The deepest feeling pervaded the people of town to-day as they returned from viewing the mangled bodies of this cruelly murdered family. Let us take warning and keep prepared for the future, both in town and in the ranches through the territory, where Indians are wont to visit or pass by.

Since writing the above we have had a conversation with a Mr. Follett, who has just arrived from Running Creek. Mr. F. is one of the party that went after the bodies. He says that the woman was found about four hundred yards from the house, with the children both in her arms -- one a babe of three or four months, and one, a little girl about two years old. The bowels of the younger one were ripped open, and its entrails scattered by the side of the mother and children. The body of the man was found about two miles from the house, but his whip was found at the ruins, and some other marks seemed to indicate that he had been first attacked there, and finding himself overpowered, had made an effort to escape. The residents of all that part of the country are leaving their homes with the greatest alarm, and coming toward Denver, bringing along their stock and moveable property, but leaving their farms and crops unprotected. Some of them will probably reach here this evening and every possible aid should be rendered to make them comfortable. The men are all ready to join in the pursuit of the atrocious murderers of their neighbors, and will render valuable service in this time of need.[119]

The theme in this second story is obvious -- a group of "innocents" has been savagely killed by a specific "outgroup" incorrectly identified as "Cheyennes." The cautionary tone of the first story is replaced by the undeniable specifics which now all citizens have observed. Since all <u>did</u> have the opportunity to view the butchery, one might question the necessity for the detailed description of the "sights." But there is an air of "grim satisfaction" present here. The myth of the savage Indian had been brought home to all so that life "in death" proved savage propensities in a very personal manner. By viewing the mutilated bodies together the frightened community now could participate actively in the myth. Unlike the first simple narrative of events, this second retelling celebrates the "art form" of the myth which "connects to daeomnic world of reason" (or the empirical world) with the fantasies of the myth "by a verisimilitude that conforms to each."[120]

As implied in the last paragraph of the story, the "massacre" created fear throughout the territory. A few days later, citizens of Denver panicked when a misled, inebriated horseman galloped through the streets broadcasting the approach of hordes of Indians who were going "to burn and massacre." Women and children were rushed into either the secure confines of the Denver Mint or the Commissary building while the men stood guard outside. For several hours the city stood under apparent siege. Three women who had looked upon the Hungates described "that horror," while, perhaps, other passed around the written description published in the <u>Commonwealth</u>. Some

Denverites broke into the military warehouse to procure arms and ammunition to fight off the impending Indian attack.[121]

The News returned under the sole editorship of Byers on June 24, 1864 but there was little mention of Native Americans until July. The "army" of Indians feared by Denver citizens and settlers of outlying areas failed to materialize and in fact never existed. For a month after the Hungate tragedy no Indian depredations were reported in Colorado. Based upon reports in the official record, at this point in the "Indian War," Indian fatalities outnumbered White fatalities by sixty-one to nine.[122] Absent real depredations, a brief report in the July 5, 1864 edition of the News served as a reminder of the myth. After rejoicing in the "rubbing out" of six "Cheyenne," the News asserted, "Cheyennes arrived on the lower Arkansas having those scalps of the Hungate family. Twenty or thirty of the mules and horses stole, near Van Wormer's ranch got away from them and were delivered by Arapahoes to the commander of Fort Larned." Thus, a definition of the Cheyennes as the enemy dictated that evidence, which could have easily convicted a band of renegade Arapahoes, be interpreted so as to maintain the original identification.[123] The report of the Hungate scalps also was totally unsubstantiated. Who had made the identification and how such an identification could be made was not stated by the News.[124] Thus, the immutability of myth provided that "observation cannot disprove it, but can provide material that is perceived as evidence for its validity."[125]

Prior to this report, on June 27, Governor Evans had issued a message printed in the News, "To the Friendly Indians of the Plains," requesting that "friendly Indians" proceed to "places of safety." He also warned that "The war on the hostile Indians will be continued until they are all effectively subdued." He cautioned against killing friendly Indians, but did not state exactly how such a determination of friendship was to be made.[126] The result was that many Whites simply assumed that all Indians were hostiles. Thus, when Left Hand, confirmed by Byers to be a "friendly Indian," approached Fort Larned under a flag of truce to offer the services of his men in the pursuit of some real hostiles -- the Kiowas under

Satanta -- he was fired upon.[127] This act angered the young braves with him who then joined with the Kiowas in making raids upon the Whites.[128]

These raids up and down the Platte took place between July 17 and July 20, 1864. The News reported these incidents (actually occurring miles from Denver) in a manner which made danger appear imminent to the jittery Denver population. Savage Indians were symbolized "Attacking Emigrants," and kidnapping White women and girls.[129] "Raid" after "Indian raid" was reported while "A general Indian War [was] anticipated . . . the excitement is intense."[130] The White deaths reported amounted to "five killed and one wounded," but were described in detail in the News. Given that "one hundred and fifty" braves were reported to be participating in these raids, and that the emigrants were generally unprotected, the number of deaths hardly apeared to justify the appellation "Indian War." Perhaps Byers sensed this when he added to the excitement by describing the wounding of cattle and horses; fifteen cattle were reported "cut all to pieces."[131] A more ominous note was given to these raids by Byers. The raids were not simply the work of "outlaw" Cheyennes as reported by the "friendly Cheyenne chiefs (who were, Byers hinted, not to be trusted) but the raids had been

> . . . regularly planned. All the accounts agree in putting the times at which the principal depredations were committed between ten o'clock a.m., and two o'clock p.m., of Sunday, the 17th Inst. The Indians must have divided into three or four parties, and made several descents at an hour agreed upon.[132]

Indians capable of "regular planning" were more threatening than Indians making senseless raids. Intentional of not, the News' reporting of raids down the Platte again emphasized the nature of the "enemy," and the proper solution. The "war" which such raids were supposed to illustrate existed only in Kansas, Nebraska, and according to Janet Lecompte, in "the columns of the Rocky Mountain News."[133]

The Election of 1864

A rival Denver newspaper agreed with Ms. Lecompte. While Byers in the News was the primary spokesman for the pro-state forces, the Black Hawk Daily Mining Journal played a similar role for those individuals opposed to statehood at this time. The previous winter Congress had authorized the Territory to frame a state constitution and elect the necessary state officials. The News and the Union Administration Party strongly favored statehood and named a slate of candidates including Chivington and Evans. Byers served as chairman of the state constitutional convention.[134] The Black Hawk Journal and its editors, Frank Hall and Orvando Hollister, opposed statehood primarily because they thought it would increase the cost of government and thus increase taxes on Colorado's miners. More importantly, the Journal accused Byers, Evans and Chivington of using the statehood question to further their own political ambitions. Specifically, the Journal argued that Territorial officials (Evans and Chivington) had mismanaged Indian affairs so as to increase the appeal of statehood. Therefore, the Journal accused Byers of "pure fabrication" in half his reporting regarding the Indians raids of late July, 1864. The Journal pointed out that most of the incidents had occurred east of Fort Kearney, over four hundred fifty miles from Denver. Moreover, the Journal implied that Byers, Evans and Chivington "cooked" up the Indian war together to prove that only as a state could Colorado get sufficient troops to control her Indians . . . ."[135] While this justification was used by the News, there is no evidence of a conscious collaboration among Byers, Evans and Chivington.[136]

On July 14th, Byers had clearly laid out the position of the News on the statehood question. Byers declared, "We are for the Constitution because we believe that its adoption will be of incalculable advantage to Colorado." He promised to advocate the cause of statehood "with all the ability and zeal" possible. Moreover, he bragged implicitly that the prestige of the News and his own position in the community assured success: "we are vain enough to believe that our efforts will be effective." As evidence for this effectiveness, Byers remarked:

> The News never yet had been beaten. No cause it ever espoused has failed. Its ticket has every time been victorious. That was true, though a rough compliment that was paid it by a 'rough,' one evening after the counting of the votes cast

at a certain city election . . . . Although a
hot canvas, it had been remarked that, for once,
the Rocky Mountain News was on the side doomed to
defeat. So well satisfied were our opponents of
the assumed fact, that they freely backed their
opinion with their money at heavy odds. The
count of the votes told a different tale; and it
was in the interchange of expressions of mutual
condolence that one said to another -- 'By G-d,
that d----d Rocky Mountain News never goes for a
thing but it fetches it!' He was right [emphasis
original].[137]

Two editions later Byers provided the advantages of
statehood. Eighth on the list was the securing "of
power and influence" for the people of Colorado to
better control their own Indian affairs.[138] To help
achieve statehood, with all its positive advantages,
Byers had promised the use of "all fair means" and to
be "terribly in earnest!"[139] Whether "fair means"
included intentionally promoting an "Indian war" based
upon "pure speculation" is probably not provable.
However, by the middle of August, the Cheyennes and
Arapahoes were engaged in raids which were close to
Denver and not pure fabrication.

In early August, Denver reached a near-hysterical
state because of rumors regarding "Rebel Guerrillas"
and the usual reports and false rumors of Indian
activities. Various rumors reached Denver that a
large body of rebels was in the Territory robbing and
plundering.[140] In fact, the "large body of rebels"
was only a gang of nine men led by former Coloradan,
Jim Reynolds, which had engaged in a series of
robberies and hold ups.[141] Again citizens of Denver
flew into a panic when two "befuddled" drunks related
a story "of one or more parties of guerillas" in the
near vicinity. The story spread "like wildfire and
lost nothing by frequent repetition." As a result,
the News reported, "many nervous people were seriously
alarmed, and didn't sleep well last night."[142] Byers
debunked this particular rumor and provided advice
regarding the interpretation of such stories:

> We suggest that those who have the ability to
> think and reason upon tolerable common sense
> principles, should bear in mind that an enemy,
> such as this was supposed to be, who designs
> attacking Denver, will not show himself within

sight of town . . . . He will not be seen with
<u>spy glasses</u> . . . nor will his mounted force
. . . go careening over the hills inside the
corporation just when we are all sitting down to
tea [emphasis original].[143]

Of course had the same sort of "common sense" been
applied to Byers' stories of the previous month, his
prestige might have suffered. But, as if recognizing
the appeal of the guerrilla scare, Byers spiced his
"Indian War" with hints of conspiracy among
Confederate agents and hostile Indians.[144] However,
other than the Reynolds gang (captured and eventually
shot by Chivington's command) no authentic Confederate
threat to Colorado this late in the war has been
documented.[145]

Initially the <u>News</u> may have speculated about a
Confederate role in the depredations to overcome
intermittent apathy in the Territory and thereby
encourage enrollment in the militia. On August 10th,
Byers remarked that "Except for the moment of alarm, a
most remarkable state of apathy has thus far prevailed
among our people." He continued, "There is no
assurance that troops will be sent." He then referred
to Kansas which had organized its own troops to "beat
back the savages."[146] But, by August 24, real events
had aided Byers in his call to arms.

Starting in the second week in August, Kiowas,
Cheyennes, Arapahoes and Sioux raided extensively on
the Platte route, near Fort Lyon and south of the
Arkansas. The philosophy of punishment used by
military authorities during the Spring in Kansas,
Nebraska and Colorado Territory had succeeded in
uniting some of the Plains Tribes against the Whites.
Even Indians described as "friendly" now hesitated to
approach military posts (although Evans had requested
the "friendly" to do so) for fear of being shot at.
The death of Lean Bear was widely known as was the
fact that Left Hand had been fired upon while under a
flag of truce.[147] Additionally, Byers was correct in
noting the inadequate military protection available to
Coloradans. The troops under Chivington's command
were able to stir the Indians up but not to provide
adequate protection. Moreover, the extensive depredations on the overland route in July stimulated Major
S.R. Curtis, Commander of the Department of Kansas, to

redraw district lines, removing Fort Lyon from Chivington's district. This redistricting effectively reduced the number of available soldiers for protection of emigrants and farmers in Colorado.[148] During August, along the Platte route alone, fifty unprotected emigrants were killed by raiding Indians. In addition, on the Sante Fe trail, three trains were intercepted by Indians with at least eleven White men killed. Several women and one child were also kidnapped and other assorted depredations reported.[149] While Denver was not directly attacked, between August 15 and September 29, 1864, Denver was cut off from travel and mail from the east. Since no supplies could arrive, food became scarce in Denver and prices increased drastically. For example, the price of flour spiraled from nine dollars per hundredweight to twenty-five dollars, when a plague of grasshoppers devoured much of the wheat crop on the South Platte.[150] Terrified ranchers and farmers left their stock and undamaged crops in the field and fled to Denver where the populace panicked at rumor after rumor. Three women reportedly lost their minds from fright.[151] Shortly after the depredations of August 7th and 8th, and only forty five days after issuing his proclamation to the "friendly Indians," Governor Evans issued several important messages. On August 10, 1864, the News printed an "Appeal" from Evans to the people.[152] He had not yet been given the authority to raise the regiment of citizen soldiers and so requested that each settlement "organize" for its own protection, declaring, "Any man who kills a hostile Indian is a patriot." The News responded with support for the appeal and also set forth the position which now comprised Byers' attitude toward the Indian problem. Although events had not yet proven the "uprising" to be general in the Territory, Byers stated that it was "general" and even argued that it pervaded the entire country west of the Mississippi. He supported the Governor and hinted at the material rewards available to the interested recruits:

> In this emergency the Governor calls for the organization of military companies. When organized, he will supply arms. They will be entitled to all the horses and other property they may capture, and, in addition, he promises to use his influence to procure their payment by the general government. There is but little

doubt that it can be effected. The first companies in the field will have the best opportunity to serve their country and the best chance for large pay.[153]

While reported thefts of stock had been the impetus for the first forays against the Indians in April and May, the record indicates that Whites fulfilling their "patriotic duty" to kill hostile Indians actually acquired more Indian stock and property than was ever lost to the Indians. Once a given Indian or group of Indians had been "rubbed out" or "bit the dust" they could be defined as "hostile" whether this was the case or not and their valuable property was forfeit. The appeal of such a "pay off" to the "floaters" in the Territorial population is obvious. Moreover, there is evidence that even Army regulars profited from such an arrangement.[154] This is not to say that there were no hostile Indians who had not committed depredations, but only that it paid equally well to kill all Indians. The effect upon "friendly" Indians is predictable if one recalls Jim Beckwourth's admonition of 1860 that Indians were as sensitive as the Whites to acts of injustice. However, while the News had supported Beckwourth on that occasion, clearly, now Byers supported another position:

> Eastern humanitarians who believe in the superiority of the Indian race will raise a terrible howl over this policy, but it is no time to split hairs nor stand upon delicate compunctions of conscience. <u>Self preservation demands decisive action, and the only way to secure it is to fight them in their own way. A few months of active extermination against the red devils will bring quiet and nothing else will</u> [emphasis added].[155]

While Evans had requested that only "hostile" Indians be killed, Byers made no such distinction in his definition of the enemy -- the "red devils." The wording of the editorial implied that matters of conscience were not worth splitting hairs over.

On August 11th, the News published another "Proclamation" by the Governor. The Governor declared that the "evidence" was now "conclusive" that most of the Indians on the Plains were "hostile." He urged citizens to "pursue, kill and destroy" hostile Indians but to avoid those Indians who had responded to his proclamation of June. The News supported the Governor's call and printed an appeal from George Tritch, Captain of the Denver City Guards calling for increased enrollment.[156] On August 13th, the News provided space for yet another Proclamation from the Governor informing the Territory that he had finally been granted the authority by the Secretary of War to raise "a regiment of cavalry to serve 100 days to fight the Indians." Again the Governor demanded the destruction of "all hostile Indians."[157] Again Byers and the News concurred. But, until after the Territorial election on September 12, 1864, Byers seldom distinguished hostile from friendly Indians while advocating "extermination" as a solution. Thus, by August 24th, the News was suggesting, "Shall we not go for them, their lodges, squaws and all?" Somehow, similar language appeared again in a report of a "battle" on October 10th, 1864, between Company D of the Colorado Third and a small group of Cheyennes comprised of six warriors, three squaws, a teenage "brave" and two papooses. The soldiers "went for them in earnest, and in a very short time they raised the white flag but too late. They [the Cheyennes] went under, one and all . . . ."[158]

To the frightened citizens of Colorado, the actual intervening events between August 10th and August 24th appeared to justify such a solution. Added to the actual events were scores of rumors and misguided reports. Of particular worry was the fear of Indian conspiracy. Not only was the uprising "general," as Byers had declared, it was also planned with the help of renegade Whites or Confederate guerrillas. Thus on August 13th, the ever-vigilant News informed its readers that

> Another dispatch, received here this afternoon, says that Chief Twoface and six Brulah Sioux arrived at Kearney, bringing back some stolen stock from the Cheyennes. The Chief told the Post Commander that in a short time, that Fort, and other points along the road would be attacked by the combined forced of Cheyennes, Arapahoes, Kiowas, Comanches, Utes, Snakes and Yanctons, in sufficient strength to 'clean the country of the Whites and the soldiers.' This Chief, whose truthfulness is proverbial among all who know him in Nebraska says that the above tribes now number

four thousand warriors, fully equipped and eager for an onslaught. Also that those Indians are generally led by white guerillas.[159]

Just as Parkman provided an exceptional leader in Pontiac to head the great conspiracy, so Byers hinted at White leadership. As inferior beings the savages did pose a threat, but only the threat of uncontrolled violence. The addition of White leadership strengthened the appeal of the conspiracy by providing a cunning which had been lacking in Indian nature as previously defined.

A similar conspiracy was revealed on August 18th, although the "spice" of White leadership was not included. The <u>News</u> warned that "It is ascertained from reliable sources that in twenty days a simultaneous attack will be made by the combined bands of Cheyennes, Kiowas, Utes, Snakes, Commanches, and Arapahoes, on Fort Kearney, Fort Cottonwood and along the Platte valley." An accompanying "release" probably made Coloradans feel even more threatened and isolated:

> Washington, Aug 16. -- It is not thought at the Indian Bureau that the outbreak of Indians on the plains is general, or stimulated by rebel agents but that a few Indians are taking retaliation for wrongs committed against them.[160]

There was no comment on this message by Byers. But the conspiracy rumors and several other atrocity stories in the same issue -- the results "of those thieving, scalping sons of butchery" -- probably functioned as a counterdefinition of the situation. Moreover, the <u>News</u>, by presenting the apparent truth of the situation, emphasized its role as a reliable, prestigious source of information. Additionally, by printing the various "Proclamations" issued by Evans, the <u>News</u> could convey the impression that Evans was working against the evil plotters. A story in the August 26th edition brought the "conspiracy" together with Evans and illustrated how he was "keeping matters under suveillance" and a "potent force for changing the plotters' behavior."[161] Under the title, A NARROW ESCAPE, the <u>News</u> revealed that

> Few are aware how narrowly the people of Colorado escaped a general Indian massacre less than a week ago. The Indians had collected on a camp on

Beaver Creek, to the number of near one thousand. There were none but warriors; all mounted, and without tents or baggage. On a certain time, which was to have been last Monday night, or on the first or second one thereafter, they were to divide and strike simultaneously upon all the frontier settlements. About three hundred warriors were to attack Pueblo and then sweep the settlements along the Arkansas and Fountaine-qui-Boulle; two hundred warriors were to aim for the head waters of Cherry Creek, destroying the settlements right and left; a force of one hundred was to attack Fort Lupton and the settlers therabouts, and a fourth party of three hundred were to take Latham and then clean out the settlements along down the Platte to the Junction or beyond. Their plans were admirably laid, and had they been carried out, the most wholesale Indian massacre ever known would have visited our unfortunate Territory ere this.

When almost ready for its execution, two Cheyenne under chiefs visited the trading post of an old plains trader for whom they had a strong friendship, and warned him what was coming. They told him he must move himself and family and drive his stock away, or they would share the fate of the balance. He instantly mounted his horse and in company with a third Indian chief who had remained friendly rode sixty miles without stopping. He laid his information before the Governor; military couriers were at once dispatched to all the threatened points, and every possible precaution taken to circumvent the savages. Fortunately it was in time to prevent the most awful consequences. The Indians found the whites on the alert and the threatened blow was deferred for the present at least.

Thus a friendly Indian has performed the most signal service and saved hundreds of lives. But for his devotion, the horrors of Minnesota, upon a far larger scale would have been reenacted in our very midst.[162]

Ironically, while the "old plains trader" was in Denver warning the Governor, the "friendly Indians" took his stock.[163] But neither the "four thousand" nor the "one thousand" warriors ever appeared, and only ten riders, assumed to be Indian warriors, were

174

actually sighted at the "certain time."[164] Just as Parkman used a questionable letter not since located to support his allegations of conspiracy, Evans (and the News) took the word of a gullible farmer. However, whether the report was true or not, it allowed the News to convey the impression that favored Territorial authorities could control the situation while hinting that the situation of danger was only "deferred for the present."

As the September election date approached, Evans, Chivington and their "mouthpiece," the News, were increasingly attacked by anti-state forces and the Black Hawk Journal. The Journal disagreed implicitly with Byers' conspiracy theory by arguing that the "Utes were friendly" and that rumors to the contrary were "absurd." Byers responded sarcastically that "The cold blooded murders of Doctors Shank and Kennedy almost in sight of where the above item was written," along with other "butchery," and "slaughter" committed by these "friendly" Utes, were evidence of only a "playful mood" of "ye gentle savages." So too were the "Arrapahoes and Cheyennes just a while ago," but Byers concluded "None of them are to be trusted" [emphasis added].[165] Thus, Byers implied again that no distinction between friendly and hostile Indians was possible.

The Journal was not at this point denying that some Indians had committed depredations. Rather, the Indian issue had become politicized as the Journal blamed Evans and Chivington for allowing troops to be called out of the Territory without attaining alternative protection. The News responded in kind by directly denying the Journal's attacks, linking the advancement of statehood with the control of the Indians and placing blame for the Indian War on other Territorial officials opposed to statehood.[166]

Byers labeled the Journal's attack as "shameful," arguing that the fault lay not with Chivington and Evans but with "the orders of their superiors." Evans and Chivington long had been requesting assistance but had been unheeded.[167] In his characteristic manner, Byers name-called the editor of the Journal: he was a "dirty dog" who had "utter disregard" for "truth and decency," and his "recklessness" should be taken as "evidence of his insanity." Hollister, the editor of the Journal, by his attack upon Evans and Chivington

175

was engaged in "Political Malignity," "Political Schemes," and "A Conspiracy as Black as Hell."[168] Also, Byers accused the Journal and Hollister of opposing statehood and attacking the Union because of Rebel sympathy.[169] Since Hollister had served with the Colorado First during the Battle of Glorietta and was a "hero" of Glorietta, Byers' charge was unfair. But Byers was not above lying and he had promised to win, so he went a step further and accused Hollister of being "A deserter from the United States Army who left his regiment in company with an avowed and loud-mouthed secessionist . . . day by day he blackens the characters of good and faithful officers by the publication of outright and inexcusable lies."[170]

In addition, Byers directly supported Governor Evans. Hoping to gain sympathy for his friend and silent partner, Byers wrote that "Never in the history of any country or campaign was there a man more grossly abused, more foully misrepresented . . . than has been Governor Evans within the last two months by the Black Hawk Journal . . . ." "Steadily," and "faithfully, day and night" Evans had worked by telegraph and letter to solve the problem. Probably the News had printed Evans' "Proclamations" of July and August as proof of this "steady labor." But the Journal's attack continued unabated. To prove that the Governor had "done all that any man could under the circumstances" [emphasis original], on August 25 and 26, 1864, the News reprinted all of Evans' correspondence regarding the Indian war of 1864.[171] Since the News was suffering a severe paper shortage, the decision to publish this correspondence at the expense of other potential stories reflects some desperation on Byers' part.[172] But the News was not successful in providing Evans the needed credibility. On September 1, 1864, Evans announced his withdrawal from the election as a candidate for the U.S. Senate on the pro-state ticket because "his favoring the measure was being used as the greatest obstacle to the success of the state question . . .."[173] At this juncture, Byers expressed no bitterness over this forced withdrawal. The state faction hoped that Evans' withdrawal would mollify those in the anti-state faction who objected not to statehood, but to the personalities associated with it.[174]

With Evans' personality no longer a question in the election, the News and Byers went on what would be a too-short offensive, arguing for the positive benefits of statehood. For about ten days, the News emphasized that benefit to statehood jeered at by the Journal -- the ability of a "state" to secure better protection from hostile Indians. While this advantage had been "eighth" on Byers' original list of arguments for statehood, shortly before Evans' withdrawal it was raised to "fourth."[175] Thereafter until the election, a vote for the "constitution" became a vote for safety from Indians. Likewise, Byers insisted, "A vote against the Constitution is a vote for the Indians . . . ." [emphasis original].[176] For proof Byers referred to Oregon and Minnesota. Byers insisted that had Evans been the governor of a sovereign state, his appeals would have been "speedily granted." Byers stated that Oregon and Minnesota, like Colorado, were ignored by the Federal Government while trying to solve their initial Indian problems. However, the problems of the two former Territories were solved almost "immediately" after receiving statehood. The "solution" he wrote about in both cases was the payment of Indian war claims to Whites suffering losses in these Territories prior to statehood. Neither incident really proved that Evans' requests for more troops or permission to raise a militia would have been more speedily granted if Colorado were a state.[177]

Byers also attempted to shift the blame for the "Indian War." Since the Treaty of Fort Wise in 1861, Byers and others in the Territory had been "nervous" regarding the status of White claims to land in Eastern Colorado. Evans had been unsuccessful the year before in gaining the cooperation of non-signatory Indians with his interpretation of that treaty. Two Colorado Justices, Harding and Armour, added fuel to this worry by finding the mountains and plains to be, legally, Indian Lands.[178] Byers stated that such findings actually had instigated the Indian War, since, somehow, the Indians knew that the Federal Government would not come to the aid of illegal White interlopers. But Byers found solace in the "patriotism" of Colorado's people: "They will beat back the advancing waves of this merciless war instigated by the decisions and opinions and acts of Federal Judges and other officers sent to administer the laws over the people of Colorado."[179] Byers believed that the population of the Territory could solve their own problems "by the adoption of a state government." The question, he insisted, was not one of state versus anti-state interests but of "Indian vs. White Man."[180] For example, rejecting the Constitution also was rejecting authority by which those men who had served in the militia could be paid: "He who votes to reject the Constitution really votes against paying Captain Tyler and his men for their brave and patriotic services."[181] Thus, Byers attempted to transform a referendum on statehood to a vote for or against Indian savagery. He appealed:

> In the name of our dearest rights as American citizens! In the name of the bleeding and suffering victims of this horrible Indian war! In the name of humanity itself, we call upon the people to vote <u>for the Constitution</u>, and for Judges of a State Supreme Court that will administer the laws of the state justly and righteously, and who will not leave our all in the hands of the merciless savages.[182]

But the statehood supported by Byers in 1864 was not to materialize. Apparently he was not successful in convincing his audience of the necessity of statehood for the solution to the Indian problem. The proposed state constitution was rejected by a majority of three to one.[183] Moreover, not only had Evans been forced to withdraw during the course of the election, but Chivington and the rest of the Union Party slate also were rejected at the polls. Although the <u>News</u> had never been beaten, in this election, Byers and the <u>News</u> were <u>soundly</u> beaten.

Byers and the state forces underestimated the independent nature of the population they were dealing with. The enabling act allowing Colorado (as well as Nevada and Nebraska) to vote on statehood had been hastily pushed through Congress. The Republican Party feared that defeats on the battleground might be translated into decreased political strength. Nine additional electoral votes for the Republicans (renamed the Union Party for this election) could have made the difference in the fall election.[184] The same sense of urgency at the Territorial level blinded pro-state forces to the importance of procedure to their independent audience. To save time, pro-state forces (who controlled the Territorial convention) proposed a slate of candidates to fill state offices so that voters could vote on the constitution and their choices for Senators and Congressman at the same time.[185] In implementing this procedure, pro-staters created a leadership for the opposition in men who believed that they had been excluded unfairly from the ballot. Additionally, many who supported statehood opposed the ticket because they believed they had been left out of the selection process. Therefore it was not difficult for Hollister and the Journal to convince a majority that the Evans/Chivington/Byers faction was more concerned with personal advancement than the welfare of Colorado. Perhaps Evans' withdrawal reflected a too-late realization of the depth of this resentment.

Moreover, the continued presence of Evans on the State ticket had restricted the rhetorical options open to Byers and the News. If Evans remained as a candidate, it would have been difficult for Byers to stress the protection from Indians offered by Statehood. Such an approach implicitly admitted that Evans had failed to solve the problem. Byers manifestly intended the publication of Evans' correspondence concerning Indian matters to illustrate that "all had been done that could have been done." However, the correspondence included fears of Indian conspiracy expressed as early as 1863. Such statements implied Evans' continued inability to get the attention of the Federal Government or to provide a viable solution. The "bleeding and suffering victims" of the Indian War also were reminders of this inability. Thus Byers and the News were able to utilize the symbol of the savage Indian as an explicit argument for statehood only during the two weeks after Evans withdrew. Nor was it made clear exactly why or how statehood would be superior to a Territory in providing protection against Indians. In other words, Byers and the News waited until too late to utilize their strongest argument. After the Hungate Massacre the Territory was united in fear and anxiety in regard to Indians. Had Byers been able to prove statehood was the proper solution to these fears, perhaps the outcome of the 1864 election might have been different. But, regardless of the actual outcome of the election, the symbol of the Native American utilized by Byers to further his goal reminded his readers of the nature of Colorado's Indians if it did not convince them of the necessity of statehood.

Sand Creek Reported

After the election, the News was somewhat subdued -- although stubbornly Byers refused to admit defeat for over a month.[186] The urgency of the preceding weeks had vanished as ballots had been cast. Recruitment for the regiment of "Hundred-Daysers" authorized by Governor Evans was well underway. After early September no depredations were reported closer than Julesburg in extreme northeastern Colorado.[187] Byers now noted the friendliness of the Utes as being "rather comforting."[188] During the last ten days of September, the News carried reports of an "Indian Expedition" under the command of Major Wynkoop.

Earlier that year, Wynkoop had written that he believed his purpose was to pursue and to kill Indians. However, on September 3, he received two letters signed by Black Kettle, the principal chief of the Cheyennes, stating that he held some White prisoners taken during the raids on the Platte route, whom the Indians desired to turn over to the authorities and that they wished to make peace with the Whites.[189] Wynkoop had also learned that three thousand Cheyennes, Arapahoes and Sioux were camped together near the headwaters of the Smoky Hill River. Against the advice of his officers, Wynkoop decided to visit the Indian camp although he realized he might be walking into a trap. His purpose was to recover the White prisoners. Taking only 130 men and two howitzers, Wynkoop went to the village. Described as a persuasive talker, Wynkoop managed to enter the armed camp, containing at least 800 armed warriors, to avoid trouble between his nervous troops and obstreperous Cheyenne "Dog Soldiers," and to leave with Black Kettle, six other Cheyenne Chiefs and four White captives. Wynkoop took these Chiefs and their White captives to a "council" at Camp Weld, near Denver, with Governor Evans and Colonel Chivington.[190]

Initially, Byers expressed his opposition to any more "rubber treaties" with the Indians. He argued that it was only the approaching winter, scarce game and potential government handouts that made these Indians interested in "peace."[191] But, in the very next issue of the News, Byers changed his position. He revealed that "a long conversation" with Wynkoop had altered his opinion and recommended "prudence" and "compromise" in dealing with the Cheyennes and

Arapahoes. He concluded, "So far as we are concerned, we are convinced that peace with the neighboring tribes is best. Yesterday we would have been as loth to compromise as anyone could be."[192] Subsequent issues of the News recounted events at the council "with which all seem pleased" and the implication was that peace now existed with the Cheyennes and Arapahoes in Black Kettle's band. The News also carried a "Memorial to Major Wynkoop" signed by forty citizens of the Arkansas valley, which stated that Wynkoop's efforts had brought peace and security to their section of Colorado.[193] The Cheyennes and Arapahoes returned to Fort Lyon where they surrendered their arms to Wynkoop and moved to a camp near Sand Creek. However, Wynkoop soon was relieved by Major Scott Anthony who returned the Indians' weapons to them because he did not have the supplies to feed them.[194]

In Denver, absent Wynkoop's persuasion, Byers returned to presenting Indian depredations, mostly from afar, since the Territory was still quiet. On October 1, 1864, a few days after advocating "prudence," the News' lead article was titled "The Indian War" in which it related "Our exchanges from every direction, east and west, north and south, that are published in the Territories and frontier states are filled with accounts of Indian depredations and outrages." The story, a review of which tribes were hostile in the west, concluded that the Utes were the "only Indians of any considerable force that are friendly disposed."[195] Subsequent issues included stories of various depredations and troop movements, but in a matter-of-fact way. There were no depredations reported in the Territory. East-west transportation and mail service had been restored and reports of the larger war indicated that the struggle had turned in the Union's favor.[196] The Colorado Third, comprised of "Hundred Daysers" had been filled out but almost mutinied when it was rumored that a peace treaty was to be signed with Black Kettle. In mid-November the Third was ordered by Chivington to proceed to Fort Lyon. An editorial in the Black Hawk Journal revealed this movement and the cynical attitude of the Journal toward the Third and the current Territorial administration:

181

> We learn from reliable sources that a large portion of the 3rd regiment has been moved to Fort Lyon though for what purpose we do not know unless it be to permit the Indians to resume their pastime of throat cutting and scalping without fear of interruption. Every mountain man has been sent away out of their reach, and now we may look forward to lively times on the Platte. On the 13th of next month the term of their enlistment will have expired and our brave mountain boys will be sent home to enjoy the reputation of 'Bloodless Hundred Dazers.' What a brilliant administration we are living under to be sure.[197]

The News, as always, was supportive of Evans and Chivington and railed against the Journal's implied attacks on Evans in the December 1st edition. But the News paid no notice to the movement of the Third mentioned by the Journal. The only mention of the Third in the News prior to December 7th was an erroneous wire from a Captain Backus which read:

> . . . the Captain states that there are no Indians near Ft. Lyon as reported here nor any prospect of there being a brush between them and the 3rd and the First unless the latter hunt after them for hundreds of miles in each direction.[198]

Probably this wire was ordered sent by Chivington who had surrounded the movements of the First and the Third with mystery.[199] Thus, Denver viewed in amazement this bulletin in the News on December 7th:

Big Indian Fight

> The first and Third Regiments have had a battle with the Indians on Sand Creek, a short distance northeast of Fort Lyon. Five hundred Indians are reported killed and six hundred horses captured. Captain Baxter and Lieutenant Pierce are reported killed. No further particulars. A message is hourly expected with full details. Bully for the Colorado boys [emphasis original].[200]

The News received the "full details" -- a copy of the "Official Report" forwarded by Chivington to Major-General S.R. Curtis.[201] Byers responded with bold headlines in the News which read:

Great Battle with Indians!
- - - - - - - - - - - - -

The Savages Dispersed!

- - - - - - - - - - - - -

500 INDIANS KILLED

Byers endorsed this "needed whipping of the redskins by our 'First Indian Expedition' . . . ." Moreover, he declared that "the members of the Third and First . . . who collectively 'cleaned out' the confederated savages on Sand Creek, have won for themselves and their commanders . . . the eternal gratitude of dwellers on these plains."202 Byers never hesitated in support of his friend, Chivington, nor in support of the "solution" which Sand Creek suggested. Throughout December, Byers and the News heaped praise upon the Colorado regiment. A victory for his friend, Chivington, offset somewhat the stinging loss in the recent election. Thus no hyperbole regarding the "battle" and the bravery exhibited by its White participants could be too overstated. Sand Creek was "Among the brilliant feats of arms in Indian warfare." The "battle would stand in history with a few rivals and none to exceed it in final results." Sand Creek, he insisted, was "the most effective expedition against the Indians ever planned and carried out." Further, he implied that going for them in their villages was the "only way." Moreover, not only could peace and order be restored by frightening the Indians into submission but the "hauteur of the treacherous tribes" also would be brought down. A savage Indian was bad enough but a presumptuous savage Indian was even worse; or so Byers seemed to imply.203

When Byers finally got around to writing a version of the battle, he provided a narrative which justified the event as a "brilliant feat." In his mythic story of Sand Creek, a group of heroes suffered great adversity, performed almost superhuman deeds and battled worthy but hostile opponents. The events of interest took place during the "great snowstorm." The brave volunteers "marched for days through the driving, blinding clouds of snow . . . ." After their arrival in their base camp (Bijou Basin), they experienced weeks of an "Artic climate." Their "sufferings were intense" and made worse because of the shortage of tents and blankets. But the soldiers were undaunted and, after a month spent in these conditions, marched

> a distance of <u>two hundred and sixty miles in less than six days</u>, and so quietly and expeditiously had the march been made that the command at the Fort was taken entirely by surprise [emphasis original].[204]

After just a few hours rest at Fort Lyon, the soldiers made a "forced midnight march of forty two miles" and then "dashed upon the enemy with yells that would put a Camanche army to the blush."

Byers' "Colorado Heros" were not attacking just any Indian camp, but one comprised of antagonists worthy of heroic attention. Nine hundred warriors fought in "genuine Indian fashion." Their "chiefs fought with unparalleled bravery; falling in front of their men. One of them charged alone against a force of two or three hundred . . . ." Additionally, these worthy foes were prepared for the battle as the "camp was well supplied with defensive works" -- the rifle pits which Chivington would later argue proved the hostility of the Indians. Byers did not overtly argue that this group of Indians was hostile. Rather, he referred only briefly to the one bit of evidence mentioned by Chivington in his report, "one white man's scalp was found . . . ." Not much proof was needed. The assumption made by most participants and the majority of the Colorado population was that Indians were hostile. No one noted that Black Kettle and Left Hand were listed among those Indians killed. Surely Byers must have recalled that, two months before, Wynkoop had brought Black Kettle seeking peace to Camp Weld and had persuaded Byers that "compromise" and "prudence" should guide solutions to the Indian problem. Left Hand was his "friendly Indian" who had tried to save Rice and Pierson. But such considerations were contradictory to the stylized world described in Byers' version of the conspiracy myth. Therefore, Byers only noted that "there were neither wounded nor prisoners." By definition, Indians were <u>the</u> enemy. Byers had implied this conclusion through 1863 and the Hungate incident further confirmed this well-known fact. The Camp Weld Council might have never occurred since Byers did not refer to it again after September 30th. The only inquiry he engaged in to ascertain his "facts" came from "those who participated in it" [Sand Creek]. Of course, these participants were White participants who were supportive of Chivington's interpretation as exemplified in his official report.

Byers concluded the two column story with a brief summary of his mythic interpretation:

> Whether viewed as a march or as a battle, the exploit has few if any parallels. A march of 260 miles in but a fraction more than five days, with deep snow, scanty forage and no road is a remarkable feat, whilst the utter surprise of a large Indian village is unprecedented. In no single battle in North America, we believe, have so many Indians been slain . . . .
> A thousand incidents of individual daring, and the passing events of the day might be told, but space forbids. We leave the task for eye witnesses to chronicle. All acquitted themselves well and Colorado soldiers have again covered themselves with glory.[205]

Byers had declared that he was "not prepared to write its history." But he was also not prepared to accept any other facts inconsistent with his interpretation of Sand Creek. No other interpretation ever appeared in the pages of the News, except as an interpretation to be scorned.[206]

On December 29, 1864, the News published an item which provided Byers his initial opportunity to express scorn. A dispatch from Washington revealed that an investigation would be made of the Sand Creek Battle because of "letters received from high officials in Colorado" which had reported that "the Indians were killed after surrendering and that a large proportion of them were women and children."[207] Byers responded the next day with his best cutting sarcasm:

> The <u>confessed</u> murderers of the Hungate family -- a <u>man and wife</u> and their two little babes, whose scalped and mutilated remains were seen by all our citizens -- were 'friendly Indians' we suppose, in the eyes of these 'high officials.'

They fell in the Sand Creek battle. The confessed participants in a score of other murders of peaceful settlers . . . must have been friendly or else the 'high officials' wouldn't say so.

Byers' source for these "confessions" was not stated, but he furthered the process of providing "proof" of the hostility of the Indians at Sand Creek. Although Chivington's report had mentioned only a white scalp not more than three days old, Byers revealed more such "evidence":

> Probably those scalps of white men, women and children -- one of them fresh -- not three days taken -- found drying in their lodges were taken in a friendly, playful manner or possibly those Indian saddle blankets trimmed with the scalps of white women, and with braids and fringes of their hair, were kept simply as mementoes of their owner's high affection for the pale face. At any rate these delicate and tasteful ornaments could not have been taken from the heads of the wives, sisters or daughters of these 'high officials' [emphasis original].[208]

Chivington also was later to refer to saddle blankets fringed with white scalps but there is no record of support for such articles in any official reports or testimony regarding the battle. This "evidence" also was not mentioned in Byers' original version of the battle in which he only referred to "one white man's scalp."[209] Moreover, in this December 30th evidence, Byers stated that the Indians had not "surrendered" but "the savages fought like devils to the end, and one of our pickets was killed and scalped by them. . . ." But an account published in the December 12th edition of the News contradicted Byers on this point. An eyewitness, whom Byers had stated that he depended upon for the true history of the event, stated that "the Indians did not scalp any of our men."[210]

Prior to any questioning of events at Sand Creek, the News, on December 22nd, playfully had noted that there was "no exaggeration in stating that no two men give the same version of the big battle, and, of the stories of a score of them, there ain't three alike, respecting[211] the minutiae of the great, glorious victory." But once Byers had taken a position supporting the official version of the battle, he again had placed his prestige on the line, not to mention his friendship for Chivington. Moreover, having declared the "Indian War" the previous spring and consistently illustrated "true" Indian nature, Byers oculd do nothing else but support Sand Creek as a great and glorious victory justified by the hostility of the Indians at the site. Thus, he concluded,

> It is--unquestioned--and--undenied--that--the--site--of--the Sand Creek battle was the rendezvous of the thieving and marauding bands of savages who roamed over this country last summer and fall. . . . By all means let there be an investigation but we advise the Honorable Congressional committee who may be appointed to conduct it, to get their scalps insured before they pass Plum Creek on their way out" [punctuation original].[212]

Byers never waivered from his position. His audience, at least, was convinced of the desirability of the "solution" suggested by Sand Creek.

The first investigative committee, "The Committee on the Conduct of the War," concluded that Sand Creek was "the scene of murder and barbarity," that Chivington's actions disgraced "the veriest savage," and that Evans' testimony regarding the Indian war was characterized by "prevarication and shuffling."[213] Moreover, the committee called for the removal of the officials "responsible" for the outrage and President Johnson asked[214] for and received Governor Evans' resignation. But the report of the committee was never published in Colorado. Only Byers' "summary" was available for examination by an already "partial" Colorado audience.[215] When another committee was appointed, comprised of three Congressmen, and traveled west to examine the site of the battle, Byers rejoiced that these distinguished members of Congress would "vindicate" Sand Creek.[216] But, after visiting the site of the battle, Senator Doclittle wrote that they had "picked up skulls of infants whose milk-teeth had not yet been shed, perforated with pistol and rifle shots . . . ." Appalled at what they saw at Sand Creek and what they heard in "sworn accounts given of the scalping and mutilating of women and children by White men under Colonel Chivington," the committee traveled to Denver to "have a full and frank discussion of the Indian problem." Later, Senator Doolittle gave a measure of the position which Byers' audience now supported regarding the "problem." Doolittle and his colleagues met with Governor Evans on the stage of the Denver Opera House. Doolittle wrote to a friend:

> When I had referred in a cool and matter-of-fact way to the occasion of conflict between the whites and Indians, growing out of the decrease of the buffalo and the increase of the herds of cattle upon the plains of Kansas and Colorado and said: the question has arisen whether we should place the Indians upon reservations and teach them to raise cattle and corn and to support themselves or whether we should exterminate them, there suddenly arose such a shout as is never heard unless upon some battlefield -- a shout almost loud enough to raise the roof of the opera house -- 'EXTERMINATE THEM! EXTERMINATE THEM!'[217]

Therefore, Byers and his audience had arrived at the same conclusion regarding the "solution" to the Indian problem: "Those whose opportunity has ever been best for observation have invariably arrived at the one conclusion, that it admits of but one solution; that [of] the extermination of the red man . . . ."[218]

Conclusions

Between 1861 and 1865, William Newton Byers, editor and founder of the Denver Rocky Mountain News, moved from supporting conciliation and negotiation with the Indians in Colorado to seeking a war of extermination against the same people. The principal justifications provided for such a change in attitude included stories of depredations and outrages committed by the "red devils" against innocent Whites. Moreover, in 1863 and 1864 such depredations were explained as the result of a conspiracy among the Plains tribes and between various Plains tribes and rebel guerrilla forces. While Byers' manifest intention had been to "send forth reliable information," stories symbolizing Native Americans during this period also served latent functions.

The latent functions of such stories included increasing the sense of identification (or "congregation") in an otherwise politically fragmented community, reminding the reading audience as to the "nature" and inevitable fate of Native Americans and allowing Byers to work as an apparent force for good against "evil plotters."

Kenneth Burke has written of "identification by antithesis, the most urgent form of congregation by segregation." In this sense, identification or a sense of unity among diverse elements is brought about by a focus upon an external foe or scapegoat.[219] Byers' independent audience had difficulty reaching agreement on many of the questions of the day. They had come from diverse backgrounds and resented most external authority. However, "Indian scalping stories" served not just to frighten them but also to bring about a sense of community or congregation regarding at least this one issue. By consistently evoking the myth of the innocent, brave White settler conspired against by the evil forces of savagery, the News could try to promote conformity and bolster the favored leadership on other specific issues such as statehood.[220] Moreover, as a "Formative Event," the importance of the so-called "Hungate Massacre" in increasing the sense of community cannot be underestimated.

Richard Merritt has described four types of Formative Events:

> . . . those making strong ties of community even firmer; those strengthening newly formed ties of community, or ties that the passage of time has weakened; those jolting a population [or part of it] into an awareness of significant differences between it and another population [or segment of the population]; and those leading separate groups to an awareness of their need for a greater degree of integration. <u>The outstanding characteristic of such events is that they vividly impress themselves upon the consciousness of the population experiencing them</u> [emphasis added].[221]

The report of the "Hungate Massacre" printed in the Commonwealth/Rocky Mountain News could have functioned in all four ways. Certainly the population of Denver after the experience appeared to be united as never before as "From the throats of thousands," wrote one observer, "went up the cry for redress."[222] Byers himself demonstrated that he understood this function of the Hungate Massacre. At least he appeared to a little over a year after the event when he wrote:

> During all this time people took no steps toward retaliation. It was not until last season . . . that they seemed to really awake to the danger of the situation . . . it was not until the butchered mutilated bodies of the Hungate family were brought into the city that they really appreciated the barbarity of the red devils.[223]

The Hungate affair might have united and mobilized the population absent the publicity provided in the Commonwealth under the editorship of Byers and Whitely. Certainly just the exhibition of the bodies would have created fear and anger. The population would have been "nervous" in any event because of the "Great Flood," apparent Rebel guerrilla infiltration, other Indian depredations and perceived inadequate military protection.[224]

However, attachment to the conspiracy myth in the concrete form exemplified by the Hungate Massacre was facilitated by the publicity provided to it.[225] By putting the scene into written symbols, the writer increased the likelihood of similarity of interpretation. Those who had viewed the bodies would be reminded of what they had witnessed. Those denied the opportunity could share in the community experience through the written symbols.[226]

Once the Hungate incident was recorded and experienced either directly or indirectly by many citizens, it became a symbol or myth which could be appealed to without explanation to secure action. As an event it was referred to in military and civilian correspondence. Thus, Evans wired frantically Commissioner Dole regarding "Extensive Indian Murders" and to Secretary of War Stanton that "One settlement [was] devastated 25 miles east of here; murdered and scalped bodies brought in today" (not mentioning the number of bodies). Later, Byers also would refer to the "butchered, mutilated bodies of the Hungates" as justification for the "irrepressible conflict," which could only end in the extermination of the Red Man.[227] Various defenses of White excesses at Sand Creek referred to the murders of the Hungates as evidence of Indian hostility.[228]

Whereas the "enemy" of Colorado Whites had not been specifically identified in previous stories, the enemy in "A Horrible Sight" was clearly identified to be the Cheyennes. This public "naming," combined with the mass experience of the tragedy, "jolted" the Denver population into an awareness of the "significant differences" between themselves and the "red devils." Although the "enemy" had been incorrectly identified, at least in the Hungate instance, the myth resisted change and experience only proved the correctness of the myth. This enemy, identified in "A Horrible Sight" and consistently mentioned by the Rocky Mountain News throughout the summer and fall of 1864, was an enemy which could mobilize and create allies. This enemy resembled in all respects the treacherous, dark, violent savage symbolized in Parkman's prototype. As the number of "Indian raids" apparently increased, the presence of such a savage must have appeared immanent to the jittery Denver population. "Friendly Indians" were forgotten since it was safer to assume that all Indians were inwardly hostile. The fate of the Hungates at least implied this conclusion. Murray Edelman explains the potency and potential functions of such a definition:

> The enemy themes that most surely and consistently evoke mass arousal and anxiety are those that make it hardest to take the enemy as a significant other: those that emphasize the respects in which he does not share our human traits and potentialities for empathy, for compassion and for social attachments. The alien, the stranger, or the subhuman are the theme struck repeatedly. These typifications most efficiently symbolize resolute malevolence. . . .it is in some variation of these themes that we see, and encourage others to see, our enemies, for people can deliberately hurt and kill only what they do not see as an exemplification of themselves and a component in their own self-concepts.[229]

Thus, the definition of the enemy hinted at in Byers' stories of 1863 was specified and completed by the "Hungate Massacre." The Cheyennes had committed "unnatural, brutal butchery" for which they deserved execution. Reports during the rest of the summer and fall provided further support for this definition. It is not surprising that, when ordering the cavalry charge upon the Cheyenne village near Sand Creek on November 29, reportedly Chivington ordered his men to "Remember the Hungates, remember our slaughtered women and children."[230]

The grisly details present in the story, "A Horrible Sight," as well as in other stories reported through 1864 provided proof of the suffering and sacrifice offered by the "innocent white victims." Faced with such suffering, the populace at large would not dare to spurn service in the needed militia, or at least not deny the need for such service. Thus, the implication was that "Victory" was only possible through self-sacrifice and "obedience" to Byers' friends Evans and Chivington.[231] Moreover, the story, "A Horrible Sight," also revealed a collective course of action agreed upon by the "hundreds of spectators." If some Whites did not agree to this solution (implicit destruction of Native Americans), events described in the story illustrated that extermination was justified. Additionally, the "recorded" agreement illustrated that the proper "solution" had been sanctioned by the community. Therefore Byers, Evans and Chivington could write and speak of extermination without violating community standards. As Morse Coffin indicated, the idea was "general" that a war of extermination was to be waged.[232] Doolittle's experience would seem further to emphasize this pervasiveness.

Prior to Byers' prediction in April, 1864, regarding "This very promising Indian War," the relationship between Whites and Indians in Colorado could have been characterized as "ordinary." Governor Evans had promised to solve the boundary question through negotiation. Although Byers had detailed the depredations and outrages "natural" to Indian character, he had also written that Colorado's Indians were "at present on friendly terms with the whites." But he also had hinted that those "acquainted with Indian character" could not guarantee their indefinite "amnity and good will."[233] Therefore, consistent with

Parkman, Morton and Nott, Byers' definition of Indian character promised inevitable hostility. When he finally declared "The Indian War," Byers was doing so only on the immediate basis of two small brushes with ill-defined groups of Indians. But no more evidence was needed. Everyone knew that such a "War" was inevitable. After the Hungates were brought to town a war of extermination was believed to be justified and after Sand Creek, such a solution was defended as a positive good.[234] Hence, Byers' Indian war with subsequent catalogued atrocities and depredations helped to change the definition of the situation from an "ordinary" one which "ordinary solutions" could control to an extraordinary situation in need of extraordinary solutions. The News' publication of Evans' "Proclamation to the Friendly Indians of the Plains," illustrated that an ordinary mechanism had been attempted and continuation of Indian hostilities proved the failure of mere persuasion. As Daniels and Kitano have theorized, "extraordinary solutions" to racial problems "logically follow" the perceived failure of "ordinary solutions." They explain:

> Extraordinary solutions are reactions to perceived extraordinary situations -- the majority group perceives a threat to its existence. The triggering mechanism related to apartheid, expulsion and extermination may be couched in a formal declaration of war or it may arise from incidents related to other boundary maintenance stages. The incident may lie outside the control of the target groups . . . or it may lie in the target group's reaction to its pariah status.[235]

Byers' declaration could have served as a formal declaration of war since no one in the Territory had the legal authority to declare war on the Indians. To Congress was reserved the right to make "just wars" with the Indians but Congress was busy with a more important war. Dispatches from Washington illustrated that the Federal Government did not share the urgency of the situation anyway. Byers' stories also illustrated that the "target group" was out of control and that Native Americans were at fault in every instance. Indian motives (outside of their "natural" propensity to steal and kill) were not examined and the possible role of incompetent military enforcement and White provocation as causes of the target group's depredations not mentioned. What was important was the perception created of threat from the Indians. The greater the perceived threat the more drastic the solution sought by the anxious Coloradans.[236]

Events of that spring and summer added to the urgency of the situation. To frightened Coloradans nature probably appeared to unite with their enemies, the Indians, as a threat to their existence. In the Spring, their town was swept away by the Great Flood, and rumors of Rebel guerrillas inspiring and directing "More Indian Raids" increased their anxiety. The mangled corpses of the Hungates proved the irrational violence of the enemy they faced. Finally, cut off from the east, confronted by food shortages and apparently ignored by a preoccupied Federal government, Coloradans were left to their own problem-solving devices. As a group they characteristically utilized expedient, violent solutions. Moreover the perceived threat was great, justifying the "most drastic solution." This solution also had been publicly symbolized by the News and the News/Commonwealth attested to the public support for the "solution."

It was not surprising that events of the Camp Weld Council which ran counter to the popular conceptions of Indian nature and beliefs regarding Indian hostility were ignored. Events were already set in motion: the "Hundred Daysers" had been raised to fight Indians; the Hungate Massacre proved the identity of the enemy and the hostility of the Cheyennes. If the Cheyennes and Black Kettle now said they were at peace, this claim was irrelevant since inwardly all Indians were treacherous. It was better to "go for them one and all" or "make a clean thing of it" since surviving Indians were only tomorrow's problems. It was no accident that Major Wynkoop and his men were the most vocal critics of White deportment at Sand Creek during and after the event.[237] Their direct experience with Black Kettle and his band of Cheyennes and Arapahoes was a type of "free empirical inquiry" into the real nature of Native Americans. Byers' audience had no such direct experience and "responded to the special stylized world that is created and given meaning by a collectively held myth . . . ."[238]

Whether Byers shared the myth he disseminated is problematic. Professor Perkin believes that Byers "knew better" because of Byers' own first-hand experience with Indians.[239] Byers' temporary change of heart because of Wynkoop's persuasion indicates some early flexibility. But this change was prior to the declared loss of prestige suffered because of the election. After the election and particularly after the controversy over Sand Creek began, Byers never admitted any other interpretation of Indian character. He embraced the conspiracy myth totally and even tried to justify it to his eastern audience. He admitted that "we see the Indian from one standpoint, whilst our Eastern friends look upon him from another and quite a different one." He argued that the eastern states "could not dream of the hardships endured by the frontiersman at the hands of his savage neighbors." Byers demanded "respect" for the "rights" of the opinions of the frontiersmen. The "opinion" he claimed as a "right" was an open expression of the conspiracy myth:

> This war of civilization against barbarism is no four year's struggle. It has lasted from the discovery and the first settlement of the American continent to the present day. In our own land its gory field stretches from Plymouth Rock to the Golden Gate. Its monument have been and still are smouldering ruins, decimated settlements, lonely graves and human bones bleaching in the sunshine, from Maide [sic] to Oregon -- from the Lakes to the Gulf. Its sufferings -- who can tell? . . . History proves that necessity [extermination of Native Americans], and whilst a few rare exceptions may be pointed out, they barely suffice to prove the rule. If this country was intended for a civilized people, the savage must submit and adapt himself to the new order of things. If it was not, then the white man should leave it in its wilderness and return to the crowded old world, which is other ages underwent the changes that this is undergoing now. The Indian is always the same, since his character has been known to white men, and he promises ever so to remain. He is the natural enemy to advancement, civilization and enlightenment. All that is wanted to prove this to every man living is the knowledge of the facts, as they exist, and which substantially prove it.[240]

The "facts" were the reports provided by the News of various Indian depredations since Byers had arrived in Colorado in 1859 and Chivington's official version of Sand Creek.

Perhaps Byers' interpretaton of the "facts" may be explained by anxieties to his role. He saw himself as one of the "oldest and most respected" members of Denver society and obviously had a high opinion of his influence since the News "had never been beaten." With defeat in the election, his position as a prestigious source was decreased, and his goal -- gaining statehood for Colorado -- temporarily foreclosed. To preserve his prestige in the News, Byers "reflected back" to his reading audience a perception upon which all could agree. He traded on a "congregation" with his audience which segregated the scapegoat or target group. Edelman hints at this function when he writes regarding public elites, "When they feel threatened, the empirical facts are translated into the forms that provide acceptable meanings and justify action to retain privileges."[241] Probably Byers' choices were made unconsciously as there is no evidence that he deliberately set out to unjustly propagate symbols of extermination. It would have been gratifying for Byers to believe that he was performing a vital service in his reporting of the "facts" with which he symbolized the "guilty." He was thus engaging in a "meaningful struggle against evil and in behalf of [his] fellow man."[242] Byers probably believed that he had defined an enemy only based upon the manifest threat presented by Native Americans. Latently, however, he symbolized an enemy likely to create and mobilize allies and one which was vulnerable to the extraconstitutional assumptions of the frontier population. A.K. McClure later observed:

> How the settlers and miners will end Indian depredations, the Chivington Massacre at Sand Creek correctly foreshadows . . . . Nine out of ten of the Western people excuse the act. They feel the Indian is in their way . . . and they look hopefully to the day when he shall have offered the last of his race as a sacrifice to the progress of civilization.[243]

Thus, American Indians were the most desirable scapegoats, since their destruction provided the very group interest -- land and mineral wealth -- which they impeded.

By the end of 1864 and early 1865, Byers and his audience were convinced of the threat posed to the territory by the Indians. Moreover, there was a consensus regarding the proper solution to the problem. The mythic themes and "facts" traded upon by Byers had served in part so as to "facilitate and rationalize aggression without limit."[244] The symbols and themes evoked by other public elites involved in the Sand Creek controversy served similar functions.

CHAPTER IV

NOTES

[1] Robert L. Perkin, The First Hundred Years, An Informal History of Denver and the Rocky Mountain News (Garden City, New York: Doubleday & Company, 1959), pp. 154, 135. For a brief history see Douglas C. McMurtrie and Albert H. Allen, Early Printing in Colorado (Denver: A.B. Hirschfeld Press, 1935), pp. 17-45. Although the editorials in the Rocky Mountain News were mostly unsigned, Byers originated and authored the major editorial position of the News (see Perkin, p. 154). It should also be noted that the spelling and grammar which appeared in these columns were "eccentric" and do not necessarily reflect errors in transcription.

[2] Quoted in Perkin, p. 135. Byers' Journal has been published in Byron G. Hooper, Jr., Overland News (May, June, July and August, 1958).

[3] Quoted in Alfred Sorensen, The Story of Omaha (Omaha: 1920), p. 73.

[4] Quotations from this guidebook are available in LeRoy R. Hafen, ed., Pikes Peak Gold Rush Guidebooks of 1859 (Glendale, California: Arthur H. Clark, 1941), pp. 212-224.

[5] Hafen, p. 223. Byers also provided a small temperance lecture cautioning, "Brandy is intended for medicine, rainy days, and Fourth of July, and should always be used very sparingly . . . .", p. 218.

[6] Perkin, p. 15. This discussion of Byers' biography is taken from Perkin, pp. 134-140 and pp. 14-17.

[7] Perkin, pp. 140-142. A biographical sketch is printed in the Rocky Mountain News (hereafter cited as RMN), January 4, 1908. Dailey kept a journal recording his experience in the Colorado volunteers: "Journal of John L. Dailey 1864," (MS in Western History Collection, Denver Public Library).

[8] See Perkin, pp. 10, 17; and McMurtrie and Allen, pp. 19, 23.

[9] Byers helped Evans establish Denver University, was supportive of the "Arts," campaigned for a "permanent bridge" over Cherry Creek and Postal Services to Denver. See Perkin, pp. 145-164, 217, 221; and McMurtrie and Allen, p. 43.

[10] William H. Lyon argues in The Pioneer Editor in Missouri, 1808-1860 (Columbia: University of Missouri Press, 1965), pp. 163-66, that the pioneer editor was a mirror of his society, "Bound and hemmed in" by the norms of his frontier community. An editor could not become too eccentric or else his paper would fail. Robert G. Athern in The Coloradans (Albuquerque: University of New Mexico Press, 1976), pp. 45-46, argues that in the Denver area specifically, "newspapers were obliged to respond to local pressures," or be forced out of existence. Other interpretations of the relationship between the frontier editor and his audience also exist. See: Olvier Knight, "The Frontier Newspaper as a Catalyst in Social Change," Pacific Northwest Quarterly, (April, 1967), 74-81; Robert Dykstra, The Cattle Towns (New York: Knopf, 1971), pp. 380-383; Donald P. Whisenhunt, "The Frontier Newspaper: A guide to Society and Culture," Journalism Quarterly, 45 (Winter, 1968), 726-729. For a review of the literature see William H. Lyon, "The Significance of Newspapers on the American Frontier," Journal of the West, 19 (August, 1980), pp. 3-12.

[11] McMurtrie and Allen, p. 40.

[12] RMN, April 23, 1859.

[13] RMN, April 23, 1859.

[14] RMN, April 23, 1859.

[15] Byers described this "effect" in a letter to Hubert H. Bancroft in 1884. This letter is in an unpublished collection, "Byers Autobiography, His Story called 'The Newspaper Press of Colorado,' and Letters on the Sand Creek Affair," in the Western History Department of the Denver Public Library.

[16] McMurtrie and Allen, p. 34.

[17] RMN, April 23, 1859.

[18] RMN, September 10, 1859.

[19] RMN, June 18, 1859.

[20] See Perkin, "The Editor is Kidnapped," pp. 165-184.

[21] For an eyewitness account of Greeley's trip see "Henry Villard to the Leavenworth Times, June 20, 1859," in Colorado Gold Rush Contemporary Letters and Reports, 1858-1859, LeRoy R. Hafen, ed. (Glendale, California: Arthur H. Clark Company, 1941), pp. 372-373.

[22] RMN, April 23, 1861.

[23] See RMN, April 23, April 26 and June 14, 1861 for descriptions of "good" Indians. For a more negative description see RMN, September 1, 1860.

[24] RMN, August 27, 1860.

[25] RMN, September 11, 1860.

[26] RMN, May 9, 1861. See also RMN, June 18, 1860.

[27] RMN, May 22, 1861.

[28] RMN, April 18, 1860.

[29] RMN, April 18, 1860.

[30] RMN, September 5, 1861.

[31] RMN, September, 1, 1860.

[32] RMN, August 31, 1860.

[33] RMN, September 1, 1860.

[34] RMN, June 25, May 6, 1861; July 11, 12, 1862.

[35] RMN, April 23, 1861.

[36] RMN, April 24, 1861. See also May 6, 1861 edition.

[37] Perkin, p. 132.

[38] RMN, January 26, March 29, 1862.

[39] For an explanation of the difference between Byers' immediate audience and Eastern humanitarian sentiments see Robert Winston Murdock, The Reformers and the American Indian (Columbia: University of Missouri Press, 1971), pp. 85-106.

[40] Perkin, p. 204. See also Lilian B. Shields, "Relations With the Cheyennes and Arapahoes in Colorado to 1861," Colorado Magazine, 4 (August, 1927), 148-153; George Bird Grinnell, The Fighting Cheyennes (1915; rpt. Norman: University of Oklahoma Press, 1955), p. 127.

[41] RMN, September 6, 1861.

[42] Quoted in Thomas L. Karnes, William Gilpin, Western Nationalist (Austin: University of Texas Press, 1970), p. 255.

[43] Susan R. Ashley, "Reminiscences of Colorado in the Early Sixties," Colorado Magazine, 13 (November, 1936), 226; Mollie D. Sanford, Mollie: The Journal of Mollie Dorsey Sanford in Nebraska and Colorado Territories, 1857-1866, Donald F. Danker, ed., (Lincoln: University of Nebraska Press, 1959), p. 162.

[44] RMN, April 7, 1863.

[45] RMN, April 7, 1863.

[46] RMN, August 19, 1861.

[47] Grinnell, p. 128.

[48] Grinnell, p. 128.

[49] RMN, September 2, 1861.

[50] Thomas Karnes characterizes Gilpin as a "Western Nationalist" who carried a message to the American people "that the west was a glorious place in which to live and that only by exploiting that region could the nation fulfill its God-given role." p. 3.

[51] RMN, September 5, 1862.

[52] RMN, March 21, 1862.

[53] RMN, March 29, 1862.

[54] RMN, February 20, 1862.

[55] Obviously, Byers consciously argued that irresponsible reporting would negatively affect immigration. There is no evidence that such stories did affect such travel. It is not clear whether Byers was aware that he was creating a political difference, which did not exist between the News and the Herald. However, during all the periods studied, Byers consistently attacked his "competition." (Ironically, the News was on better terms with the "secesh" Mountineer than with the Herald during this early period.)

[56] Perkin, pp. 130-32.

[57] RMN, March 31, 1862.

[58] Perkin, p. 257.

[59] RMN, June 24, 1862.

[60] RMN, March 26, 1862.

[61] RMN, March 26, April 26, May 2, May 5, May 28, June 24, June 30, July 8, July 14, July 17, July 23, July 24, December 20, 1862.

[62] RMN, July 11, 1862.

[63] On March 26, April 26 and May 2nd the News reported on "Our Indian Neighbors." See RMN, July 14 and 17th 1862 for a more negative view.

[64] RMN, July 23, 1862.

[65] RMN, July 24, 1862.

[66] Grinnell, pp. 130-31.

[67] RMN, September 5, 1862; Donald J. Berthong, The Southern Cheyenne (Norman: University of Oklahoma Press, 1963), p. 159.

[68] "Governor Evans Message," RMN, July 19, 1862.

[69] RMN, June 13, 1863.

[70] RMN, September 10, 1863.

[71] RMN, August 6, 1862.

[72] The sample used was as complete as is available. Some portions of the microfilm were unreadable and not all issues of the News have survived the ravages of time. For this analysis, all the stories available from 1863 were scanned for the word "extermination" or its equivalents. These equivalents included "should be wiped out" (used once) and "the General Harney Treatment," used twice (General Harney led a punitive expedition against the Sioux in 1855 in which all Sioux -- men, women and children -- were killed. Grinnell, p. 108ff). The two positive stories were optimistic regarding the future relations with Colorado's Indians. See RMN, September 10, October 2, 1863. The latter story concerned "The Caddo Indians," who Byers later said never existed in Colorado, RMN, June 14, 1865.

[73] RMN, March 24, 1863.

[74] RMN, April 2, 1863.

[75] See: RMN, June 2, June 15, July 25, August 13, 1863.

[76] RMN, April 4, 1863.

[77] RMN, July 13, 1863.

[78] RMN, April 24, 1863.

[79] RMN, April 20, 1863.

[80] RMN, April 27, 1863.

[81] Berthong, p. 163; Grinnell, p. 131 and Stan Hoig, The Sand Creek Massacre (Norman: University of Oklahoma Press, 1961), p. 24, all agree that the Arapahoes and Cheyennes were relatively friendly during 1863. The official record also supports this claim. See Letter from Colley to Dole, September 30, 1863, "Report of the Commissioner of Indian Affairs for 1863," Report of the Secretary of the Interior, 38th Cong., 1st Sess., 1864, Doc. No 1, p. 252.

[82] "Treaty of Fort Laramie, September 17, 1851," in Wilcomb E. Washburn, The American Indian and the United States: A Documentary History (New York: Random House, 1973), IV, 2477-2480. For discussions of the treaty see: Perkin, pp. 77-79; Dee Brown, Bury My Heart at Wounded Knee: An Indian History of the American West (New York: Bantam Books, 1970), pp. 68-70; Grinnell, pp. 100-101.

[83] RMN, September 6, 1860.

[84] Francis Paul Prucha, American Indian Policy in the Formative Years: The Indian Trade and Intercourse Acts, 1790-1834 (Cambridge: Harvard University Press, 1962), p. 262.

[85] RMN, September 6, 1860.

[86] Printed in RMN, March 16, 1861.

[87] Quoted in RMN, June 13, 1863.

[88] RMN, September 22, 1863; A few months before, Governor Evans had been informed of a "secret" conference among the Cheyennes, Arapahoes and Sioux for the purpose of driving all Whites from the country. After the unsuccessful conclusion of his fall treaty efforts, the report of this apparent conspiracy was reenforced. See Hoig, pp. 303-4 and the next chapter of this study for discussion.

[89] "Evans to Dole, November 10, 1863," in The War of the Rebellion: A Compilation of the Official Records of the Union and Confederate Armies (Washington, G.P.O., 1891), Series I, Vol 24, part 4, p. 100. Hereafter this source will be cited as Rebellion Records or RR.

[90] William Unrau, "A Prelude to War," Colorado Magazine, 45 (Fall, 1964), p. 306.

[91] Janet Lecompte in "Sand Creek," Colorado Magazine, 41 (Fall, 1964), p. 320, believes that many of Byers' stories were "pure fabrication." Her conclusion is probably based upon a charge in the rival Black Hawk Daily Mining Journal, August 22, 1864. See below for further discussion of this rivalry and charge.

[92] See: RMN, September 29, 1859, March 30, 1860.

[93] A.K. McClure in Three Thousand Miles Through the Rocky Mountains (Philadelphia: J.P. Lippincott, 1869) documents this attitude throughout the frontier based upon his personal observation. See pp. 51, 66-67, 73-76, 83-87. His observations were made in 1867, after Sand Creek.

[94] Perkin, p. 258.

[95] See the next chapter for a discussion and analysis.

[96] This is not an argument that there was deliberate design behind the stories in the News or any collusion between Byers and Evans in this regard, only that such stories tended to illustrate the "nature" of Native Americans.

[97] RMN, July 14, 1864.

[98] For reports of atrocities by Colorado's Indians see RMN, April 12, 14, 15, 19, 20, May 4, July 5, 18, 19, 20, 23, August 4, 5, 1864. The August 10th edition calls for extermination. Reports of other atrocities committed by Colorado's Indians may be found in the August 11, 16, 18, 24 and 27th editions. See also September 19, 24, 27 and 28th issues, 1864. Reports of atrocities committed by non-Colorado Indians may be found in the January 8, 9, 11, April 21, 28, July 17, August 9, 27, September 9, 19, October 1, 6, 15, 17, 18, November 5 or 6 and November 29, 1864. Reports of "conspiracy" among Native Americans and Rebel agents are in the August 4th, 5th, 13th and 24th editions, 1864. Indians are related to the political concerns of the day in the August 11, 23, 24, 25, 26, 27 and 30th editions. See also September 1st, 5th, 7th, 9th and 28th for arguments linking the necessity of statehood with protection from the Indians.
For the few positive symbolizations regarding Native Americans see September 19, 24 and October 20th editions of the RMN, 1864.

[99] RMN, January 8, 9 and 11th, 1864.

[100] RMN, April 12, 1864.

[101] RMN, April 15, 1864.

[102] Exactly which Indians were to be punished was not specifically stated. Both Dunn and Downing initially were unsure regarding the identity of the "bands" they encountered. Eayre was reported, incorrectly, to have encountered Sioux. See Chapter V for a discussion; Grinnell, p. 142; Hoig, pp. 37, 43.

[103] For accounts of this encounter see: Rebellion Records, Series I, Vol 34, part 1, 883, 884-85, 887-88. For doubts regarding White claims regarding Indian depredations see Grinnell, pp. 142-143.

[104] Hoig, p. 40, Grinnell, p. 141.

[105] RR, Series I, Vol 34, part 3, 167.

[106] RR, Series I, Vol 34, part 1, 907-908.

[107] Again the White claims of deliberate Indian theft were never substantiated. Cheyenne witnesses claimed that Lean Bear was shot without provocation. Grinnell, pp. 145-146. Major T. I. McKenny's criticism of Eayre's expedition also tends to support the Indian claims. See RR, Series I, Vol 34, part 4, 402-404.

[108] Hoig, p. 53.

[109] RMN, April 14, 1864.

[110] Again, I am not arguing that Byers purposefully chose these symbols, only that the symbols could have functioned in the manner indicated. The symbol "war" was also not reflective of Native American interpretations. Robert L. Munkres, in "Indian-White Contact Before 1870: Culture Factors in Conflict," Journal of the West, 10 (July, 1971), 457, explains, "To the tribes there was no clear understanding of the distinction drawn by white man between a "battle" and a "war," nor of the relationship between the two. The imperatives of a nomadic existence rendered full-time and continuous warfare a literal impossibility" [emphasis added].

[111] For these symbols see RMN, April 19, 1864. Bruner quoted in Murray Edelman, Politics as Symbolic Action: Mass Arousal and Quiescence (Chicago: Markham, 1971), p. 53.

[112] Perkin, pp. 210-211.

[113] Reprinted in Perkin, pp. 212-220; especially see p. 213.

[114] Denver Weekly Commonwealth, May 25, 1864.

[115] Perkin, pp. 219-222. The exact nature of Byers' relationship to the Commonwealth between May 10th and June 26th is not clear. The editor of the Commonwealth was Simeon Whitley -- actually the Federal agent for the Middle Park Indian Agency. However, this "Agency" was never established and was only a ruse to enable Whitley to enter Colorado and form the Colorado Council of the Union League of America -- an organization to promote the Union cause. See Harry Kelsey, "Background to Sand Creek," Colorado Magazine, 45 (Fall, 1968), pp. 294-297. Like Byers, Whitley began working for statehood as soon as he entered the Territory. While editor of the Commonwealth, he supported editorial policies identical with those of Byers in the News. But Whitley's work has been described as "inept, erratic and often misdirected" (Kelsey, p. 296). Possibly, Governor Evans supported Byers in his purchase of the Commonwealth, recognizing Byers as the more effective campaigner. During the period between the Flood and June 26, 1864, Byers "assisted" Whitley but the exact authorship of various items in the Commonwealth is not clear. This identification is less important than the symbols used to describe the so-called Hungate Massacre which the two editors probably agreed upon.

[116] Donald J. Berthong, The Southern Cheyennes (Norman: University of Oklahoma Press, 1963), pp. 190-191; Ralph K. Andrist, The Long Death: The Last Days of the Plains Indians (London: Collier Books, 1964), pp. 80-81.

[117] Denver Commonwealth, June 15, 1864.

[118] Quoted in Hoig, p. 58.

[119] Denver Commonwealth, June 15, 1864.

[120] Edelman, p. 54.

[121] Susan Riley Ashley, "Reminiscences of Colorado," p. 75; RR, Series I, Vol 34, part 4, 449.

[122] See various reports in Rebellion Records, Series I, Vol 34, parts 1-4. Additionally see Janet Lecompte's discussion, 318-319.

[123] RMN, July 5, 1864; Historians have since concluded that Roman Nose and a small band of Northern Arapahoes were responsible for the Hungate tragedy. See: Lecompte, p. 318; Lonnie J. White, "From Bloodless to Bloody: The Third Colorado Cavalry and the Sand Creek Massacre," Journal of the West, 6 (October, 1967), p. 542; Grinnell, p. 150, Berthong, pp. 190-191; Hoig, p. 59. There was also evidence of this blame from contemporary records. For military reports see Rebellion Records, Series I, Vol 34, part 4, pp. 320-21, 330, 354-55, 461; Black Hawk Daily Mining Journal, June 15, 1864.

[124] There is no reference to the "Hungate Scalps" in correspondence contained in the Rebellion Records.

[125] Edelman, p. 80.

[126] Rebellion Records, Series I, Vol 41, part 1, 964.

[127] See United States Congress, Senate, "Sand Creek Massacre," Report of the Secretary of War, Senate Executive Document 26, 39th Congress, 2d sess. (Washington, G.P.O., 1867), p. 126; Lecompte, p. 319, Hoig, p. 80.

[128] Hoig, pp. 80-81.

[129] RMN, July 17, 18, 19, 20, 23, 1864.

[130] RMN, July 18, 1864.

[131] RMN, July 23, 20, 1864.

[132] RMN, July 23, 1864.

[133] Lecompte, p. 320.

[134] White, pp. 545-546; RMN, August 1, 1864.

[135] Black Hawk Daily Mining Journal, August 22, 1864; Lecompte, pp. 320-321.

[136] Lecompte, p. 321.

137 RMN, July 14, 1864.

138 RMN, June 16, 1864.

139 RMN, June 14, 1864.

140 RMN, July 29, 1864.

141 Hoig, pp. 64-65; Perkin, pp. 250-252.

142 RMN, August 4, 1864.

143 RMN, August 4, 1864.

144 See RMN, August 5, 23, 24, 1864 and discussion below.

145 See Hoig, pp. 84-85; Perkin, pp. 250-252.

146 RMN, August 10, 1864.

147 See Hoig, pp. 85-90; Berthong; pp. 201-204; Grinnell, p. 155-157 and Lecompte, pp. 321-322.

148 Grinnell, p. 204; Hoig, pp. 91-92. See correspondence in Rebellion Records, Series I, Vol 41, part 2, pp. 369, 483, 613-614.

149 Berthong, pp. 205-206.

150 Grinnell, pp. 156-157; RMN, August 10, 1864.

151 Lecompte, p. 322; Also see correspondence in U.S. Congress, House, "Report of the Commissioner of Indians Affairs for 1864," Report of the Secretary of the Interior, 38th Cong., 2nd sess., 1865, Doc. No. 1, pp. 380-82.

152 RMN, August 10, 1864.

153 The general nature of the "uprising" in the territory did not become obvious until the following week. RMN, August 10, 1864.

154 See Report of the Secretary of War, pp. 15, 52, 112 for testimony regarding the profitability of killing Indians.

[155] Compare Byers' statements of October, 1860, written in support of Beckwourth's position with these statements of August 10, 1864.

[156] RMN, August 11, 1864.

[157] RMN, August 13, 1864.

[158] Quoted in White, p. 555.

[159] RMN, August 13, 1864. Also see the August 5th, 23rd and 24th editions.

[160] RMN, August 18, 1864.

[161] Edelman, p. 82, indicates this as one technique of rhetorical evocation used by public officials.

[162] RMN, August 26, 1864.

[163] Lecompte, p. 321; Berthong, p. 205; Grinnell, p. 157.

[164] Report, Secretary of the Interior, 1864, p. 363; Grinnell, p. 157; Rebellion Records, Series I, Vol 41, part 2, pp. 843, 844-45, 864-65; Berthong writes that only "small parties" of warriors appeared, (p. 205).

[165] RMN, August 24, 1864. After the election Byers and the News agreed that the Utes were friendly and that a peace treaty with the Cheyennes and Arapahoes was desirable. RMN, September 19, 28, 1864.

[166] The actual number of stories concerning Indians in the RMN peaked during August and September, clustering in late August and early September with 20 total Indian stories appearing in August and 13 in September. In August, 10 of these stories were concerned with actual or perceived depredations (including conspiracies) and only two such stories appeared in September. The other ten stories in August concerned political themes with five strictly political stories recorded in early September.

[167] RMN, August 11, 1864.

[168] RMN, August 11, 23, 26, 30, 1864.

[169] RMN, August 24, 1864.

[170] Perhaps Byers had been inspired by Tom Gibson's old, defunct Herald, which had circulated a similar lie regarding Byers in 1863. Perkin, p. 133; RMN, August 30, 1864.

[171] RMN, August 25, 1864.

[172] The paper stock of the News was shipped in from the East. With travel and supplies cut off, Byers compensated by reducing the size of the paper, limiting the runs and sometimes printing on scrap paper. Perkin, pp. 266-267.

[173] RMN, September 1, 1864.

[174] Carl Ubbelohde, Maxine Benson, and Duane A. Smith, A Colorado History, 3rd ed. (Boulder, Colorado: Pruett Publishing Co., 1972), pp. 134-35.

[175] RMN, August 27, 1864.

[176] RMN, August 30, 1864.

[177] RMN, September 7, 1864.

[178] RMN, August 30, 1864.

[179] RMN, August 30, 1864; Also see September 7th issue.

[180] RMN, September 5, 1864.

[181] RMN, September 7, 1864.

[182] RMN, August 30, 1864.

[183] The final vote was 1,520 for the Constitution to 4,676 against. Ubbelohde et al., p. 135.

[184] Ubbelohde, pp. 133-34.

[185] Ubbelohde, pp. 134-35.

[186] Byers did not "admit" defeat until November 4. RMN, November 4, 1864.

[187] RMN, November 29, 1864.

[188] RMN, September 19, 1864.

[189] RMN, September 24, 1864.

[190] White, pp. 546-548. Controversy surrounds this "Camp Weld Council" and Chivington's and Evans' remarks there. See the next chapter for an analysis.

[191] RMN, September 24, 27, 1864.

[192] RMN, September 28, 1864.

[193] RMN, September 24, 29 and October 20, 1864.

[194] Wynkoop was relieved because he bypassed regular Army channels in taking his "peace party" to Denver; he should have proceeded through his commanding officer in the Department of Kansas. White, p. 548. There is also controversy over the demeanor of the Cheyennes and Arapahoes who "came in" to Fort Lyon with Wynkoop testifying that they were non-hostile and that the Indians believed the Camp Weld Council had established peace with the Whites. Anthony argued for the opposite conclusion. See the next chapter for analysis.

[195] RMN, October 1, 1864.

[196] RMN, October 6, 15, 18, November 6, 28, 29, 1864.

[197] Black Hawk Daily Mining Journal, November 28, 1864.

[198] RMN, November 30, 1864.

[199] Officers at Fort Lyon related that the arrival of Chivington and his troops took them totally by surprise. Nor did Chivington notify General Curtis of his plan. White, p. 558.

[200] RMN, December 7, 1864.

[201] RMN, December 8, 1864; In this report, Chivington claimed to have marched 300 miles, the last 40 miles in one night. He claimed to have attacked a hostile Cheyenne village of 900 to 1,000 warriors and to have killed 400 to 500 Indians, including Black Kettle and Left Hand. A White man's scalp "not more

than three days old," was also reported found. Most of this report is subject to controversy, particularly as to the size of the village and the number and sex and age of the Indians killed. See chapter six for discussion.

[202] RMN, December 8, 1864.

[203] RMN, December 8, 12, 13, 17, 1864.

[204] RMN, December 17, 1864.

[205] RMN, December 17, 1864.

[206] At various times Byers argued that other interpretations of the event slandered Evans and Chivington (RMN, December 30, 1864, September 4, 1865, September 21, 1864) caused increased Indian outrages (October 26, 1865) and was part of a "conspiracy" to keep Colorado out of the Union (November 6, 1865, April 6, 1866, May 14, 1866, May 24, 1866). As late as 1880 he was still defending Sand Creek to the Eastern audience (New York Daily Tribune, February 5, 6, 22, 1880).

[207] RMN, December 29, 1864.

[208] RMN, December 30, 1864.

[209] John Chivington, "Speech to the Pioneer's Club," in Alice Polk Hill, Tales of the Colorado Pioneers (Denver: Pierson and Gardner, 1884), pp. 91-92; RMN, December 27, 1864.

[210] RMN, December 12, 1864.

[211] RMN, December 22, 1864.

[212] RMN, December 30, 1864.

[213] U.S. Congress, Senate, "Massacre of Cheyenne Indians," Report of the Jonit Committee on the Conduct of the War, 39th Cong., 2d Sess. (Washington: G.P.O., 1864), I-VI.

[214] Edgar C. McMechen, Life of Governor Evans (Denver: Wahlgreen Publishing Co., 1924), pp. 139ff.

[215] RMN, June 24, 1864. Only statements consistent with Chivington's interpretation were printed in this "Synopsis of the Sand Creek Investigation."

[216] RMN, July 19, August 19, 1865.

[217] "Letter of Senator Doolittle to Mrs. L.F.S. Foster, March 7, 1881, Notes and Documents," New Mexico Historical Review, 26 (April, 1951), 156-57.

[218] RMN, July 24, 1865.

[219] Kenneth Burke, "The Rhetorical Situation," Communication: Ethical and Moral Issues, ed. Lee Thayer (New York: Gordon and Beach Science Pub., 1973), pp. 268-69.

[220] Edelman, p. 78.

[221] Richard L. Merritt, Symbols of American Community, 1735-1775 (New Haven: Yale University Press, 1966), p. 27.

[222] This is an especially interesting and important "observation." It was recorded by Second Lt. Harry Richmond of the Third Colorado Cavalry, a participant at Sand Creek, after that encounter and in reaction to White criticism of White participation in the affair. At least the observation indicates that he perceived that "extermination" was the solution favored by the majority. It also reinforces Coffin's statements referred to in Chapter Two. "Letter of Harry Richmond, The 'Chivington Massacre,' the other side of the question," RMN, May 29, 1865. Additionally, historians appear to agree that the "Hungate Massacre" brought about a consensus of the proper "solution" to the Indian problem. See: White, p. 541; Andrist, p. 80; Lecompte, p. 319, Grinnell, p. 151; Elmer R. Burkey, "The Site of the Murder of the Hungate Family by Indians," in 1864," Colorado Magazine, 12 (July, 1935), p. 139.

[223] RMN, July 24, 1865.

[224] Ashley, p. 72; Colin B. Goodykoontz, "Colorado As Seen By a Home Missionary, 1863-1868," Colorado Magazine, 12 (March, 1935), 65-66.

[225] Burkey implies this conclusion, p. 139, as does Grinnell, p. 150.

[226] Thomas Dye in Understanding Public Policy (Englewood Cliffs, N.J., Prentice-Hall, 1972), pp. 74-75 implies that media reporting of public acts of violence can increase the community's reactions to that violence -- perhaps with more drastic violence.

[227] "Evans to W.P. Dole, June 14, 1864," Indian Affairs Letter Books, John Evans Collection, State Historical Society of Colorado. A reproduction of this telegram was also printed in the August 25, 1864 edition of the RMN; "Evans to E.M. Stanton, June 14, 1864," Rebellion Records, Series 1, Vol 34, part 4, 305; RMN, July 24, 1865.

[228] Reply of Governor Evans of the Territory of Colorado to That Part of the Report of "The Committee on the Conduct of the War," headed "Massacre of Cheyenne Indians," Executive Department and Superintendency of Indian Affairs, Colorado Territory, Denver, August 6, 1865, xvii; John Chivington, "Speech Given to the Pioneer Meeting," in Hill, p. 91; RMN, December 30, 1864.

[229] Edelman, p. 115.

[230] Quoted in Perkin, p. 271. The testimonies of Jim Beckwourth, Lt. James Gannon and A.J. Gill in the Report on the Conduct of the War, pp. 67, 110, 179, generally support that Chivington uttered these words or a message very similar. After the "Hungate Massacre" Chivington ordered at least one member of his command not to "encumber" himself "with prisoner Indians." Rebellion Records, Series I, Vol 34, page 4, 330.

[231] Edelman, p. 78.

[232] Morse H. Coffin, The Battle of Sand Creek (Waco, Tex: W.M. Morrison, 1965), pp. 9-10. For Chivington and Evans' statements in this regard, see Chapter five and six.

[233] RMN, April 4, 1863.

[234] In the spring of 1865, the Union Administration Party, the dominant political party in Colorado at this time approved resolutions calling for "more Sand Creek battles." In the subsequent election, Union

Administration Candidates generally were successful. White, p. 575; Also see contemporary accounts in the RMN, November 27, 30, December 20, 1865.

[235] Roger Daniels and Harry H.L. Kitano, American Racism: Exploration of the Nature of Prejudice (Englewood Cliffs, N.J.; Prentice-Hall, 1970), pp. 11, 13.

[236] Edelman implies this relationship between perceived threat and proposed solution, pp. 162-63.

[237] See the last chapter for an analysis.

[238] Edelman explains this relationship between the attachment to the myth and attempts to verify reality, p. 79.

[239] Perkin, p. 262.

[240] RMN, July 24, 1865.

[241] Edelman, p. 98.

[242] Edelman, p. 128.

[243] McClure, p. 51.

[244] Edelman, p. 114.

MAP
COLORADO TERRITORY

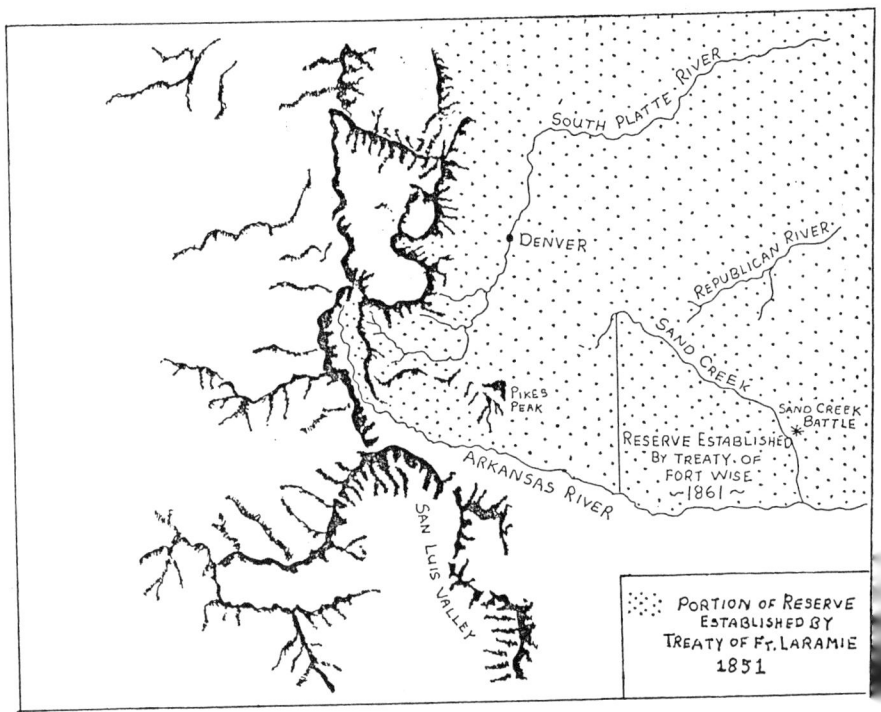

CHAPTER V

GOVERNOR JOHN EVANS: ELITE SYMBOLS OF NATIVE
AMERICANS AND THE LEGITIMATION OF EXTERMINATION

Background

John Evans was not born to the elite, but was a self-made man, eventually achieving personal and financial success in two of his three careers.[1] Evans was born into a devout Quaker family on March 9, 1814. His biographer, Edgar Carlisle McMechan, has credited Evans' mother Rachel with being the "overshadowing" influence on the young Quaker's early life. Apparently Evans, the oldest of eleven children, was not influenced to a great extent by his father, a businessman. Instead his mother, his paternal grandmother and his Quaker religion molded his early creative talents in the direction of social service.[2] McMechan believes that the "principle of probity, temperance and toleration" which Evans acquired in his youth, "guided him throughout his life."[3] Yet, there is an air of hard ambition surrounding the many apparently altruistic activities in which Evans engaged. Almost all of his concerns were tremendously successful financially. Whatever his goal, he set about it as deliberately as possible, expecting success and reluctant to admit defeat. He was most successful as a medical doctor and financier. He never achieved all of the goals he set for himself in his "political career."[4]

After his early education at the "Academy" in Richmond, Indiana, he attended several small boarding schools around Philadelphia. After graduation, and against his parents' wishes, he decided to attend medical school and did so at his own expense. By 1841, he had established a successful medical practice in Attica, Indiana, and married his first wife. While living in Attica, he was influenced greatly by Matthew Simpson, the founder and first president of De Pauw University. Bishop Simpson soon became a close friend and through Simpson's influence, both Evans and his wife were converted from Quakerism to Methodism.[5] Within two years Evans had established himself as "one of the most influential citizens in that section of the country." He was instrumental in founding and establishing the State Hospital for the insane in Indiana. Initially he served on the board of directors, but in 1845 he moved to Indianapolis to act as superintendent of that hospital. Thereafter his interest shifted to the Chicago area as a center for science, culture and commerce. At first he concentrated his energies at a distance, remaining at home in Indianapolis while serving as the first editor of the Northwestern Medical and Surgical Journal. He also helped to found Mercy Hospital and Rush Medical School in Chicago and was a visiting professor at Rush in the late 1840's. As a leader in the medical profession, he developed the prototypes of surgical instruments still in use today and stimulated a medical controversy by publishing a paper in which he stated that cholera was a communicable disease spread by interpersonal contact. It was ten years before the medical profession as a whole would arrive at the same conclusion. Eventually Evans moved his family to Chicago where his interests shifted to investments and politics. He amassed his fortune based upon wise investments in real estate while he also dabbled in the newly emerging railroad industry in Chicago.[6] Soon, he became active in the young "Republican" party in Chicago -- still a minor local party -- comprised of abolitionists as well as "know nothing" elements. In 1856 he sought nomination for Congress on the Republican ticket but apparently was defeated because of disagreement with the know nothings. He was a "prominent speaker" at both the Illinois State Convention and the National Convention of the newly founded Republican Party in 1859.[7]

Evans' political beliefs bore the influence of his Quaker background -- especially regarding the issue of slavery. In 1856 he said that he believed "it to be the duty of the general government in all cases where it has the authority over the subject to exercise its positive influence in favor of freedom and against slavery." By 1861 he was advocating emancipation of all slaves and their enrollment in the Union Army.[8] His active service for the Republican Party in 1860 apparently brought every vote in favor of Lincoln from the Indiana delegation. He was rewarded shortly after Lincoln's inauguration with an offer of the Governorship of Washington Territory which he declined. He believed that Washington was too far from his Chicago business interests. However, when he was offered the Governorship of Colorado Territory in the spring of 1862, he accepted, hoping that the Colorado climate would improve his daughter's health.[9]

During his Chicago years, Evans also became a close friend and business partner of Orrington Lunt who worked with Evans to establish a "University of Chicago" under the patronage of the Methodist Episcopal Church. Evans himself purchased the site of the University, later named Evanston. McMechan writes that it was Evans' wise financial advice and considerable personal donations that determined Northwestern University's financial stability in its early years.[10]

John Evans arrived in Denver, Colorado Territory, on May 18, 1862. While a young physician in Attica, Indiana, he had indicated the intended goals of his life. He wanted, he declared, "to build a city, found a college, become governor of one of the states of the Union, go to the U.S. Senate, amass a fortune and make himself famous." By May of 1862, he had achieved all of these intentions except going to the U.S. Senate. He could now pursue this goal while Governor of Colorado Territory and Superintendent of Indian Affairs of that Territory.[11]

However, Evans' dual role as Governor and Superintendent complicated his quest for an elected political career. As Governor, he was responsible for protecting and representing the interests of the Territory's White population; as Indian Superintendent, he was responsible for protecting Indian rights and providing for their general welfare. The White Colorado population regarded Indians as obstructing civilization and the White group interest -- land and mineral wealth. The Indians believed the Whites to be interlopers on constitutionally promised Indian land. Thus, Evans' dual roles were often irreconcilable and the solutions to the problems of policy he faced contradictory.[12]

Evans sent messages regarding his Indian charges to two principal audiences: a White audience comprised of governmental and military authorities and White civilians and a Native American audience made up of the Territorial tribes. While Evans sought consciously to serve both his White and Indian audiences, his symbolizations of his Native charges tended to function so as to serve and to reflect the interests and fears of the White Coloradan population.

White Audience

Evans to Government Agencies

In his early reports to Commissioner of Indian Affairs Dole, Evans stressed the benefits of a civilization policy -- of inculcating his Indian charges with White values. Evans believed that such a policy would bring about improved relations between Whites and Native Americans in Colorado. He especially emphasized the importance of teaching the Indians the benefits of owning private property. At the same time he pressured the Commissioner to give him the authority to "concentrate" the Arapahoes and Cheyennes on a reservation in southeastern Colorado. Additionally (and contrary to the assumptions of his civilization policy), Evans communicated to the War Department messages requesting increased authority over military matters in Colorado. His primary means of persuasion in this regard were messages filled with the symbols of Indian conspiracy. During this time Evans also called the citizens of Colorado to arms against the hostile Indians. Ultimately Evans abandoned his role as Superintendent of Indian Affairs and from November of 1863 through the Summer and Fall of 1864 Evans communicated only the key symbols of the conspiracy myth.

Initially Evans appeared to share the optimism expressed by Byers and the News regarding the likelihood of a negotiated settlement with the Indian tribes for land already occupied by the Whites.[13] Probably his Quaker background did provide him with "enlightened" beliefs regarding the potential of all men. Evans wrote, regarding the Utes, one of Colorado's mountain Indian tribes:

> It was part of my policy to try to civilize them [the Indians], but I decided that it is impossible to civilize a man until you show him how he can obtain a subsistence . . . I took the appropriations for these tribes and bought an

immense herd of sheep . . . gave a certain number of sheep and cattle to each family, instructing them not to kill the animals, but to save the cows for the milk they would give and the sheep for the wool . . . .[14]

Evans wrote to Commissioner Dole regarding some land set aside by the Treaty of Fort Wise for the Arapahoes and Cheyennes: "[the land] is a choice grazing country . . . [the Cheyennes and Arapahoes can] readily learn to take care of cattle and sheep. They keep large droves of ponies in good condition. By this means the Indians of the Plains may all readily be taught to procure a livelihood for themselves." He also urged the use of boarding schools as a method of "civilizing" the Cheyennes and Arapahoes. By removing Indian children from the influence of their parents, Evans concluded, the "wild influence of their aboriginal state" could be suspended.[15]

Later, while attempting to dissociate himself from events at Sand Creek, Evans characterized his Indian policy as "humane." He had hoped, he said, "to get everybody to live together without fighting."[16] But soon after his arrival in Denver, Evans began sending messages which could account for all eventualities. He favored concentrating the Indians in an area out of the way of the Whites. Manifestly he argued that this policy would permit the Indians to begin appreciating the value of property and agriculture and allow for education. However, such removal also could solve land boundary questions, allow for White advancement and assure Evans continued support from his White audience.

The situation Evans faced upon his arrival in Denver in 1862 had brought immediate tension between his two roles. The 1861 Treaty of Fort Wise was an attempt by Whites to supplant the provisions of the Fort Laramie treaty of 1851. The provisions of the latter treaty had provided the Cheyennes and the Arapahoes all the land east of the Rockies between the North Platte and Arkansas Rivers. Additionally the treaty reassured those Indians that White emigrants would only pass through this Indian land and not remain. The treaty also provided compensation to the Indians for grass, timber and game destroyed by the emigrants.[17] With the discovery of gold in Colorado, arrival of the White "fifty-niners" and establishment

223

of illegal Jefferson Territory, pressure mounted for a new treaty. The Treaty of 1861 provided that the Cheyennes and Arapahoes would cede all of the Fort Laramie treaty lands, except for a small reservation in southeast Colorado near the junction of the Arkansas River and Sand Creek. However, only the peace chiefs of the Southern Cheyennes and Arapahoes signed the treaty. But the more militant "Dog Soldiers" nominally represented by the chiefs refused to recognize the treaty. Another division of the Cheyennes, the "Platte bands" also did not recognize it.[18]

Evans believed that somehow the Fort Wise Treaty had to be extended to all Cheyennes and Arapahoes. As he expressed the problem to Commissioner Dole, "If this is not done the mining territory and in fact all the settled portion of Colorado are subject to Indian title and by our Organic Act not under the Territorial Government at all. Our laws are null and we are in anarchy [emphasis added]."[19] Thus, as Indian Superintendent, Evans was aware of the Indians' legal land rights. Moreover, as Governor he recognized that all White accomplishments in Colorado were at risk if the Treaty of 1861 was not extended (this included eventual statehood -- a condition for his desired Senate seat). Evans' language in this letter tended to favor his role as Governor. In the same letter he urged Dole to let him extend the treaty provisions without the formal acceptance of the nonsignatory Indians. Evans implied that the non-signing Arapahoes and Cheyennes, "poor wanderers over a country too large for them to traverse in a year," would quietly accept the loss of their hunting lands. Reference to the militant "Dog Soldiers" was not made in this message.[20]

Initially, Dole was not persuaded by Evans' appeal. S.E. Browne, U.S. Attorney in Colorado had written to Dole that Federal laws for the protection of Indians' land rights were being "hamstrung."[21] Therefore Dole denied Evans' request as moving too quickly toward a policy of "concentration" and accepted Browne's ruling that "the area north of the South Platte the site of the mines and the territorial capital at Golden City was off limits to settlers."[22] White reaction within the Territory was immediate and vocal and Dole was forced to reconsider. Evans, with the entire support of the Territory behind him, warned

Dole that the decision had incited the miners and settlers and that the "dangers of an Indian War" were now imminent.[23]

Apparently Dole realized that implicit in Evans' message regarding the "danger of an Indian War" was a conflict initiated by disgruntled miners who would volunteer to solve the boundary dispute in their own expedient way. He also received pressure from Territorial officials. Probably fearing that he would be held responsible for any loss of life in Colorado Territory, Dole reversed himself.[24] He wrote to Evans that "the treaty of 1861 ceded by its express terms all lands not owned, possessed or claimed by the Cheyennes and Arapahoes, wherever situated." The $450,000 provided to the Indians over a period of fifteen years, Dole rationalized, was too large for the few Indians formally included under the treaty. Therefore, Dole found that "the treaty was in reality meant for all, and you must go ahead with a council and get the rest to agree to the Treaty of 1861."[25] Since Evans had communicated to Dole the difficulty of accomplishing such a council, Dole extended to Evans the authority to "adopt such a policy as may be found expedient." Thus, Dole's reversal allowed for an increase in Evans' power over the Indian affairs in the Territory. If Evans' attempts to gain the acquiescence of non-signatory Cheyennes and Arapahoes to the Treaty failed, he could utilize such measures as he found to be expedient.[26]

After Dole's reversal, Evans sought the ratification of the Treaty of 1861. Throughout the spring, summer and fall of 1863, he sent his Indian agents and scouts in search of recalcitrant bands of Cheyennes and Arapahoes in an attempt to gather the Indians together to persuade them of the benefits of the treaty. In the spring, he also began corresponding with the War Department about his Indian charges.

After an encounter with a small Cheyenne band in March of 1863, Lieutenant Hawkins of the Colorado First reported to Evans that "the Indians talk very bitterly of the whites -- say they have stolen their ponies and abused their women, taken their hunting grounds and that they expected they would have to fight for their rights."[27]

Apparently Evans was impressed by this report and his communications with the War Department that spring reflect a more ominous view than the view he had expressed to Dole. As Evans reported it to General Schofield, Commander, Department of Missouri,

> I sent a special messenger to Washington in reference to Indian difficulties, and should have an answer soon. Indians have given notice we must fight or leave. Have just had report of a big secret conference between Sioux, Arapahoes and Cheyennes, about 100 miles north. May want our forces strengthened in a few days . . .[28]

Thus Evans generalized the views of one small and disgruntled band of Cheyennes. Moreover, he hinted at the beginnings of a conspiracy -- "a secret conference" -- which was not so secret that he did not know about it. By these words he did not overtly declare Colorado tribes to be "at war" or hostile, but the potential for hostilities is clearly allowed for in his mention of the possible request for more forces. He lacked any specific evidence (other than Hawkins' report) of general Indian hostility. But he sought to gather and persuade the non-signatory Cheyennes and probably wished to solve the boundary question through persuasion. However, if the Indians succumbed to their natural conspiratorial nature, military force was another "expedient" which could be utilized.[29]

Although Evans tried various modes of persuasion, his attempts to convince the Dog Soldiers and the Platte River Bands of the desirability of the 1861 Treaty were met with consistent frustration. A group of Cheyennes, Arapahoes and Ute chiefs were sent to visit the Great Father in Washington so they might be impressed with the power of the United States.[30] He sent messages to the Indian participants in the "big, secret conference" that they risked "extermination" if they made war upon the Whites.[31] He sent his agents, Elbridge Gerry, S.J. Colley and John Smith to gather various groups of Cheyennes and Arapahoes for a great conference.[32] However, whether because of failure by his agents or reluctance of the Indians to become involved in another Treaty session, Evans did not even succeed in gathering the Indians together. Evans himself met only with Roman Nose, the leader of a small party of Arapahoes. Roman Nose claimed to be a

226

"friend" but steadfastly refused to sign the Treaty.[33] Moreover, by the fall, several of the Indian chiefs who had consented initially to the Treaty now rejected it as a "swindle" and denied that they had ever signed it.[34]

Although unsuccessful in these persuasive attempts, in October of 1863 Evans was writing confidently that hostility on the part of the Plains tribes was not expected.[35] Reports from his agents also confirmed that general hostility was not a problem.[36] However, less than a month later, Evans began writing of a "league" between the Arapahoes, Cheyennes, Sioux and Kiowas for the purpose of making war on the Whites in the spring.[37] He had received "evidence" confirming this league as the outcome of the "big, secret conference" he had informed General Schofield about. The evidence came to Evans in the form of a letter from one Robert North. North, a White man, had been living among the Arapahoes with an Arapahoe wife. Although North could neither read nor write, apparently he had dictated a letter which was then brought to Evans. Evans forwarded a copy of the letter to both Dole and Secretary of War Stanton. As North related the facts:

> Having recovered an Arapaho prisoner, a squaw, from the Utes, I obtained the confidence of the Indians completely. I have lived with them from a boy, and my wife is an Arapaho. In honor of my exploit in recovering the prisoner the Indians recently gave me a 'big medicine dance' about 55 miles below Fort Lyon, on the Arkansas River, at which the leading chiefs and warriors of several of the tribes of the plains met. The Comanches, Apaches, Kiowas, the northern band of Arapahos, and all of the Cheyennes with the Sioux, have pledged one another to go to war with the whites as soon as they can procure ammunition in the spring. I heard them discuss the matter often and the few of them who opposed it were forced to be quiet and were really in danger of the loss of their lives.[38]

Evans wrote to Dole that he was "fully satisfied" with the "truthfulness" of North's information and promised "to ferret out any step in progress of this foul conspiracy among these poor, degraded wretches."[39]

Evans was to refer to this "conspiracy" throughout his correspondence of the following year and in his testimony and defense of his role in events leading to Sand Creek.

It is somewhat surprising that Evans accepted North's statement without question or investigation. North seems to have been an unsavory character. His loyalty to the Whites especially should have suspect since he assisted later in the massacre of 80 soldiers near Fort Phil Kearney in 1866 and was eventually hanged by a group of White vigilantes for his reported crimes against the Whites. However, North's character was not obvious in 1863. Additionally, such a negative judgment would have been difficult since North's name was not circulated with the letter.[40] Perhaps with the final rejection of his Treaty efforts by Roman Nose on November 9, 1863, Evans was susceptible to additional information which reenforced his message in May to General Schofield.[41] This is not to assert that North's statement caused Evans immediately to abandon his attempts to solve the land problem by Treaty.

In December, Evans traveled to Washington to seek the consent of President Lincoln and Commissioner Dole to negotiate an entirely new Treaty with the Cheyennes and Arapahoes. One block in negotiations had been the undesirable nature of land contained in the proposed Arkansas River/Sand Creek Reservation. Therefore Evans sought permission to procure additional land better suited to the Indians' need. Apparently he was not granted this request since no reference to it is made in later correspondence.[42]

Evans also sought increased military protection for the Colorado population. Prior to his arrival in Washington, he had sent a message to Secretary of War Stanton requesting this increase.[43] Evans argued that the alliance described in North's message "taken in connection with the extensive depredations recently committed on the settlers of Colorado" justified further strengthening of Colorado's defenses. The extensive depredations referred to by Evans consisted of the theft of horses from Mr. Van Wormer. No White deaths or injuries had been reported.[44] Evans also requested that the Commander of the district be given the authority to call out the militia of Colorado "in case of a formidable combination of hostile tribes as

228

is foreshadowed in the papers referred to." Evans was rightly concerned regarding the availability of military forces in Colorado since only abut 300 soldiers could have been mustered if needed. Without authority to call out the militia Evans feared that

> An alliance of several thousand warriors beginning on the sparse settlements at various points along our extended frontier, as these wild savages propose to do, might sweep off our settlers by thousands and devastate a large part of our settlements before relief could be provided by your orders . . .[45]

In this letter, Evans provided symbolization of "several thousand warriors" plotting to strike at "various points" along the frontier. Interestingly, even the few details provided by Evans in this message bear a resemblance to a "plot" which would not be enacted and discovered until the next August. However, by the time of its "discovery" Evans would have already written on several occasions of the threat of "simultaneous attack" upon "various points"[46] of the frontier by thousands of savage Indians. Perhaps Evans was remarkably astute regarding Indian methods.[47] It is more likely that events throughout 1864 were interpreted by Evans as fulfillment of his previous symbolizations.[48]

On this occasion Stanton and Lincoln were unmoved by Evans' requests.[49] When Evans returned to Colorado, he had no permission to negotiate another Treaty and no increased authority to raise a militia. He had received promise of some carbines for use by the soldiers in Colorado. In spite of the failure of this initial message, his subsequent letters to the military commander of Colorado Territory and the War Department followed a similar pattern. This pattern included: references to Indian conspiracy, exaggerated claims of Indian depredations and dire predictions if his requests for more troops were not granted.

In the months immediately following, a severe Colorado winter restricted Indian-White contacts. Evans had no reason to write for military aid until the spring of 1864. In the meantime, General Schofield was replaced by Major-General S.R. Curtis, providing Evans with a new audience for his requests in the spring and summer of 1864.[50]

On April 11, 1864, Evans began his correspondence with Curtis. Evans enclosed copies of North's statement "For fear the papers referred to . . . may not have come to your notice." Evans decried the "indifference" his previous correspondence had received. Claiming the reports were "well authenticated" Evans cited "recent events" as a "confirmation" of the "alliance." The "recent events" were reports of cattle theft attributed to the Cheyennes. Although the actual thefts were never substantiated, Evans declared that the information "threw doubts" upon the "peaceable dispositions" of the Indians. He pledged to Curtis to keep him informed with "authentic accounts of the situation."[51] On April 26, 1864, Evans followed up with his first "authentic account."

Again he referred to his letter of the previous fall. Evans wrote:

> I have now to inform you that in pursuance of the plans then divulged to me through spies, they have commenced by the robbing of settlers and stealing of stock in large quantities, and attacking soldiers sent out for their recovery. I am confident that those powerful tribes are allied . . . . Unless supported from the east of the plains, we will have difficulty in protecting settlements and punishing depredations.[52]

A professional soldier, Curtis probably did not find Evans' unsigned statement from North and his vague reference to "spies" to serve for the facts expected in military correspondence. The General's own correspondence illustrates that he was familiar with the military "facts" of the events referred to by Evans.[53] However, Curtis made no reference to any "alliance" in his various replies to Evans. He believed that Governor Evans' problems with the Indians were solvable through the organizaton of a local militia and "kindness" expressed by the Whites toward Indians.[54]

By the end of May, Evans' messages to Curtis had become longer and filled with more emotional appeals. Yet, most of the arguments made were repeats of previous information sent to Curtis. Evans utilized more ink and paper vindicating his conspiracy explanation of events that spring, than he did requesting more federal troops. In his letter of May 28, again he enclosed copies of North's statement and reexplained the "alliance." Perhaps Evans hoped that Curtis had not acknowledged the "alliance" only because he had not received or fully read all of Evans' previous requests. Evans wrote that he was reluctant to send forward (to the Eastern front) any more Colorado troops. He complained that "Now we have but half the troops we then had [in early April] and are at war with a powerful combination of Indian tribes, who are pledged to sustain each other and drive the white people from the country . . . ."[55] Evans argued that a militia was not serviceable for the defense of sparse settlements "scattered along streams in single tiers of houses, from 2 to 4 miles apart for hundred of miles . . . ." He referred to a large force of "hostile" Indians located vaguely on the headwaters of the Republican River. Moreover, he defended his earlier letters:

> The depredations have commenced <u>precisely as foretold in my communication to the department last fall</u> . . . all of the Cheyennes a most warlike and powerful tribe, with the Kiowas and Comanches, are allied and now carrying out their hellish purposes according to their agreement [emphasis added].[56]

Thus, Evans declared the Cheyennes hostile and the uprising general, although events had not yet justified this declaration.[57] He concluded this message imploring Curtis "in the name of humanity" not to remove any more troops. Evans continued his hyperbole a few days later, warning that it would be "destruction and death" to Colorado if Curtis did not see to the protection of Colorado's lines of communication with the East.[58] Curtis responded tersely, ". . . you must act on your own authority and discretion in calling out militia. I hope you will do so and allow the Federal troops to come forward soon."[59] Again Curtis made no reference to the alliance claimed by Evans.

Reports of the Hungate tragedy became available on June 11th. On the basis of that event, Evans appealed directly to Commissioner Dole and Secretary of War Stanton. He wrote to Dole that

> Extensive Indian murders, burning houses &c. on Box Elder Creek, twenty-five miles east reliably reported. The war I reported last fall begun in earnest. Spies report large numbers in alliance. Please ask War Department to strengthen our defenses, and also to authorize by telegraph to call out militia in United States service.
> Portion of Cheyennes, Arapahos, Sioux, Kiowas and Camanche Indians friendly. To keep them so it is necessary to collect them at agencies or other places, and feed them. Shall I order this done immediately?$_{60}$

To Stanton, Evans "reported":

> Indian hostilities on our settlements commenced, as per information given you last fall. One settlement devastated 25 miles east of here; murdered and scalped bodies brought in today. Our troops near all gone. Can furnish 100-days men, if authorized to do so, to fight Indians. Militia cannot be made useful unless in the U.S. Service to cooperate with troops. Shall I call a regiment of 100 days' men or muster into U.S. service the militia?$_{61}$

Given the lack of "military fact" in these two reports, it is not surprising that Evans bypassed Curtis. Evans was aware that the "Extensive Indian murders" and "devastated settlement" involved four Whites. Curtis received the same information.$_{62}$ The exaggerated impression given in both reports was that of a large scale uprising by the Indians. It is difficult to believe that Evans was not aware of the extent of this exaggeration. In a sense, the Hungate tragedy had the symbolic significance of a large-scale attack on the Whites. But Evans' reports were descriptive, implying that literally an extensive attack had occurred. One must conclude that Evans utilized exaggerated misrepresentation in an attempt to persuade the War Department to grant him the authority to raise a regiment. Such claims could also vindicate his warning of the previous fall.$_{63}$

Evans also adapted these two messages to the roles served by the men to whom they were addressed. Dole was included in the Interior Department and could make a direct appeal on Evans' behalf. By requesting directions regarding the "friendly" Cheyennes,

Arapahoes, Sioux, Kiowas and Comanches, Evans emphasized his role as Indian Superintendent and that he was not seeking to fight all Indians (and also contradicted his declaration to Curtis that <u>all</u> Cheyennes, with the Kiowas and Comanches, were united in a "hellish" plot). Evans made no distinction between the hostile and friendly Indians to Stanton whose purpose was coordination of military resources. Since the war between the states made a heavy demand upon these resources, Stanton, in Evans' view, would have been less likely to grant Evans the requested authority, if all the Territorial tribes were not hostile. Evans received no response from Stanton but Dole indicated his support for Evans' plan to separate hostile from friendly Indians.[64]

On June 16th Evans tried again to persuade Curtis of the reality of the Indian alliance. He repeated his explanation as to why a militia was impractical in Colorado. Again he provided "copies of letters to show you that this is the programme set forth in my communications last fall." Evans warned that the alliance was becoming stronger daily. He also sent a new letter from North repeating the existence of the alliance and that the Cheyennes were the instigators. A second letter from a Sioux "Squaw man," William McGaa alias Jack Jones, was included naming the Cheyennes as the "ringleaders" of the conspiracy.[65]

By June 22, 1864, relations between Evans and Curtis were deteriorating. From Superintendent Lane, the Governor learned that Curtis doubted his interpretation of the situation in Colorado. Defensively Evans addressed the "doubt":

> I had supposed that the information I have given you was sufficient to satisfy you that this Indian War is no myth but a terrible reality to a community situated as we are, so exposed and so far from our base of supplies with a scarcity of subsistence already . . .

Evans challenged Curtis to disprove the alliance:

> If you have evidence that my information of Indian hostilities and alliances for war are not well founded, I shall be most happy to be informed of it; yes to satisfy me that I am mistaken will be the greatest favor you can

confer upon me and the people of Colorado generally. But how can any evidence disprove the facts which are furnished I am at a loss to perceive, and how the multiplied and numerous assurances from friendly Indians, Indian traders and people who suffer, and our troops who have had several engagements with them, being attacked in nearly every instance, can fail to prove our dangers, I am at a loss to understand . . . . As requested I shall from time to time furnish you with such reliable evidence only of either danger or its absence as may come to my knowledge.

In the mean time, general, believe me to be respectfully your obedient servant,

John Evans[66]

Although Evans thus implored Curtis to believe him, apparently the difference in perception between the two men revolved around their interpretation of what was "reliable evidence." Evans relied upon general anecdotal evidence but many Colorado citizens would have testified to its veracity (most of the supporting materials provided by Evans to Curtis were comprised of such testimony).[67] On the other hand, Curtis demanded that Evans provide him the "facts" so that he might "know" Colorado's "disasters."[68] Curtis' response to Evans' message of the 22nd clarified that facts were observed events -- not predictions of future catastrophes, or generally held opinions.

Curtis remarked upon the ambiguity of the evidence provided by Evans and pointed out that the facts (military reports) proved only that "small portions" of Indians had united to commit the hostilities near Denver. "I may not have all you have seen and heard," Curtis cautioned, "But I am sure I have a great deal on the subject which you have not seen or heard . . . ."[69] Curtis concluded with an admonition regarding the importance of establishing fact in Indian/White relations:

> All my conversation with agent Lane was intended to express to him and through him to you that however much we may have reason to apprehend a general Indian War, we should not conclude them as such a thing in actual existence before doing all in our power to prevent such a disaster. It

is not demonstrated by the report then before me. But be it a great or small matter, we would be culpable if we did not do all in our power to suppress it . . . .[70]

Had Curtis followed his own advice later in August and September, the probability[71] of a battle at Sand Creek may have been decreased. Evans did not communicate with Curtis again for over two weeks. Thereafter he communicated infrequently with Curtis, seldom initiating communication, only responding to inquiries from Curtis. When he did write to Curtis, the messages sent were short and specific.

In August, Evans appealed not just to the War Department and Curtis for aid against the "allied savages" but also to the White citizens of Colorado. Faced by the raids and killings which occurred in the second week in August and without promise of Federal help, Evans sought to raise a large militia to combat the alliance.

Evans to the People of Colorado

On June 27, 1864, Evans had issued a message "to the friendly Indians of the Plains" requesting that the "friendly Indians separate themselves from the hostile" and proceed to places designated as safe.[72] Whether the agents placed in charge of informing the various bands of scattered Indians adequately carried out their task is not clear.[73] Nevertheless, on August 11, 1864, only 44 days after requesting this separation of hostile from friendly, Evans issued an "Appeal" to the citizens of Colorado. The Appeal followed reports of depredations on the Platte in July and the murder of Whites and capture of White women and children on Plum Creek around August 7th or 8th. Additionally, Evans' Appeal was presented in the Rocky Mountain News along with Byers' views of Indian nature.[74] Evans' rhetoric printed in the News generally was more temperate than were the stories circulated by Byers. Perhaps because of his role as Indian Superintendent, sanctioned in Washington by Commissioner Dole, Evans believed it necessary to distinguish between hostile and friendly Indians. He could not totally abandon his role as Indian Superintendent without risking his appointed position.

However, his messages as Governor tended, for his White audience, to function so as to legitimize the destruction of all Indians.

Evans' message of August 10th provided information to nervous citizens and called upon them to act. He had hoped, he declared, to secure protection from the War Department "against the merciless savages." However, he reported, "I am informed now that we must, ourselves, defend our settlements." He provided directions instructing the citizens "how to" organize. He explained that "organization" was required before either government pay or government arms could be provided. Additionally, he proclaimed, "any man who kills a hostile Indian is a patriot . . . ." However, he warned that not all Indians were hostile and cautioned his readers that killing "friendly Indians" would only result in "greater difficulty." He made a final appeal for orderly action and made reference to his political critics:

> He is the true patriot who goes to work and prepares for defense in the only legal and proper way of doing so in time of danger. Those who refuse to cooperate with him and throw barriers in his way belong to another class.[75]

Evans may have been describing himself as the "true patriot" since he was engaging in the only apparent legal and proper method for protecting the Territory. The campaign for statehood was in full swing and the Black Hawk Journal had been criticizing Evans for failing to maintain adequate military protection within the Territory.[76] Many Denver merchants probably recalled money they had lost due to the "bogus" Gilpin drafts of 1862. Therefore they were reluctant to support the raising of another militia without guaranteed government support. In this "Appeal," Evans did admit that volunteers would "have to look to Congress for pay . . . ." But he promised the "patriots" who volunteered "all the property belonging to hostile Indians that they capture . . . ."[77]

Apparently Evans did not believe that this "Appeal" was enough to arouse the lethargic citizens of Colorado to enlist. Therefore, in the very next

236

issue of the News he issued an official "Proclamation." Printed at the head of the editorial page of the News was the following:

Proclamation by Governor Evans, of Colorado Territory

PROCLAMATION

Having sent messengers to the Indians of the Plains, directing the friendly to rendezvous at Fort Lyon, Fort Larned, Fort Laramie, and Camp Collins for safety and protection, warning them that all hostile Indians would be pursued and destroyed, and the last of said messengers having now returned, and the evidence being conclusive that most of the Indian tribes of the plains are at war and hostile to the whites, and having to the utmost of my ability endeavored to induce all of the Indians of the plains to come to said places of rendezvous, promising them subsistence and protection, with a few exceptions they have refused to do:

Now, therefore, I, John Evans, governor of Colorado Territory, do issue this my proclamation, authorizing all citizens of Colorado, either individually or in such parties as they may organize, to go in pursuit of all hostile Indians on the plains, scrupulously avoiding those who have responded to my said call to rendezvous at the points indicated; also to kill and destroy, as enemies of the country, wherever they may be found, all such hostile Indians. And further, as the only reward I am authorized to offer for such services, I hereby empower such citizens, or parties of citizens, to take captive, and hold to their own private use and benefit, all the property of said hostile Indians that they may capture, and to receive for all stolen property recovered from said Indians such reward as may be deemed proper and just therefor.

I further offer to all such parties as will organize under the militia law of the Territory for the purpose to furnish them arms and ammunition, and to present their accounts for pay as regular soldiers for themselves, their horses, their subsistence, and transportation, to Congress, under assurance of the department commander that they will be paid.

The conflict is upon us, and all good citizens are called upon to do their duty for the defense of their homes and families. In testimony whereof, I have hereunto set my hand and caused the great seal of the Territory of Colorado to be affixed this 11th day of August, A.D. 1864.

JOHN EVANS[78]

With these words Governor Evans proclaimed war upon the Indians of the plains and fulfilled Byers' predicted "Indian War" of April, 1864. Furthermore, Evans implied that persuasion, an ordinary mechanism, had failed and that a military solution was now required. He provided no specific conclusive evidence that most of the tribes were hostile. Somewhat later he testified that he considered the failure of the Dog Soldiers and Platte Tribes to meet with him as proof of their hostility.[79] However, the citizens of Colorado needed no more conclusive proof. The Hungate "Massacre" had already accomplished this persuasion.

In the second paragraph of the Proclamation, Evans indicated his official approval for White volunteers to "kill and destroy" all hostile Indians. While his appeal of the previous day had emphasized the importance of "organization" and "order," now in his official capacity as Governor he allowed for individual action in the destruction of these "enemies of the country." The message also implied that individuals or groups could count only on captured Indian property as their reward. Perhaps Evans was more certain of this "reward" than Curtis' promise that the costs of the militia organization would be reimbursed by Congress.

In this Proclamation, again Evans differentiated hostile from friendly Indians. "Hostile" Indians were to be distinguished from friendly Indians based upon their response to Evans' Proclamation in June. Apparently if individuals or groups of Indians had relocated near to the points indicated, they were to be considered "friendly." Evans did not name the "few" who had responded to his call. He did equate failure to do so with refusing to do so -- an important distinction since failure to come in could have resulted from events beyond the tribes' control.[80]

While probably Evans had good intentions in issuing this Proclamation and did attempt to distinguish which of the enemy were to be killed, the Proclamation could have functioned otherwise. Without a <u>precise</u> definition of who was a hostile Indian and since officially most were hostile, the safest act for any patriot was to kill all Indians. It also paid equally well to kill all Indians.

Two questions were also left unanswered by the Proclamation: Did <u>all</u> hostile Indians include Indian women and children? Could friendly Indians still proceed to safe places?

Evans wrote nothing about prisoners. Clearly his instructions said to "kill and destroy" <u>all</u> such hostile Indians. Evans may have believed that such a distinction was implicit in his message and that Christian gentlemen naturally would make such an allowance and not kill women and children. While such an omission may seem slight, an official rejection of an "extermination policy" could not have been taken lightly by Colorado's more responsible citizens. However, if Evans had made such a statement, probably he would have received criticism regarding it. Pressure from a White constituency and the coming election discouraged such a statement.[81]

It was also not clear in the Proclamation if its issuance negated the conditions of Evans' June message to the "friendly Indians." Obviously even if they were still officially permitted to "proceed to safe places," unofficially it still paid for Whites to destroy them while they were attempting to follow Evans' request.[82] Thus, this Proclamation of August 11, 1864 functioned as an official sanction for a war of extermination against all of Colorado's Indians.

The guaranteed rewards of Evans' Appeal and Proclamation limited the scope of potential White action against hostile Indians. Absent a guarantee of Government pay, a large militia organization was unlikely. However, on August 13, 1864, Evans received formal authorization from the Secretary of War to raise a regiment of 100-days men "to fight the Indians." Therefore Evans issued another Proclamation to the "Patriotic Citizens of Colorado."[83]

He provided assurances that personal expenses would be promptly paid and information regarding the formation of the regiment. He urged Coloradans to enlist or otherwise support the cause and made the purpose of the regiment clear:

> Let this regiment be filled at once in co-operation with the large force from the states asked for, pursue, kill and destroy all hostile Indians that infest the plains, for thus only can we assure the permanent and lasting peace.[84]

Evans did not rescind the provisions of his Appeal of August 10th and Proclamation of August 11th, allowing for the capture of hostile Indian property as pay. Technically such rewards were now not necessary for the members of the Colorado Third since the Government paid them a salary, in addition to all expenses. However, captured Indian stock added profit to this small salary. This profit may have been especially appealing to the "floaters" in the Territory. Professor Carey has hinted that many of the men who enlisted in the Third needed little excuse to kill all Indians. However, Evans' messages implying that all hostile Indians were to be destroyed gave them official sanction to do so. For more stable elements in the Third, there was the assurance that such destruction was an act of patriotism. The members of the Colorado First had earned their glory in New Mexico two years before. With Governor Evans' blessing the new members of the Third could "pursue, kill and destroy all hostile Indians" while seeking similar glory. Moreover, if Indian property was forfeited to those engaged in such patriotism, one logical conclusion was that victory provided Whites with the one Indian possession that Whites most coveted -- Indian land. It would be difficult to prove that these messages caused any unjust killing and mutilation of Indians by Whites. However, the wording of these messages could have facilitated such actions.[85]

But Evans was not successful in bringing about the filling of the Third Regiment through the use of persuasion alone. Recruitment in Denver was especially slow and on August 17th, Colonel Chivington declared martial law and ordered the District Provost Marshal to enroll all able bodied males in some sort of military service.[86]

While appealing to Coloradans to support the raising of a militia and then the 100-days regiment, Evans had continued trying to convince the War Department to provide him with additional authority and troops for the protection of Colorado. However, actual events in late July and during the first two weeks in August made persuasion by Evans less necessary.

Between July 17 and July 20th Indian raids did take place on the Platte in which Whites were killed.[87] Starting in the second week in August raids up and down the Platte River resulted in a significant number of White deaths.[88] General Curtis himself went into the field to help restore the Overland Stage and mail service, but encountered no Indians.[89] On August 8, 1864, Evans wrote Curtis in a curt and self-assured manner:

> Of course you have news of outrages near Plum Creek. We are in a desperate condition on account of our communications being cut off by Indians. The route will have to be patrolled or we are cut off. Militia law is so defective we can't hold troops away from home. Station camps at points along the line as far up as Junction and gather emigrants along in companies and escort from camp to camp.[90]

This message from Evans to Curtis was probably in response to Curtis who had noted on July 30th that "I have not heard a word from you since your dispatch concerning new troubles on the Platte." Curtis expressed "anxiety" over this lack of communication. "It seems impossible to get intelligence of the enemy," he wrote and admitted that "the Kiowas, Big Mouth's Arapahoes, and Comanches seem certainly engaged in this affair . . . ."[91] On August 10th, Evans telegraphed both Dole and Stanton again seeking authority. He stated to Dole that:

> I am now satisfied that the tribes of the plains are nearly all combined in this terrible war, as apprehended last winter. It will be the largest Indian war this country has ever had, extending from Texas to the British lines, involving nearly all the wild tribes of the plains. Please bring all the force of your department to bear in favor of speedy reenforcement of our troops, and get me

authority to raise a regiment of 100-days' mounted men. Our militia law is inoperative, and unless this authority is given we will be destroyed [emphasis added].$_{92}$

This time he made no reference to "friendly" Indians. He addressed Dole not as protector of Indian rights in Colorado Territory but as Governor and protector of White interests. To Secretary of War Stanton, preoccupied with the Civil War, Evans wrote:

> The alliance of Indians on the plains reported last winter in my communication is now undoubted. A large force, say 10,000 troops will be necessary to defend the lines and put down hostilities. Unless they can be sent at once we will be cut off and destroyed.$_{93}$

The next day, August 11, 1864, Evans wrote similar statements to Curtis, "The alliance of all the tribes, as I have reported to you is now undoubted. If they sweep west, as they probably will, we shall be in great danger of being destroyed." But, in contrast to his message to Stanton, Evans estimated that only 5,000 additional troops were needed.$_{94}$

This time Evans' reference to the alliance and hyperbolic claims were partially rewarded. As discussed, on August 13th he received permission to raise a force of 100-days' men, citizen soldiers from the Colorado population.$_{95}$

But Evans' petitions to the War Department did not end after he received permission to raise the Colorado Third. Probably motivated by a genuine fear exacerbated by events mentioned in the previous chapter, Evans continued to symbolize Colorado's situation as perilous. But now his requests centered on recalling more troops to the Territory. For several weeks after August 15th, the Indians cut off travel and mail over the Overland Trail. Evans wanted the route patrolled and more protection for Colorado settlers. The regiment of 100-days' men was hampered by a lack of adequate saddles, mounts and weapons. Thus Evans wrote to Stanton on August 18th of "Extensive Indian depredations . . . thirty miles south of Denver. Our lines of communication are cut . . . Large bodies of Indians are undoubtedly near to Denver . . . I earnestly request that Colonel Ford's regiment, Second Colorado Volunteers, be immediately sent to our relief. It is impossible to exaggerate our danger."[96] Evans wrote to Curtis that without help the situation was "hopeless." But Evans wasted little time on Curtis, who still refused to believe that the Indian war was general. Evans revealed to Secretary Stanton that the conspiracy written of the previous fall was about to come to fruition. "Unlimited information of contemplated attack by a large body of Indians . . . ," he warned Stanton. The attack would be "along the entire line of our settlements."[97] Two weeks later he was still requesting "positive orders for our Second Colorado Cavalry to come out . . . Unless escorts are sent . . . we will have a famine in addition to this gigantic Indian war . . . . Through spies we get knowledge of the plan of about 1000 warriors in camp to strike our frontier settlements in small bands simultaneously in the night for an extent of 300 miles." But, Evans, recorded, "It was frustrated at the time, but we have to fear another such attempt soon."[98] While Evans did receive permission to purchase the necessary equipment and mounts, no Federal troops were returned to Colorado. The entire Federal Government was busy countering the threat from Quantrill's raids and Price's Missouri expedition.[99]

Thus, in these messages of the spring, summer and fall of 1864, John Evans provided symbols of Native Americans to military and governmental authorities and White Coloradans. His manifest intent with messages directed at the War Department was to gain increased protection for Colorado's White citizens. His primary appeal to persuade both Commissioner Dole and the military of the necessity for increased protection was the image of an "alliance" led by Cheyenne ringleaders. This alliance threatened Colorado's destruction with its "hellish" plots. In his communication of this conspiracy, Evans often exaggerated events and seldom provided the specific facts of these disasters. There is no evidence that anyone in Evans' governmental or military audience ever adhered to Evans' interpretation of events in Colorado.[100] His continual messages symbolizing doom and disaster for Colorado could have worked at cross-purposes. By predicting imminent events (death and destruction) as early as June which did not occur, Evans decreased the credibility of his later messages. Moreover, it became necessary for him to continue to

243

exaggerate in order to prove that his previous messages had been correct. Whether intentional or unintentional, these symbolizations illustrating the hostility of the Territorial tribes could have facilitated a military solution to the boundary question.[101] However, it appears that actual events in Colorado in late July and during the second week in August finally convinced the War Department to provide Evans with the authority to raise an army. Evans did not receive the 10,000 Federal troops he had requested of Stanton. Therefore Evans would have to rely on a regiment of citizen-soldiers raised from within Colorado Territory. Evans sent several messages to White Coloradans first calling on them to organize for their own defense and then supporting the raising of the 100-days' regiment. However, these messages alone did not achieve Evans' intent. Persuasion failed and the regiment was filled through the invocation of Martial Law in Denver. Latently, Evans' messages functioned as a declaration of war against the Indians, linking patriotism with the destruction of hostile Indians. But his Proclamation blurred the distinction between hostile and friendly Indians. All of these messages tended to favor Evans' role as Governor over his role as Indian Superintendent. Later, Commissioner Dole condemned Evans' behavior during this time. This condemnation probably contributed to Evans' forced resignation the following year.[102]

By engaging in acts which appeared to facilitate the protection of White Coloradans while securing their land interests, Evans may have hoped that he would increase his chances in the September election. His forced withdrawal may be taken as evidence that he was not successful in this regard. But the messages sent by Evans to his White audience had their most significant effects upon his behavior toward Native Americans at the Camp Weld Conference.

Evans to American Indians

John Evans encountered consistent frustration in his communications with his Indian charges. Not all of the reasons for this failure were under his control but his communications were based upon impractical and ethnocentric assumptions which assured failure. His initial intent was the control of the Indians and the maintenance of peace. He proposed to accomplish this by "civilizing" the Indians. He indicated to Commissioner Dole that he believed that he could instill in the Indians an appreciation for private property and farming. As a former Quaker and a devout Methodist, Evans believed in the perfectability of all men. If the Indians' external conditions were altered, "savage" methods and customs would be abandoned. But like many Jeffersonians before him, Evans' assumptions granted Indian cultures nothing of value. He assumed that the Indians would perceive quickly the superiority of White-like civilization. Moreover, he proposed an identical policy -- instruction in farming and raising livestock -- for the Utes, the Cheyennes and the Arapahoes. That is, he assumed that all "Indians" were the same when there were significant cultural differences between the Cheyennes and the Utes. He$_{103}$ was relatively successful in "civilizing" the Utes. However, the Cheyennes, one of the most conservative and proudest$_{104}$of the Plains tribes, were not so easily persuaded. One Indian, Bull Bear, recalcitrant leader of the Cheyenne Dog Soldiers, the most influential and powerful of the Cheyennes' warrior/military societies, reacted negatively to Evans' civilization policy. He questioned Evans' scout and special agent Elbridge Gerry:

    'Does the Great Father want us to live like white men?'
    'The Great Father will help you to live comfortably,' replied Gerry, 'he will build schools and educate your papooses.'
    Again Bull Bear demanded, 'Does the Great Father want us to live like white men?'
    'Yes,' said Gerry. 'That is what he wants.'
    'You tell white chief,' was the scornful answer, 'Indian may not be so low yet.'$_{105}$

The Cheyennes were as ethnocentric as the Whites. They resented especially Evans' attempts to get them to curb their war-making customs. Evans made it his habit to address groups of Indians urging them to adopt White ways and to stop fighting one another. But when Evans demanded that the Cheyennes stop raiding their traditional$_{106}$ enemy, the Utes, he alienated the Cheyennes. He could have only insulted them more by asking them to become$_{107}$ brothers with their most despised enemy, the Crows.

The Cheyennes were relative newcomers to the Plains and had had to fight to maintain their place thereon. Moreover, for the male Cheyenne warrior no value was placed higher than illustrating military virtue. An individual male Cheyennes' prestige was dependent on proven battlefield bravery. Display of such bravery was an end in itself and, contrary to White perceptions, killing and scalping an enemy was less important than such a display. E. Adamson Hoebel provides an excellent ethnographic description of the importance of valor in the Cheyenne life-way:

> [For the Cheyenne] Prestige drives override the more limited military requirements for the defeat of the enemy. The show-off tends to supersede the mere soldier. War has been transformed into a great game in which scoring against the enemy often takes precedence over killing him.
> The scoring is in count of coup -- touching or striking an enemy with hand or weapons. Coups counted within an enemy encampment rank highest of all. By extension, any heroic deed in battle counts as a coup: saving a wounded comrade, being first to locate an enemy . . . or charging a body of enemies alone while the rest of the Cheyennes watch to see the results. A man's rank as a warrior depends on two factors: his total 'score' in coups and his ability to lead successful raids in which Cheyenne losses are low. Actual killing and scalping get their credit too, but they do not rate as high as the show-off deeds.[108]

Evans believed that he was trying to insure peace in his attempts to stop inter-tribal raiding. As the Cheyennes interpreted it, he was asking them to abandon their manhood and reason for living. Without war, the male Cheyenne became an "old squaw." Living in peace with the entire world was inimical to the Cheyennes' way of life. Moreover, different value assumptions regarding war were major contributors to conflict between Coloradans and the Cheyennes.[109]

War Declared

Both Indians and military authorities agreed that the events of April and May, 1864 were the beginnings of the "war" of 1864.[110] Probably it is impossible to determine the true nature of events from the reports from the conflicting sides. However, one instance does provide an example of the conflicting interpretations of "war." It also illustrates the type of information upon which Evans based his claims to General Curtis in May of 1864 that "recent events" proved his allegations to General Schofield.

On April 11, 1864, a certain White rancher named Ripley reported that the Indians had been stealing stock along Bijou Creek and driving people from their ranches. On April 12, Lieutenant Clark Dunn was dispatched with forty men to chase the Indians, disarm them and recover the stock. Ripley himself was to be their guide. Eventually Dunn and his command encountered a party of fifteen or twenty Indians and a conflict ensued. Dunn reported that after a march of 75 miles (in one day) he "discovered the Indians . . . evidently intending to steal a herd of horses and mules grazing near Fremont's orchard . . . ." He continued:

> . . . when upon approaching them [the Indians] I discovered a herd of horses [in their possession] . . . When near enough to speak to them Mr. Ripley, a ranchman who had lost all the stock he had, and who had informed us of their depredations said that they were the Indians, and pointing to the herd said there were his stock. Feeling the great responsibility that was resting upon me and not desiring to bring about an Indian war . . . I dismounted, walked forward to meet their chief and tried to obtain the stock without any resort to violence. After requesting the chief to return the stock, who replied only by a scornful laugh, I told him I would be compelled to disarm his party, at the same time reaching forward as if to take the arms from one of the Indians, when they immediately commenced firing . . . . We killed some 8 or 10 of the Indians and wounded 12 or 15 more.[111]

A certain Bouser, an interpreter for Governor Evans, gave a different version of these events. He reported:

> The first difficulty between the Cheyennes and Arapahoes and whites occurred on the 11th of April, 1864. A white man came into Camp Sanborn

and reported that he had cattle stolen. A detail of 20 men was sent after the Indians to get the cattle. The commander of the detail, Lieutenentt Clark Dunn, had orders to disarm and fetch in the Indians; if they refused, to sweep them off the face of the earth. A fight occurred, and some Indians were wounded, also four soldiers, two of whom afterward died. There was no interpreter along with the detail . . . . I know an Indian named Spotted Horse . . . he told me that he was in the affair with Lieutenant Dunn. He said the Indians took three head of cattle; there were 100 warriors. There was snow upon the ground, and the Indians were hungry and took the cattle; they would have come into Denver if their horses had been in condition. They went south of the river with the cattle intending if the soldiers came after them to settle for the cattle by giving some of their ponies. Before they had time to cross the river and kill the cattle the soldiers overtook them. The soldiers had no interpreter, had no talk with the Indians, gave them no time even to deliver the cattle, but pitched into them . . . . Spotted Horse seeing that there was going to be war, threw up his chieftainship, and with it some one hundred head of ponies, and came in to Governor Evans. I acted as interpreter, and he told substantially to Governor Evans the above. This same chief traded four of his ponies to ransom a White woman -- Mrs. Kelly.[112]

Captain Sanborn, Dunn's immediate commander, provided a somewhat[113] contradictory summary of Dunn's experience. He communicated to Chivington and Evans that "these Indians . . . were evidently on the warpath, as they did not talk anything but fight."[114] Given that the Whites had no interpreter it is unclear how either Dunn or Sanborn could have reached this conclusion. Apparently Governor Evans did not accept Spotted Horse's account of this encounter, since he made no reference to this report in his correspondence. Similar conflicting interpretations are available of other Indian/White skirmishes in the spring of 1864.[115] Evans appears to have accepted the military reports of these encounters and to have ignored any evidence which might disprove the "alliance."

Black Kettle and the Cheyennes did not immediately interpret the encounter with Dunn as indicative of a continuing war as defined by the Whites. Rather, events at Fremont's Orchard were characterized as a "fight."[116] While the Cheyennes eventually described these events as part of a "war," there was still no real understanding on the part of the Cheyennes as to what White men characterized as "war." For the Whites, being in a state of war implied all-out strategic efforts by both sides to kill as many of the enemy as possible. From the White standpoint, wars were to be avoided and their perpetrators were to be punished. After war, peacemaking meant a total surrender by one side with the conditions for surrender determined at the victor's discretion. Admittable motives for going to war were property theft (depredations) and unprovoked murder.

The Cheyennes' interpretation was in marked contrast. For the Cheyennes, a "war" involved limited and specific objectives with revenge being a primary motivation stimulated by prestige needs. A warrior who did not avenge a relative's unpaid-for death was a coward. For the Cheyennes "making war" was more often the result of individual action than "official" tribal policy. That is, any warrior could decide to make war for his own reasons. Those acquaintances of his who shared his concerns might go with him. Young warriors could be influenced by older chiefs or warriors but were under no obligation to desist from seeking their own ends. Therefore, rather than large groups of Indians, most Cheyenne raiding parties were small with limited firepower. A small size allowed for quickness of movement and maximization of individual acts of bravery. Additionally, rather than engaging in long-term planning, Cheyenne warriors in the 1860's were more likely to respond to the "here and now." Too much planning might make an individual warrior appear to be a coward and hurt his prestige. Moreover, Cheyenne practice permitted remuneration rather than punishment to set things right again. Thus, the group encountered by Dunn believed they could simply trade their horses for stolen stock. Similar payment was also allowable in the event of intra-tribal homicide.[117] Once things were set straight, Cheyennes seldom carried grudges. For the Cheyennes, peacemaking during a "war" did not require total surrender and such opportunities were viewed as a means to increase trade and exchange gifts.[118] Consistent with their "here and now" orientation, peacemaking on a given day did not preclude raids in the near or far future. The theft of horses from non-Cheyennes was a pastime and renumeration was not required unless the thief was caught. Such a conception of war tended to keep Cheyenne losses at a minimum while maximizing individual warriors' chances to count coup. As Robert L. Munkres has concluded, "To the [Plains] tribes there was no clear understanding of the distinction drawn by white men between a 'battle' and a 'war,' nor of the relationship between the two. The imperatives of a nomadic existence rendered full-time and continuous warfare <u>a literal impossibility</u>" [emphasis added]. Such a limitation also would decrease the likelihood of any effective alliance among the Plains tribes.[119]

Sanborn, Evans and Byers characterized the fight at Fremont's Orchard as the Indians being on the "warpath," and "alliance" or a "promising Indian war." Dunn feared (so he said) instigating an "Indian War." But with the Indians characterized as at "war," every unexplained loss of stock became another depredation and every group of Indians a group of "hellish savages." Thus, in the spring and summer Chivington's men behaved as if they were in a "war." As such it was a war against "Indians" without differentiation on the basis of age, sex or tribe. John Smith testified:

> A short time after this occurrence [Dunn's fight] took place a village of squaws, papooses and old men . . . who were perfectly unaware of any difficulty having occurred between any portion of their tribe [Cheyenne] and the whites, were attacked by a large party of soldiers and some of them killed and their ponies driven off.[120]

For the Cheyennes, such events ultimately meant, in Black Kettle's words, that "war was inevitable and they immediately commenced to retaliate."[121]

It is clear that Evans believed the Cheyennes were "on the warpath" when he issued his "Proclamation to the Friendly Indians of the Plains." He sent the message on June 29th to Indian agent Colley directing him to use "every means" to communicate the message to the Indians.[122] Overtly, this message was an attempt to provide protection to Indians "still friendly" to the Whites. Acting in his role as Superintendent, Evans believed also that the policy might induce the Indians to cease hostilities. By providing a "safe refuge," Evans hoped to, in his words, "collect those who became tired of war and desire peace."[123] However, the offer was limited and incorrect in its assumption that the Cheyennes would tire of war.

The means to provide for the Indians who would come in were limited. In his message to Indian agent S.G. Colley, Evans warned Colley to "use the utmost economy in providing for those who come in, as the Secretary of the Interior confines me to the amount of our appropriations, and they may be exhausted before the summer is out." The $3,000 he sent to Colley to provide for the friendlies who came into Fort Lyon may have been adequate to the task. However, Colley could have used these annuities for his own purposes.[124] Colley sent letters to Evans in August which tended to reenforce Evans' fear of an alliance.[125] In his testimony to the Committee on the Conduct of the War of 1865, Colley said that the impression of an alliance was a "misunderstanding" and that the Cheyennes and Arapahoes were not active in such an "alliance." Colley also testified to the Committee that the previous year he had received "nothing at all" for the Indians. What became of the annuity grant or Evans' permission for Colley to requisition supplies for the friendly Indians is not stated.[126] But on September 29, 1864, the day after the Camp Weld Conference, Evans informed Colley that the state of war which still existed between Black Kettle's band and the military removed the responsibility of the Indian Bureau for their care.[127] Colley may have been relieved, since with his charges declared hostile (as represented by him to Evans in August) no one would listen to Indian complaints that they had not received their annuities or supplies.[128] Whatever Colley's motivation, some of the friendlies who "came in" did not stay, preferring to hunt rather than settle for sparse military rations. Colley may have testified at the hearings in favor of the Indians out of spite for Chivington. Reportedly $30,000 worth of Colley's goods were destroyed or "acquired" by Chivington's troops at Sand Creek.[129]

Evans also assumed that the Cheyennes wanted the "war" to end. It was Cheyenne custom to "raid" and steal stock during the summer months. For the Indians actually engaged in the raids, there was little incentive to stop. Remuneration could always be provided injured Whites in the fall, when the raiding season ended.

Evans' plan might have worked if given time and if the cooperation of the military had been assured. In time, the raiding season would have elapsed, and most of the Indians would have proceeded to the designated places of refuge. However, the punitive philosophy adopted by Chivington and local volunteers whipped Indians not even involved in the raiding into a retaliatory mood and escalated the conflict. Moreover, nervous guards at the "places of refuge" fired upon friendly Indians attempting to do as the Governor requested. Such behavior also caused some cooperative Indians to become hostile.[130]

In effect Evans had set an impossible standard by expecting Indian compliance in only 45 days. The "Proclamation to Friendly Indians" had been his attempt as Indian Superintendent to control the situation. His Appeal and Proclamations as Governor directed at a White audience contradicted and negated that attempt. Even in spite of provocation by Chivington's troops, on September 4, 1864, the initial Proclamation to the Indians was still partially functional. Evans received a letter from Colley stating that Black Kettle and some other chiefs desired to meet with Evans to make peace.[131] Major Wynkoop brought Black Kettle and several other Indians to Denver on September 28th for a conference with Governor Evans and other authorities.[132]

The Camp Weld Council

Major Wynkoop arrived in Denver two days before the rest of the party who were following in a wagon under military escort. Initially, Evans refused to see Wynkoop. When Wynkoop finally did get to see the Governor, the Major told Evans that the chiefs would arrive in two days to hold council with Evans. According to Wynkoop's testimony, Evans replied that he was sorry Wynkoop had brought in the Indians and that he (Evans) wished to have nothing to do with them. As far as Evans was concerned, the Indians were at war with the United States and belonged in the hands of the military authorities. Reportedly Evans also said that it was poor policy to make peace with the Indians "until they were properly punished, for the reason that the United States would be acknowledging themselves whipped." Wynkoop replied that it would be "strange if the United States would consider themselves whipped by a few Indians." Moreover, Wynkoop drew Evans' attention to the fact that

> . . . as a United States officer, I had pledged myself to these Indians to convey them to Denver, to procure and interview with himself; that I had brought these Indians a distance of nearly four hundred miles from their village with that object in view; and desired that he would furnish them an audience.$_{133}$

Evans replied "querulously," that he was unable to see the chiefs as he was to visit the Ute Indian agency on the following day, "besides he did not want to see them anyhow." Wynkoop continued to try to persuade the Governor to meet with the Indians and eventually succeeded. But not before Evans stated what may have been his real reason for not wanting to do so. According to Wynkoop:

> He [Evans] then referred to the fact that the third regiment of one-hundred day men, having been raised and in camp, were nearly ready to make an Indian campaign. He further said that the regiment was ordered to be raised upon his representations to Washington that they were necessary for the protection of the Territory, and to fight hostile Indians; and now, if he made peace with the Indians, it would be supposed at Washington that he had misrepresented matters in regard to the Indian difficulties in Colorado, and had put the government to useless expense in raising and equipping the regiment; that <u>they had been raised to kill Indians, and they must kill Indians.</u> Several times in our conversations . . . he made the remark 'What shall I do with the third regiment, if I make peace?' [emphasis added].$_{134}$

On September 28, 1864, a council was held at Camp Weld outside of Denver. Governor Evans presided over the session. In attendance were several military officers, including Chivington and Wynkoop, John

Smith, and the official interpreter, Amos Stock (or Steck), a Denver attorney and Ute agent Simeon Whitley. Representing the Indians were: Black Kettle, a Cheyenne chief, White Antelope, another Cheyenne chief, and Bull Bear, leader of the Cheyenne Dog Soldiers. Three other Indians also were present representing the Arapahoes and Left Hand, who was ill. Simeon Whitley was asked by the Governor to make a record of the proceedings. Traditionally, historians have accepted his record as a representation of the events at the council.[135]

As a record, Whitley's interpretation illustrates that the agenda of this conference was controlled by Evans as a forum for White grievances against the Indians. It was not an opportunity for the Indians to state their complaints against the Whites. An additional record may illustrate that Whitley's record was either incorrect or altered.

In Whitley's version of the events at the council, the council opened with Governor Evans asking the Indians what they had to say. Black Kettle responded, saying that the Indians desired peace -- that he had done everything in his power to keep the peace. He had brought four White prisoners as evidence of his good faith and accompanied Major Wynkoop to the council. Also he said that other Indians would abide by any agreement reached during the session.[136] Evans replied that he was sorry that the Indians did not respond to his Proclamation at once. He accused them of allying with the Sioux and "however much a few individuals may have tried to keep the peace, <u>as a nation you have gone to war</u>." He told of trying to gather them together the previous fall, but instead of meeting with him "your people went away and smoked the war pipe with our enemies." The Indians denied Evans' allegations but acknowledged that their actions could have been interpreted in this manner.[137] The council continued:

> <u>Gov. Evans</u>: So far as making a treaty is now concerned, we are in no condition to do it. Your young men are on the warpath. My soldiers are preparing for the fight. You, so far, have had the advantage, but the time is near at hand when the plains will

swarm with United States soldiers. I understand that these men who have come to see me now, have been opposed to the war all the time, but their people have controlled them and they cannot help themselves. Is this so?

The Indians agreed that this had generally been the case. Evans then declared his inability to make peace with them -- saying that power had passed to the great War Chief. White Antelope inquired as to how his people could be protected from the soldiers on the plains. Evans said again that "You must make that arrangement with the Military Chief." White Antelope stated that he feared that his people would be killed while he was at the conference and Evans agreed, "There is great danger of it." On four different occasions Evans declined to make peace. In two instances he did vaguely suggest that the Indians could prove their friendship by allying with the soldiers against hostile Indians.[138]

Throughout the conference Evans did not make his "evidence" for the alliance known. When the Indians denied his claims about their alliance with the Sioux, Evans replied "No matter who said this, your conduct has proved to my satisfaction that was the case."[139] His only direct sources of evidence regarding the establishment of the alliance were North and McGaa. Apparently his mind was set on this issue and on the necessity of making war as he had hinted to Wynkoop on the 26th. Additionally his statement that "M<u>y</u> soldiers are preparing for the fight . . ." signified some personal involvement in their purpose. He passed on the responsibility of making peace to the military. He did imply that his offer to the friendly Indians was still good, but this promise was contradicted by a statement which he made that a "failure" to make arrangements with the military would result in all being treated as enemies. Establishing an arrangement with the military also had a hollow ring given the well-known fate of Lean Bear (Bull Bear's brother) and the firing upon of Left Hand by the soldiers. Amos Stock testified that Lean Bear's killing was mentioned by the Indians during the course of the council. Stock recalled that:

255

They said (which one I don't remember) in reply to what the governor had said about coming to the post under his proclamation, that as soon as it was read to them by a half-breed . . . they wrote a paper, which Bull Bear's brother [Lean Bear] carried to a commander of soldiers . . . that he got off his horse and tied him to one of the wagons of the command and was advancing unarmed, with the paper in his hand toward the military when he was shot down and killed. <u>The governor made no inquiry about this killing, no allusion whatever</u> [emphasis added].[140]

Whitley's version contained no reference to the Indian version of the killing of Lean Bear. Stock also testified that the governor stated that the Indians could show good faith by joining with the soldiers to "punish the Indians that were hostile." In Whitley's record Evans vaguely said that "the only way . . . is by making some arrangement with the soldiers to help them."[141]

The remainder of Agent Whitley's account consisted of Governor Evans inquiring after various depredations. He asked about the Hungate murders. Neva, an Arapahoe representative, said that Roman Nose and a party of Northern Arapahoes were to blame. A somewhat confusing exchange followed with Whitley himself remarking in the record, "That cannot be true . . . ." Evans queried "where is Roman Nose now?" and Neva responding, "you ought to know better than me. You have been nearer to him." The topic was dropped. In his testimony, Stock did not mention Whitley's statement and summarized Neva's reply as "He (Neva) said that he had gone off North somewhere, and that he had not seen him (Roman Nose) but he knew that he did it and his people knew that he did it."[142]

Evans inquired regarding the encounter at Fremont's Orchard. White Antelope remarked, "I would like you to know that this was the beginning of war, and I should like to know what it was for, a soldier fired first." In Whitley's record, Evans replied, "The Indians had stolen about forty horses, the soldiers went to recover them and the Indians fired a volley into their ranks."

Stock provided a different version stating that after White Antelope's remark, "'There governor is the beginning of this war,' the Governor made no inquiry respecting it, made no answer. They appeared anxious to tell it, but the subject was changed and the governor directed the interpreter to other matters."[143]

Later, near the end of the council, Evans emphasized again his unwillingness to make peace: "I cannot say anything about those things (peace) now." The conference ended with a cryptic statement from Chivington:

> <u>Col. Chivington</u> -- I am not a big war chief, but all the soldiers in this country are at my command. My rule of fighting white men or Indians is to fight them until they lay down their arms and submit to military authority. They are nearer Major Wynkoop than any one else and they can go to him when they are ready to do that.

Exactly what Chivington meant by this statement and what was concluded at the conference because of it has been subject to some controversy. Nevertheless, the Indians departed and submitted themselves to Wynkoop as Chivington appeared to request.[144]

With a message to Indian Agent Colley the following day, Evans made clear his overt intentions relative to the council. Emphatically, he declared, "I have declined to make any treaty with them, lest it might embarrass the military operations . . . The Arapahoe and Cheyenne Indians now being at war with the United States Government must make peace with the military authorities." He also asked Colley to make sure to "impress" upon the Indians that the council was only for clarification and "Not to offer them anything whatever."[145] Such instruction to Colley may indicate that Evans did not believe that his statements to the Indians the previous day were as clear as they could have been.

Evans' ignorance of Indian ways is also apparent in his recorded behavior at the council. He assumed that the purpose of the "Chiefs" or Cheyenne leaders was to control individual Indians. A Cheyenne chief held his position by influence. Neither the chief nor

257

the tribe had the right to forbid or to regulate the actions of individual warriors -- especially actions regarding the making of "war." That Black Kettle or Bull Bear had been unsuccessful in persuading the young Dog Soldiers not to raid the Whites was no real indictment of their leadership. It was a fact of life and indicated only individual free action. In Evans' view, the actions of individual Indians meant that Cheyennes "as a nation" were at war. But he was unwilling to let individual Indians who apparently represented a significant number of Plains tribes make peace with him.

Evans' interpretations of the events at Camp Weld ran counter to other interpretations given to the council by both the Indian and the White participants. Even Evans' ally, the Rocky Mountain News, concluded that the Governor had stated that the Indians could prove they were friendly by placing their tribes in "aid in the war upon the hostile tribes of the plains." The News stated also that Evans and Chivington had referred the matter to Major Wynkoop who was "familiar with their dispositions, wants and necessities." Yet, later Evans denied any such interpretations. Evans relied primarily upon Whitley's record to support his contention that no promises had been made by him to the Indians.[146]

At this point it is clear that Evans had tried to abandon his role as Indian Superintendent. As Governor he had determined a course of action. He communicated as if his messages directed at the Indians were also to be interpreted by a White audience. From his statements to Wynkoop, it appears that Evans felt that his options were restricted by his previous rhetoric directed at the War Department. If he made peace he feared "they would suppose at Washington that he had misrepresented matters . . . ." Thus, his behavior at Camp Weld was tyrannized by his own exaggerated claims and requests of the previous spring and summer. Evans' statements as Governor had made it difficult for him to make peace as Indian Superintendent. He had rhetorically painted himself into a corner. Having symbolized the situation as "hopeless" and the adversary as "savage," he did not believe he could admit to any other interpretations.

Whitley and Evans were friends and political allies. Although there is no direct evidence of collusion, Whitley's account of events at Camp Weld favored Evans' interpretation of the situation. Without reference to Indian complaints regarding White behavior, Whitley's account tended to emphasize the hostile acts committed against innocent Whites with the knowledge and perhaps the complicity of the Indians present. Additionally, Whitley's account does not include more than a hint of statements by Evans regarding a future course of actions for the Indians to follow. The testimony of Stock and others contradicts the impression in Whitley's record on both of these counts. Perhaps Evans decided prior to the council that his best course of action was no action and no commitment on his part. It was possible that Stock was incorrect in his note-taking or that Whitley missed comments during the course of the council. However, after Sand Creek and in his defense regarding his behavior as Indian Superintendent, Evans argued substantially that:

1. Statements made by the Indians at Camp Weld proved their hostility.

2. He did not send the Indians to Fort Lyon, rather he left them in the hands of the military.

3. The statements he made to the Committee on the Conduct of the War were not "prevarications."[147]

Whitley's account provided strong support for Evans' positions and was Evans' major source of evidence.

Evans' unwillingness to make peace at Camp Weld did not keep the Indians present from believing that hostilities were over. Even the News remarked that all present at the council seemed "satisfied." Before their departure, the chiefs embraced Evans and Wynkoop. In the Indians' view, if they went with Major Wynkoop and surrendered to him all would be well. Several White witnesses also testified that this arrangement was their understanding.[148] Thus, Black Kettle, White Antelope, Bull Bear and the Arapahoes returned to their people, in Byers' words, "to induce their tribes to lay down their arms." Upon their return to Fort Lyon, Black Kettle's Cheyennes turned in their arms and met with Major Wynkoop who promised them military rations for sustenance and gave his word of honor that they were in his safekeeping.

Black Kettle and Bull Bear went out to persuade more Cheyennes to come in and surrender. A short while later, Wynkoop was relieved of his command by Major Scott Anthony. Anthony was skeptical of Wynkoop's actions but reported that the Indians appeared to "want peace." Apparently he renewed Wynkoop's agreement with the Indians but sent them to Sand Creek, about twenty-five miles northeast of Fort Lyon so that they could hunt game. He expressed his real intentions to headquarters: "My intention . . . is to let matters remain dormant until troops can be sent out to take the field . . . ." When Chivington arrived on November 28, 1864, with 1,000 men, Anthony wrote that he appreciated the men "as I believe the Indians will be properly punished."[149]

By his apparent overt statements at Camp Weld, Evans attempted to reject peace with the Cheyennes and Arapahoes. Covertly, the council functioned to reassure the Indians that, for the present, hostilities were over. For them "war" was a series of battles and the lull between was peace. Probably Evans was correct that Indian raids would be renewed again in the spring. His apparent message to them was that they must surrender unconditionally to the military. But the Cheyenne had little understanding of such a "surrender," since making peace was a process to be enjoyed. They had enjoyed speaking with Evans and the other Whites; they intended to speak with other Indians to persuade them to stop raiding. In the Indian perception of the "here and now," they had established peace. But, in effect, the Council made the Indians at Sand Creek easy targets for Chivington's Third Regiment. As Anthony wrote on November 6th:

> Their arms [the Indians] are in very poor condition and but few with little ammunition. Their horses far below the average grade of Indians' horses. In fact, these that are here could make but a feeble fight if they desired war.[150]

Although there was much movement by Indians to and from the vicinity near Fort Lyon, the group of Indians attacked by Chivington and his men on November 29, 1864, were those Indians represented at the Camp Weld Council in September.[151]

What were Evans' motives and intentions in the fall of 1863 and throughout 1864? Later Evans declared that he should bear none of the responsibility for any abuses at Sand Creek since he had been out of the Territory at the time.[152] Certainly Evans may have had no perverse motives in the conduct of Indian policy. His background does not suggest any race hatred. In fact, his abolitionist sentiments expressed in 1856 illustrate opposite beliefs regarding the Negro race. Whether this radical bent extended to his beliefs about Indians is not entirely clear. Until he arrived in Colorado, Evans had no direct experience with Native Americans. But his attempts to "civilize" the Cheyennes and the Arapahoes suffered from implicit ethnocentric judgments. When his new charges refused to meet him and talk about a treaty which would embody his civilization policy, it may have been easy for Evans to believe North's information. Without past experience with Indians, their refusal to meet him and their sporadic raids could have indicated to him that the tribes were planning a major uprising. His exaggerated appeals to the War Department may have been a result of fear for Colorado's safety. The same fear could have motivated his appeals to Coloradans to mobilize against hostile Indians.[153] However, such "fear" does not explain his behavior at Camp Weld. If Evans truly feared for Colorado's safety, he should have wanted to make peace with any group of potentially threatening Indians. But perhaps his fear was salved by the raising of the Third Regiment through which he could now protect the Territory. Moreover, his fear of loss of prestige with his White constituents also affected his behavior. Thus, he rejected peace to maintain his elite position which he now saw as dependent upon his previous statements.

Even if fear was Evans' primary motivation, it is also clear that if Colorado was threatened by hostile Indians, a military solution could solve the boundary question. Forced to surrender, the Indians would have to accept conditions as dictated by the Whites. Colorado's potential statehood along with Evans' elected political career depended upon the solution to this problem. With his forced withdrawal prior to the election, Evans may have felt his prestige was at a low ebb, and refused to make peace as the policy he believed to be the most popular with the majority of his White constituents.[154]

Whatever Evans' motivations, it was the latent effects of his messages which worked against the interests of the Native Americans in Colorado. In his statements to Indians at Camp Weld, Evans held out no offer of peace. Yet, the Indians present there subsequently conducted themselves as if they were "at peace." Certainly the attack on the Indians at Sand Creek would have been less likely if Evans had made peace at Camp Weld. That he was not precluded from doing so was implied by Commissioner Dole. Dole reminded Evans of his forgotten role and duties as Indian Superintendent. In October, 1864, Dole wrote to Evans that "it is your duty to hold yourself in readiness to encourage and receive the first intimations of a desire on the part of the Indians for a permanent peace . . . ." Almost as if he were predicting events in November and the following year, Dole concluded, "I cannot help believing that much of the difficulty on the plains might have been avoided, if a spirit of conciliation had been exercised by the military and others."[155] Dole's message implied that any peace made by Evans would have been respected in Washington.

Thus, Governor John Evans did not order the attack on the Indians at Sand Creek. But the messages he sent may have helped to sharpen the knives wielded by Chivington's men on November 29, 1864.

CHAPTER V

NOTES

[1] Edgar Carlisle McMechen in Life of Governor Evans, Second Territorial Governor of Colorado (Denver: Wahlgreen Press, 1924), says that Evans pursued three careers: one as a medical doctor, one as a businessman and one as a politician. But Evans was never successful in being elected to public office (see pp. 1-191). For a brief biography of Evans see the Rocky Mountain News, July 1, 1979, p. 4.

[2] Quoted in McMechan, p. 12.

[3] McMechen, p. 8.

[4] Two historian have been critical regarding Evans' ambitions. Jerome C. Smiley in his History of Denver (Denver: Times-Sun Publications, 1961), pp. 493-494, writes that "His [Evans'] ambitions were divided between two great purposes; one to develop Colorado resources; the other to enter the United States Senate. Therefore his administration was bent, swayed and influenced by his political aims." Hubert Bancroft (quoted in the Rocky Mountain News, July 1, 1979, p. 18) was even less complimentary calling Evans a "cold-blooded mercenary." Donald J. Berthong in The Southern Cheyennes (Norman: University of Oklahoma Press, 1963), pp. 167, 169, also is not complimentary. Berthong argues that Evans tried "systematically" to prove hostility on the part of the plains tribes when no general hostility existed. My contention is not that Evans sought consciously to engage in evil acts but that his efforts tended to function so as to illustrate the savage nature of Native Americans.

[5] McMechen, p. 36.

[6] McMechen, pp. 23, 40-42, 51-53, 77-78.

[7] McMechen, pp. 82, 83.

[8] McMechen, pp. 81, 83.

[9] McMechen, pp. 84-88.

[10] McMechen, pp. 60-64.

[11] Evans quoted in McMechen, p. 30.

[12] This analysis was stimulated by William M. Neil's "The Territorial Governor as Indian Superintendent in the Trans-Mississippi West," The Mississippi Valley Historical Review, 43 (September, 1956), 236.

[13] Rocky Mountain News, June 13, 1863, (hereafter this source will be cited as RMN).

[14] Evans quoted in McMechen, p. 122.

[15] Evans to Dole, August 6, 1862, quoted in Berthong, p. 159.

[16] See Evans' comments in United States Senate "The Chivington Massacre," Reports of the Committee, 39th Congress, 2d session, (Washington, D.C. G.P.O., 1867), p. 133. (Hereafter cited as "The Chivington Massacre.") "Massacre of Cheyenne Indians," Report on the Conduct of the War, 38th Congress, 2d session, (Wasington, D.C. G.P.O., 1864), p. 38. (Hereafter cited as "Massacre of Cheyenne Indians").

[17] "Treaty of Fort Laramie, September 17, 1851," in Wilcomb E. Washburn, The American Indian and the United States: A Documentary History (New York: Random House, 1973), IV, 2477-2480; for discussions of the treaty see: Robert L. Perkin, The First Hundred Years, An Informal History of Denver and the Rocky Mountain News (Garden City, New York: Doubleday & Company, 1959), pp. 77-79; Dee Brown, Bury My Heart at Wounded Knee: An Indian History of the American West (New York: Bantam Books, 1970), pp. 68-70; George Bird Grinnell, The Fighting Cheyenne (1915; rpt. Norman: University of Oklahoma Press, 1958), pp. 100-101.

[18] Berthong, pp. 149-151, 155, 156; also see Raymond Carey, "The Puzzle of Sand Creek," Colorado Magazine, 41 (Fall, 1964), 304-307.

[19] Evans to Dole, March 19, 1863, Letters received by the Office of Indian Affairs, Upper Arkansas Agency, National Archives (Hereafter cited as OIA, LR, Upper Arkansas). Available on microfilm at the Federal Records Center in Atlanta.

[20] Evans to Dole, March 19, 1863, OIA, LR, Upper Arkansas.

[21] S.E. Browne to the Secretary of the Interior, December 29, 1862, OIA, LR, Colorado Superintendency.

[22] Dole quoted in William Unrau, "A Prelude to War," Colorado Magazine, 41 (Fall, 1964), 310.

[23] Evans to Dole, April 10, 1863, OIA, LR, Colorado Superintendency; Also in RMN, August 25, 1864.

[24] One of these officials was Hiriam P. Bennett, Territorial Delegate to Washington and a close ally of Evans. Unrau, p. 311. Dole's retraction is in "Dole to Evans, May 18, 1863, OIA, LS (Letters Sent): also see "Benjamin F. Hall to Dole, May 24, 1863," OIA, LR, Colorado Superintendency.

[25] Dole to Evans, May 18, 1863.

[26] Dole's exact words were for Evans to "Adopt such a kind of policy as may be found expedient." Dole to Evans, May 18, 1863.

[27] Hawkins quoted in United States Interior Department, Bureau of Indian Affairs, Report of the Commissioner of Indian Affairs, 1863 (Washington, G.P.O., 1880-1901), 122, 128-129.

[28] Evans to General Schofield, May 27, 1863, United States War Department, The War of the Rebellion: A Compilation of the Official Records of the Union and Confederate Armies, Washington, G.P.O., 1880-1901, Series 1, Vol 22, part 2, 294 (Hereafter cited as Rebellion Records or RR). Berthong concludes that Hawkins' report was the basis for Evans' message to General Schofield, pp. 162-163. For a similar view, see "Evans to Dole, April 10, 1863," quoted in RMN, August 25, 1864.

[29] While Berthong argues that Evans deliberately and systematically set about to prove to the War Department that the Plains Indians were hostile, there is no direct evidence that this was his intent (Berthong, pp. 167-169). In his interpretation, Berthong ignores evidence that illustrates Evans' attempts to utilize other mechanisms well after

Berthong says that Evans had decided upon proving the Indians to be hostile. Given Evans' Quaker background, it would have been difficult for him to engage in overt arguments which sought Indian destruction. Unconsciously he may have desired such destruction, since such destruction would further his goals and increase his standing with his White supporters. It is less problematic to view Evans' messages as potentially proving or illustrating "true" Indian nature to their receivers. It is also clear that Evans had no official power over the military in Colorado and that he had to persuade the War Department of the necessity for military aid. See Neil, pp. 231 ff, for a general explanation of the problems faced by civilian authorities in the territories relevant to their perceived military needs.

[30] Stan Hoig, The Sand Creek Massacre (Norman: University of Oklahoma Press, 1961), p. 25; RMN, April 27, 1863.

[31] Annual Report of the Commissioner of Indian Affairs, 1863, pp. 239-246.

[32] Berthong, pp. 166-167.

[33] Evans to Commissioner Dole, November 9, 1863, printed in the RMN, August 25, 1864.

[34] Berthong, p. 168; Report, Commissioner of Indian Affairs, 1863, pp. 129-230; One reason for the reluctance of the Indians to negotiate with the Whites was the shooting of an Indian, Little Heart, by a soldier at Fort Larned (Grinnell, pp. 132-133).

[35] Report, Commissioner of Indian Affairs, 1863, p. 121.

[36] Grinnell, p. 134.

[37] Evans to Colley, November 7, 1863; Evans to Commissioner Dole, November 9, November 10, 1863; Evans to Chivington, November 9, 1863; Evans to Secretary of War Stanton, December 14, 1863, all quoted in RMN, August 25, 1864; Also see RR, Series 1, Vol 24, part 4, p. 100.

[38] North's account is recorded in RR, Series 1, Vol 24, part 4, p. 100.

[39] RR, Series 1, Vol 24, part 4, p. 100.

[40] North has been described as the "murderous white chief of an outlawed band of the Northern or Big Horn Arapahoes." Some have reported that North was insane. See Joseph H. Taylor, "Sketches of Frontier and Indian Life on the Upper Missouri and Great Plains," in The Renegade Chief (Bismarck, N.D., 1897), 224ff. Also see Grinnell, p. 134; Hoig, p. 33. Evans did know that North had made this statement. RR, Series 1, Vol 24, part 4, p. 100. Evans also received supporting testimony in this regard from agent John Loree. Loree's character was also questionable. See Robert L. Munkres, "Indian White Contact Before 1870: Cultural Factors in Conflict," Journal of the West, 10 (July, 1971), 460-61. While some historians have accepted that a "conspiracy" of some type actually did take place in 1864, it should be noted that a conspiracy or "alliance" in the White sense of these terms was contrary to Indian nature and probably a practical impossibility. First of all, each Plains tribe considered itself to be the chosen race. The name Cheyenne literally means "The People." Secondarly, individual actions in the Cheyennes' definition of war were more important than group goals. Thus, each individual Cheyenne was more interested in furthering his own prestige by battle than driving the Whites away. An "alliance" by definition would imply that the Cheyennes alone were not able to control their world and, with more Indians engaged in fighting, decrease the chance for individual glory. Third, to sustain an alliance or "conspiracy" requires planning for the future and the Plains Indians seldom planned battle strategy. The Cheyennes were concerned with the "here and now" not some unknown future. Finally, individual small raids for stock with chances for individual bravery were the norm. Such a norm would account for the sighting of only small groups of Indians when large-scale simultaneous uprisings were predicted as in the RMN story, "A Narrow Escape." See George Bird Grinnell, The Cheyenne Indians: Their History and Way of Life (New York: Cooper Square Publishing, 1962), II, 1-47; E. Adamson Hoebel, The Cheyennes, Indians of the Great Plains (Chicago: Holt, Rinehart and Winston, 1960), pp. 69-79, 82-89.

[41] In November 9th correspondence with Commissioner Dole, Evans indicated that he feared

"failure" of the treaty negotiations and that Roman Nose "does not seem much disposed to go to the Arkansas . . . ." (Reprinted in the RMN, August 25, 1864). As an individual, Evans was unused to failure and may have perceived the alliance explanation as a method for avoiding failure.

[42] Berthong, p. 173; McMechen, p. 128. This is the evidence not considered by Berthong in his examination of Evans' "systematic" attempts to prove the Plains Tribes to be hostile.

[43] Evans to E.M. Stanton, December 14, 1863, reprinted in RMN, August 25, 1864.

[44] Evans later referred to these "extensive depredations" in his testimony to the Joint Committee in 1865. He admitted that the horse had been stolen by a band of Arapahoes with whom North lived and that the Indians involved had made restitution for the animals which were not returned ("The Chivington Massacre," p. 46; Grinnell, The Fighting Cheyenne, p. 135). It was at Van Wormer's (sometimes spelled Van Wirmer) ranch in June of 1864 that the Hungates were killed.

[45] Grinnell, The Fighting Cheyenne, p. 130, makes the estimate of the number of soldiers available in Colorado Territory in 1863. "Evans to Stanton, December 14, 1863," reprinted in RMN, August 25, 1864.

[46] Recall the story of "A Narrow Escape," in the RMN, August 26, 1864, discussed in the previous chapter which was a report of events similar to those hinted at by Evans in this earlier message. Also see: Evans to Gen. S.R. Curtis, April 11, 1864, April 26, 1864, in RMN, August 25, 1864; Evans to Curtis, May 28, 1864, RR, Series 1, Vol. 34, part 4, 97-99; Evans to Stanton, June 14, 1864, RR, Series 1, Vol. 34, part 4, 381; Evans to Curtis, June 16, 1864, RR, Series 1, Vol. 34, part 4, 421-423; Evans to Stanton, August 10, 1864, RR, Series 1, Vol. 41, part 2, 661; Evans to Stanton, August 10, 1864, August 22, 1864, RR, Series 1, Vol. 41, part 2, 765, 809. In a letter to Secretary Stanton, September 7, 1864, RR, Series 1, Vol. 41, part 3, 98, Evans finally reports that the "Plan" of the "alliance" was frustrated but that another attempt was expected soon. On September 30,

1864, in his "Address to Captain Tyler, Officers and Men," Evans made specific reference to this "plot" (RMN, September 30, 1864).

[47] Grinnell says that Gov. Evans "was quite ignorant of Indians," this statement, while biased, is probably true (The Fighting Cheyenne, p. 135). At this point Evans had been in Colorado less than a year and had had only limited direct experience with Indians. Moreover, he depended upon his Indian agents and military friends for most of his information about Indians. These individuals were not always the most honest or dependable sources of information. See Harry Kelsey, "Background to Sand Creek," Colorado Magazine, 35 (Fall, 1968), 279-299.

[48] This explanation will be expanded upon more fully below in the discussion of the Camp Weld Conference.

[49] Reportedly Lincoln said to Evans, "Well Governor, you go back to Colorado and handle things as your best judgement dictates during this terrible war, and I will try to handle the situation here," (McMechen, p. 128). Evans was not successful in achieving any of the increased military aid he sought until September of 1864.

[50] Actually Schofield had succeeded Curtis as Commander of the Department of Missouri in May of 1863, but in a reorganization (of which there were many during the Civil War), Curtis succeeded Schofield in January of 1864 with Colorado Territory now included in the Department of Kansas military district. See Arthur P. Wade, "The Military Command Structure of the Great Plains, 1863-1891," Journal of the West, 15 (July, 1976), p. 11. Neil indicates that jurisdictional jealousy was often a problem between military commanders and territorial governors. Curtis may have preferred to act upon "military" information rather than information originating with Evans (Neil, pp. 231ff).

[51] Evans to Major General Curtis, April 11, 1864, reprinted in RMN, August 25, 1864. For accounts of the "recent events" see RR, Series 1, Vol. 34, part 1, 883, 884-85, 887-888. For doubts regarding White claims of cattle theft see Grinnell, The Fighting Cheyenne, pp. 142-43; Hoig, pp. 41-42. Curtis was a

graduate of West Point and commanded the victorious Union forces at Pea Ridge, Arkansas. While the military commander in Missouri, he became involved in factional politics and Lincoln was forced to remove him from command. See Albert Castel, "War and Politics: The Price Raid of 1864," The Kansas Historical Quarterly, 24 (Fall, 1958), 132.

[52] Evans to Curtis, April 26, 1864, reprinted in RMN, August 25, 1864.

[53] See Curtis to Major General Halleck, April 16, 1864, RR, Series 1, Vol. 34, part 3, 188.

[54] Curtis to Evans, May 9, 1864, RR, Series 1, Vol. 34, part 3, 531.

[55] Evans to Curtis, May 28, 1864, RR, Series 1, Vol. 34, part 4, 98.

[56] RR, Series 1, Vol. 34, part 4, 98.

[57] It was August before any widespread organized depredations were reported. See RR, Series 1, Vol. 41, part 2, 642, 670-71.

[58] Evans to Curtis, June 3, 1864, RR, Series 1, Vol. 34, part 4, 206.

[59] RR, Series 1, Vol. 34, part 4, 353.

[60] Evans to Commissioner Dole, June 14, 1864, reprinted in RMN, August 25, 1864.

[61] Evans to Hon. E. M. Stanton, Secretary of War, June 14, 1864, RR, Series 1, Vol. 34, part 4, 381.

[62] Evans wrote to Chivington regarding the facts of the Hungate tragedy, "he (a messenger) says that yesterday afternoon the Indians drove off his stock, burned Mr. Van Wormer's house, and murdered a man who was in Mr. Van W.'s employ, his wife and two children and burned his house . . . ." RR, Series 1, Vol. 34, part 4, 319.

[63] There is no direct proof of this conclusion but no other settlement was destroyed during this time period to which Evans could have been referring. The only "murdered and scalped bodies" brought in were

those of the Hungates. Evans may have believed that the exaggeration was necessary to provide adequate future protection for the population of Colorado.

[64] Evans to Hon. H.P. Bennett, June 24 1864, reprinted in RMN, August 26, 1864.

[65] Evans to Curtis, June 16, 1864, RR, Series 1, Vol. 34, part 4, 421-23; Both McGaa and North, with ties to other tribes (the Sioux and Arapahoes, respectively) had motives to blame the Cheyennes for the depredations.

[66] Evans to Curtis, June 22, 1864, RR, Series 1, Vol. 34, part 4, 512-13.

[67] See: RR, Series 1, Vol. 34, part 4, 100, 206-207, 319, 421-23.

[68] Curtis to Evans, August 11, 1864, RR, Series 1, Vol. 44, part 2, 661.

[69] Curtis to Evans, July 5, 1864, RR, Series 1, Vol. 41, part 2, 53.

[70] Curtis was probably influenced by a report from one of his confidential staff members, Major T.I. McKenny. McKenny had written to Curtis in June that "If great caution is not exercised on our part there will be a bloody war. It should be our policy to try and conciliate them . . . [we should] stop these scouting parties that are roaming over the country who do not know one tribe from another and who will kill anything in the shape of an Indian." RR, Series 1, Vol. 34, part 4, 401-405.

[71] While Curtis never came to believe in the "alliance" supported by Evans, in early August, Curtis adopted a policy that guilty Indians should be "chastised." See Curtis to Commander, Fort Kearney, August 10, 1864, RR, Series 1, Vol. 41, part 2, 644; Curtis to General Blunt, September 22, 1864, RR, Series 1, Vol. 41, part 3, 314; Curtis to General Wood, August 10, 1864, RR, Series 1, Vol. 41, part 2, 645. Curtis wrote to Chivington on the day of the Camp Weld Conference that "I want no peace until the Indians suffer more . . . . It is better to chastize before giving anything . . . . No peace must be made without my directions." (Curtis to Chivington,

September 28, 1864, RR, Series 1, Vol. 41, part 3, 462). Curtis' orders may explain Evans' reluctance to make peace with the Indians at Camp Weld. However, it is not clear whether Evans had received the order prior to the council. But Evans was not subject to Curtis' order. Nevertheless, Evans cites Curtis' orders in his defense of his conduct at Camp Weld, (John Evans, Reply of Governor Evans of the Territory of Colorado to that Part Referring to Him of the Report of 'The Committee on the Conduct of the War,' Headed 'Massacre of Cheyenne Indians.' Executive Department and Superintendency of Indian Affairs, Colorado Territory, August 6, 1865. This Reply is reprinted in "The Chivington Massacre," 80-87, see especially p. 82.

[72] RR, Series 1, Vol. 41, part 1, 964.

[73] Evans claimed that he had sent the Proclamation by special messengers "through every practicable channel . . . to all the tribes of the plains." (Evans quoted in U.S. Senate, "Sand Creek Massacre," Report of the Secretary of War, 39th Cong, 2d session, Senate Executive Document 26 (Washington, D.C.: G.P.O., 1864). Hereafter this source will be cited as Report, Secretary of War or Report). However, the "special messengers" have been described as ignorant and incompetent (Kelsey, pp. 279-299).

[74] John Evans, "Appeal to the People," RMN, August 10, 1864.

[75] RMN, August 10, 1864.

[76] Black Hawk Mining Journal, August 15, 1864.

[77] RMN, August 10, 1864.

[78] RMN, August 11, 1864.

[79] Evans' testimony in "The Chivington Massacre," pp. 45-47.

[80] At the Camp Weld Conference Black Kettle indicated that he had only recently learned of Evans' offer. Forty-four days was not much time to communicate a specific message to widely dispersed groups (Report of the Proceedings of the Camp Weld Meeting in Report, Secretary of War, pp. 213-218).

[81] There is an implication in Evans' "Proclamation to the Friendly Indians of the Plains" on June 27, that he intended no such distinction -- or at least that he did not expect military authorities to make such a distinction. "None but those who intend to be friendly with the whites must come to these places. The families of those who have gone to war with the whites must be kept from among the friendly Indians. The war on hostile Indians will be continued until they are effectively subdued" (RR, Series 1, Vol. 41, part 1, 964). As previously discussed, the election was scheduled for early September and the campaign was actively ongoing by August 1, 1864. Moreover, the "mouthpiece" of the "antis" favored extermination as a policy and had made Evans' Indian policy a campaign issue. Thus, Evans would have wanted to avoid additional controversy without compromising his role as Indian Superintendent.

[82] Even "payment" was not required. Edward Wynkoop testified that from his conversations with Black Kettle he learned that when "friendly" Cheyennes had tried repeatedly to approach the designated forts, they had been driven off and Lean Bear had been killed (Report, Secretary of War, p. 86).

[83] Curtis' request for a militia on August 11 resulted in a company of only 95 men by August 15, (RMN, September 30, 1864). For the 100-days' men Proclamation see RMN, August 13, 1864.

[84] RMN, August 13, 1864.

[85] Pay for a private was $11.00 per month (or $.40/day), for a Corporal, $13.00 and a Sergeant received $17.00 per month ("Pay of Army Officers and Soldiers," RMN, August 31, 1861). Allowance for plunder taken from the Indians was also an important recruiting device as explained by Raymond G. Carey, "The 'Bloodless Third' Regiment, Colorado Volunteer Cavalry," Colorado Magazine, 38 (October, 1961), 278. For evidence regarding the profit involved in killing Indians see Report, Secretary of War, pp. 15, 52, 112. Janet Lecompte in "Sand Creek," Colorado Magazine, 41 (Fall, 1964), 322 says that somehow the wording of Evans' proclamation "Lodged in the minds of those who became "hundred daysers" who proceeded to "kill Indians" without compassion.

[86] RMN, August 23, 1864.

[87] See: Hoig, pp. 85-90; Berthong, pp. 201-204; Grinnell, The Fighting Cheyenne, pp. 156-67 and Lecompte, 321-22.

[88] Berthong, pp. 205-206; also see correspondence in RR, Series 1, Vol. 41, part 2, 642, 670-72, 765.

[89] Curtis to Evans, July 30, 1864, RR, Series 1, Vol. 41, part 2, 484.

[90] Evans to Curtis, August 8, 1864, RR, Series 1, Vol. 41, part 2, 613.

[91] Curtis to Evans, July 30, 1864, RR, Series 1, Vol. 41, part 2, 484.

[92] Evans to Dole, August 10, 1864, RR, Series 1, Vol. 41, part 2, 644.

[93] Evans to Stanton, August 10, 1864, RR, Series 1, Vol. 41, part 2, 644.

[94] Evans to Curtis, August 11, 1864, RR, Series 1, Vol. 41, part 2, 661.

[95] Charlot to Chivington, August 11, 1864, RR, Series 1, Vol. 41, part 2, 644, 695.

[96] Evans to Stanton, August 18, 1864, RR, Series 1, Vol. 41, part 2, 765.

[97] For Curtis' doubts see correspondence in RR, Series 1, Vol. 41, part 3, 179-80, 181, 260, 294-95, 334-35; Evans to Stanton, August 22, 1864, RR, Series 1, Vol. 41, part 2, 809.

[98] Evans to Stanton, September 7, 1864, RR, Series 1, Vol. 41, part 3, 98.

[99] Hoig, p. 109.

[100] Obviously Curtis did not adhere to the "alliance" explanation. Nor were Dole and Stanton ever convinced enough by Evans to provide the requested troops (Dole to Evans, October 15, 1864, Report, Commissioner of Indian Affairs, 1864, p. 256). The one exception in Evans' military audience was

Chivington. However, Chivington only referred to the "alliance" in testimony defending the necessity of the Sand Creek battle. The alliance is never referred to in any of Chivington's official or unofficial reports and correspondence (Testimony of John Chivington, "Massacre of Cheyenne Indians," p. 106).

[101] This military solution could have taken the form of official policy. However, the assumptions of Indian hostility displayed by Chivington's men brought about an Indian reaction which seemed to confirm Indian hostility.

[102] Dole to Evans, October 15, 1864, Report, Commissioner of Indian Affairs, 1864, p. 256.

[103] McMechen, pp. 122-23.

[104] Hoebel, p. 1.

[105] Quoted in McMechen, p. 118.

[106] Report, Commissioner of Indians Affairs, 1862, p. 229; Grinnell, p. 131.

[107] Hoebel, p. 69.

[108] Hoebel, p. 70.

[109] See Robert L. Munkres, "Indian-White Contact Before 1870: Cultural Factors in Conflict," Journal of the West, 10 (July, 1971), 439-473; Theodore Balgooyen, "A Study of Conflicting Values: American Plains Indian Orators Vs. the U.S. Commissioners of Indian Affairs," Western Speech, (Spring, 1962), 76-83.

[110] White Antelope made such a statement at the Camp Weld Conference, see p. 216 in Report, Secretary of War.

[111] RR, Series 1, Vol. 34, part 1, 884-85.

[112] Bowsers' testimony is in "The Chivington Massacre," pp. 72-73.

[113] Dunn reported that he had not learned to what tribe the Indians belonged; Sanborn reported that Dunn said "They represented themselves [the Indians] to be Cheyennes . . . (RR, Series 1, Vol. 34, part 1, 883, 885).

[114] RR, Series 1, Vol. 34, part 1, 883.

[115] For official reports see RR, Series 1, Vol. 34, part 1, 880-88; for discussion of contrasting points of view see Grinnell, The Fighting Cheyenne, pp. 137-44 and Hoig, pp. 36-53.

[116] See Wynkoop's testimony in Report, Secretary of War, p. 85.

[117] See discussion in Hoebel, pp. 69-79 and Grinnell, The Cheyenne Indians, II, 1-47. Also see Munkres, p. 457 and Balgooyen, pp. 76-77. A Cheyenne who murdered another Cheyenne was thought to "stink" thereafter and usually was ostracized for a time (Hoebel, pp. 50-52).

[118] Balgooyen, p. 82.

[119] Munkres, p. 457.

[120] Testimony of John Smith, Report, Secretary of War, p. 32.

[121] Black Kettle quoted in Report, Secretary of War, p. 85.

[122] RR, Series 1, Vol. 41, part 1, 964; In his "Reply," Evans said that the Proclamation was issued only "months after the war had become general." See "The Chivington Massacre," p. 78.

[123] Evans to Colley, June 16, 1864, RR, Series 1, Vol. 41, part 1, 963.

[124] Hoig, p. 63; Testimony of William Bent in United States Congress, Condition of the Indian Tribes, Report of the Joint Special Committee, (Washington, D.C., G.P.O., 1867), p. 95. Also see Testimony of John Dodds, Testimony of Asbury Bird and Testimony of Robert Bent, pp. 65, 72, 96.

[125] Kelsey, pp. 284-86.

[126] Testimony of S.J. Colley, "Chivington Massacre," pp. 35-36. Evans had instructed Colley on June 16th to make "requisition" with the Commander at Fort Lyon for the "subsistence" of the "friendly" Indians (RR, Series 1, Vol. 41, part 1, 1863).

[127] Evans to Colley, September 29, 1864, RR, Series 1, Vol. 41, part 3, 495.

[128] John T. Dodds testified that Black Kettle, Lean Bear and Left Hand had complained that they had to pay for the goods given to them by the "Great Father." Condition of the Indian Tribes, p. 65.

[129] Reginald S. Craig, The Fighting Parson: The Biography of Colonel John M. Chivington (Los Angeles: Westernlore Press, 1959), pp. 203-205, 208.

[130] Testimony of Major Wynkoop, Report, Secretary of War, p. 86.

[131] Colley to Evans, September 4, 1864, RR, Series 1, Vol. 41, part 3, 195.

[132] See Wynkoop to Lieutenant J.E. Tappan, September 18, 1864, RR, Series 1, Vol. 41, part 3, 242-43; Also see Wynkoop's testimony in Report, Secretary of War, pp. 84-85.

[133] Testimony of Edward Wynkoop, "The Chivington Massacre," p. 77; also see Report, Secretary of War, p. 90.

[134] "The Chivington Massacre," p. 77.

[135] Whitley's record is on pp. 213-17 in Report, Secretary of War.

[136] Report, Secretary of War, p. 213.

[137] Report, Secretary of War, pp. 213-14.

[138] Report, Secretary of War, pp. 404-405.

[139] Report, Secretary of War, p. 404.

[140] Testimony of Amos Stock (or Steck), Report, Secretary of War, 41; Stock also kept notes during the council (Testimony of Joseph Cramer, Report, Secretary of War, p. 60). Although the wording of his version is not exactly as recorded by Whitley, his version follows the general development of speeches as recorded (supposedly) verbatim by Whitley. For example, Stock recalls the similes used by Black

Kettle as recorded by Whitley. The differences in the two accounts will be explained. Whitley was a close ally of Evans, Stock was not.

[141] Report, Secretary of War, pp. 40, 215.

[142] Report, Secretary of War, pp. 216, 42. Also see Whitley's explanation of this remark on pp. 217-18; This analysis is intended to illustrate that Whitley's account may not have been accurate.

[143] Report, Secretary of War, pp. 216, 42. In his testimony, Captain Silas Soule said that the Indians were led from making statements regarding White depredations against them "by other questions" (p. 27).

[144] Report, Secretary of War, p. 217. Whitley also testified that he was not certain if all the statements made by the Governor had been made directly to the Indians (p. 45).

[145] Evans to Major S.G. Colley, September 29, 1864, RR, Series 1, Vol. 41, part 3, 495.

[146] RMN, September 29, 1864; Also see: Testimony of Edward Wynkoop, Silas Soule and Joseph Cramer in Report, Secretary of War, pp. 91, 9 and 61. For Evans' statements in this regard see his "Reply" in the "The Chivington Massacre," p. 82 and his testimony on p. 47 of the same document.

[147] Evans' "Reply" in "The Chivington Massacre," p. 86.

[148] RMN, September 29, 1864; Wynkoop's testimony in Report, Secretary of War, pp. 91, 100; Soule's Testimony, Report, p. 10; Testimony of Joseph Cramer, Report, p. 61.

[149] See Wynkoop's testimony in Report, pp. 91-92; Reports of Major Scott Anthony, November 6-16th, 1864 -- Affairs at Fort Lyon, Colorado Territory, RR, Series 1, Vol. 41, part 1, 912-914; Anthony to Lieut. A. Helliwell, November 28, 1864, RR, Series 1, Vol. 41, part 4, p. 708.

[150] Robert M. Utley has concluded that the chiefs departed the council content that peace had resulted

but were not aware "of the nuances that qualified the agreement in the minds of Evans and Chivington." Frontersman in Blue: The United States Army and the Indian, 1848-1865 (New York: Macmillan, 1967), p. 291. Also see reports of Major Scott Anthony, November 6, 1864, RR, Series 1, Vol. 41, part 1, 913.

[151]Testimony of Joseph Cramer, Report, Secretary of War, p. 50.

[152]"The Chivington Massacre," p. 78.

[153]It would be impossible to prove absolutely if Evans shared the myth he helped to propagate. He did have access to information which disproved or tended to disprove the "alliance." Evans received a letter from Robert B. Mitchell, Commander of the District of Nebraska which dismissed the possibility of "combined efforts of the Indians in this district . . ." (RR, Series 1, Vol. 41, part 2, 168). He also received a letter from S.E. Browne on August 25, 1864, discounting "the story about Indians being seen . . ." which was the basis for the plot which Evans referred to in his letter to Stanton on September 7 (RR, Series 1, Vol. 41, part 2, 864). Evans did not waiver from his "alliance" explanation in any of the statements or defenses studied.

[154]This conclusion is similar to that of Lonnie J. White in "From Bloodless to Bloody: The Third Colorado Cavalry and the Sand Creek Massacre," Journal of the West, 6 (October, 1967), 550.

[155]Dole to Evans, October 16, 1864, Report, Commissioner of Indian Affairs, 1864, p. 256.

CHAPTER VI

COLONEL JOHN CHIVINGTON: ELITE SYMBOLS OF NATIVE AMERICANS AND THE LEGITIMATION OF EXTERMINATION

Background

Like his friend, John Evans, John Chivington was a self-made man. Chivington was born on January 27, 1821 in Warren County, Ohio. Beyond this fact, little reliable evidence has been located regarding Chivington's early life. In Chivington family tradition, his father has been described as a bigamist and alcoholic who "came to a sad end in a roadside snowbank with a half-filled jug clutched in his congealed hand."[1]

However, Chivington's only biographer, Reginald Craig, has portrayed Chivington's father as an honest, hardworking woodsman. Additionally, Craig presents Chivington in an idealized manner. As Professor Carey describes it, "as remarkably similar to an idealized, youthful Lincoln."[2] Amid Craig's sanitized anecdotes of Chivington's life (including his role at Sand Creek), is some information which appears to be reliable. Like Evans, Chivington was a convert to Methodism, opting for the ministry in 1844. Between 1844 and 1860, Chivington preached in five different states: Ohio, Illinois, Missouri, Kansas and Nebraska. He started preaching as a "circuit rider" but he arrived in Denver in 1860 as a presiding elder of Denver's First Methodist Episcopal Church. Also like Evans, Chivington declared abolitionist beliefs and was a loyal Union man and Republican. While in Missouri, Chivington served as missionary to the Wyandot Indians. Throughout his life, Chivington was also an active Mason, founding lodges in Kansas and Colorado.[3]

Little else is known about Chivington's early life. It is apparent that prior to his arrival in Denver, he had worked hard enough in his various ministries to be given more responsibility. However, his rise was not rapid and, until he arrived in Denver, he appears to have had no other ambitions besides his church work. He had little military experience and while he had maintained an interest in politics, he had not sought political office.

However, by August of 1861, Chivington had become a Major in the First Colorado Regiment. Apparently he had put his life in the ministry behind him. Reportedly when offered the position of Chaplain with the Colorado Regiment, Chivington declined the offer and demanded a "fighting commission" instead. The reasons for his shift of life interests are obscure. Craig credits Chivington's patriotism and his wish to destroy slavery as being among the primary causes.[4] No doubt, Chivington did believe these to be good reasons for his change of careers. However, the selection of a purely secular role after fifteen years in the ministry is surprising. Perhaps Chivington believed he could serve his new community best in this new role. Additionally, his last child had just been married, lessening his responsibility at home. After fifteen years of a relatively sedate life, he may have desired more excitement and physical activity. Moreover, if he were an ambitious man, he could have perceived involvement in military life as a more direct route to a position of influence or simply another position from which he could influence the community.[5]

Whatever his motivations, Chivington illustrated quickly a flair for the military life. Although his only prior military experience was a short term in an Ohio militia company, he was soon placed in charge of the training of new recuits at Camp Weld.[6] Eventually Chivington and the rough and undisciplined volunteer troops were ordered to New Mexico to assist Colonel Canby of the Department of New Mexico. While in New Mexico, the Colorado troops were instrumental in stopping an attempted Confederate invasion of Colorado. It is generally conceded that Chivington's leadership was responsible for cutting the supply lines to the Confederate forces. This action made the difference for the outnumbered Union forces.[7] As a reward, Chivington received a field promotion from Major to Colonel of the First Colorado Regiment, which was later signed by Colorado Governor John Evans.[8] A few months after returning to Denver, Colonel Chivington was appointed Commander of the Military District of Colorado. As Commander, he was responsible for protecting the civilian inhabitants of

Colorado from Rebel invasion and Indian depredations. Moreover, he was also faced with the de facto duty of keeping the overland mail and stage route open. In 1863 and 1864 Chivington also became involved in Territorial politics, running for Congress on the pro-state ticket.

Chivington sent three general types of messages regarding Native Americans between 1863 and 1865: official orders directed to his subordinates; official reports directed to his superiors, and "unofficial" statements made prior to and during the engagement at Sand Creek. These messages, taken together, tended to legitimize and to justify extermination as the solution to the Indian problem.

Official Correspondence

The official messages sent by Chivington to his subordinates were uncomplicated. White interests were always to be favored over American Indian concerns. His written orders for dealing with apparent Indian depredations against Whites were brutally direct: pursue the offenders, force restitution and "kill" those responsible. In his reports and correspondence to his superiors, Chivington was more circumspect. His official reports and messages illustrate a gradual development from a policy of "prudence" to "chastisement" and finally to "cleaning them [the Indians] out." These reports may have tended to persuade General Curtis that pursuit, restitution and punishment should be the military's policy towards the Plains tribes. Moreover, these same reports provide hints that Chivington was considering a military action against the Indians similar to Sand Creek.[9]

Upon his return to the Territory in June of 1863 after the New Mexico campaign, Chivington appeared confident in his new command. He wrote to District Headquarters that the Indians were "restive" but predicted that "they may be gotten along with without fighting, by a firm and prudent course on our part." However, like Evans, he made it clear that an adequate number of troops was necessary to assure continued peace.[10] Except for the ongoing conflict between the Utes and the Cheyennes, and a few minor Indian raids, Chivington and his troops were not involved much in

Indian affairs. When military action was required "chastisement" was the policy and caution was urged by Chivington "toward any party of Indians who are peacefully disposed."[11]

The spring of 1864 brought increased conflict and Chivington demonstrated a harsher attitude. On April 13, 1864, he reported to General Curtis the events at Fremont's Orchard. Also, he sought permission for an apparent change of policy, writing, "I shall chastise them severely unless you direct differently."[12] But he did not allow Curtis to respond before making his own policy change. The same day that he wrote to General Curtis, he informed the Commander at Fort Laramie about Dunn's fight, warning that the Indians "have gone with stolen stock in your direction," and urged the Commander to "Look out for them and kill them."[13] By April 16th, Chivington appeared to be sharing Evans' interpretation of events. He wrote the commanding officer of Fort Union, New Mexico, "The long anticipated difficulties with Indians in this Territory appear to have reached a crises." However, probably Chivington wanted only to impress upon the Commander that all of Colorado's troops were needed in Colorado.[14] By the 29th of April, Chivington was reassuring General Curtis that further Indians troubles did not seem "probable." He also undercut Evans' attempts to gain the authority to call out the militia writing to Curtis that "Don't think they [the militia] will be needed but possibly they may."[15]

But, by the end of May, Chivington was worrying about the Indians again. He predicted to Major Charlot that "These Indians [the Cheyennes] are going to give our settlements a bad time this season."[16] Therefore, Chivington instructed Major Wynkoop that "The Cheyennes have to be soundly whipped before they will be quiet. If any of them are caught in your vicinity, kill them, as that is the only way." Chivington's change of expression is not entirely attributable to external events since Indian depredations in May occurred at approximately the same level as April.[17] He may have been responding to erroneous information which rumored that a good portion of Lieutenant Eayre's expedition had been destroyed by the Cheyennes. Chivington knew that Denver was "filled with rumors" regarding Indian threats and depredations.[18] Additionally, a state constitutional convention had just been called to write a "constitution" to be voted upon and Chivington was an active delegate. He emerged as the pro-staters' nominee for Congress.[19] His shift to a harsher policy could have been a result of his own anxieties which he shared with the population at large. He may have believed that a harsh stand could help to increase his prestige in the nervous community.

But Chivington's message to General Curtis via Major Charlot was more restrained than that message he sent to Wynkoop. Chivington commented that "The Kiowas and Cheyennes are determined on war and will have to be soundly thrashed before they will be quiet."[20] After the Hungate Massacre, Chivington ordered Captain Davidson of the First Colorado Regiment to pursue the Indians responsible but encouraged Davidson not to "encumber your command with prisoners." The meaning was clear -- the Indians were not to be captured but killed.[21] Such strong feelings were understandable, given the nature of the Hungate tragedy.

However, Chivington did not present such frank language to Major Charlot and General Curtis. He informed Curtis that:

> Their policy [the Indians] seems to be to keep their families and stock on the Cimarron and other tributaries of the Arkansas, south side, and send out parties to kill and steal . . . . My judgement is that the only way to conquer a peace is to follow them to their settlements and there chastise them . . . . Does this meet the approbation of the major general commanding?[22]

There was a foreshadowing of Chivington's military action at Sand Creek in this message. With his question directed at Curtis, he may have sought approval for such a policy. However, Curtis did not respond. For several weeks thereafter there was no communication between Chivington and Curtis. This "silence" occurred during approximately the same time period that Curtis and Governor Evans did not correspond. When Curtis finally wrote to Chivington, it was to reprimand him for not keeping him informed of events in Colorado. Curtis had requested information from Chivington fearing that he was not receiving authentic accounts of "Indian barbarities."

He demanded "careful reports" from Chivington.[23] When he received no information, apparently Curtis concluded that Chivington was too preoccupied with politics in Colorado to comply. Therefore on July 30th, Curtis warned Chivington that:

> I fear your attention is too much attracted by other matters than your command, and hope you will feel the importance of concluding a good record, which you commenced in the line of your present duties, whatever turn other matters of public interest may take in Colorado. I have [had] no news from Colorado . . . . I did not get your dispatches sent to me from this place, as they had not arrived when I left Fort Leavenworth. I shall expect to find them on reaching my headquarters . . . .

Three days later Curtis was also demanding that Evans send him the "facts."[24] Obviously Curtis felt out of touch with events in Colorado. He did not believe that Evans was a reliable source of information. Thus he reprimanded Chivington severely. He wanted the military facts and Chivington should have been his best source since the Major had a good military record when he "commenced" his duties.

Curtis appears to have been ignorant, or at least unrealistic, regarding the war-making potential of the Plains tribes. Like many military men, his education and experience did not provide him with adequate understanding of Indian customs.[25] He illustrated this lack of understanding on June 29th when he informed Chivington that ". . . a good company or two, with two howitzers well-attended, is no doubt sufficient to pursue and destroy any band of Indians likely to congregate anywhere on the Plains, and it is bad economy to divert needless numbers in pursuit of Indians." This attitude would also help to explain the futility of Evans' frantic demands throughout the summer. Curtis' misconceptions of the Plains Indians' war-making potential were similar to the misconceptions of George Armstrong Custer.[26] It is problematic whether Curtis realized his misconceptions. However, threats to distant settlements from roving bands of Indians were secondary to his primary duty of holding Missouri, Kansas and Colorado Territory safe from the Confederacy. With a perceived information vacuum and little time to personally investigate the situation in

Colorado, Curtis ultimately may have accepted Chivington's information and policy recommendations without careful critical analysis. That is, once Curtis was reassured regarding Chivington's performance of his duties, he may have been especially susceptible to information originating with Chivington. Curtis' complaint had been about a lack of information originating with Chivington, not the nature of the information.

Chivington's letter to Curtis of August 8, 1864 contained the necessary reassurances. Chivington apologized for the delay in reports, provided his excuses and assured Curtis that he had been performing and would continue to perform his required duties.[27] Chivington made no promises regarding increased communications with Curtis but maintained more regular correspondence thereafter. Moreover, these messages contained concise information about Native Americans' conduct in Colorado which tended to reinforce a policy of punishment. Chivington sent Curtis recommendations for the relocation of various military posts in Colorado. He also hinted that extermination might be the best way to solve the Indian problem. For example, he speculated:

> . . . should our national troubles terminate soon these posts should be needed but a few years, as then we should be able to either kill off those Indians or make them settle on reservations and go to work, and I confess the former of these propositions looks most feasible to me. Of this last point I do not speak so positively but of the first I don't think there is a doubt.[28]

Thus Chivington stated again that "killing Indians" was his favored policy and it was a policy which was enacted at Sand Creek. Additionally, this "hint" accompanied information useful to Curtis and was available for consideration if Curtis was unsure of what actions to take.[29] Throughout September of 1864, Chivington sent information to Curtis. He reported that Indians were "all around"; that there were large forces of Indians "congregated eighty miles from Fort Lyon 3,000 strong."[30] When Chivington learned that Wynkoop was bringing Black Kettle and the other chiefs to Denver, he telegraphed Curtis that information, hinted at the Indians' "real" reason for seeking peace and provided Curtis with the policy which should be recommended:

I have been informed by E.W. Wynkoop, Commanding Fort Lyon, that he is on his way here with Cheyenne and Arapahoe Chiefs and four white prisoners they gave up. Winter approaches. Third Regiment is full, and they know they will be chastised for their outrages and now want peace. I hope the Major-General will direct that they make full resitution and then go on their reserve and stay there. Would like to know by telegraph.[31]

Curtis replied, following Chivington's lead with an order which effectively negated the possibility of any permanent peace on the part of the Whites after Camp Weld:

I shall require the bad Indians delivered up; restoration of equal numbers of stock; also hostages to secure. I want no peace till the Indians suffer more . . . . It is better to chastise before giving anything but a little tobacco to talk over. No peace must be made without my directions.[32]

After this order, Chivington was not afraid to make an open statement of his policy toward Indians to Curtis. On July 5th, he hinted to Curtis that the way to "conquer a peace" was to chastise the Indians in their villages. By October 10th, the policy was in process. Thus Chivington reported that:

Captain Nichols, Third Colorado Volunteer Cavalry, surprised and killed 10 Indians, Cheyennes, captured 11 ponies and 1 mule this morning near Valley Station. <u>We will clean them out of country between Platte and Arkansas directly</u> [emphasis added].[33]

Chivington did not mention that this "village" was comprised of only two lodges inhabited by six warriors, three squaws, a youngster about fifteen years old "who shot an arrow well," and two babies. One of the volunteers present that day was Morse Coffin. He wrote, years later, that the women and children were killed in cold blood after the men had been killed and over the objections of some of the volunteers. This was the village whose inhabitants "went under one and all . . ." as suggested by the

Rocky Mountain News. Chivington's orders to his subordinates to "kill all the Indians you come across" had been followed to the letter.

Therefore, Chivington's official orders to his subordinates legitimized a policy of extermination. By ordering that "all Indians" be killed, he helped to negate any chance for "friendly Indians" to proceed to safe places. Moreover, such a phrase also allowed for the killing of women and children. No order to the contrary was included in any of Chivington's orders.

With his reports to General Curtis, Chivington "educated" Curtis in a policy of punishment for Colorado's Indian tribes. Whether because of Chivington's information or actual events, or both, after August 10, 1864, Curtis officially endorsed a "punishment" policy. Although Curtis did not approve the indiscriminate slaughter of all ages and sexes, Chivington felt free to report to Curtis Captain Nichols' action near Valley Station.[34]

Unofficial Messages

Statements attributed to Chivington before and during the Sand Creek Battle contributed to a legitimation of extermination as policy. While it is not clear if all of Chivington's statements were intended as orders or stimulated any in his command to engage in indiscriminate slaughter, scalping or other atrocities, apparently he made no statements precluding such actions.[35]

In a sense, the entire military action at Sand Creek was "unofficial." Although the planning for movement of men and materials to the site of the battle had to be started well in advance, Chivington made no overt mention of his intentions to General Curtis. Moreover, the location of the battle, near Fort Lyon in southeastern Colorado, was out of Chivington's command.[36]

In mid-October, 1864, Chivington began ordering his troops out of the Denver area. Any large-scale military action had been delayed because of the lack of proper mounts, saddles and weapons. However, on the 15th of October the necessary saddles arrived and Chivington ordered various units of the Third to Bijou

Basin, about seventy miles southeast of Denver. He wrote to Wynkoop requesting his aid in speeding up delivery of some needed arms so that he (Chivington) could go after a "large number" of Indians located somewhere on the Republican River. While the existence of this "large number" of Indians has been disputed, it is unclear whether Chivington believed he was going in pursuit of these Indians. Chivington probably believed that he had to appear to be doing "something."[37]

The morale of the volunteer troops was at a low ebb. They had been called the "Bloodless Third" by skeptical Coloradans. Chivington himself had just received a resounding defeat in the September election.[38] He was also under continuing pressure from Ben Holladay, owner of the Overland Stage Line, to keep the route open and safe from Indian raids. Chivington was threatened further in late October when he learned that Holladay had pressured Secretary of War Stanton into turning the protection of the Overland trail over to Brigadier-General P.E. Connor. Apparently, it was a worried Chivington who telegraphed Major Charlot:

> Have department lines been changed? If not, will I allow him [Connor] to give direction to matters in this district? Line perfectly protected to Julesberg. The line this side Julesberg ought to be in this district, as my troops are taking care of it.[39]

In the meantime, the troops at Camp Elbert in Bijou Basin had been stopped from further movement by severe winter storms. The storms resulted, according to a participant, in an "almost universal howl of discontent among the men." They had joined up to kill Indians, but so far only the ranks of the Third had been thinned by deaths from exposure and by desertion.[40] On that same date[41] Chivington issued marching orders to the Third. Years later, Chivington wrote that Connor expressed to him doubts about the chances of Chivington and his men catching any Indians. Chivington recalled:

> To which I could only reply, 'I may not general, but I think I will catch them.'
> I promised him I would do so, when he looked back at me and said: 'colonel where are these Indians?'

290

I said 'General that is the trick that wins in this game, if the game is won. There are but two persons who know their exact location, and they are myself and Colonel George L. Shoup.'$_{42}$ Chivington responded to this challenge from Connor not by setting a course toward the Republican but by setting a "secret course." Later he explained that previous$_{43}$Indian campaigns had failed for lack of secrecy.

By November 24th, Chivington and his troops were encamped at Spring Bottom, a stage station along the Arkansas River. Here, one James Combs from Fort Lyon encountered Chivington and his officers. According to Combs' testimony, Chivington questioned him regarding the status of the occupants at Fort Lyon and whether Chivington's troop movements were known. Combs replied that Chivington's activities were unknown and that Major Anthony had recently replaced Major Wynkoop as Commander. According to Combs, Chivington responded "Oh! You must be mistaken; I think Left Hand was in command before Major Anthony came here." Thereafter Combs related that Chivington questioned him closely about the demeanor of the Indians near Fort Lyon. Combs commented that there was "promiscuous conversation" among Chivington and his men about scalps, "where they were going to arrange them, etc. He [Chivington] spoke up said that 'scalps are what we are after.'" Combs then told Chivington that 400-500 scalps were within a day's march of Fort Lyon and that they could be taken with fifty men because "they [the Indians] had given up their arms to Major Anthony and were unarmed now." Additionally, Combs said he informed Chivington that some of the Indians were away on a buffalo hunt. Reportedly Chivington responded that "he would give them a lively buffalo hunt." Then Chivington drew himself up in his chair and declared "'Well I long to be wading in gore.'"$_{44}$

Chivington had made statements regarding his policy toward Indians prior to his November words and actions. S.E. Browne testified that in a public speech delivered in late August, Colonel Chivington announced "that his policy was to 'kill and scalp all little and big; that nits made lice.'" A.C. Hunt testified similarly that Chivington's policy was "to exterminate the Indians -- to kill them all."

Lieutenant Cramer also reported that "I heard him [Chivington] say he was in favor of killing all the Indians he came to."[45]

By the 27th, the Third was ten miles from Fort Lyon where Chivington and his officers encountered Lieutenant Silas Soule and Second Lt. Minton. Soule, also a hero of the Glorietta campaign, testified that he was surprised to encounter Chivington and his troops. Soule and Minton were on a scouting expedition and believed initially that the fires of the Third were Indian campfires. Chivington asked immediately if there were Indians at Fort Lyon. Soule replied that a few Cheyennes and Arapahoes were camped at Sand Creek. Soule emphasized, he said, that the Indians were not dangerous and were considered as prisoners of war. One of Chivington's officers responded "They won't be prisoners after we get there." The statement drew laughter from a number of the soldiers with Chivington.[46]

After the Third arrived at Lyon, Soule consulted with two other officers: Lieutenants Cramer and Baldwin. The three agreed that Chivington's plan to attack the Indians at Sand Creek was ill-conceived. Therefore Soule approached Major Anthony to determine if Anthony would help them to dissuade Chivington. Anthony's cooperation was crucial to Chivington, since Fort Lyon was not included in his command. Anthony could have stopped or at least delayed the attack until he contacted his superior for instructions. However, Anthony (Soule said) indicated that he would support Chivington's expedition since Chivington had promised to spare the "friendly Indians." Moreover, Anthony told Soule that the real objective of the expedition was a much larger group of hostile Indians at Smoky Hill. Anthony also warned Soule that Chivington had made threats against Soule for his opposition.[47] Cramer had a similar discussion with Anthony with the same results. Cramer testified that he approached Chivington to dissuade him:

> I had some conversation with Major Downing, Lieutenant Maynard and Colonel Chivington. I stated to them my feelings in regards to the matter; that I believed it to be 'murder,' and stated the obligations that we of Major Wynkoop's command were under to those Indians. To Colonel Chivington I know I stated that Major Wynkoop had

pledged his word as an officer and a man to those
Indians, and that all officers under him were
indirectly pledged in the same manner that he
was, and that I felt it was placing us in very
embarrassing circumstances, to fight the same
Indians that had saved our lives, as we all felt
they had. Colonel Chivington's reply was, that
he believed it right or honorable to use any
means under God's heaven to kill Indians that
would kill women and children, and 'damn any man
that was in sympathy with Indians,' and such men
as Major Wynkoop and myself had better get out of
the United States service.[48]

Later, the same day, Lietenants Minton and Cossit
addressed Chivington, also trying to convince him not
to attack the Sand Creek encampment. Again Chivington
responded, "Damn any man who is in sympathy with an
Indian." He also threatened to arrest officers who
did not comply with his orders.[49] That same evening
between 700 and 1000 troops left Fort Lyon for Sand
Creek. Chivington was in command and old Indian scout
Jim Beckwourth, always a friend to the Cheyennes, had
been forced into service as a guide. The troops rode
all night and came upon the encampment of Indians in
the early dawn. Prior to leading the charge upon the
village Chivington addressed his troops. Morse Coffin
was in the best position to witness the statement.
Coffin related that:

. . . Colonel Chivington, turning to the command
said: 'Boys, I shall not tell you what you are
to kill, but remember our slaughtered women and
children,' or words similar and I think the above
is correctly nearly word for word . . . . As he
said this his countenance showed deep feeling and
agitation and I think his lips quivered. I
noticed both his expression and words, as I was
probably not more than 30 to 40 feet from him.[50]

Jim Beckwourth testified to a slightly different
version of Chivington's statements. He declared:

His remark, when he halted up in the middle of
Sand Creek was this: 'Men strip for action!' He
also said 'I don't tell you to kill all ages and
sexes, but look back on the plains of the Platte,
where your mothers, fathers, brothers, sisters
have been slain, and their blood saturating the
sands of the Platte.'

Robert Bent, Lieutenant Cannon and A.J. Gill testified to hearing similar remarks.[51]

With Chivington's statements to remind them of the mutilated visages of the Hungates, Governor Evans' assurances that killing Indians was a patriotic act and their own personal frustrations as the "Bloodless Third," the volunteers, according to one observer, rushed into the encampment "like so many wild fellows."[52]

The exact nature of events at the battle of Sand Creek has been subject to some controversy.[53] What is obvious from the testimony in the three different investigations is that the volunteers fought with much disorder. The wounds of several volunteers were attributed not to the Indians, but to other volunteers. Silas Soule refused to order his company to fire. "Captured" Indian property and stock disappeared and was never accounted for.[54] If the independent volunteers did want to commit acts of butchery upon the outnumbered Indians, it is unclear that orders to the contrary would have been obeyed. However, it is apparent that Chivington did not attempt to prevent such actions. As James Cannon testified ". . . to the best of my knowledge and belief these atrocities that were committed were with the knowledge of J.M. Chivington and I do not know of his taking any measures to prevent them." Major Anthony believed such a order to the contrary would have been obeyed since all other orders had been obeyed.[55] Jack Smith, in particular, suffered for lack of such a contrary order.

Jack Smith was the son of John Smith, Indian scout and Evans' official Indian translator. Young Smith, a half-breed, was at the Indian camp visiting his mother. In the course of the battle, Jack Smith was captured. The evening after the battle, talk began circulating that the volunteers were threatening to kill Smith. When Chivington was told that the soldiers were planning to kill Jack, he replied," I have given my instructions, have told my men not to take any prisoners."[56] Jim Beckwourth related the results of Chivington's muteness:

> He [Jack Smith] was sitting in the lodge with me; not more than five or six feet from me, just across the lodge. There were from ten to fifteen

soldiers came into the lodge at the time, and there was some person on the outside and called to his father, John Smith. He, the old man, went out, and there was a pistol fired when the old man got out of the lodge. There was a piece of the lodge cut out where [when] the old man went out. There was a pistol fired through this opening and the bullet entered below his [Jack Smith's] right breast. He sprung forward and fell dead . . . .$_{57}$

Colonel Shoup testified that he heard Chivington order that John Smith was not to be harmed, but "that he did not intend to take any Indian prisoners."$_{58}$ That is, John Smith, a White man, was to be preserved but his son Jack, a half-breed, was an expendable Indian.

Chivington's "unofficial statements" functioned both to stifle opposition and to legitimize extermination as policy. The extermination of Native Americans was a popular policy. Informally, it was as difficult for Soule, Cramer and Minton to express their contrary views to Chivington as it was for a Denver citizen to disagree with the majority decision of a peoples' court. Formally, the dissenters were faced by the requirements of military procedure. Failure to obey Chivington could result in their arrest. Chivington's threats served at least to silence the opposition. With no contrary views expressed a policy of extermination would have been facilitated. Murray Edelman provides some insight into such suppression of communication. He writes:

> Hostile speeches [about enemies] . . . force political spectators either to perceive the targets of these actions as malevolent or to perceive the government as deceptive. In the absence of other cues the great majority will predictably resolve such dissonance in favor of the official regime . . . .$_{59}$

Thus, the borderline volunteers who may have been uncomfortable with Chivington's apparent policy, in the absence of conflicting data, "went along."

The content of Chivington's informal statement could partially account for Morse Coffin's belief that the feeling was "general" that a war of extermination was to be waged against the Indians. Such statements which originated with a perceived military authority -- the military authority in Colorado Territory -- could only tend to legitimize extermination as policy. The so-called "floaters" and other less desirable elements in the Third may have been prone to killing and mutilating Indians absent any statement from a superior officer. However, the same procedures which allowed Chivington to silence his officers, may have decreased the probability of abuses. If Major Anthony was correct, at least the most stable elements of the Third would have obeyed orders.

Sand Creek Reported

Chivington presented unequivocal reports of the engagement at Sand Creek: a large force of hostile Cheyennes was attacked, 400-500 Indians were killed and all the volunteers "did nobly." His first report from the scene was terse but set the mold for his detailed version of the battle as well as his officers' reports. Chivington reported:

> In the last ten days my command has marched 300 miles, 100 of which the snow was two feet deep. After a march of forty miles last night I, at daylight this morning attacked Cheyenne village of 130 lodges, from 900 to 1,000 warriors strong; killed chiefs Black Kettle, White Antelope Knock knee and little Robe [little Raven], and between 400 and 500 other Indians . . . . All did nobly, Think I will catch some more of them eighty miles, on Smoky Hill. Found white man's scalp, not more than three days old, in one of the lodges.[60]

Chivington's longer report written on December 16th expanded upon his original "facts." Chivington provided a detailed explanation of the movements of various regiments of the Third during the battle. He informed Curtis that a planned expedition to Smoky Hill had been cancelled because of the weather and weariness of the stock. Moreover, Chivington assured General Curtis that the "evidence" was "conclusive" that "these Indians were the worst that have infested the routes . . . during the last spring and summer . . . ." Confidently he wrote, "On every hand the evidence was clear that no lick was struck amiss."[61] The reports of Chivington's officers followed his[62] lead but Major Anthony was not entirely supportive.

By December 15th, Chivington's decision to abandon the pursuit of the Indians at Smoky Hill became known to Anthony. Anthony disagreed with this decision and directly contradicted Chivington's statements about the weather and transportation. Anthony wrote:

> I now regret exceedingly that Colonel Chivington's command could not have pursued the Indians farther. We were not to exceed from two to three day's march from the main hostile Indian camp. I think, with a force sufficient to have whipped them. The command must have seventy wagons for 700 men. The weather fine for this season of the year; the proper time for an Indian campaign . . . . I sincerely regret that so good an opportunity was lost to follow the Indians up.[63]

Anthony also provided the first hints that the so-called "battle" involved abuses not mentioned in Chivington's official reports. Anthony was not opposed to a "massacre" of Indians as policy but, perhaps remembering his promise to Black Kettle, implied that the attack upon the Indians at Sand Creek was not justified:

> The Indians did not scalp our killed, but our men must have scalped 100 of theirs. One prisoner [halfbreed] son of John S. Smith, Indian interpreter, was taken and afterward killed in camp . . . . The massacre was a terrible one and such a one as each of the hostile tribes on the plains richly deserve. I think one such visitation to each hostile tribe would forever put an end to Indian war on the plains, and I regret exceedingly that this punishment could not have fallen upon some other band.[64]

But until "high officials" called for an investigation into the battle, Chivington and his officers did not have to defend their actions and reports at Sand Creek.

Chivington sent messages to Byers and the <u>Rocky Mountain News</u> in praise of the battle and its White participants. The engagement was "one of the most bloody Indian battles ever fought . . . to avenge the horrid deeds of those savages we have so severely handled." "One of the most powerful villages of the Cheyenne Nation" was reportedly destroyed. Chivington's hyperbolic statements in praise of the battle were probably an inspiration for Byers' similar versions of the incident.[65]

With the advent of the various investigations into the incident, other versions of the "battle" emerged. These accounts were in direct contrast with Chivington's claims. Those witnesses critical of Chivington and the conduct of his command at Sand Creek were comprised of officers from Fort Lyon, Indian agent Colley, White traders William Bent and John Smith and Indian scout, Jim Beckwourth. The testimony of this group called into question every claim made by Chivington in his reports. The total number of Indians in the village was estimated at much less than the 1,000 claimed by Chivington and his officers. The total number of Indians killed was calculated to be closer to 100 than the 600 mentioned by Chivington. Moreover, various witnesses claimed that two-thirds of those Indians killed were women and children. These witnesses described despicable acts of butchery and brutality performed by Chivington's men and apparently with his knowledge. Some of these witnesses did have motives to impeach Chivington, but others did not.[66]

The various interpretations available of the action at Sand Creek are a result of these testimonies about the event. However most of the historiographic controversy revolves around the <u>extent</u> of the atrocities committed; not whether such atrocities did occur. Historians have generally agreed that all sexes and ages were killed and their bodies mutilated and scalped.[67] But even if few atrocities were committed by Whites, the general population believed that the encounter at Sand Creek was a "signal punishment," implying extermination of the Cheyennes.[68] Thus, this policy was viewed as a positive good. White Coloradans received Chivington's reports as evidence of such a policy and even with some amusement. On December 22nd, the <u>News</u> noted, tongue-in-cheek, that "Cheyenne scalps are getting as

298

thick here now as toads in Egypt. Everybody has got one and is anxious to get another to send east."[69] Apparently one hundred Cheyenne scalps balanced the one White scalp found by Chivington's command.[70]

Colorado's White citizens expressed few initial doubts regarding either the necessity or the benefits of the action at Sand Creek. For them, Chivington's reports functioned as evidence that the "savages" who infested their plains had been punished. Even General Curtis, who had condemned Chivington's actions, believed such punishment decreased the threat for the Plains tribes. For one and all the policy of extermination had become a legitimate means of solving the Indian problem and Chivington's reports were symbolic of this policy's success. The very "fact" that an attack had occurred created a White perception of Indian hostility, guilt and proper punishment.[71]

The exact motives for Chivington's actions and words may never be isolated, but several reasons seem obvious and his rhetoric contains hints of motives probably even unknown to Chivington.

Chivington may have made no specific plans regarding the object of his winter campaign prior to ordering the Colorado troops from Bijou Basin. His recent defeat in the election, the impatience of the "100 Daysers" and the threat from General Connor pressured him to do something. Perhaps Chivington started with a vague intention of locating the reported group of Indians on the Republican. However, upon encountering Combs at Spring Bottom Station, he received information about the group of Indians camped at Sand Creek which "fifty men" could defeat. If he wanted to restore prestige lost in the recent election, an easy victory with minimal White losses may have seemed like the thing to do. General Connor, who threatened Chivington's military command, had earned his rank as Brigadier General by killing Indians at the conjunction of Battle Creek and Bear Creek in Idaho. Connor and his troops, after a forced winter march of 140 miles, surprised the Indian camp at daybreak and overwhelmed and killed most of the Indians camped there.[72] Connor's victory could have inspired Chivington's action. Lieutenant Cossit testified that, after the Sand Creek battle, he heard Chivington remark "that he thought that [the battle] would put a star on his shoulder." Chivington had hoped for a generalship after the New Mexico campaign but had been turned down.[73]

It is difficult to reconcile Chivington's reported deeds and motives and words with his religious background. However, partial explanation may be found in the pressures of his roles and the personal functions provided by his words and deeds.

As an elder in the Methodist church, Chivington was expected to perform various Christian duties. Such duties included the bringing of God's word to the flock. As Commander of the Colorado Military District, he was expected to protect the White population. As a candidate for Congress on the pro-state ticket he had to gain the approval of a potential White constituency. He would have been aware of the beliefs of this population regarding the general worth of Indians and the best solution to the Indian problem. Like Evans, his actions and words favored White interests over Indian interests, perhaps reflecting the pressure from potential voters.

Chivington's rhetoric is unequivocal in favoring White interests. No positive statements about Native Americans are apparent. Also conspicuous for their limited appearance are Biblical or religious references. After fifteen years of immanent involvement with Christianity, such an absence of religious images and messages implies the repression of such references. Such repression makes logical sense as homilies about Christian charity and tolerance would be difficult to reconcile with statements that papooses should be killed since "nits make lice." The few vague references of a religious nature which can be found in Chivington's rhetoric tend to justify the killing of Indians as Chivington's personal scapegoats.

In a declaration reported by Lieutenant Cramer, Chivington stated that "he believed it to be right or honorable to use any means under God's heaven to kill Indians . . . ." With such words, Chivington implied that the destruction of Indians was God's work. He also stated that those who sympathized with Indians should be "damned," implying, in a Burkeian sense, that killing Indians would bring salvation. If his officers wanted to share salvation or redemption with

Chivington, if they wanted to avoid the threat of pollution or disorder, they would follow his commands. Chivington expressed little doubt about the "order" implicit in his policy and the "disorder" which was imminent if his policy was not followed. In a message "To the Public" written after Sand Creek, he declared, "It is not surprising that the Indian believes himself to be the White man's superior. White men of the frontier, do you desire to become the servile dogs of a brutal savage? If you do this policy [Wynkoop's peace policy] will suit you, though I thought differently and acted accordingly."[74] Under a peace policy Indian interests would tyrannize white interests; Chivington believed that death was preferable. Sarcastically he commented

. . . it will not do to make the Indians <u>angry</u>: it is better to feed them than to fight them. If the soldiers at Camp Sanborn had done thus you would have branded them as cowards, and rather than done this it were better to have killed them, as a true soldier prizes his honor more than his life [emphasis and grammar original].[75]

To avoid the pollution threatened by the loss of honor which military men would suffer by a "peace policy," Chivington proposed, implicitly, what he labeled as a "holy horror."[76] He had stated to Curtis that following the Indians to their villages and chastising them there in order to "conquer a peace" was the best way. In Chivington's new order redemption would result from such a "holy horror." A signal punishment as reported by Captain Nichols or as symbolized by Sand Creek was "holy" since it helped to maintain White superiority. In Chivington's "Appeal to the Public" it is not surprising that Chivington did not address the controversy over the nature of the Sand Creek "battle" or "massacre." Both he and his audience believed that the only way to "salvation" was the destruction of Native Americans.

Although Chivington could repress overt statements of theology, he could not repress a tendency to dichotomize the world into good and evil. Those who worked with him and agreed with him were "brave men." Those men who refused were "malignant cowards . . . crawling vipers . . . venomous as reptiles and cowardly as curs." The sources of all his troubles were external to him in the guise of

"Government employees conspiring . . ." against him. Their mark of guilt, he implied, was their closeness to the Indians: "one an <u>Indian</u> agent, the other an <u>Indian</u> interpreter" [emphasis added]. Colley and Smith, according to Chivington, manipulated the Committee on the Conduct of the War and made its members

> . . . the innocent tools of two ignorant old Indian trappers and traders to wreak disgrace and ruin upon Col. Chivington and Colorado soldiers generally. Truly these two old gentlemen, Colley and Smith must have read the scriptures for they appear to have been in Washington, as innocent as lambs and as wary as foxes.[77]

Finally, in this message directed at the public, Chivington extracted the "doctrine" of his experience. He revealed that the Indians and his White enemies belonged in the same company:

> Lo the poor Indian in thy untutored greatness you have proved yourself with the assistance of high officials, your friend a good diplomat. You have long been a bone of contention and many a villainous swindle has been perpetrated upon the Government in thy name and humanity, which would put to blush the unaparalled Commander of the sons of sin. His satanic Majesty, the Devil [punctuation original].[78]

Thus, the brutal savages were symbolized by Chivington so that he could kill them. The evil they represented was external, "not here in me." As Chivington and other Colorado settlers encountered Indians they were reminded of repressed desires which they, as civilized men, thought they had left behind long before. It became necessary to destroy the Indians in order to preserve White culture from being subverted. As Chivington stated, not to control the Indians was to risk becoming "servile dogs." As a member of the ministry, Chivington had been forced to live within a specified code of conduct. It may have been useful for him to project the evil impulses he encountered within himself onto the "brutal savages." Killing them would purge his polluted state. Thus Indians were simultaneously his devils and scapegoats.[79]

His overt justification for calling for the killing of Indians had included the fact that ". . . they would kill women and children . . . ." Yet, his soldiers killed more women and children than any one group of Cheyennes.[80] This signal punishment which was supposed to sow fear among the Plains tribes was followed by Indian raids and killing of Whites worse than any such actions prior to Sand Creek. The "savages" which Chivington sought to kill at Sand Creek finally fulfilled this White man's conception of their nature.[81]

Summary

Manifestly, John Evans and John Chivington sought to protect Coloradans. Accordingly they addressed messages to specific audiences to achieve this end. Evans' messages were directed primarily at White audiences and, incidentally, to an Indian audience. Chivington's statements were sent to White audiences with an emphasis upon the Colorado Third Volunteer Regiment.

Initially Evans attempted to preserve peace and engender "civilization." Eventually he sought to protect Coloradans by seeking to persuade the War Department to provide increased troops for Colorado. Also, he requested increased authority to finance and raise a Territorial militia. His principal proof for the necessity of these requests was a "conspiracy" or "alliance" among the Plains tribes which threatened the destruction of Colorado Whites. Simultaneously, he called the Colorado population to arms and sent messages to Native Americans in an apparent effort to preserve peace.

John Chivington's messages were comprised of official orders and reports and unofficial statements. It was his duty to protect White Coloradans and to maintain order on the plains.

Both of these men were faced with threats against their elite positions and both men desired elective office as a representative from Colorado. Thus the messages they sent and the actions they took were influenced by pressure from their White audience. Not surprisingly, these words and actions worked to the detriment of Native Americans in Colorado.

Latently, their messages about Native Americans complemented many of the functions served by Byers' messages in the News. The enemy was defined and the situation was characterized as urgent. Most importantly, the messages of Evans and Chivington tended to legitimize extermination as "official" government policy.

Latently, John Evans' messages defined "hostile Indians" as enemies of the state. He exhorted Colorado Whites and volunteers to action against the "merciless savages" who "infested" the plains.[82] However, other than vague distinctions between hostile and non-hostile Indians he did not expand upon the image of the "merciless savage." The enemy was the conspiring savage, irrationally violent and with no redeeming qualities.[83] Evans had encountered the same symbols in the News as had the rest of Byers' reading audience. With his (Evans') limited direct experience with Indians, he may have been susceptible to direct education from the News about the nature of Native Americans. Moreover, his personal friendship with Byers would have allowed for interpersonal discussion of the stories and events reported in the News. If such discussions occurred, the direct persuasion of Byers' symbols would have been reinforced.[84] Therefore, with the dimensions of the enemy apparent to Evans and White Coloradans, there was no need for Evans to provide further definition.

With the impression created that "hostile plotters" were conspiring against innocent Whites, Evans had to provide reassurance that he was an effective leader who could protect the threatened Whites from danger. Stories about his actions in this regard in the News could have been helpful in creating this impression. His "Appeal" and two "Proclamations" also could be interpreted as attempts to solve the problem. Intentional or not, Evans' statements reassured Whites that most Indians were hostile enemies of the state and that the destruction of such enemies was a legitimate action sanctioned by the government.

After Sand Creek, Evans wrote a "Reply" to the charges made against him by the Committee on the Conduct of the War. This "Reply" was addressed to the "People of Colorado." In this defense, Evans attempted to distinguish his "Appeal" and first official "Proclamation" from his "Hundred Day's Proclamation." He argued that the language in the first two messages was necessary to motivate the formation of the militia. As he explained it, "without means to mount or pay militia . . . could any other course be pursued?" Further, Evans stated that the militia was "disbanded" months prior to Sand Creek.[85] But his first two messages still would have been perceived by his audience as statements by a government official. Even if Evans did not intend for the "100-Daysers" to be influenced by the appeals in his first two messages, the functions of the language of these messages remained. The Colorado Third perceived that their task was to pursue, kill and destroy hostile Indians as a patriotic act. Moreover, the property of these hostile Indians was forfeited as part of their pay.

Like Evans' messages, Chivington's messages contributed little to furthering the definition of the enemy. Chivington does not appear to have attempted persuasion about Indian nature until after the battle. There is no evidence that his communications with Curtis were deliberate attempts to convince Curtis of his point of view. Chivington seems to have been direct and uncompromising in his views. Initially Indians were friendly, then they became hostile; there was little middle ground in Chivington's symbolizations of them. His statements help to illustrate that he was, in Hugh Carey's[86] words, "a prominent, aggressive personality . . . ." As such, Chivington seems to have written and uttered his words with authority and conviction. The men he led, while independent, rough and undisciplined, would also have been anxious. Most had no prior military experience. All were marching into an unknown situation and the very definition of the enemy they were familiar with made "it" a formidable threat. Under these conditions Chivington's statements would have been especially persuasive to his immediate audience. Some research indicates that individuals tend to be the most influenced by autocractic leadership when they "feel threatened and helpless."[87]

Chivington also occupied a formal authority role. if all persuasion failed, his word was final. Like Evans, Chivington's occupation of a governmental role made all of his statements function as official statements. Therefore Chivington's statements became clear, unambiguous orders which legitimized a policy of extermination. Moreover, these orders were energized by his perceived effectiveness. Such an analysis would support Major Anthony's belief that orders <u>not</u> to exterminate and <u>not</u> to scalp would have been obeyed.

Murray Edelman has written about the particular power and unique functions served by "Government behavior and cues." It is his view that government does not continue to exist based solely on its satisfaction of popular demands. Rather, he states that governments help to create the very expectations and demand which they satisfy. He writes:

> Government affects behavior chiefly by shaping the cognitions of large numbers of people in ambiguous situations. It helps create their beliefs about what is proper; their perceptions of what is fact; and their expectations . . . .[88]

The chief instrument for such persuasion is the use of myth which is influential in ambiguous and anxiety-ridden situations.[89] Government acts and cues are "an especially potent influence upon behavior" because:

> for the great mass of political spectators cues to group status and security, and especially as to their future status and security, can come chiefly or only from governmental acts. This is one of the few forms of activity perceived as involving all groups and individuals in society and as reflecting the range of public interests, wants and capabilities . . . only government can evoke fairly confident expectations of future welfare . . . can create the perceived worlds that in turn shape perceptions and interpretations of current events and therefore the behaviors with which people respond to them.[90]

Therefore, the statements of Evans and Chivington "symbolized the whole" to Colorado Whites. They provided cues as to the meaning of events for Colorado Whites and vocalized a popular sentiment which would provide a solution. Even Evans' and Chivington's political enemies recognized the correctness of these pronouncements about Indian nature, propensities and required fate. They might disagree on political issues but all could agree on the threat from apparent Indian actions. Thus, in 1864, Evans' and Chivington's messages functioned to legitimize a regime of extermination against Native Americans.

CHAPTER VI

NOTES

[1] Reginald S. Craig, The Fighting Parson, the Biography of Colonel John M. Chivington (Los Angeles: Westernlore Press, 1959), p. 24; Raymond G. Carey, "Colonel Chivington, Brigadier General Connor and Sand Creek," Denver Westerner Brand Book, 16 (1960), 108-109.

[2] Carey, p. 109.

[3] Craig, pp. 29-46. See also Stan Hoig, The Sand Creek Massacre (Norman: University of Oklahoma Press), p. 9, for a brief biographical note.

[4] Craig provides a "conversation" between Chivington and Gilpin in which he quotes Chivington as declining the Chaplain's position by saying, ". . . I feel compelled to strike a blow in person for the destruction of human slavery and to help in some measure to make this a truly free country. Therefore I must respectfully decline an appointment as a non-combatant officer, and at the same time urgently request a fighting commission instead." No source is provided for this quotation. Hoig generally agrees that Chivington declined the Chaplain's position in favor a Major's commission (p. 9).

[5] Craig, p. 52. Determining Chivington's motives generally is difficult since he left no records of his inner thoughts. He does not appear to have been an introspective individual (Carey, pp. 107-108).

[6] Craig, p. 67.

[7] Ovando J. Hollister, History of the First Regiment of Colorado Volunteers (1863; rpt. Lakewood: The Golden Press, 1949), p. 62; Craig, p. 123; Robert Perkin, The First Hundred Years: An Informal History of Denver and the Rocky Mountain News (Garden City, New York: Doubleday, 1959), pp. 235-252.

[8] Craig, p. 131.

[9] Chivington probably was not aware of the different symbols he utilized in addressing his subordinates vs. his superiors. However, in at least

one instance, he sent messages on the same day indicating to his superiors that "chastisement" was his policy and to his subordinates to "kill them" (the Indians). (John Chivington to General Curtis, April 13, 1864, Chivington to Lieutenant Colonel William O. Collins, United States War Department, The War of the Rebellion: A Compilation of the Official Records of the Union and Confederate Armies (Washington, G.P.O., 1880-1901), Series 1, Vol. 34, part 3, 149, 150. Hereafter this source will be cited as Rebellion Records or RR). It is not clear what was intended by the term "chastise." Its common meaning "to inflict pain for the purpose of punishment" may have been intended. An order to kill would seem to be somewhat different in meaning from an order to "chastise." To "severely chastise" would be a harsher punishment than to chastise. It is possible that "chastise" was a code word for killing, illustrating the reluctance of upper levels of command to openly admit such a policy. Such a distinction without a difference seems unlikely if Marcus Cunlife's discussion in Soldiers and Civilians, The Martial Spirit In America 1775-1865 (Boston: Little, Brown and Company, 1968), pp. 270-272, is accepted. He contends that Army regulars "detested" volunteer troops for their brutality towards Indians. Chivington's superiors appear to have shared this detestation. After Sand Creek and during the subsequent investigation and recriminations Curtis wrote that he "abhorred" the style of warfare utilized by Chivington and the Colorado Volunteers (Curtis to General Halleck, January 12, 1865, RR, Series 1, Vol. 48, part 1, 416, 489).

[10]Chivington District Headquarters, June 11, 1864, Chivington to Major General John M. Schofield, September 12, 1863, RR, Series 1, Vol. 22, part 2, 303, 437.

[11]Chivington to General Schofield, July 13, 1863, Silas Soule to Wynkoop, June 30, 1863, Soule to Wynkoop, July 10, 1863, Chivington to Assistant Adjutant General, Dept. of Missouri, August 7, 1863, RR, Series 1, Vol. 22, part 2, 369-371, 437.

[12]RR, Series 1, Vol. 34, part 3, 149.

[13]Chivington to William O. Collins, April 13, 1864, RR, Series 1, Vol. 34, part 3, 150.

[14] RR, Series 1, Vol. 34, part 3, 190.

[15] Chivington to Curtis, April 29, 1864, RR, Series 1, Vol. 34, part 3, 354. There are two messages to Curtis on this date.

[16] Major Charlot was Assistant Adjutant General and reports addressed to him were usually forwarded to Curtis. Chivington to C.S. Charlot, May 28, 1864, RR, Series 1, Vol. 34, part 4, 100.

[17] Chivington to E.W. Wynkoop, May 31, 1864, RR, Series I, Vol. 34, part 4, 151.

[18] Chivington to Lieutenant G.L. Shoup, May 29, 1864, RR, Series I, Vol. 34, part 4, 116. Both Chivington and the rest of the Denver population were also still reeling from the "Great Flood" on May 19th.

[19] See The Denver Commonwealth, May 25, 1864 for the minutes of the "District Convention."

[20] Chivington to Major C.S. Charlot, June 11, 1864, RR, Series I, Vol. 34, part 4, 318.

[21] Chivington to Captain J.C. Davidson, June 12, 1864, RR, Series I, Vol. 34, part 4, 330.

[22] Chivington to Major Charlot, July 5, 1864, RR, Series I, Vol. 41, part 2, 54.

[23] Curtis to Chivington, June 29, 1864, RR, Series I, Vol. 34, part 4, 595.

[24] Curtis to Chivington, July 30, 1864, Curtis to Evans, August 11, 1864, RR, Series I, Vol. 41, part 2, 483-484, 661.

[25] Robert Utley in Frontier Regulars: The U.S. Army and the Indian, 1866-1891 (New York: Macmillan, 1974), pp. 45-47, concludes that regular army officers "consistently" failed in conventional warfare with Native Americans because of lack of a "formal doctrine" related to Indian warfare and customs. Such a doctrine was never developed because the Army assumed each Indian "war" was the last. Hoig agrees and says that Curtis was "ignorant" regarding Indians (p. 94).

[26] Curtis to Chivington, June 29, 1864, RR, Series I, Vol. 34, part 3, 595.

[27] Chivington to Curtis, August 8, 1864, RR, Series I, Vol. 34, part 2, 613.

[28] Chivington to Curtis, August 11, 1864, RR, Series I, Vol. 41, part 2, 660.

[29] Curtis' attitude in the spring and early summer has been previously noted (see note 70 in Chapter V). By August 10, 1864, Curtis had adopted a policy of punishment. While events alone could have changed his policy, only the "information" he received from Chivington provided a solution to these events.

[30] Chivington to Charlot, August 18, 1864, RR, Series 1, Vol. 41, part 2, 766; Chivington to Curtis, September 13, September 19, September 23, 1864 in RR, Series 1, Vol. 41, part 3, 181, 261, 335.

[31] Chivington to Charlot, September 26, 1864, RR, Series 1, Vol. 41, part 3, 399.

[32] Curtis to Chivington, September 28, 1864, RR, Series 1, Vol. 41, part 3, 462. Hoig suggests that Curtis was following Chivington's lead (p. 112). This telegraph apparently was received *after* the Camp Weld conference had concluded.

[33] Chivington to Headquarters, District of Colorado, October 10, 1864, RR, Series 1, Vol. 41, part 1, 883.

[34] Morse Coffin, The Battle of Sand Creek (Waco, Texas: Wm. Morrison, 1965), p. 8. Nichols did not mention the two papooses in his official report to Chivington (D.H. Nichols to Chivington, October 11, 1864, RR, Series 1, Vol. 41, part 3, 798-99). Curtis had issued emphatic orders that women and children be spared (General Field Order No. 1, Headquarters, Dept. of Kansas, July 27, 1864, RR, Series 1, Vol. 48, part 1, 503-505). In his orders to his subordinates Chivington made no such distinction and made no comments to Nichols about the squaws killed by his command (Chivington to D.H. Nichols, October 14, 1864, RR, Series 1, Vol. 41, part 3, 87).

[35] All of the "unofficial statements" to be considered are taken from testimony and affidavits contained in the transcripts of the three investigations. As a first hand observer, Morse Coffin's statements will also be included. While Chivington may not have said the exact words to be examined Perkin says that it is probable that Chivington made similar statements (p. 274).

[36] Testimony of Scott Anthony, United States Congress, House of Representatives, "Massacre of Cheyenne Indians," Report on the Conduct of the War, 38th Cong. 2d sess. (Washington D.C., G.P.O., 1864), p. 29 (hereafter this source cited as "Massacre of Cheyenne Indians"). From a communication a day before the battle at Sand Creek, it appears that General Curtis knew nothing of Chivington's plans (Curtis to Carleton, November 28, 1864, RR, Series 1, Vol. 41, part 4, 709).

[37] Chivington to Wynkoop, October 16, 1864, RR, Series 1, Vol. 41, part 4, 23-24; General Curtis had telegraphed to Cottonwood Station on September 29th, to check Evans' claims of a "large Indian force on the Republican" (RR, Series 1, Vol. 41, part 3, 494). On the 29th and 30th he received two replies that there was "no evidence" of such a force (RR, Series 1, Vol. 41, part 3, 494, 524). Apparently Curtis had not passed his information on to Chivington. Curtis was preoccupied with Price's Missouri expedition (Chivington makes reference to this fact in his correspondence with Wynkoop on the 16th).

[38] Raymond G. Carey, "The 'Bloodless Third' Regiment Colorado Volunteer Cavalry," Colorado Magazine, 38 (Fall, 1961), 275-298.

[39] Chivington to Major C.S. Charlot, October 26, 1864, RR, Series 1, Vol. 41, part 4, 259.

[40] "Entry for October 31, 1864," Journal of John L. Dailey, 1864, (MS in Western History Department, Denver Public Library). Also see Lynn I. Perrigo, "Major Hal Sayr's Diary of the Sand Creek Campaign," Colorado Magazine, 15 (March, 1938), 48-57.

[41] Rocky Mountain News, November 16, 1864. Evans left the Territory for Washington, D.C., on November 16th.

[42] Quoted in Hoig, pp. 135-36; originally published in The Denver Republican, May 18, 1890.

[43] Testimony of John Chivington, "Massacre of Cheyenne Indians," p. 106.

[44] All direct quotations taken from Testimony of James Combs, U.S. Senate, "Sand Creek Massacre," Report of the Secretary of War, 39th Cong., 2d sess., Senate Executive Document 26 (Washington: G.P.O., 1867), 116-117 (hereafter this source will be cited as Report of the Secretary of War or Report).

[45] Affidavit of S.E. Brown in United States Senate, "The Chivington Massacre," Reports of the Committees, 39th Cong., 2d sess., (Washington, D.C.: G.P.O., 1867), p. 71 (hereafter this source will be cited as "The Chivington Massacre"). Testimony of A.C. Hunt, "Massacre of Cheyenne Indians, 45-46; Testimony of Lt. Cramer, Report of the Secretary of War, 63. Coffin also refers to the expression, "Nits make lice" (pp. 9-10). Perkin writes that Chivington's speech had been delivered late in August as a campaign speech. In the speech Chivington declared that his policy was to "kill and scalp all, little and big," because "nits make lice." Perkin concludes that the "Speech was warmly applauded and the phrase became a fighting slogan for the Third." (p. 209).

[46] Hoig, p. 140; Testimony of Silas Soule, Report, pp. 13, 21.

[48] Testimony of Lt. Joseph Cramer, Report, p. 47.

[49] Testimony of W.P. Minton, Report, p. 147; Testimony of Lt. C.M. Cossit, Report, p. 153; Testimony of Indian Agent Colley, "The Chivington Massacre," p. 34; Also see pp. 73-74 of the "The Chivington Massacre."

[50] Coffin, p. 19.

[51] Testimony of James Beckwirth, Report, pp. 68-69; Affidavit of Robert Bent, "The Chivington Massacre," p. 96; Testimony of Lt. Cannon, Report, p. 110; Testimony of A.J. Gill, Report, p. 179.

[52] Andrew J. Templeton, "Life and Reminiscences" (MS in Pioneers' Museum, Colorado Springs, Colorado), p. 6. At least one officer of the Third, Lt. Leavitt L. Bowen, referred to Chivington's "language" prior to the battle as the inspiration for the "signal punishment meted out to the savages." Bowen also stated "the Third Regiment cannot any longer be called in Denver the bloodless Third," (RR, Series 1, Vol. 41, part 1, 957).

[53] See below discussion for an analysis of the reports of the battle.

[54] Testimony of Silas Soule, Report, pp. 12, 13, 15; Testimony of Dr. Caleb S. Birdsal, Report, pp. 202-203; "Silas Soule to his Mother, December 18, 1864" (Unpublished collection, Western History Department, Denver Public Library); Coffin, pp. 36-37.

[55] Testimony of James D. Cannon, "The Chivington Massacre," p. 53. Soule made similar remarks (Report, p. 14). Testimony of Major Scott Anthony, "Massacre of Cheyenne Indians," p. 27.

[56] Testimony of Major Scott Anthony, "Massacre of Cheyenne Indians," pp. 22-23. Also see Testimony of Silas Soule, Report, p. 28; Testimony of John Smith, "Massacre of Cheyenne Indians," p. 10; Testimony of Lt. Cramer, "The Chivington Massacre," p. 74.

[57] Testimony of James Beckwirth, Report of the Secretary of War, p. 71.

[58] Testimony of Colonel Shoup, Report, p. 177. Shoup was testifying as Chivington's witness.

[59] Murray Edelman, Politics as Symbolic Action (Wisconsin: Markham, 1971), p. 37.

[60] Chivington to Headquarters, District of Colorado, November 29, 1864, RR, Series 1, Vol. 41, part 1, 948.

[61] Chivington to General S.R. Curtis, December 16, 1864, RR, Series 1, Vol. 41, part 1, 948-50.

[62] See the reports of Lt. Kennedy, Lt. Dunn, Col. Shoup, Lt. Leavitt, Major Hal Sayr and Captain

Theodore Cree in RR, Series 1, Vol. 41, part 1, 954-59. Major Anthony's initial reports were also supportive (same source, 951-52).

[63] Anthony to Headquarters, Fort Lyon, Colorado Territory, December 15, 1864, RR, Series 1, Vol. 41, part 1, 953.

[64] Historians have generally ignored this statement by Anthony. Like Coffin's statements, Anthony's statements may be judged as good evidence since they tend to indict his involvement with the battle (RR, Series 1, Vol. 41, part 1, 954).

[65] Rocky Mountain News, December 8, 1864, December 22, 1864.

[66] See: Testimony of Samuel Colley, "The Chivington Massacre," p. 29; Testimony of John Smith, "The Chivington Massacre," p. 42; "Massacre of Cheyenne Indians," p. 9; Testimony of James D. Cannon, "The Chivington Massacre," p. 53; Report, pp. 111, 113; Affidavit of Private David Louderback, "The Chivington Massacre," pp. 53-54; Report, pp. 11, 23; Testimony of James Beckwith, Report, pp. 69-71. In his defense Chivington argued that various Indian traders (Bent, Smith, Colley and Louderback, who was their employee) had vowed to "get Old Chiv," because of investments that were lost at Sand Creek (John Chivington, To the People of Colorado, Synopsis of the Sand Creek Investigation (Originally published Denver, June 1865), p. 3; available on Micro card F 776, Western History Collection, Denver Public Library). Soule, John Smith and Lt. Cramer were all present at the September 11th council with Black Kettle and may have testified against Chivington because he forced them into action against Indians who were their friends. However, Soule in particular, seems to have been a person of high principle. Initially, he wrote favorably of Chivington (Soule to Annie, July 16, 1864, unpublished letters, Western History Collection, Denver Public Library) but wrote to his mother on December 18, 1864 and January 8, 1865 of the "horrable massacre" and that he had refused to order his company to fire. He wrote also, "I think I stand better than he [Chivington] does in regard to his great Indian fight . . . not more than 130 killed but most were women and children and all of them scalped." Shortly after completing his testimony to the Military

Commission, Soule was assassinated on the streets of Denver (Rocky Mountain News, April 24, 1865). Nor would Anthony appear to have a perverse motive to "get" Chivington. His testimony indicted his behavior as well as Chivington's. In his "Defense" Chivington said that if he had unjustly killed Indians, it was Anthony's fault -- perhaps hinting that Anthony's less than favorable report had upset him (Chivington) (Chivington, To The People, p. 5).

[67] Michael A. Sievers, "Sands of Sand Creek Historiography," Colorado Magazine, 49 (Fall, 1972), 126.

[68] Calls for more Sand Creeks have been noted previously. Also see the June 6th and January 13, 1865 editions of the Rocky Mountain News. It was reported that the Colorado Legislature was considering offering bounties for scalps of hostile Indians and utilizing bloodhounds to pursue and exterminate "roving bands of warriors."

[69] Rocky Mountain News, December 22, 1864.

[70] Joseph Cramer testified that the one scalp found in the Indian camp was "very old, the hair being much faded" (The "Chivington Massacre," p. 73).

[71] Curtis to Gen. Halleck, January 12, 1865, RR, Series 1, Vol. 48, part 1, 502-503; Murray Edelman writes "Actual attacks upon the target group are especially potent in creating a perception of their hostility and their guilt," p. 38.

[72] See RR, Series 1, Vol. 40, part 1, 185-87.

[73] Affidavit of C.M. Cossit, "Massacre of Cheyenne Indians," p. 74; Craig claims that after Glorietta, Secretary of War Stanton offered Chivington a star if he would stay in Washington and help train the new troops. But, Chivington supposedly turned Stanton down so that he could return to Colorado (pp. 141-42). This claim seems to be false (Carey, "Col. Chivington, Connor," 131-33), that Stanton offered Chivington a star.

[74] John Chivington, "To The Public," p. 5.

[75] "To The Public, " p. 3.

[76]"To The Public," p. 7.

[77]"To The Public," p. 8.

[78]"To The Public," p. 8.

[79]This analysis was stimulated by Peter Lowenberg's "The Psychology of Racism," in Gary Nash and Richard Weiss, eds., The Great Fear, Race in the Mind of America (Chicago: Holt, Rinehart and Winston, 1970), pp. 186-201; Also see William Rueckert, Kenneth Burke and the Drama of Human Relations (Minneapolis: University of Minnesota Press, 1963), pp. 131, 156-57.

[80]The Cheyennes seldom killed women and children as policy, although individual renegades might do so. Such killings were usually because the Indians did not believe they could travel quickly enough with the prisoners. In the Cheyennes culture, all children were revered and treated with respect (George Bird Grinnell, The Cheyenne Indians: Their History and Way of Life (New York: Cooper Square Publishers, 1962), I: 104, 106).

[81]Sievers writes that "most writers agree . . . that Sand Creek did result in a general outbreak" (p. 128). Donald J. Berthong, in The Southern Cheyennes (Norman: University of Oklahoma Press, 1963), contends that a unity was created among the tribes that otherwise might not have happened (p. 225). John Selby in The Conquest of the American West (Totowa, New Jersey: Rowman and Littlefield, 1976), argues that the plains were set "aflame" as a result of the Sand Creek encounter (p. 208).

[82]Rocky Mountain News, August 10, 13, 1864.

[83]See David J. Finlay, Ole R. Holsti and Richard R. Fagen, Enemies in Politics (Chicago: Rand McNally, 1967), pp. 1-24, for an informative discussion of "Theoretical Dimensions of the Idea of the Enemy."

[84]See Robert G. Meadow, Politics as Communication (Norwood, N.J.: Ablex Publish Corp., 1980), pp. 102-103 for a discussion of the direct educational effects of the media and the indirect effects. Such consultation would account for the similarity of Evans' and Byers' views without necessarily indicating a conspiracy between them.

[85] "The Chivington Massacre," p. 85.

[86] Carey, "Col. Chivington, Connor," p. 109.

[87] Finley, Holsti and Fagen, p. 12.

[88] Edelman, p. 7. This statement does not mean that Chivington and Evans consciously manipulated Coloradans to a point of view contrary to their beliefs. Rather, they made statements which may have reflected popular sentiments but their pronouncements of these statements gave them official sanction.

[89] Edelman, pp. 54-55.

[90] Edelman, pp. 8-9.

CHAPTER VII

CONCLUSIONS AND IMPLICATIONS:

FROM SAND CREEK TO MY LAI 4

>"The chief counsel to First Lieut. William L. Calley, Jr., said today that the lieutenant did not feel he was killing humans when he ordered and participated in the execution of two groups of Vietnamese civilians at My Lai."
>
>New York Times,
>February 18, 1971

Embedded in the rhetoric surrounding Sand Creek are key symbols which were used by White Americans to justify the treatment of Native Americans. The attitudes reflected in these key symbols about "enemies" and violence are not restricted to 1864 or to the treatment of the Indian. Subsequent American actions in Vietnam illustrate the continuing nature of these key symbols in a conspiracy myth.

Conclusions Specific to Sand Creek

The rhetoric of Sand Creek may be characterized as encrusted with key symbols of the conspiracy myth and "wishes" for the extermination of American Indians. Byers' rhetoric, Evans' rhetoric and Chivington's rhetoric are replete with such representations.

Two groups of symbols are ubiquitous throughout the rhetoric of these three men: symbols related to the "deficient" or "savage" Indian and symbols of "extermination." Clustering around the idea of "Indian" were such pejorative symbols of identification as "savage," "redskin," "the poor Indian," and "vermin." Symbols of expectation provided the acts performed by Native Americans.

"Depredations," "massacres," "murders," and "outrages" were results of Indian actions against Whites. However, "fights," and "battles" were initiated by Whites to bring accounting for such acts. Savages "slaughtered," "murdered," "butchered" and "massacred." "Redskins were "killed," "trapped," "pursued," "punished" or "chastized."

More neutral terms were also utilized. Formal tribal designations and personal individual Indian names occurred during situations of relatively little conflict and in formal reports to authorities. Thus, throughout 1864 the stories about American Indians in the News were characterized by banal language. But there was a pause in the use of this kind of language during the reporting of the Camp Weld Conference. Moreover, Chivington's reports to his superiors were circumspect in the language he used to describe Indians but his orders to his subordinates and in battle may be classified as "banal" in their expression.

Evans' symbols of Native Americans were more restrained than those propagated by Byers and Chivington. In his messages to the War Department, Evans did not go beyond the term "Indian" as a symbol of identification. Rather, his symbols were those of expectation: the Indians engaged in "hellish plots" which threatened the "destruction" of Colorado and the danger of this destruction "could not be exaggerated." In his messages to White Coloradans, Evans did distinguish hostile from friendly Indians. However, competing messages (like Byers') and personal anxieties made this identification a distinction without a difference.

With his symbols of demand, John Chivington called for action against all Indians. Unlike Evans he made no distinctions in the Indians he identified. All Indians were to be given the same treatment. There is no evidence that Chivington qualified his official and unofficial orders to exclude non-hostile Indians and Indian women and children. It was Chivington's intention to "kill" all the Indians that he encountered.

Extermination and the "deficient Indian"

One assumption of the myth acknowledged by Byers and implied by both Evans and Chivington was that "destiny" dictated the Indians' doom. If Whites were truly superior, how could inferior savages offer any real threat? Of course, there was little emphasis on this assumption. And, as if to ensure an "active doom," rather than waiting for passive extinction, demands for extermination became linked with various symbols of Native Americans. Mere motion was not enough, action was required. The primary vehicle for this linkage was the definition of the Indian as enemy.

A definition of Indians as the enemy was not just symbolic. Indians had engaged in battle with Whites. Thus, it would be natural for Whites to label specific Indians or groups of Indians as military opponents. But, after only limited engagements with small groups of Indians, Evans and Chivington declared a general Indian war and by implication a generalized Indian/Enemy. Byers' stories helped to identify and to define this enemy: Indians were not only deficient but their acts, as recorded by Byers, illustrated a threat. His reminders made the image of the bloodthirsty, violent and treacherous savage more salient to those individuals in Denver who had not encountered hostile Indians. Controlled by their nature, the savages attacked, killed and tortured innocent Whites who suffered greatly while performing acts of bravery. Such stories required that their readers also be willing to sacrifice without complaining. Additionally, in his recording of the Hungate tragedy, Byers revealed a solution accepted by all Whites. Salvation was possible through the extermination of Indians. Few of Byers' contemporaries would have argued that the enemy present in such images should not be exterminated.

The extermination of Native Americans was a predominant symbol in Byers' rhetoric and a matter-of-fact statement in Chivington's rhetoric. The frequent occurrence of this sentiment in the recorded statements studied hints of more frequent expression in daily interpersonal conversation, unrecorded speeches and newspapers not examined.[1] The pervasiveness of the idea provided a situation characterized by statements that symbolized Indians as requiring extermination. Such immanent symbolization construed a scene/situation in which the act of extermination was contained. That is, a situation was created favorable to extermination as an act. Kenneth

Burke explains the "principle of selectivity" which bears upon actors in a given situation. He writes that, "One set of scenic conditions will 'implement' and 'amplify' given ways and temperaments which in other situations would remain mere potentialities, unplanted seeds . . . ."² Certainly as actors, Chivington and his men had other choices in dealing with the Native Americans at Sand Creek. However, with the situation defined as urgent and the enemy as representative of the antithesis of all that was good, another choice seems unlikely. The publicly endorsed choice was extermination. The apparent external conflict evidenced the danger of the situation. Moreover, the internal conflict within Coloradans when confronted by beings representative of what they might become demanded action. The "disorder" perceived by Chivington required solution. Indians were simultaneously unredeemable enemies, convenient scapegoats and possessors of the group interest desired by Colorado Whites. The sacrifice of Native Americans camped at Sand Creek was consistent with the scene.³ Some historians have despaired that historical evidence provides no absolute proof that Sand Creek was indeed a "massacre" of Indians by Whites. But a Burkeian interpretation of historical rhetoric illustrates that another choice was unlikely.⁴

Myth and Reality in Colorado
White/Native American Relationship

Symbols propagated initially by Whites were predictions of eventual outcomes between Whites and Native Americans in Colorado. Fulfillment of Indian "nature" was predicted by Evans as early as the fall of 1863. Byers prounounced a "war" in the spring of 1864. Yet neither symbolization was justified by the facts. But Whites in general and Chivington's men specifically responded to the characterization of the situation provided by Byers and Evans. With the Indians engaged in conspiratorial war, any actual or perceived encounter with Indians was given greater significance. The reported theft of stock was explained as evidence of the Indian propensity to steal. Actual thefts by specific Indian bands brought blame to all Indians in Colorado. The acts of renegade Indians like Roman Nose proved that all White women and children were threatened by any Colorado

Indian. Therefore, when encountering specific Indians, Whites were already mobilized against them and interpreted Indian actions (or even nonactions) as evidence of hostility. White volunteers knew, because of Indian nature, that all Indians were the same and that the "redskin" of the Indians was a physical indication of identical inward nature. Therefore, the dehumanized "redskin" could be actually hostile, ambivalent or a past friend to the Whites. But almost any response fulfilled White expectations of hostility. The fate of Lean Bear and the firing upon of Left Hand illustrate a common White behavior. Various groups of Indians reacted to White behavior by joining the retaliatory raids further fulfilling White expectations of an "Indian War." In turn, Whites symbolized ways of dealing with the solution. The News suggested that Whites "should go for them [Indians] one and all." Evans urged the destruction of hostile Indians. Chivington stated that to "conquer" them in their villages was the "only way" and that "nits made lice." With these images available for interpretation, Captain Nichols and his men staged a rehearsal of events to come. Eventually a larger White action followed at Sand Creek. After this encounter, Indian raids increased and a general Indian war did follow. Indians fulfilled the role predicted for them the previous year. The myth was produced and finally imitated. Thus, the White view of Indian nature was self-sealing.[5]

The Myth and Choice

Although Kenneth Burke admits that scenes influence acts, he does not construe this relationship to be totally deterministic. Human beings are capable of more than mere motion. The nature of the defined situation may make one choice more "appropriate" than another. But other choices are possible.

For example, while most men in Chivington's command responded to the stylized world of the conspiracy myth and attacked the Indians at Sand Creek, others refused to do so or did so reluctantly. Among those men who were unwilling participants were Silas Soule, Joseph Cramer, Charles Phillips and John Smith. All of these individuals had been present at a meeting between Black Kettle and other chiefs of the Arapahoes and Cheyennes and the Commander of Fort

Larned, Major Edward Wynkoop.[6] This meeting had taken place on September 10th and 11th, 1864, prior to the Camp Weld Conference but after Wynkoop had received a letter signed by Black Kettle stating a desire to make peace with the Whites.[7]

Before this encounter, Wynkoop had written that he believed it his duty to kill Indians.[8] Thus, he was skeptical of Black Kettle's request which included an offer to exchange prisoners with the Whites. Two Indian representatives, One-Eye and Min-im-mie, delivered the letter to Wynkoop and invited Wynkoop to Smoky Hill and informed him that about two thousand Indians were congregated there. Suspecting a trap, Wynkoop told One-Eye that he (One-Eye) and Min-im-mie would be held hostage and killed at the first sign of Indian treachery. One-Eye replied that the Cheyennes did not lie and if Indian treachery did occur, he would not care to live anyway.[9] Wynkoop was impressed. Later, he wrote:

> I was bewildered with an exhibition of such patriotism on the part of the two savages and felt myself in the presence of Superior beings; and these were the representatives of a race that I heretofore looked upon without exception as being cruel, treacherous, and bloodthirsty without feeling or affection for friend or kindred.[10]

Eventually Wynkoop, accompanied by his officers and about 125 soldiers, traveled to Smoky Hill where they met with Black Kettle. During the course of the conference, a portion of the huge gathering of Indians threatened to destroy the outnumbered Whites. However, Black Kettle intervened, diffusing the tense situation and the negotiations ended successfully with the release of four White prisoners. Moreover, Black Kettle and some other Indians prepared to go with Wynkoop to Denver to discuss peace with Colorado authorities.[11]

Wynkoop was not present at Sand Creek during the battle; however, he was highly critical of Chivington's conduct of that engagement. Wynkoop believed that he had given his word of honor to the Indians camped there that they would be safe.[12] Soule, Cramer and Smith, who were all at the Sand Creek battle, testified against Chivington. They believed that the Indians destroyed at Sand Creek had saved their lives at Smoky Hill.[13] As a group, Wynkoop and his officers rejected Chivington's interpretation of the events at Sand Creek.

Why did some Coloradans, like Wynkoop and Soule, reject the conspiracy myth while many other adhered to it? The answer to this question is problematic. However, as a part of the scene, certain conditions may minimize susceptibility to myth, while other conditions increase susceptibility.

Wynkoop and his officers were placed in a context which encouraged "individual observation."[14] Rather than hearing about the enemy, or engaging with him in battle as he "proved" his nature, Wynkoop was faced with two living, breathing individuals. Confronted by a reality in which an <u>Indian</u> disavowed treachery and offered his life as proof, Wynkoop was forced to reassess his past assumptions. Similarly, his officers were impressed by the efforts of Black Kettle to protect them while at Smoky Hill and later interacted on a regular basis with Black Kettle and other Indians who proceeded to Sand Creek. Rather than the faceless, violent savage, they found, in Black Kettle's words, that there were "good men and bad men" on both sides. Thus, for these Whites, the conference at Smoky Hill acted as a formative event which illustrated the inadequacies of the myth. Wynkoop and his men, a relatively small group, were placed in a scene apart from a White "mass response" to Indians. Absent authoritative and group pressure to conform to the accepted definition of the enemy, they relied upon a direct empirical inquiry to arrive at their own conclusions.[15]

Murray Edelman isolates another set of conditions that may decrease susceptibility to myth. He believes the individuals occupying roles in which "widespread belief in the myth will be harmful or self-defeating" will be less likely to ascribe to the myth.[16] Such a condition may help to explain General Curtis' refusal to adhere to Evans' messages. Although Curtis underestimated the military capabilities of the Plains Indians, he could not have responded to all of Evans' requests for increased military aid without compromising the protection of Missouri. But Evans engaged in behavior contrary to this condition.

325

Evans' continued strident statements of the myth worked against him. His behavior was self-defeating as it illustrated his continued inability to solve for the "future catastrophes" he predicted. Evans' fate may demonstrate that elites who are overly constrained by myth may be less successful rhetorically, than elites capable of creating or recognizing myth.[17]

Several conditions also may provide influence for the attachment to myth. Edelman explains that "(1) The degree of anxiety the myth rationalizes and (2) the intensity with which the particular expectation that forms the central premise of the myth is held, may facilitate attachment to myth."[18] Another condition would also seem appropriate: (3) The extent to which the role provided in the myth is ego-relevant to the individual.[19]

Numerous authors have emphasized the role of anxiety as a condition which increases attachment to myth.[20] Certainly conditions in Colorado in 1864 generated great anxiety and fear for Whites. Coloradans had experienced the Great Flood, the grasshopper infestation and a commodity shortage, all indisputable events. A few Whites experienced Indian raids and all knew that such raids and "depredations" had occurred. Some Whites had viewed the butchered visages of the Hungate family. Most Whites read accounts in the News which reported that Denver and other valuable land upon which Whites had settled was considered legally by the courts to belong to the Indians.

Other fear-generating cues were available in the News as it reported the Hungate tragedy and accounts of other Indian activities. Evans' messages provided evidence that the Government believed the situation to be urgent and that all could expect a "future catastrophe" unless something was done. These statements of the conspiracy myth both intensified White Coloradan anxiety and rationalized a "solution" which would remove the cause of the anxiety. This solution also helped to reduce internal conflict and personal insecurities. Professor Finlay explains:

> . . . the means used against the enemy are of secondary concern for any means may be justified because of our equitable and upright stature and cause and his immoral and unholy nature and

designs. However, self-righteousness also is a means of reducing needs for security or emotional release and catharsis; it is a method of reducing inner conflicts by displacing them onto external scapegoats.[21]

In the vivid images provided by the myth, Whites could both anticipate certain destruction at the hands of the savages and appreciate the innocent nature of those good Whites who had fallen prey, or could fall prey, to treacherous Indians. With the wickedness of the enemy revealed, each White participant could visualize a personal heroic role in the removal of such an evil threat. For a population prone to vigilante-type, expedient solutions, the "execution" of the threat may have seemed to most an appropriate act. For specific White men in the Colorado Third, such heroic righteousness was ego-relevant with the potential for equaling the heroism of the Colorado volunteers at Glorietta -- or at least of divesting themselves of the epithet, "The Bloodless Third."

The collective course of action rationalized by the myth also provided potential benefits for both Chivington and Evans and was definable as serving the public interest.

For John Chivington, an enemy was provided whose successful destruction might provide him a "substantial benefit."[22] Indeed, killing Indians was an accepted manner of gaining military status and recognition. Moreover, Indians provided Chivington a personal devil whose destruction could purge him of evil impulses. By destroying this devil, Chivington ensured that his actions were righteous and that the "good" (superior Whites) would triumph over the "evil" (inferior savages). With the Indian defined as the enemy, it was also in the public interest to remove this threat.

For Evans, attachment to the myth became necessary to maintain his status (or so he might have perceived it). A change in his original position contrary to a conspiracy interpretation would illustrate that his past messages had no meaning. With an enemy defined as "out there," he may have hoped to deflect attention from his controversial political career and to unite his audience behind him. He too stood to gain from being identified as a leader of the self-righteous in the battle against evil. Thus, the benefits which Chivington and Evans might have received plus the fear and anxiety from actual and perceived events made them as susceptible to the conspiracy myth as the larger Colorado population.

White Rhetoric and Native Americans

It is clear, from the preceding pages, that White American rhetoric about Native Americans suffered from distortion. Diverse examples of rhetoric including Parkman, Morton, various constitutions, Byers, Evans and Chivington imply the extent of this distortion in mid-nineteenth century White rhetoric. Certainly the substance of White American rhetoric regarding Native Americans contains the three assumptions related by Robert Berkhofer: the deficient savage, the inferiority of native cultures and the stereotype of the Indian.[23] However, this "substance" went beyond simple stereotypes to include deterministic mythic assumptions regarding Native and White American relations. As mythic elements, such conceptions resisted change and were not falsifiable.

Thus, evidence which could have proven that Roman Nose and renegade Araphoes had murdered the Hungates was interpreted as evidence of Cheyenne hostility. Additionally, John Evans rejected evidence not consistent with his interpretation of the "alliance" and construed Cheyenne statements of non-hostility at Camp Weld as "proof" of their actual hostility. With the Indian described as the enemy, there was constant tension against any symbolizations by Native Americans disputing their demeanor. Not only could Native American cultures offer nothing of value to Whites, Indians could say nothing of value. The mythic Indian was mute. Therefore Evans suggested to Superintendent Dole that the 1862 treaty be extended to non-signatory Cheyennes without consulting them. This impulse continued and by 1871 Congress had assumed "plenary power" over all Indian affairs. Indian utterances in treaties before that time were to be interpreted as Congress saw fit. Indian utterances after that time were irrelevant as the process of treaty making was abandoned.[24]

Behind Evans' role as Superintendent of Indian Affairs in Colorado was the presumption that one function of the Federal Government was to facilitate relations between White and Native Americans. The 1862 treaty, the Kansas-Nebraska Act and various court decisions were the constitutional basis which defined the "wishes" that Evans was to fulfill. However, contrary demands were presented in the News, by Evans himself in his role as Governor and in Chivington's declarations. Since Colorado's Native Americans could not speak for themselves and since only a few Whites defended them, there was no contest. The removal of any possibility of communication between groups in conflict could only increase the likelihood of aggression and violence.[25]

In its continued efforts to negotiate with and eventually to protect Native Americans, the Federal Government had to reconcile constitutional statements protecting Native Americans with contrary popular White assumptions. Subsequent government policy has reflected the continuing tension between contradictory assumptions regarding Native Americans. Turnabouts and extreme changes have marked this policy, with the Indian the ultimate loser to the "color reaction" of White Americans. Thus, while its Indian policy established the Federal Government as the agent of change for the ameloriation of racial disharmony, the outcome of its policies in this regard established the expectation of government failure.

Edmund Leach has stated that "myth" is one way of accounting for unobservable realities in terms of observable phenomena. The White rhetoric examined provides examples of observable differences; differences explained by unobservable myth. For Colorado Whites, physically observable racial characteristics reflected permanent Indian inferiority; Indian "savage" customs provided proof of Indian savagery and White "victories" like Sand Creek were "signal punishments" of Native Americans justified by their inferiority and savage state. The persistence of such unreal assumptions regarding Native Americans so distorted White perceptions of reality that Whites met consistent frustration in their attempts to deal with Native Americans.[26] But White elites found the conspiracy myth useful in their definitions of the situation.

Once the tenets of the conspiracy myth were assumed, the immutability of myth and minimal proof burdens for a conspiracy theory allowed White elites to define any actions to be taken against Native Americans as appropriate. Thus, the failure of the Cheyennes to respond to Evans' requests for a peace conference in the Fall of 1863 was construed by Evans as "proof" of Cheyenne hostility. Moreover, one letter from an unsavory White renegade was accepted by Evans as evidence of the "alliance." Relatively small and isolated acts of various Indian bands were provided greater and more significant meaning in Evans' reports and pleas to the War Department and in the pages of Byers' Rocky Mountain News. Each Indian incursion heightened Evans' warnings that the danger could not be exaggerated. Therefore Evans called for the pursuit and "destruction" of hostile Indians. Once the situation had been defined as a conspiracy, "extraordinary actions" were called for to deal with the emergency. Only 44 days after he had issued his Proclamation to the "friendly Indians," Evans issued messages to Colorado Whites clearly indicating that talk or rhetoric to control the problem was at an end, if it ever had been considered a viable alternative.

For use by elites, the conspiracy myth was most powerful in its portrayal of Indian violence against Whites and its rationalization of White violence (extraordinary actions) against Indians. As described in the News and as constantly symbolized by Evans, lurid bloodthirsty violence was characteristic only of the Indian -- thus, in the myth, only the Indian/Enemy was perceived as really violent. Each episode of Indian atrocity or threatened Indian atrocity was presented by White elites in a manner which illustrated that outnumbered Whites had been unjustly attacked or were about to be attacked by merciless savages. Seldom were Indian motives provided any fair hearing. Rather, such attacks were presented as a result of irrational and uncontrolled violence inherent in the Indians' savage nature. Such presentations also implied that Indians utilized violence on a much larger scale than did Whites. As Evans predicted it, if help was not forthcoming, huge numbers of hostile Indians threatened "total destruction." The News added to these impressions by giving seemingly endless accounts of unprovoked Indian violence. Not only were Colorado's Indians violent, but stories from afar illustrated that all Indians were violent and that the violence was widespread.

With the Enemy/Indian defined by such acts or threatening future acts, it remained only for those in authority to pronounce "sentence." In this White point of view, Indian/Enemy violence was "a crime against the state and finally against the state of civilization; a criminal conspiracy...."[27] As violent murderers of White women, children and soldiers, Indians became subhumans to be ruthlessly executed.

Indian violence justified any White action taken against them. Yet such White actions were not <u>really</u> violent. To "chastise," was not uncontrolled violence but justifiable retribution against an unfeeling, uncaring enemy. Thus, the myth resolved a logical inconsistency and allowed Whites to engage themselves in the very acts for which the Indian/Enemy was condemned. The White use of violence was apparently restrained, cool and determined. Fighting against superior numbers, the Whites displayed bravery, cleverness and sacrifice. White motives were therefore unimpeachable while Enemy/Indian motives remained unexamined.

Such a conception also allowed Whites to overlook the non-physical violence committed against the Enemy/Indian culture and person. White land frauds, theft of Indian annuities and refusal by Whites to honor any treaty obligations were overlooked as "reasons" for Indian actions against Whites. Chiefs, like Black Kettle or Pontiac, who fought (and negotiated) in defense of their people were "patriot Indians" but portrayed by Whites as savage killers. As Newton Garver has hinted, this destruction of unique, individual human qualities is a type of violence against the person.[28] Viewing all Enemies/ Indians as identical destroyed the humanity and personhood of the enemy. Moreover, by implication, since Indians were irrationally violent, they could not be negotiated with as a "people" but "must suffer more." The Indians' nonhumanity reenforced their muteness and required that only extraordinary means could be used to reestablish White control.

With the situation characterized as "extraordinary," events seemed to move inexorably to a determined conclusion. The myth effectively deflected contradictory information. Thus, Cheyenne attempts to make peace were ignored and the protests of Major

Wynkoop's men brushed aside. No peace was to be made until the Indians suffered more. "Aggression without limit" had been rationalized and the solution "logically" followed.[29] In the previous century, similar logic characterized other outcomes of White and Native American relations.[30] The "logic" could be represented as follows:

> physical differences(R) + cultural differences(R) + anxiety(R) + possession of a group interest = violence, repression and extermination
>
> R = conspiracy myth.

That is, the greater the perceived physical and cultural differences (as revealed in the myth), the greater the personal and social anxieties (as called forth by the myth) and the more valuable the White interest possessed by the target group (not admitted in the myth), the greater the probability that Whites would react to Native Americans with acts of repression, violence and extermination.

The myth was central to this equation. Except for the group interest, every component of the equation was "translated" by the myth. That is, the myth defined how enemies were to be identified (by their color and physiognomy) and the nature of these enemies (by their acts). Because of their evil acts, Native Americans might appear to be an active and strong threat. However, even a strong and active enemy is no great threat if he is not near. Thus, for Coloradans, the Hungate massacre (a single instance) illustrated the true meaning of past events. Moreover, the tragedy emphasized that the enemy was different from the good Whites. Indians were not like Whites, but were the opposite -- the very antithesis of White values. Thus, as Wynkoop described him, the mythic Indian was "without exception, a being cruel, treacherous and blood-thirsty without feeling or affection for friend or kindred." Stripped of human qualities by the myth, Indians became targets, their scalps trophies for collection.

Probably violence was inevitable between Whites and Indians. But the equation predicts that the level of violence was a function of mythic assumptions and White desires for Indian land. As Whites responded to

Indians that did not exist, they used means they believed justified by the nature of the enemy. Savage means were thought necessary to control "savages." But such means also polarized ambivalent and friendly Indians against the Whites, increasing the level of violence. In turn, Whites became more convinced of the correctness of their self-righteousness and hostilities escalated. The first victim of such increased violence was dialogue between the two races. Communication and violence were mutually exclusive, yet White rhetoric to justify and legitimize the necessary violence increased. However, this communication was directed inward within the White society. The images present in these communications provided hints of the intentions of their White users. Thus, in his correspondence with Curtis, Chivington provided images of his actions at Sand Creek prior to ordering that engagement. His "holy horror" lived in symbols before it was carried out.

Also present in the equation, but not admittable, was the White desire for Indian land. Limited by the constitutions of a self-conscious democracy, Whites could not overtly state that they fought Indians solely to take their lands. But the procurement of Indian land was a by-product of White/Indian conflict. Virtually every victory by Whites over Indians brought Whites more Indian land through subsequent peace treaties.[31]

Overt goals of constitutions concerning Native Americans included establishing peace, regulating trade and maintaining boundaries. Of course, the establishment of peace, regulation of trade and boundary maintenance were to be based upon White terms. Although Native Americans might participate in the negotiations, their words were meaningless for reasons previously discussed. Thus "peace" was given to the Cherokees on the basis of White conditions and "peace" was denied Black Kettle and the Cheyennes on a similar basis. A "just war" as defined in either treaty or act was to be determined solely by the Whites and therefore an "Indian war" was identified as such by the Whites.

Similarly, trade was regulated on the terms of the Whites. While some legislators sought to protect the Indian from the evil practices of White traders, most shared the practical view that trade must be regulated so that the natives would not attack the Whites until the Whites were ready for such an attack. The record reveals that the justice guaranteed Native Americans in land and trade dealings with Whites was seldom provided. Government enforcers lacked the resources, the will or the encouragement to protect Indian land and property rights. The Federal Government's inability to guarantee its promises was a continuing cause of conflict between White and Native Americans and cynicism on the part of the natives regarding the treaty making process.

Although keeping peace was an on-going goal of treaty making, boundary maintenance in a fashion favorable to Whites ultimately became the most important goal of White/Indian policy. The early treaties and acts contained long geographical descriptive "Articles" drawing the line between White land and Indian land. Specific clauses were eventually replaced with variable clauses like a clause in the 1834 Intercourse Act. Indian land was no longer any specific parcel or section, but an abstraction subject to the definition of the Government at any particular time.[32] Manifest destiny required land where the young nation could grow. If various constitutions allowed the Government to define whatever land was needed as White land, expansion was assured. Better yet, if, through treaty making, the Indians would formalize particular cessions, they were bowing to their destiny to give way.

The "assignment" of Native Americans to their own land was a latent statement of their potential place in American society. A "line" between Whites and Indians not only fulfilled the peculiar need (in the Indian's view) of the Anglo to mark and possess his territory, but also restricted contact between multiple Indian cultures and an emerging European-American culture. The fervor of the Georgian removal forces may have been aroused simply because the "Cherokee nation" had become intrusive upon the White man's consciousness. Allowed to remain where they were, the Cherokees would have become an island in the middle of White civilization. With continued progress toward White-like civilization they would have become evidence of the potential equality (on White terms) of Native Americans. Moreover, given Native American progress Whites would have been faced with the decision of granting constitutional guarantees to Native Americans. As the fate of the 1834 Act granting Territorial privileges to Indian country demonstrated, the majority of legislators were reluctant to do so. The myth of Anglo superiority disallowed the extension of such rights. While many legislators believed that Anglos had an obligation to civilize "inferior" peoples, like Native Americans, for them, civilization was not necessary coterminous with constitutional guarantees of equality.[33] The myths associated with Indian inferiority were threatened less if the Native Americans were out of sight. The "moral gulf" between the two races, noted by Parkman and Morton, was sustained more easily by a literal gulf between the two races. Some legislators were so anxious regarding contact between the races that a neutral strip of land five miles between the lands of the two races was proposed on which all settlement was to be prohibited.[34] A demilitarized zone usually is used to separate absolute enemies.

The fate of the Cherokees indicates that Indian possession of White-coveted land was by itself enough to stimulate White anxiety and violence. But the conspiracy myth as a "constitution beneath the constitution" provided the justification and "right" requested by Reverend Gray. A savage, by definition, had no use for land. With the Indians' "doom" manifest, anxious Whites protected themselves but acquired Indian land in the process.

It was rhetorically useful for Whites to subscribe to a conspiracy myth of Native American tactics. Whites sought to symbolize that which they needed to overcome "so as to kill it." What resulted was not a positive statement of what nineteenth century civilization could become, but a mythic process for justifying the doom of Native Americans and providing for White salvation.

Implications for White/Non-White Rhetoric

What meanings can a conflict which occurred over one hundred years ago have in the 1980's? The Indian wars of the last century were among the first "foreign" wars in American history. Moreover, in the Indians, the new country faced its first non-White antagonists. White perceptions of Indians functioned as a pre-enactment of more recent U.S. relations with developing countries of "color." America's proclivity to violence when dealing with its Native peoples has formed and influenced its behavior toward peoples of other cultures. One historian credits the Indian wars as exercising the most "brutalizing influence on the American character."[35] Whites no longer expect to encounter treachery and violence at the hands of Native Americans; that enemy was vanquished long ago.[36] But perhaps because of White perceptions of history, any "enemy" of another culture, especially a darker enemy, is an expected conspirator. Therefore, American perceptions of "colored enemies" are as likely to be as distorted as nineteenth-century White perceptions of Native Americans. The U.S. experience in Vietnam generally and the conduct of Charlie Company at My Lai 4 further illustrate such a view.[37]

The Deficient Vietnamese Savage

Some American soldiers stationed in Vietnam displayed implicit assumptions of White superiority. Certain Vietnamese customs were viewed as evidence of the "uncivilized" nature of the Vietnamese civilian. For example, some G.I.'s complained that the Vietnamese, as a people, didn't care about their own children. It was reported that mothers attempted to leave their children behind when being evacuated to safety by American forces. "[I] saw it with my own eyes," reported a G.I., "A woman hopped up on the chopper after setting her baby down on the ground. When I picked it up and handed it to her, she shouted and pointed to the ground and wouldn't accept the baby from me."[38] Peasant women in Quang Ngai, where the the soldier was stationed, believed that it was unlucky to carry a baby across a threshold. Therefore a "good" mother always set the child down, stepped through and then reached back and retrieved the child.[39]

Another soldier complained that "you can't help these dinks. They like to live like pigs in hovels, and even when you build them new houses, they won't live in them."[40] The G.I. was unaware of the customs among the Vietnamese in the area where he was assigned and so he judged the apparent custom by White standards. However, ancient practice required that married women had to live in houses with full, double sloped roofs. The houses provided by American aid had single-slope roofs. Thus, most married peasant women refused to live in the new huts; no "good" wife would do so.⁴¹

The attitude of many Americans toward all Vietnamese, not simply the Viet Cong, was apparent in many of the terms used to refer to Vietnamese. Popular Army terminology branded Vietnamese civilians as "gooks," "dinks," and "slopes." Even when being cared for in the "friendly" confines of an American military hospital, Vietnamese were provided with American "names." For example, a civilian who had lost an eye was called "bubbles," "Ohio," or "cyclops."⁴² Thus, some Americans granted no value to Vietnamese culture and depersonalized even those they were helping. A "favorite joke" shared among marines in Quang Ngai reflected the general contempt held toward all Vietnamese by some American military: "The loyal Vietnamese should all be taken and put out to sea in a raft. Everybody left in the country should then be killed, and the nation paved over with concrete, like a parking lot. Then the raft should be sunk."⁴³ Indeed, from the statements of some G.I.'s, it appears that there was hardly a distinction drawn between friendly Vietnamese and the "enemy" Viet Cong.

The Vietnamese as "Enemy"

A letter from a G.I. published in the Congressional Record in 1969 provides one view of the nature of the "enemy" perceived by some Americans:

. . . you learned enough about the Oriental mind to find nothing incongruous about a Viet Cong woman advancing with her baby in her arms . . . . They know our reverence for soft women and helpless children and know how to capitalize on this strictly Judeo-Christian hangup. Caucasians simply can't fight these people according to western precepts and the grunts in the field learn this often after they have been half wiped out.⁴⁴

Therefore the "different" nature of the enemy was emphasized while implying the color difference. The writer hinted that, as a rule, Whites rejected making war against women and babies but that the circumstances and type of enemy encountered justified any means: only savage means could control savages. Such "acts" committed by the Vietnamese were used to justify a general "scorched earth policy" which affected all Vietnamese. While official Army policy forbade the killing of women and children (and "friendly civilians"), in practice such distinctions were seldom made.[45] Moreover, anxiety and fear generated a belief reminiscent of earlier American mythology that "The only 'good' dink is a dead dink."[46]

Terry Reid, an American soldier from Wisconsin, was a member of the Americal Division stationed in Vietnam. He reported that indiscriminate massacre of Vietnamese civilians was commonplace by his unit. After several of his fellow G.I.'s were killed in a mine accident, Reid said that his unit retaliated by killing sixty civilians -- "women, children and old men." He explained that it was assumed that all young Vietnamese "are supposed to be in the army. If you see one and he is not . . . he is free game to be shot [as a Viet Cong]."[47] Charles West, a member of Charlie Company, explained the "logic": "It's hard to distinguish a mama-san from a papa-san when everybody has on black pajamas."[48] Innocent victims were often included in official reports of the day's statistics as "enemy" kills. Problems of definition were solved by concluding that "Anything that's dead and isn't White is a VC."[49] But the case of Charlie Company at My Lai 4 demonstrates that death was not always a prerequisite for such definition.

Charlie Company and Captain Medina's Rhetoric

On March 15, 1968, Charlie Company, 1st Battalion, 20th infantry, lost Sergeant George Cox to a "mine accident." A Viet Cong booby-trapped artillery round had exploded, killing Cox. Captain Ernest Medina, the company's commanding officer, addressed the company at Cox's funeral.[50] Reportedly, Medina provided solace to the group, telling them that he felt their pain and loss but that he didn't show it because he was the leader. However, he said, there was no reason for them to hold back. He told them "to let it out, let it go." His objective, he testified later, was to "fire them up, to get them ready to go . . . ."[51] He also took the opportunity to inform the men about their mission on the next day. Charlie

Company was to destroy the 48th Viet Cong Battalion, reportedly in strength at My Lai 4. Medina ordered the company to "burn and destroy My Lai 4, and to kill all livestock and destroy other food stuffs found in the area."[52] Exactly what else Medina ordered that day has been subject to controversy. However, the Peers Commission Report concluded regarding how Medina's statements functioned. The Report stated that "CPT Medina's orders and instructions concerning the inhabitants of My Lai 4 left little or no doubt in the minds of a significant number of men in his company that all persons remaining on the My Lai 4 area at the time of combat assault were enemy, and that C Company's mission was to destroy the enemy" [emphasis added].[53] Statements made by various members of Charlie Company support this conclusion.

Harry Stanley testified that he believed that Medina "ordered us to 'kill everything in the village.' The men in my squad talked about this among ourselves that night . . . because the order . . . was so unusual. We all agreed that Medina meant for us to kill every man, woman and child in the village."[54] Charles West recalled that the Captain said that after the attack,[55] "nothing [in the area] would be walking or crawling." Herbert Carter believed that Medina had been explicit. "Well boys," he said Medina remarked to them, "this is your chance to get revenge on these people. When we go into My Lai, it's open season. When we leave nothing will be living. Everything's going to go."[56] Michael Bernhardt remembered Medina saying something similar: "They're all VCs, now go in and get them. We owe them something . . . ." Bernhardt also said that Medina "didn't have to specifically say [to kill] women and kids."[57]

Perhaps Medina made these remarks in an unofficial sense, as several members of Charlie Company denied that Medina directly ordered them to kill women and children. Gregory Olsen stated that "He (Medina) told us to shoot the enemy." Then, Olsen recalled, "Someone asked 'Who is the enemy?' Medina defined the enemy as anybody that was running from us, hiding from us, or who appeared to us to be the enemy. If a man was running, shoot him; sometimes even if a woman with a rifle was running, shoot her. He never at any time said 'Slaughter the people.'"[58] Of course, with this definition of the enemy, almost any Vietnamese could "appear to be the enemy."

Henry Pedrick may have judged the situation most correctly. He stated that "The orders could be interpreted in different ways to different persons according to their emotional structure . . . one person just might interpret it to kill if he wanted to."[59]

Certainly the men of Charlie Company had been placed in a situation which did not really allow for empirical examination. Anxiety, frustration and fear prepared the men of Charlie Company to accept a meaningful explanation of why they were there, what they were to do and who they were to deal with. Michael Terry had asked the question of Medina as to who was the enemy. Terry recalled that "Guys were asking when they would have a chance to fight instead of marching around and getting blown up."[60] Indeed, Charlie Company had been inactive and was "impatient for action." Hostility and frustration had built up as various members had been lost to snipers and mines.[61] Thus, Terry explained Medina's behavior and statements. Terry believed that "like a good Captain, Medina tried to appease them." The effect, Terry concluded, was that Medina "gave the impression -- he never specifically said -- that they could kill the people . . . that they could kill anybody they saw . . . . It seemed like there would be a whole lot of killing the next day."[62]

Whatever Medina specifically said, Robert Pendleton remembered a consensus after the speech: "That evening, as we cleaned our weapons and got our gear ready, we talked about the operation. People were talking about killing everything that moved. Everyone knew what we were going to do" [emphasis added].[63] The next day between 175 and 400 civilian men, women and children were killed by Charlie Company at My Lai 4.[64]

Like Chivington's rhetoric, Medina's rhetoric seemed, to his audience, to call for undifferentiated action against the "enemy." Also similar to Chivington, there is no evidence that Medina spoke to stop such actions. His muteness in this regard at least legitimized such a policy. Michael Bernhardt stated that as far as Medina was concerned, "Everything that walked and didn't wear a uniform was a VC . . . ."[65] Such a perception legitimized brutality at the platoon level of command. Charles

Hall explained that "On the lower level squad leaders and platoon leaders didn't enforce the rules -- like for beating people. This happened every day; every day there was disregard for the people."[66]

For the men of Charlie Company, what culminated at My Lai started with personal fears which were followed by small acts of brutality, followed by more brutal acts. As Ron Grzesik of Charlie Company admitted, "It was like going from one step to another worse one . . . . First, you'd stop the people, question them and let them go. Second, you'd stop the people, beat up an old man, and let them go. Third, you'd stop the people, beat up an old man, and then shoot him. Fourth, you go in and wipe out a village."[67] But the spiral of violence represented in this progression started with the violence done to the humanity and individuality of the individual Vietnamese as they were symbolized by their benefactors. Like their predecessors at Sand Creek, the members of Charlie Company, under stress, assumed that the Vietnamese families at My Lai 4 were deserving of execution simply because they were "dinks," "gooks" and "slopes."

The effect of actions like Charlie Company's on neutral and non-Communist Vietnamese was predictable. Like Colorado's Natives, the Vietnamese fulfilled the definition of their nature provided by the Americans. As Jonathan Schell realized:

> when we go into a village . . . we classify all the people into different categories. But these categories do not depend on something we perceive about them; they depend on what we do to them. If we kill them, they are Vietcong. If we capture them and tie them up, they are Vietcong suspects. If we grab them and move them to a camp, they were hostile civilians. Having done this to many people who were in fact innocent, the definitions we have imposed became real. The men who have been tied up or tortured actually become our enemies and shoot real bullets at us, but we are facing the shadow of our own actions.[68]

Nguyen Bat, a former resident of My Lai 4, was not a communist at the time of the massacre. But after the shooting, he said [69] "all the [surviving] villagers became Communists."

Many Americans at large refused to believe that the massacre had occurred at all. Others justified the act as necessary or no worse than Viet Cong actions.[70] Members of Charlie Company returned home and puzzled over why they had performed such actions. How could "good" American boys engage in such acts?

Similar to the events at Sand Creek, a situation was created favorable for extermination as an act. The scene seemed to call for brutal acts by its American participants against those identified as the enemy. One G.I. reported that Vietnam was a "fantasy-land" in which violent acts were expected and acceptable. But, after his return he recognized that ". . . it wasn't like it was supposed to be."[71] Professor Hans Morgenthau believes that incidents like My Lai were a "logical consequence" of the situation. He explains:

> . . . if you are engaged in a war directed not against a distinguishable army, not against a particular group within a population as a whole, it becomes perfectly logical . . . to regard every man, woman and child as an actual or potential enemy who has to be eliminated.[72]

Thus, in the "fantasy-land" of My Lai, the definition of the enemy called for extermination. Since any Vietnamese could be a potential enemy, the logical action was to kill all Vietnamese. The external features of the "slopes" marked them for death as potential conspirators against the good Americans.

The contributors to <u>War Crimes and the American Conscience</u> have noted the importance of race and official legitimation as factors at My Lai and other racially directed violence.

> The pattern of violence at My Lai does not resemble a riot or mass psychosis. But it does have its counterparts in certain American traditions: genocidal attacks on American Indians in the nineteenth century and mass lynchings which persisted until the 1930's . . . . [This] is an all too rational response to the encouragement, spoken or unspoken of their community leaders. . . . It is important that at My Lai, as at the mass lynchings of blacks and the genocide of the Native Americans, the victims were of a different race.[73]

342

The role of race in American acts of violence deserves further study. It does appear that projection as a mechanism for coping with internal anxieties occurs most easily in situations when Americans confront a "darker race."[74] Both the members of the Colorado Third and Charlie Company collected "trophies" from the bodies of their "colored" enemies.[75] Whether this "enemy" is faced in Vietnam or at the "new" battle of Wounded Knee in 1973, America's perceptions of her motives are "predicated on a self-image of moral rectitude."[76] Implicit in this image is a suppressed racism, ethnocentrism and insensitivity which elevates American culture above that of the "lesser developed" culture. Moreover, a Manichaean, good-versus-evil approach based upon perceived American historical experience dictates that the good Americans can expect violence from darker or different peoples. An enemy from another culture is an expected conspirator. American expectations become self-sealing.[77]

Thus, in the rhetoric surrounding My Lai, echoes of Sand Creek reveal the deep-rootedness of a conspiracy myth in American conflicts with darker nations.[78] The extent of this tendency is not proven by this study. However, it is clear that the outcomes of such perceptions are not in our best interests.

A Rhetoric of Extermination

A pragmatic observer might argue for the control of <u>actions</u> as the means for avoiding future Sand Creeks or My Lais. Such a view ignores the role of symbols in helping to create the reality to which men respond. Gordon Allport hints at the relationship of symbols and violence, writing that there is "never a bite without previous barking."[79] Pejorative symbols provide a redefinition of the minority group prior to any violence committed against that group. Such definitions facilitate the destruction of the "target group." The substance of Colorado White assumptions about Native Americans were promises of what was fulfilled at Sand Creek. Similarly the symbols contained in the rhetoric of Charlie Company hinted at the atrocity to come. Psychohistorian Robert Jay Lifton explains the ethical importance of isolating and explaining such key symbols:

Realities are not something bequeathed to us by some outside force; they are man-made. Therefore, the reality itself could be . . . absurd and evil. In such a case the task -- the ethical task -- becomes not to adapt oneself to that reality, but rather to transform it. Just as the reality itself was made by man, it takes men to transform and change the reality.$_{80}$

Thus, the critic who calls for the control of actions as the sole solution to the avoidance of future Sand Creeks, may only find that men adapt themselves to the "necessity" for more Sand Creeks or to the "fantasy-land" that was My Lai. As Lifton implies, the solution comes from critiquing such "evil" realities and providing alternative interpretations. Ensuring Constitutional guarantees and human rights for any individual or group of individuals would provide one reality which would decrease the probability of future Sand Creeks. However, as this study illustrates, such constitutional guarantees have not been adequate in the past. Thus, the social critic should be familiar with the rhetorical process by which such guarantees are devalued. This study suggests the following characteristics of a "Rhetoric of Extermination":

1. A Conspiracy Myth picturing the "target group" plotting the destruction of the "good" Whites or other dominant group.

2. Antilocution or what Allport calls "barking" which symbolizes the target group as enemy, i.e. savages, vermin, redskins, gooks, slant-eyes, dinks, etc. Physical differences between the dominant group and target group help to inspire such antilocution.

3. A Formative Event or "precipitating incident" which is interpreted by elites and authorities as illustrating the "true" nature of the "enemy." This event may be a real occurrence or a fiction invented by elites to increase a sense of urgency so as to mobilize allies.

4. A Group Interest (money, land, power) which will be gained through the destruction or

subjugation of the target group. This interest is not directly admitted by the dominant group.

5. Self-Sealing Results wherein provocations offered by the dominant group cause retaliation by the minority target group. The dominant group interprets such retaliation as "proof" of their previous antilocution.

6. Actual Calls for Extermination of the Target Group.

One role of the critic should be to reveal the assumptions of such a rhetoric. While myth and myth-making may serve positive social functions, in human relations myth containing the assumptions described above should not be allowed to distort our perceptions of persons of color.

Areas For Further Study

Four areas specific to an understanding of the Sand Creek incident offer potential for further study. These areas included: other newspapers, Chivington's background, other agents and Indian rhetoric.

Fragmentary records of newspapers besides the Rocky Mountain News are available.[81] A study of these records could provide useful information as none of their editors were allied with Evans or Chivington.

Further research into Chivington's background might provide increased insight into his actions and rhetoric at Sand Creek. Additionally his activities and rhetoric after he left the Denver area subsequent to Sand Creek also might provide clues as to his motivations in 1864.[82]

Besides Byers, Evans and Chivington, the words and actions of other actors influenced events at Sand Creek. General Curtis' perception of the situation and his orders in this regard were important to its outcome. In particular, the role of the information he received from Chivington in shaping his perceptions could act as a basis for more detailed study.

Major Jacob Downing and Lieutenant Clark Dunn's orders and reports addressed to Chivington also may be a source of important information. Downing appears to have used the phraseology of extermination before Chivington. Dunn's reports were the basis for Governor Evans' beliefs about the demeanor of the Indians who "took" Ripley's stock.[83]

Major Wynkoop and Lieutenant Silas Soule were Chivington's chief opponents and unique in their contrary views. Both men were popular with their contemporaries. Their actions and words might be a valuable source for an increased understanding of the situation.[84]

Finally, a more detailed study is needed of Cheyenne and Arapahoe viewpoints of the situation. Grinnell's studies are helpful in this regard but a more objective review is needed for a balanced synthesis.

In the general area of Native and White American relations further opportunity for study also exists.

The relationship of other atrocity stories to other massacres is one area which could be studied. Military doctrine and the beliefs of professional soldiers about Indian nature might illustrate the pervasiveness of beliefs about Indian nature.[85]

Additionally, more "positive" myths held by Whites about Native Americans offer another contrast to the conspiracy myth. In particular, the so-called "Noble savage" myth could be the focus of study. Moreover, the conditions favoring attachment to this myth and the functions it served for its White adherents could be contrasted with similar conditions and functions of the conspiracy myth.[86]

Finally, current myths adhered to by Whites about "Indians" need isolation and study. Concern for modern Indians and their plight is intermittent but of no great intensity or salience for most Americans. Moreover, when concern is voiced for the "poor Indians" it is measured by the extent to which its vocalist perceives that Indians do not meet White standards. Indians as complete humans are seldom the topic of White rhetoric. Perhaps a natural outcome of past adherence to the conspiracy myth is a White belief in the "non-existence" of modern Indians. Thus, current mythic beliefs need to be isolated and their implications analyzed.

In the general area of White/nonwhite relations, the role of rhetoric and myth and their functions related to racial violence need further study. Social scientists could be particularly useful in analyzing and measuring this function.[87]

Vine Deloria, modern Indian spokesman, summarizes the final intent and lesson of this study:

> . . . the understanding of the racial question does not ultimately involve understanding by either blacks or Indians. It involves the white man himself. He must examine his past. He must face the problems he has created within himself and within others. The white man must no longer project his fears and insecurities onto other groups, races and countries. Before the white man can relate to others he must forego the pleasure of defining them. The white man must learn to stop viewing history as a plot against himself.[88]

CHAPTER VII

NOTES

[1] Partial records of other newspapers exist. For a complete bibliography, see Douglas C. McMurtrie and Albert H. Allen, Early Printing in Colorado (Denver: A.B. Hirschfield Press, 1935). The Black Hawk Journal, August 30, 1864 clearly shared the extermination solution.

[2] Kenneth Burke, A Grammar of Motives (1945; rpt. Berkely and Los Angeles: University of California Press, 1969), p. 19.

[3] Burke, pp. 9, 15, 19, explains that scenes help to determine certain acts.

[4] Reginald S. Craig, The Fighting Parson: The Biography of Colonel John M. Chivington (Los Angeles: Westernlore Press, 1959), pp. 188-195; Raymond Carey, "Puzzle of Sand Creek," Colorado Magazine, 41 (Spring, 1964), 281. For empirical studies of the relationship between rhetoric and violent acts, see Monica Blumenthal et al., More About Justifying Violence, Methodological Studies of Attitudes and Behavior (Ann Arbor, Michigan: University of Michigan Press, 1975), p. 181ff. The authors concluded, "The data showed clearly that the individuals' rhetoric influenced the course of action recommended. The study thus provided concrete information supporting the widely held notion that rhetoric can inflame, that is, the words which are used to label certain actions as violence are not only pejorative but also may be used to rationalize retaliatory physical violence" (p. 181).

[5] David J. Finley, Ole R. Holsti and Richard R. Fagen in Enemies in Politics (Chicago: Rand McNally, 1967), p. 13, write, "By proclaiming the enemy's dangerous intentions and perhaps offering a little provocation on the side, such groups effect a self-fulfilling prophecy; the 'enemy' will 'respond' and in this way actually become as dangerous to the group as it accused him of being in the first place."

[6] U.S. Senate, "Sand Creek Massacre," Report of the Secretary of War, 39th Cong., 2d session, Senate

Executive Document 26 (Washington, G.P.O., 1867), p. 31. Hereafter this source will be cited as Report, Secretary of War or Report).

[7] Report, Secretary of War, 119, 169; Stan Hoig, The Sand Creek Massacre (Norman: University of Oklahoma Press, 1961), p. 98.

[8] Wynkoop had written, "My intention is to kill all Indians I may come across until I receive orders to the contrary . . . ." Wynkoop to Chivington, August, 1864, United States War Department, The War of the Rebellion: A Compilation of the Official Records of the Union and Confederate Armies (Washington, G.P.O., 1880-1901), Series 1, Vol. 41, part 1, 237-238 (hereafter cited as Rebellion Records or RR).

[9] Testimony of Edward Wynkoop, Report, Secretary of War, 84.

[10] Edward H. Wynkoop's Unfinished Manuscript, unpublished MS in Colorado History Collection, 11-20, Colorado State Historical Society, 28.

[11] Testimony of Edward Wynkoop, Report, Secretary of War, 86.

[12] Report, Secretary of War, 87.

[13] Their testimonies are in Report, Secretary of War, pp. 10, 26-27, 47 and 127.

[14] Murray Edelman in Politics as Symbolic Action (Chicago: Markham, 1971), p. 51, provides this benefit as one which decreases susceptibility.

[15] Edelman, p. 52; also see Finley, Holsti and Fagen, p. 11.

[16] Edelman, p. 51.

[17] Implied by Edelman, pp. 51-52.

[18] Edelman, pp. 55.

[19] See p. 2 in Finley, Holsti and Fagen for a discussion of the importance of ego relevance to myth attachment.

[20] Edelman, p. 54; Jerome Bruner, "Myth and Identity," in Myth and Mythmaking, ed. Henry A. Murray (New York: George Braziller, 1960), p. 279; Erik Erikson, Young Man Luther (New York: Norton, 1958), p. 111; Carey McWilliams, Brothers Under the Skin (Boston: Little, Brown and Co., 1944), p. 53.

[21] Finley, Holsti and Fagen, p. 8.

[22] Edelman, p. 51, explains that myth attachment may be facilitated by the gaining of a "substantial benefit."

[23] Robert Berkhofer, The White Man's Indian, Images of the American Indian From Columbus to the Present (New York: Alfred A. Knopf, 1978), pp. 3-25.

[24] William T. Hagan, American Indians (Chicago: University of Chicago Press, 1961), p. 173.

[25] Rollo May, Power and Innocence, A Search of the Sources of Violence (New York: W.W. Norton Co., 1972), p. 67.

[26] Leach is quoted in Robert W. Winks, The Myth of the American Frontier (Leicester University Press, 1971), p. 7. This conclusion is consistent with Roy Harvey Pearce's in Savagism and Civilization: A Study of the Indian and American Mind (Baltimore: Johns Hopkins Press, 1965), p. 242.

[27] Robert Shulman, "Parkman's Indians and American Violence," The Massachusetts Review, 12 (April, 1971), 226.

[28] Newton Garver, "What Violence Is," in Violence in America, ed. Thomas Rose (New York: Atherton Press, 1969), pp. 5-13.

[29] This "logic" is consistent with the conclusions of Roger Daniels and Harry H.L. Kitano, American Racism: Exploration of the Nature of Prejudice (Englewood Cliffs, New Jersey: Prentice Hall, 1970), p. 12.

[30] W. Eugene Hollon, Frontier Violence, Another Look (New York: Oxford University Press, 1974), pp. 129-130; Hugh Davis Graham and Ted Robert Gurr, eds., The History of Violence in America, Historical and

Comparative Perspectives, A Report Submitted to the National Commission on the Causes and Prevention of Violence (New York: Fredrick A. Praeger, 1969), p. 67.

[31]Hollon, p. 131; H.H. Powers, "The Ethics of Expansion," International Journal of Ethics, 10 (1900), 292.

[32]Francis Paul Prucha, American Indian Policy in the Formative Years (Lincoln: University of Nebraska Press, 1962), p. 262.

[33]Rubin Francis Weston makes a similar argument relating to imperialism and racism on the part of U.S. policy makers. See Racism in U.S. Imperialism: The Influence of Racial Assumptions on American Foreign Policy, 1893-1946 (Columbia: University of South Carolina Press, 1972). A conclusion regarding reasons for a reluctance to extend Constitutional guarantees to Native Americans would be consistent with Boorstin's preenactment analogy as well as Shulman's arguments.

[34]Prucha, p. 258.

[35]Richard Maxwell, Brown, "Historial Patterns of Violence in America," in Graham and Gurr, p. 67.

[36]Just below the surface, however, memories of the myth may operate as what Edelman describes as a "deep structure." For example faced with the Indian occupation of the Pine Ridge Reservation in 1973, (the "new" battle of Wounded Knee) government officials reacted in a fashion not justified by the "threat" posed by the small group of Indian militants. One observer recorded the level of potential force brought to bear by the federal government: ". . . approximately 90 U.S. Marshals and FBI agents surrounded Wounded Knee . . . by the next day, 250 Federal personnel were on duty, helmeted and armed with M-16 machine guns. The Marshals' log report [recorded the following:] 'All U.S. Marshal personnel advised to fire when fired upon . . . army convoy arrived with armored personnel carriers (APCs -- tank-like vehicles used to carry soldiers into battle!)' Two Air Force Phantom Jets were also called in." (Akwesane Notes, Voices From Wounded Knee, 1973, in The Words of the Participants (New York: Mohawk

Nation, 1975), pp. 41, 51. The need for such force may relate to old fears of Indians. Such unconscious fear might also help to explain continued government policies described by Indian spokesmen as "Institutional Genocide." (See various issues of The American Indian Journal, especially see July, 1977). Also see Hollon, pp. 124-125.

[37] These conclusions are implied by statements in Erwin Knoll and Judith Nies McFadden, eds., War Crimes and the American Conscience (Chicago: Holt, Rinehart and Winston, 1970), p. 138.

[38] Quoted in Seymour M. Hersh, My Lai 4, A Report on the Massacre and its Aftermath (New York: Random House, 1970), pp. 7-8. Hersh's book is based upon interviews with American soldiers and other first hand observers of events in Vietnam. Specifically, he interviewed various members of Charlie Company. These interviews are available nowhere else.

[39] Hersh, pp. 7-8.

[40] Hersh, p. 8

[41] Hersh, p. 8.

[42] Hersh, p. 8. These symbols are also mentioned by Gordon Livingston in Knoll and McFadden, p. 136.

[43] Hersh, p. 11. Hersh bases his recording of this "joke" and other racist remarks by G.I.s on Miss Claire Culhane's record of G.I. attitudes toward the Vietnamese found in her unpublished diary kept during her stay in Vietnam (p. 190).

[44] Congressional Record, December 29, 1969, p. E11033.

[45] See Richard Falk's statement in Knoll and McFadden, pp. 5-6.

[46] Knoll and McFadden, p. 116.

[47] Quoted in Hersh, p. 14.

[48] Quoted in Hersh, p. 53.

[49] Quoted in Hersh, p. 13.

[50] Hersh, p. 39; Joseph Goldstein, Burke Marshall and Jack Schwartz, The My Lai Massacre and Its Cover-up: Beyond the Reach of Law? The Peers Commission Report (New York: The Free Press, 1976), pp. 98-99 (hereafter cited as the Peers Commission).

[51] Hersh, p. 46; Peers Commission, p. 99.

[52] Peers Commission, p. 98.

[53] Peers Commission, p. 98.

[54] Quoted in Hersh, pp. 40-41.

[55] Quoted in Hersh, p. 41.

[56] Quoted in Hersh, p. 41.

[57] Quoted in Hersh, p. 41.

[58] Quoted in Hersh, pp. 41-42.

[59] Quoted in Hersh, p. 42. Also see Edelman's comment in this regard on p. 76. He explains that "deep structures" allow for "divergent meanings" arising from common experiences which for some, may reconcile behavior with "incompatible norms."

[60] Quoted in Hersh, p. 55.

[61] Hersh, pp. 23, 24-25.

[62] Quoted in Hersh, p. 42.

[63] Quoted in Peers Commission, p. 99.

[64] Peers Commission, p. 1; Hersh, p. 75.

[65] Quoted in Hersh, p. 24.

[66] Quoted in Hersh, p. 24.

[67] Quoted in Hersh, p. 43.

[68] Quoted in Knoll and McFadden, p. 111.

[69] Quoted in Hersh, p. 74.

[70] Hersh, pp. 155-170; Knoll and McFadden, pp. 122-124.

[71] Quoted in Hersh, p. 185.

[72] Quoted in Knoll and McFadden, p. 110.

[73] Knoll and McFadden, p. 113.

[74] Vine Deloria, Jr., Custer Died For Your Sins: An Indian Manifesto (New York: Avon Books, 1970), pp. 169-195.

[75] Reportedly, after their return from Sand Creek, the Colorado Third displayed over 100 Indian scalps at the Denver theatre (Hagan, p. 108); Gregory Olsen recalled seeing an American Troop carrier with about twenty human ears on the antenna (Hersh, p. 23).

[76] Knoll and McFadden, p. 138.

[77] Knoll and McFadden, p. 118. Walter H. Capps, The Unfinished War, Vietnam and the American Conscience (Boston: Beacon Press, 1982), p. 137. It is not my intent to offer detailed proof of this characterization. Rather, the American experience in Vietnam may be viewed as illustrating similarities with the White nineteenth century way of viewing Indians.

[78] Shulman, p. 233.

[79] Gordon W. Allport, The Nature of Prejudice (Garden City, New York: Doubleday, 1958), p. 56.

[80] Quoted in Knoll and McFadden, p. 15.

[81] McMurtrie and Allen is a complete bibliography of these newspapers.

[82] Raymond Carey makes this recommendation in "Colonel Chivington, Brigadier General Connor and Sand Creek," Denver Westerner Brand Book, 16 (1969), pp. 107-109. However, locating primary sources not already analyzed would be necessary.

[83] See RR, Series 1, Vol. 34, part 1, pp. 880-887, 906-909; RR, Series 1, Vol. 34, part 3, pp. 146, 242, 250-252, 314, 407. Major Anthony's statements particularly directed to the Indians at Sand Creek need further analysis.

[84] Major Wynkoop's unfinished manuscript has been previously noted. Also see Thomas D. Isern, "The Controversial Career of Edward W. Wynkoop," The Colorado Magazine, 56 (Winter/Spring, 1979), 1-18; Silas Soule, Unpublished Letter Collection in Western History Collection of the Denver Public Library; C.A. Prentice, "Captain Silas Soule, A Pioneer Martyr," The Colorado Magazine, 14 (May, 1927); Rocky Mountain News, April 24, 27, 1865.

[85] Robert Utley, Frontiers Regulars: The U.S. Army and the Indians, 1866-1891 (New York: Macmillan Co., 1974), pp. 45-47, cites the lack of an accurate military doctrine as one reason for the failure of the army in its conventional warfare with Indians. For a general discussion, see Marcus Cunlife, Soldiers and Civilians, The Martial Spirit in American 1775-1865 (Boston: Little, Brown and Company, 1968).

[86] For one analysis of the "noble savage myth," see Bryan R. Wilson, The Noble Savages: The Primitive Origins of Charisma and its Contemporary Survival (Los Angeles: University of California Press, 1975). Also see Wilcomb F. Washburn, "A Moral History of Indian-White Relations: Needs and Opportunities for Study," Ethnohistory, 4 (Winter, 1957), p. 56; Edna C. Sorber, "The Noble Eloquent Savage," Ethnohistory, 19 (Summer, 1972), pp. 227-236.

[87] The Contributors to Knoll and McFadden also call for social science research in this area (pp. 125-126).

[88] Deloria, p. 175.

APPENDIX

CHRONOLOGY: IMPORTANT EVENTS BEFORE AND AFTER SAND CREEK

1851	Ft. Laramie Treaty
1858-59	"Gold Rush" to Colorado region
1859	Rocky Mountain News publishes first issue
1861	Colorado Territorial Government is organized
	Ft. Wise Treaty
1862	John Evans appointed Second Territorial Governor
	Battle at Glorietta Pass (New Mexico)
	John Chivington appointed Military Commander of Colorado Territory
	Widely reported Sioux uprising in Minnesota
1863	Delegation of Colorado Indian Tribes visits Washington
	Great Fire destroys much of Denver
1864	Great Flood in Cherry Creek

April: Dunn's encounter "Battle of Fremont's Orchard"

Eayre's expedition clashes with two different groups of Indians

May: Downing's expedition kills several Indians

June 18th: Hungates murdered and bodies brought to Denver

June 27th: Evans' Proclamation "To the Friendly Indians . . ."

APPENDIX, continued

1864   August 7th and 8th: Trains and settlements attacked in eastern Colorado and western Kansas; many Whites killed and captured

       August 10th: Evans' "Appeal to the Citizens of Colorado"

       August 11th: Evans' "Proclamation" of the "Indian War" of 1864

       August 13th: Secretary of War Stanton authorizes regiment of "100 days men"

       September: Camp Weld Council

                        State Election

       October: Nichols Encounter

       November 29th: Sand Creek Engagement

1865   Evans forced to resign

       Chivington resigns

SELECTED BIBLIOGRAPHY

Manuscripts

Byers, William Newton. Byers' autobiography, his story called "The Newspaper Press of Colorado," and letters on the Sand Creek Affair. Unpublished collection in the Western History Department of the Denver Public Library.

Byers, William Newton. "The Sand Creek Affair." Handwritten Manuscript in "Byers' Papers," a Special Collection in the Western History Collection, Denver Public Library.

Chivington, John M. To The People of Colorado. Synopsis of the Sand Creek Investigation. Denver, June 1865. Microcard, Western History Collection, Denver Public Library.

Dailey, John L. "Journal of John L. Daily 1864." Manuscript in Western History Collection, Denver Public Library.

Soule, Silas S. "Papers 1861-1865." Unpublished Letters and Manuscript, Western History Collection, Denver Public Library.

Templeton, Andrew J. "Life and Reminiscences." Manuscript in Pioneers' Museum, Colorado Springs, Colorado.

Thom, William B. Eighteen Unpublished Letters. Western History Collection, Denver Public Library.

Government Documents

Letters Received by the Office of Indian Affairs, 1863. Upper Arkansas Agency, National Archives.

United States Congress, House of Representatives. "Massacre of Cheyenne Indians," Report on the Conduct of the War, 38th Congress, 2nd Session. Washington, D.C.: Government Printing Office, 1865.

United States Congress. "Investigation of the My Lai Incident." Hearing of the Armed Services

359

Investigating Subcommittee. 91st Congress, 2nd Session. Washington, D.C.: Government Printing Office, 1976.

United States Congress, Senate. "The Chivington Massacre." Report of the Committees. 39th Congress, 2nd Session. Washington, D.C.: Government Printing Office, 1867.

United States Congress, Senate. Indian Affairs, Laws and Treaties. Vol. 2. Senate Executive Document 319, 58th Congress, 2nd Session. Ed. by C.J. Kappler. Washington, D.C.: Government Printing Office, 1904.

United States Congress, Senate. "Sand Creek Massacre." Report of the Secretary of War, 39th Congress, 2nd Session. Washington, D.C.: Government Printing Office, 1867.

United States Interior Department, Bureau of Indian Affairs. Reports of the Commissioner of Indian Affairs for the Years 1851 through 1865. Washington, D.C.: Government Printing Office, 1861-1866.

United States Interior Department, Census Office. Population of the United States in 1860. Washington, D.C.: Government Printing Office, 1864.

United States War Department. The War of the Rebellion: A Compilation of the Official Records of the Union and Confederate Armies. Four Series, 128 vols. Washington, D.C.: Government Printing Office, 1880-1901.

Newspapers

Black Hawk Daily Mining Journal, 1864.

Denver Weekly Commonwealth, May 25, 1864.

Rocky Mountain News, Denver, 1860-1865.

Books

Adams, James Truslow. The March of Democracy: A History of the United States. 2 vols. New York: Random House, 1965.

Allibone, Austin S. Critical Dictionary of English Literature and British and American Authors. Philadelphia: J.P. Lippincott, 1872.

Allport, Gordon W. The Nature of Prejudice. Garden City, New York: Doubleday, 1958.

Andrist, Ralph K. The Long Death: The Last Days of the Plains Indians. London: Collier, 1964.

Athearn, Robert G. The Coloradans. Albuquerque: University of New Mexico Press, 1976.

Baker, James B. and LeRoy R. Hafen, eds. History of Colorado, 5 vols. Denver: Linderman, 1927.

Berkofer, Robert F., Jr. Salvation and the Savage, An Analysis of Protestant Missions and American Indian Response, 1787-1862. New York: Atheneum, 1976.

Berkhofer, Robert F., Jr. The White Man's Indian, Images of the American Indian from Columbus to the Present. New York: Alfred A. Knopf, 1978.

Berthong, Donald J. The Southern Cheyennes. Norman: University of Oklahoma Press, 1963.

Brown, Dee. Bury My Heart at Wounded Knee: An Indian History of the American West. New York: Bantam Books, 1970.

Burnette, Lawrence O., ed. Wisconsin Witness to Frederick Jackson Turner: A Collection of Essays on the Historian and the Thesis. Madison, Wisconsin: The State Historical Society of Wisconsin, 1961.

Byers, William N. Encyclopedia of Biography of Colorado. Chicago: Century Publishing, 1901.

Caldwell, Charles. Thoughts on the Original Unity of the Human Race. New York: E. Bliss, 1830.

Capps, Walter A. The Unfinished War: Vietnam and the American Conscience. Boston: Beacon Press, 1982.

Carlson, Lewis H. and George A. Colburn, eds. In Their Place: White America Defines her Minorities, 1850-1950. New York: John Wiley and Sons, 1972.

Carter, Samuel. Cherokee Sunset: A Nation Betrayed, A Narrative of Travail and Triumph, Persecution and Exile. New York: Doubleday, 1976.

Casey, Lee, ed. Denver Murders. New York: Alfred A. Knopf, 1946.

Coffin, Morse H. The Battle of Sand Creek. Waco, Texas: W.M. Morrison, 1965.

Cook, Jacob E., ed. The Federalist. Middleton: Wesleyan University Press, 1961.

Craig, Katherine L. Craig's Brief History of Colorado for Teacher and Student, 2nd ed. Denver: Welch-Haffner, 1923.

Craig, Reginald S. The Fighting Parson: the Biography of Colonel John M. Chivington. Los Angeles: Westernlore Press, 1959.

Cunlife, Marcus. Soldiers and Civilians, the Martial Spirit in America, 1775-1865. Boston: Little Brown, 1968.

Daniels, Roger and Harry H.L. Kitano. American Racism: Exploration of the Nature of Prejudice. Englewood Cliffs, New Jersey: Prentice-Hall, 1970.

Davies, John D. Phrenology Fad and Science: A 19th-Century Crusade. New Haven: Yale University Press, 1971.

Deloria, Vine. Custer Died For Your Sins, An Indian Manifesto. New York: Avon, 1969.

De Waalmalefijt, Annemarie. Images of Man: A History of Anthropological Thought. New York: Alfred A. Knopf, 1974.

Dixon, J. William Hepworth. New America. Philadelphia: J.P. Lippincott, 1867.

Doughty, Howard. *Francis Parkman.* New York: Macmillian, 1962.

Dudley, Edward and Maximillian E. Novak, eds. *The Wild Man Within: An Image in Western Thought from the Renaissance to Romanticism.* Pittsburg: University of Pittsburg Press, 1972.

Dunn, J.P. *Massacres of the Mountains: A History of the Indian Wars of the Far West 1816-1875.* New York: Archer House, 1958.

Dye, Thomas. *Understanding Public Policy.* Englewood Cliffs, New Jersey: Prentice-Hall, 1972.

Dykstra, Robert. *The Cattle Towns.* New York: Knopf, 1971.

Edelman, Murray. *Politics as Symbolic Action: Mass Arousal and Quiescence.* Chicago: Markham, 1971.

Eliade, Mircea. *Myths, Dreams and Mysteries.* New York: Harper and Row, 1960.

Ellul, Jacques. *Propaganda: The Formation of Men's Attitudes.* New York: Alfred A. Knopf, 1969.

Farrand, Max, ed. *The Records of the Federal Convention of 1787.* 4 vols. New Haven: Yale University Press, 1937.

Filler, Louis and Allen Guttmann, eds. *The Removal of the Cherokee Nation: Manifest Destiny or National Dishonor?* New York: Robert E. Krieger, 1977.

Finley, David J., Ole R. Holsti and Richard R. Fagen. *Enemies in Politics.* Chicago: Rand McNally, 1967.

Gale, Robert L. *Francis Parkman.* New York: Twayne Publishers, 1973.

Gardiner, Dorothy. *The Great Betrayal.* Garden City, New York: Doubleday, 1949.

Goldstein, Joseph, Burke Marshall and Jack Schwartz. *The My Lai Massacre and its Cover-up: Beyond the Reach of Law? The Peers Commission Report with a Supplement and Introductory Essay on the Limits of the Law.* New York: The Free Press, 1976.

Goode, Reverend Wililam H. Outposts of Zion with Limmings of Mission Life. Cincinnati: Poe and Hatchcock, 1864.

Gossett, Thomas F. Race, the History of an Idea in America. Dallas: Southern Methodist University Press, 1963.

Grinnell, George Bird. The Cheyenne Indians: Their History and Way of Life. 2 vols. New York: Cooper Square, 1962.

Grinnell, George Bird. The Fighting Cheyennes. 1915; rpt. Norman: University of Oklahoma Press, 1956.

Habermas, Jugen. The Legitimation Crises. trans., Thomas McCarthy. Boston: Beacon Press, 1973.

Hafen, LeRoy, ed. Colorado Gold Rush Contemporary Letters and Reports 1858-1859. Glendale, California: Arthur H. Clark, 1941.

Hafen, LeRoy, ed. Pikes Peak Gold Rush Guidebooks of 1859. Glendale, California: Arthur H. Clark, 1941.

Hafen, LeRoy R., and Ann W. Hafen, eds. Reports From Colorado, The Wildman Letters 1859-1865 with Other Related Letters and Newspaper Reports, 1859.

Hall, Frank. History of the State of Colorado, 4 vols. Chicago: Blakely, 1899.

Harmon, George Dewey. Sixty Years of Indian Affairs: Political, Economic and Diplomatic 1789-1850. Chapel Hill: University of North Carolina Press, 1941.

Hersh, Seymour M. My Lai 4, A Report on the Massacre and Its Aftermath. New York: Random House, 1970.

Hill, Alice Polk. Tales of the Colorado Pioneers. Denver: Pierson and Gardiner, 1884.

Hoebel, Adamson E. The Cheyennes, Indians of the Great Plains. Chicago: Holt, Rinehart and Winston, 1960.

Hoig, Stan. The Sand Creek Massacre. Norman: University of Oklahoma Press, 1961.

Holder, Preston. The Hoe and the Horse on the Plains, A Study of Cultural Development Among North American Indians. Lincoln: University of Nebraska Press, 1970.

Hollister, Ovando J. Boldly They Ride: A History of the First Colorado Regiment of Volunteers. 1863; rpt. Lakewood, Colorado: Golden Press, 1949.

Horsman, Reginald. Expansion and American Indian Policy, 1783-1812. E. Lansing: Michigan State University Press, 1967.

Horsman, Reginald. Race and Manifest Destiny: The Origins of American Racial Anglo Saxonism. Cambridge: Harvard University Press, 1981.

Howbert, Irving. The Indians of the Pike's Peak Region, Including An Account of the Battle of Sand Creek, and of Occurrances in El Paso County, Colorado, During the War with the Cheyenne and Arapahoes, in 1864 and 1868. 1914; rpt. Glorietta, New Mexico: Rio Grande Press, 1970.

Hunt, George T. The Wars of the Iroquois: A Study in Inter-tribal Trade Relations. Madison, Wisconsin: University of Wisconsin Press, 1940.

Jackson, Helen Hunt. A Century of Dishonor. Boston: Roberts Brothers, 1887.

Jacobs, Wilbur R. Dispossessing the American Indian: Indians and Whites on the Colonial Frontier. New York: Charles Scribner's Sons, 1972.

Jennings, Francis. The Invasion of America, Indians, Colonialism, and The Cant of Conquest. Chapel Hill: University of North Carolina Press, 1975.

Karnes, Thomas L. William Gilpin, Western Nationalist. Austin: University of Texas Press, 1970.

Kennedy, John Pendelton. The Collected Works, Memoirs of the Life of William Wirt. New York: G.P. Putnam and Sons, 1972.

Kinser, Bill and Neil Kleinmen. The Dream that Was No More a Dream: A Search for Aesthetic Reality in Germany 1890-1945. Evanston: Harper and Row, 1969.

Kirk, G.S. Myth: Its Meaning and Functions in Ancient and Other Cultures. Los Angeles: University of California Press, 1970.

Knoll, Erwin and Judith Neil McFadden, eds. War Crimes and the American Conscience, Chicago: Holt, Rinehart and Winston, 1970.

Leckie, William H. The Military Conquest of the Southern Plains. Norman: University of Oklahoma Press, 1963.

Lyon, William H. The Pioneer Editor in Missouri, 1808-1860. Columbia: University of Missouri Press, 1965.

McClure, A.K. Three Thousand Miles Through the Rocky Mountains. Philadelphia: J.P. Lippincott, 1869.

McMechen, Edgar Carlisle. Life of Governor Evans. Denver: Walgren Publishing, 1924.

McMurtrie, Douglas C. and Albert H. Allen. Early Printing in Colorado. Denver: A.B. Hirschfield, 1935.

McWilliams, Carey. Brothers Under the Skin. Boston: Little Brown, 1944.

Morison, Samuel Eliot. The Parkman Reader. Boston: Little Brown, 1955.

Morton, Samuel George. Crania Americana: or A Comparative View of the Skulls of Various Aboriginal Nations of North and South America; to Which is Prefixed an Essay on the Varieties of the Human Species. Philadelphia: J. Dobson, 1839.

Mosca, Gaetano. The Ruling Class. trans. H.D. Kahn. New York: McGraw-Hill, 1939.

Mumey, Nolie. History of the Early Settlements of Denver. Glendale, California: Arthur H. Clark, 1942.

Murdock, Robert Winston. *The Reformers and the American Indian*. Columbia: University of Missouri Press, 1971.

Nash, Gary B. *Red, White and Black: The Peoples of Early America*. Englewood Cliffs, New Jersey: Prentice-Hall, 1974.

Nash, Gary B. and Richard Weiss, eds. *The Great Fear, Race In the Mind of America*. New York: Holt, Rinehart and Winston, 1970.

Nott, J.C. *Two Lectures on the Connection Between the Biblical and Physical History of Man*. 1843; rpt. New York: Negro Universities Press, 1969.

Nott, J.C. *Two Lectures on the Natural History of the Caucasian and Negro Race*. Mobile: Thompson, 1844.

Nott, J.C. and George R. Glidden. *Types of Mankind: or, Ethnological Researches Based upon the Ancient Monuments, Paintings, Sculptures and Crania of Races, and upon their Natural, Geographical, Philological and Biblical History*. London: Trubner and Co., 1854.

Parkman, Francis. *The Conspiracy of Pontiac and the Indian War After the Conquest of Canada*. 2 vols. New York: Charles Scribner's Sons, 1915.

Parkman, Francis. *The Oregon Trail: Sketches of Prairie and Rocky Mountain Life*. New York: Charles Scribners' Sons, 1915.

Paxson, Frederic L. *History of the American Frontier 1763-1893*. Boston: Houghton Mifflin, 1924.

Pearce, Roy Harvey. *Savagism and Civilization: A Study of the Indian and the American Mind*. Baltimore: John Hopkins Press, 1965.

Peckham, Howard H. *Pontiac and the Indian Uprising*. Princeton: Princeton University Press, 1947.

Perkin, Robert L. *The First Hundred Years: An Informal History of Denver and the Rocky Mountain News*. Garden City, New York: Doubleday, 1959.

Prucha, Francis Paul. American Indian Policy in the Formative Years: The Indian Trade and Intercourse Acts, 1790-1834. Lincoln: University of Nebraska Press, 1962.

Prucha, Francis Paul, ed. Documents of United States Indian Policy. Lincoln: University of Nebraska Press, 1975.

Richardson, Albert D. Beyond the Mississippi: From the Great River to the Great Ocean. New York: Bliss, 1867.

Sanford, Mollie D. Mollie: The Journal of Mollie Sanford in Nebraska and Colorado Territories, 1857-1866. Lincoln: University of Nebraska Press, 1959.

Selby, John. The Conquest of the American West. Totowa, New Jersey: Rowman and Littlefield, 1976.

Sheehan, Bernard W. Seeds of Extinction, Jeffersonian Philanthrophy and the American Indian. Chapel Hill: University of North Carolina Press, 1973.

Shoyer, Trent. The Critique of Domination: The Origins and Development of Critical Theory. Boston: Beacon Press, 1973.

Smiley, Jerome C. History of Denver. Denver: Times-Sun, 1961.

Smiley, Jerome C., ed. Semi-Centennial History of the State of Colorado, 2 vols. Chicago: Lewis Publishing, 1913.

Smith, Duane A. Rocky Mountain Mining Camps, The Urban Frontier. Bloomington: Indiana University Press, 1967.

Stanton, William. The Leopards's Spots: Scientific Attitudes Towards Race in America 1815-1859. Chicago: University of Chicago Press, 1960.

Stevenson, Taylor W. History as Myth. New York: Seabury Press, 1969.

Stone, Wilbur Fisk, ed. History of Colorado, 4 vols. Chicago: S.J. Clarke Publishing, 1918.

Thayer, William M. Marvels of the New West. Norwich, Connecticut: Henry Bill Publishing, 1888.

Tudor, Henry. Political Myth. New York: Praeger, 1972.

Turner, Frederick Jackson. The United States, 1830-1850: the Nation and its Sections. Glouchester, Massachusetts: Peter Smith, 1958.

Ubbelohde, Carl, Maxine Benson and Duane A. Smith. A Colorado History, 3rd ed. Boulder, Colorado: Pruett Publishing, 1972.

Utley, Robert. Frontiersmen in Blue: The United States Army and the Indian, 1866-1891. New York: Macmillan, 1974.

Wallace, Anthony F.C. The Death and Rebirth of the Senaca. New York: Vintage Books, 1972.

Warmington, Eric C. and Philip G. Rouse, eds. Great Dialogues of Plato, trans. W.H.D. Rouse. New York: New American Library of World Literature, 1956.

Washburn, Wilcomb. The American Indian and the United States, A Documentary History, 4 vols. New York: Random House, 1973.

Washburn, Wilcomb. Red Man's Land/White Man's Law: A Study of the Past and Present Status of the American Indian. New York: Charles Scribner's Sons, 1971.

Weinberg, Albert K. Manifest Destiny: A Study of Nationalist Expansionism in American History. Glouchester, Massachusetts: Peter Smith, 1958.

West, Elliot. The Saloon on the Rocky Mountain Mining Frontier. Lincoln: University of Nebraska Press, 1979.

Weston, Rubin Francis. Racism in U.S. Imperialism, The Influence of Racial Assumptions on American Foreign Policy, 1873-1946. Columbia: University of South Carolina Press, 1972.

Wills, Garry. Inventing America: Jefferson's Declaration of Independence. Garden City, New York: Doubleday, 1978.

Willison, George F. *Here They Dug the Gold.* New York: Brentano's, 1931.

Wilson, Bryan R. *The Noble Savages: The Primative Origins of Charisma and its Contemporary Survival.* Los Angeles: University of California Press, 1975.

Articles

Adams, Blanche V. "The Second Colorado Cavalry in the Civil War." *The Colorado Magazine*, 8 (May 1931).

Ashley, Susan Riley. "Reminiscences of Colorado in the Early 'Sixties.'" *The Colorado Magazine*, 13 (November, 1939).

Axtell, James. "Through a Glass Darkly, Colonial Attitudes Toward Native Americans." *Essays from Sarah Lawrence Faculty*, (October, 1973).

Balgooyen, Theodore. "A Study of Conflicting Values: American Plains Indian Orators Vs. The U.S. Commissioners of Indian Affairs." *Western Speech*, (Spring, 1962).

Bass, Jeff D. and Richard Cherwitz. "Imperial Mission and Manifest Destiny: A Case Study of Political Myth in Rhetorical Discourse." *Southern Speech Communication Journal*, 43 (Spring, 1978).

Berwanger, Eugene H. "William J. Hardin: Colorado Spokesman for Racial Justice, 1863-1871." *The Colorado Magazine*, 52 (Winter, 1975).

Bowen, Francis. "Review of the History of the Conspiracy of Pontiac." *North American Review*, (October, 1851).

Bruner, Jerome. "Myth and Identity," in *Myth and Mythmaking*, Henry A. Murray, ed., New York: Brazillier, 1960.

Burkey, Elmer R. "The Site of the Murder of the Hungate Family by Indians in 1864." *The Colorado Magazine*, 12 (July, 1935).

Burnette, Donald L. "An Historical Analysis of the 1968 'Indian Civil Rights' Act." *Harvard Journal on Legislation*, 9 (May, 1972).

Campbell, Joseph. "Mythological Themes in Creative Literature and Art." in Myths, Dreams and Religion, Joseph Campbell, ed. New York: E.P. Dutton, 1970.

Carey, Raymond G. "Another View of the Sand Creek Affair." The Denver Westerners Monthly Roundup, 16 (February, 1960).

Carey, Raymond G. "The 'Bloodless Third' Regiment, Colorado Volunteer Cavalry." The Colorado Magazine, 38 (October, 1961).

Carey, Raymond G. "The Puzzle of Sand Creek." The Colorado Magazine, 41 (Fall, 1964).

Castel, Albert. "War and Politics: The Price Raid of 1864." The Kansas Historical Quarterly, 24 (Fall, 1958).

Dunklee, Edward V. "Justice Comes to Denver." The Westerners Brand Book, 1949. Denver: Artcraft Press, 1949.

Goodykoontz, Colin B. "Colorado As Seen by a Home Missionary, 1863-1868." The Colorado Magazine, 12 (March, 1935).

Gower, Calvin W. "Vigilantes." The Colorado Magazine, 41 (Spring, 1941).

Hafen, LeRoy R. "The Last Years of James P. Beckwourth." The Colorado Magazine, 5 (August, 1928).

Hill, Nathaniel. "Nathaniel Hill Inspects Colorado Letters Written in 1864." The Colorado Magazine, 34 (January, 1957).

Horsman, Reginald. "Scientific Racism and the American Indian in the Mid-Nineteenth Century." American Quarterly, 27 (May, 1965).

Isern, Thomas D. "The Controversial Career of Edward W. Wynkoop." The Colorado Magazine, 56 (Winter/Spring 1979).

Kelsey, Harry. "Background to Sand Creek." The Colorado Magazine, 45 (Fall, 1968).

Knight, Oliver. "The Frontier Newspaper as a Catalyst in Social Change." Pacific Northwest Quarterly, (April, 1967).

Lecompte, Janet. "Sand Creek." The Colorado Magazine, 41 (Fall, 1964).

"Letter of Senator Doolittle to Mrs. L.F.S. Foster, March 7, 1881, Notes and Documents." New Mexico Historical Review, 26 (April, 1951).

Lyon, William H. "The Significance of Newspapers on the American Frontier." Journal of the West, 19 (August, 1980).

Mumey, Dr. Nolie. "John Milton Chivington, the Misunderstood Man." 1956 Brand Book of the Denver Westerners, Boulder, Colorado: Johnson Publishing Co., 1957.

Munkres, Robert L. "Indian-White Contact Before 1870: Cultural Factors in Conflict." Journal of the West, 10 (July, 1971).

Muskrat, Jerry. "The Constitution and the American Indian: Past and Prologue." Hastings Constitutional Law Quarterly, 3 (Summer, 1976).

Nash, Gary B. "The Image of the Indian in the Southern Colonial Mind." in the Wild Man Within, eds. Edward Dudley and Maximillian E. Novak. Pittsburg: University of Pittsburg Press, 1972.

Neil, William M. "The Territorial Governor as Indian Superintendent in the Trans-Mississippi West." The Mississippi Valley Historical Review, 43 (September, 1956).

Paxson, Frederic L. "A Generation of the Frontier Hypothesis." Pacific Valley Historical Review, 2 (March, 1933).

Perrigo, Lynn I. "Major Hal Sayre's Diary of the Sand Creek Campaign." The Colorado Magazine, 14 (July, 1921).

Prentice, C.A. "Captain Silas S. Soule, a Pioneer Matryr." The Colorado Magazine, 14 (May, 1927).

Sanford, Albert B. "The Big Flood in Cherry Creek, 1864." The Colorado Magazine, 16 (May, 1927).

Schafer, Joseph. "Turner's Frontier Philosophy." Wisconsin Magazine of History, 16 (June, 1933).

Shields, Lilian. "Relations With the Cheyenne and Arapahoes to 1861." The Colorado Magazine, 14 (August, 1927).

Sievers, Michael A. "Sand of Sand Creek Historiography." The Colorado Magazine, 49 (Fall, 1972).

Tabor, Augusta. "Cabin Life in Colorado." The Colorado Magazine, 14 (March, 1927).

Unrau, William E. "A Prelude to War." The Colorado Magazine, 41 (Fall, 1964).

Wade, Arthur P. "The Military Command Structure of the Great Plains, 1853-1891." Journal of the West, 15 (July, 1976).

Washburn, Wilcomb. "A Moral History of Indian-White Relations: Needs and Opportunities for Study." Ethnohistory, 4 (Winter, 1957).

Washburn, Wilcomb. "The Moral and Legal Justifications for Dispossessing the Indians." in Seventeenth-Century America: Essays in Colonial History, ed. James Morton Smith. Chapel Hill: University of Norther Carolina Press, 1959.

Whisenhunt, Donald P. "The Frontier Newspaper: A Guide to Society and Culture." Journalism Quarterly, 45 (Winter, 1968).

White, Lonnie. "From Bloodless to Bloody: The Third Colorado Cavalry and the Sand Creek Massacre." Journal of the West, 6 (October, 1967).

Williams, Francis S. "Trial and Judgements of the People's Courts of Denver." The Colorado Magazine, 27 (October, 1950).

Tertiary Sources

Axtell, James T. "The Ethnohistory of Early America, A Review Essay." William and Mary Quarterly, 35 (January, 1978).

Berkhofer, Robert F. Jr. A Behavioral Approach to Historical Analysis. New York: The Free Press, 1969.

Burke, Kenneth. "Fact, Inference and Proof in the Analysis of Literary Symbolism." in Symbols and Values, ed. Lyman Bryson. New York: Cooper Square, 1964.

Burke, Kenneth. A Grammar of Motives. 1945; rpt. Berkeley: University of California Press, 1969.

Burke, Kenneth. "Interaction-Dramatism." in International Encyclopedia of the Social Sciences, vol. 7. ed. David L. Sills. New York: Macmillan and the Free Press, 1968.

Burke, Kenneth. A Rhetoric of Motives. 1950; rpt. Berkeley: University of California Press, 1969.

Burke, Kenneth. "The Rhetorical Situation." in Communication: Ethical and Moral Issues. ed. Lee Thayer. New York: Garden and Beach, 1973.

George, Alexander L. "Quanitative and Qualitative Approaches to Content Analysis." in Trends in Content Analysis, ed. Ithiel de Sola Pool. Urbana, Illinois: University of Illinois Press, 1959.

Lasswell, Harold D., Daniel Lerner and Ithiel de Sola Pool. The Comparative Study of Symbols: An Introduction. Stanford University Press, 1952.

Meadow, Robert G. Politics as Communication. Norwood, New Jersey: Ablex, 1980.

Merritt, Richard L. Symbols of American Community 1735-1775. New Haven: Yale University Press, 1966.

Merritt, Richard L. Systematic Approaches to Comparative Politics. Chicago: Rand McNally, 1970.

Read, James Morgan. *Atrocity Propaganda, 1914-1919*. New York: Arno Press, 1972.

Rief, Philip. "Psychoanalysis." in *American History and the Social Sciences*, ed. Edward N. Saveth. New York: The Free Press, 1964.

Rueckert, William H. *Kenneth Burke and the Drama of Human Relations*. Minneapolis: University of Minnesota Press, 1963.

Washburn, Wilcomb E. "Ethnohistory: History In the Round." *Ethnohistory*, 8 (Spring, 1961).

INDEX

Allport, Gordon, 343.
Anthony, Scott, 181, 260, 291, 292, 294, 297.
Articles of Confederation: Article IV, 77.
Athearn, Robert G., 102, 107.

Bannock City, 152-153.
Beckwourth (or Beckwirth), Jim, 139-140, 146, 156, 171, 293, 294-295, 298.
Bent, Robert, 294.
Berkhofer, Robert F., 19, 25, 27, 328.
Bernhardt, Michael, 339, 340.
Black Hawk Daily Mining Journal, 117, 166, 175-177, 179, 181-182, 236.
Black Kettle, 159, 180, 181, 184, 194, 249, 250, 251-252, 254, 258, 259, 287, 297, 323, 324, 325, 331.
Borden, Philip, 21.
Browne, S.E., 224, 291.
Bruner, Jerome, 10, 160.
Buell, John, 103.
Bull Bear, 245, 254, 255, 258, 259.
Burke, Kenneth: constitutions defined, 12-13; perfect atrocity story, 13-14; theory of rhetoric, 28-29; survival of constitutional titles, 76; constitutions and enemies, 89; identification by antithesis, 189; principle of selectivity, 321-323.
Byers, William N., 14, 101, 102, 104, 105, 120; biography, 131-134; goals, 134; the problem of returning emigrants, 134-136; passim, 131-195.

Cable, Rufus, 108-109.
Caldwell, Charles, 59, 68.
Campbell, Joseph, 7-8.
Camp Weld Council, 119, 180-181, 184, 194, 244, 251, 252-262, 324, 328.
Canby, Colonel, 282.
Cannon, James, 294.
Carey, Hugh, 115, 240, 281, 305.
Carlson, Lewis, 58.
Carter, Herbert, 339.
Charlot, Major, 284, 285, 290.
Cherokee Indian Removal: treaty at DeWitt's Corner, 83; Hopewell treaty, 83-84; Cherokee constitutional convention, 85; gold discovered, 85; restrictive state laws, 86; situation extraordinary, 87; Cherokee Nation v. Georgia, 88; Worcester v. Georgia, 88.

Cheyenne war-making customs, 245-246, 248, 260.
Chivington, Colonel John M., 5, 14, 15, 114, 115,
    118, 133, 159-160, 161, 167, 168, 175, 178, 179,
    180, 182-187, 192, 196, 240, 248, 250, 252, 253,
    257, 258, 260; passim, 281-303; biography of,
    281-283; official correspondence, 283-289; unofficial
    messages, 289-296; motives, 300-303.
Coffin, Morse, 117, 118-119, 192, 288, 293, 295.
Colburn, George A., 58.
Colley, S.J., 226, 250, 251, 257, 298, 302.
Colorado Third Reigment, 13, 113, 114, 115, 181;
    attitudes towards Indians, 116-121; subject to
    community pressure, 120-121; proclamation of,
    240-242; ego relevance of roles, 327.
Combe, George, 60, 61.
Combs, James, 291, 299.
Connor, P.E., General, 290, 299.
Conspiracy: Rebels and Indians, 143-144, 172-173.
Conspiracy myth, 51, 53, 55, 184, 190, 195, 319-323;
    rhetorical uses of, 329-335.
Conspiracy theory of Indian war, 45.
Constitutional debates and Indians, 78-79.
Content analysis: definition of, 25; steps for,
    25-27.
Cossit, Lt., 293, 299-300.
Cramer, Joseph, Lt. 292-293, 295, 300, 323, 324.
Crania Americana, 59, 60-75.
Crawford, Reverend William, 120.
Curtis, S.R., 169-170, 182, 229-235, 241-243, 247,
    284-289, 296-297, 299.

Daily Commonweath and Republican, 161-164, 189.
Dailey, John, 133.
Dale, Matthew, 105.
Daniels, Roger, 21, 193.
Davison, Captain, 285.
Deficient "Vietnamese Savage," 336-337.
Deloria, Vine, 347.
Denver Herald, 141-144.
Denver Mountaineer, 143.
Dog Soldiers, 180, 224, 226, 238, 245, 254.
Dole, W.P., 190, 222, 223, 224-225, 226, 227, 231-232,
    235, 241-242, 244, 245, 262, 328.
Doolittle, Senator, 187-188, 192.
Downing, Jacob, 159, 292, 346.
Dunklee, Edward, 112.
Dunn, Clark, 158-159, 247-248, 249, 284, 346.

Eayre, George, 159, 284.
Edelman, Murray: definition of myth, 7; myth and anxiety, 11; myth and enemy themes, 191; elite preservation of status, 196; elite suppression of communication, 295; susceptibility to myth, 325-326.
Election of 1864, 166, 175-179.
Elaide, Mircea, 8-9.
Ellsworth, William, 89.
Ellul, Jacques, 7.
English/Indian conspiracy, 76.
Ethnohistory, 22, 27.
Evans, John, 14, 15, 114, 133, 146, 149, 154-155, 156-157, 161, 165, 167, 170, 171, 173, 175, 176, 178, 179, 180, 187-188, 190, 192; biography, 219-221; passim, 219-260; conspiracy theory regarding Plains tribes, 226-235; Proclamation to the People of Colorado, 236-239; Proclamation to the "Patriotic Citizens of Colorado," 239-241; military version of Indian/White conflicts, 247-258; Camp Weld Council, 252-259.

Fee simple, 79.
Fifty-niners, 104, 105, 108, 110, 135.
Finlay, David, 326-327.

Garver, Newton, 331.
George, Alexander, 27.
Gerry, Elbridge, 226, 245.
Gill, A.J., 294.
Gilpin, William, 107, 143, 144.
Gliddon, George, 71.
Glorietta, battle of, 114, 120, 176.
Gobacks, 103, 137.
Goode, William, 103.
Gray, Robert, Reverend, 1.
Great fire, 160.
Great flood in Cherry Creek, 161-162.
Greeley, Horace, 110, 137.
Grinnell, George Bird, 22.
Grzesik, Ron, 341.

Habermas, Jurgen, 9.
Hagan, William T., 19, 77, 83.
Hakluyt, John, 1, 2.
Hakluyt, Richard, 1.
Hall, Charles, 341.
Hall, Frank, 103, 167.
Hamilton, Alexander, 81.

Hardin, William J., 107.
Harrison, Charley, 112.
Hill, Nathaniel, 120.
Hoebel, E. Adamson, 246.
Holder, Preston, 22.
Holladay, Ben, 290.
Hollister, Orvando, 116, 117, 119, 167, 175-176, 179.
Horsman, Reginald, 58.
Howbert, Irving, 117, 119-120.
Hungate "massacre," 161-164, 184-185, 189-192, 231-232, 238, 285, 328, 332.
Hunt, A.C., 291-292.

Ideology, 9, 18, 20.
"Indian War" of 1864, 158-160, 176, 238, 246-252.

Jackson, Andrew, 86, 87.
Jackson, Helen Hunt, 87.
Jacobs, Wilbur, 45, 46, 55-56.
"Jefferson Territory," 113, 141, 224.
Jefferson, Thomas, 59, 79, 82, 88.
Jennings, Francis, 18, 19.

Key symbols: general discussion, 11, 13, 14, 15, 25-27; of Parkman's conspiracy, 57; of "science," 75; of government constitutions, 90; of Sand Creek rhetoric, 319-322.
Kitano, Harry H.L., 21, 193.
Knox, Henry, 79, 80, 81.

Lasswell, Harold, 10, 13, 24-27.
Leach, Edmund, 329.
Lean Bear, 144, 159-160, 169, 255, 323.
Lecompte, Janet, 166.
Left Hand, 140, 165-166, 169, 184, 254, 255, 323.
Lifton, Robert Jay, 343-344.
Lincoln, Abraham, 107, 131, 143, 220, 229, 281.
Lowenburg, Peter, 21.
Lunt, Orrington, 221.

McClure, A.K., 109, 196.
McGaa, William, 233, 255.
McMechan, Edgar Carlisle, 219, 221.
McWilliams, Carey, 16.
Manifest and latent functions, 27-28, 29, 188-192, 196, 243-244, 261-262, 303-306.
Marshall, John, 86, 88.
Medina, Ernest, 338-340.

Merritt, Richard L., 28, 189.
Miner's Courts, 111-112.
Min-im-mie, 324.
Minorities, Colorado Whites' attitudes towards, 107-110.
Minton, Lt., 292, 293, 295.
Morgenthau, Hans, 342.
Morton, Samuel George, 12, 24, 59-75, 193.
Mosca, Gaetano, 4.
Munkres, Robert L., 250.
Muskrat, Jerry, 30.
My Lai Massacre, 17, 336-343.
Myth, historical, 8-11.
Myth, 7-11.

Nash, Gary, 4, 21.
Neva, 256.
Nichols, Captain, 228, 289, 301, 323.
North, Robert, 227-228, 230-231, 233, 255.
Northwest Ordinance of 1787, 77-78.
Nott, Josiah, 70-75, 193.

Olsen, Gregory, 339.
One Eye, 324.
Overland Stage route, 114, 169, 241, 283, 290.

Parkman, Francis, 11-12, passim, 45-57, 64, 66, 132, 150, 173, 191, 193.
Pearce, Roy Harvey, 3, 20.
Peoples' courts, 112.
Peckham, Howard, 46.
Pedrick, Henry, 340.
Peers Commission, 339.
Pendleton, Robert, 340.
Perkin, Robert L. 23, 112, 131, 156, 195.
Phillips, Charles, 323.
Phrenology, 61.
Pike, General Albert, 144.
Plains tribes, war-making customs, 156.
Pontiac: as the "prime mover," 47, 52; as the "best champion, 49; as a "patriotic Indian," 331.
Powhatan confederacy, 2.
Prucha, Francis Paul, 89.
Purchas, Samuel, 1.

Qualitative content analysis, 28.

Reid, Terry, 339.
Reynolds, James, 168-169.
Rhetoric, 6, 7, 18; rhetoric and action, 3, 5, 15.

COLUMBIA COLLEGE
973.7S968S   C1   V0
SAND CREEK AND THE RHETORIC OF EXTERM

3 2711 00007 8902

DISCARD

JUL 1 9 1989

SAND CREEK AND THE RHETORIC OF EXTERMINATION

A Case Study in Indian-White Relations

David Svaldi
Adams State College

UNIVERSITY
PRESS OF
AMERICA

Lanham • New York • London

Copyright © 1989 by

University Press of America,® Inc.

4720 Boston Way
Lanham, MD 20706

3 Henrietta Street
London WC2E 8LU England

All rights reserved

Printed in the United States of America

British Cataloging in Publication Information Available

Library of Congress Cataloging-in-Publication Data

Svaldi, David, 1948–
Sand Creek and the rhetoric of extermination : a case study in
Indian–White relations / David Svaldi.
p.   cm.
Bibliography: p.
Includes index.
1. Sand Creek, Battle of, 1864. 2. Indians of North America–
–Public opinion. 3. Indians of North America– –Government
relations– –1789–1869. 4. Public opinion– –United States.
5. Genocide– –United States.
E83.863.S86   1989   88–38120 CIP
973.7– –dc19
ISBN 0–8191–7314–2 (alk. paper)

973.7 S968s

Svaldi, David, 1948-

Sand Creek and the rhetoric
of extermination

All University Press of America books are produced on acid-free paper.
The paper used in this publication meets the minimum requirements of American
National Standard for Information Sciences—Permanence of Paper for Printed Library
Materials, ANSI Z39.48–1984.   ∞